Merry
to Ma
from Mom
1981

THE LIFE & TIMES OF GREG CLARK

Canada's Favorite Storyteller

Also by Jock Carroll:

THE SHY PHOTOGRAPHER (BOTTOMS UP!)
THE DEATH OF THE TORONTO TELEGRAM
THE SUMMER OLYMPIC GAMES
DOWN THE ROAD

With Pak Jong Yong:

KOREAN BOY

THE LIFE & TIMES OF
GREG CLARK

Canada's Favorite Storyteller

JOCK CARROLL

Doubleday Canada Limited, Toronto, Ontario
Doubleday & Company, Inc., Garden City, New York
1981

Library of Congress Cataloging in Publication Data

Carroll, Jock.
   The life & times of Greg Clark, Canada's favorite
storyteller.

   Includes index.
   1. Clark, Gregory—Biography.   2. Authors, Canadian—
20th century—Biography.   I. Title.
PR9199.3.C52Z6   1981   813'.52   [B]
ISBN: 0-385-17635-x   AACR2
Library of Congress Catalog Card Number 81–43040

The author expresses grateful acknowledgment to the following:
Greg Clark, Jr., for permission to reprint Greg Clark's stories
"Rejuvenation Pills" and "A Sportsman Is One"; his "Packsack"
column of September 16, 1975; the excerpts from Greg Clark's
diaries; and for permission to use family photographs.

The Montreal *Standard,* Inc., for permission to reprint Greg Clark's
stories "Miss L. Bruce—A Love Story" and "The Robin."

The *Toronto Star* for assistance in research and permission to reprint
excerpts from *J. E. Atkinson of The Star* by Ross Harkness.

Doubleday & Company, Inc., for permission to reprint an excerpt
from *O Rare Don Marquis* by Edward Anthony, copyright ©
1962 by Edward Anthony.

Charles Scribner's Sons for permission to reprint an excerpt from
Ernest Hemingway: A Life Story by Carlos Baker, copyright © 1969
by Carlos Baker, copyright © 1969 by Mary Hemingway.

GREGORY CLARK

1892–1977

"Napoo!"

Contents ──────────

Preface _____

The editor working on this book has asked me to write a few words warning possible purchasers that the book contains material they might find shocking, or harmful to their health, or that should be read subject to parental guidance.

I objected to doing this on the grounds that I saw nothing shocking in the book, nor did I think Greg's friends or relatives would see anything shocking in it. The editor argued that there were countless other Canadians who revered Greg as the lovable little gnome he portrayed in his own stories and who might be upset to learn there was more to him.

It's true Greg was a lovable little gnome, but he was also much more than that. He was a human being, for one thing—and in the company of hunters, fishermen and other low companions he was a somewhat earthy human being.

This book, then, addresses itself to more than Greg Clark's public image and his achievements. It tries to portray Greg in all his dimensions. Perhaps some people will find this shocking or harmful to their health or that of their parents. I think the editor's real concern is to make clear that if you find more Greg Clark in this book than you bargained for, there is no use trying to get your money back, because you have been duly warned.

This same editor also asks me to say something about the structure of the book, so that readers will not be confused by the order of events. For the most part, this book is a straightforward account of Greg's life, moving directly along like a train on a track. However, the train is halted now and then to permit the insertion of a chapter that is not necessarily in chronological order. In these chapters you will meet the real Greg Clark, alive and kicking.

These chapters came about because Greg asked me to write this biography many years before he died. In the ensuing years we spent a great deal of time together, on assignment, on fishing trips and in his home and mine. We both made extensive notes and I tape recorded a great deal of material. Some of these scenes have been inserted in the book just as they happened. It is my feeling that they contribute to an understanding of Greg and will enable the reader to make up his or her own mind as to what kind of man Greg was. The book begins with one of these chapters.

The book also pauses for two or three of Greg's own stories, which I think are good examples of his writing. These, too, have simply been inserted where it seemed appropriate.

That's about all there is to say about the structure of the book. Simply put, it's more dithyrambic than definitive.

Now, if the editor doesn't mind, I'd like to get a few words of my own into this author's preface. I would like to thank Greg's relatives for their generous help in gathering material—particularly Greg's son, Greg Clark, Jr., and his wife, Doreen; Greg's daughter, Elizabeth, and her husband, Hiro Wakabayashi; Greg's sister, Mabel, and her husband, Thomas Drew-Brook; and Greg's nephew Joseph A. P. Clark. I would like to thank Greg's friends —Ralph Allen, Craig Ballantyne, Morley Callaghan, Frank Chamberlain, Alex Forbes, Duncan Macpherson, Dick Malone, Bill Oille, Gil Purcell, Hugh Shaw, Gord Sinclair, Charles Vining, Bruce West and many others whose names are mentioned in the book and whose contributions will be apparent to the reader.

I am also indebted to the Canada Council for two grants, which allowed me to take time from my regular employment to work on the book. The sponsors of my applications to the Canada Council were Doug Creighton of the Toronto *Sun,* Doug MacFarlane of the Toronto *Telegram,* Gil Purcell of Canadian Press, Hugh Shaw of *Weekend Magazine* and Greg Clark, Jr.

During the years of gathering material for the book I occasionally received comments that were somewhat unsettling.

Publisher John Gray said, "It is our experience that you cannot write a biography of a man while he is still alive."

Author Morley Callaghan said, "You'll never be able to write an honest biography of Greg."

Newspaperman Gil Purcell said, "You'll never finish it."

I didn't agree with any of these statements when they were made. However, in the course of doing the book I have come to perceive an element of truth in each one of them.

Truth is elusive. With regard to those places in this book where it has eluded me completely, I would like to repeat a remark of E. J. Kahn, Jr., a writer for the *New Yorker* magazine whom I met in Korea. Kahn wrote a book about the Korean War and upon reading it I was delighted to discover that he had lost or misplaced about a million Koreans. I promptly wrote him a letter pointing out that this kind of monumental mistake was hardly in keeping with the *New Yorker*'s reputation for accuracy.

Kahn wrote back just as promptly. "In all my years of writing and reporting," he said, "I have never made a single mistake. Sometimes, admittedly, my sources of information have been wrong."

In this book I don't know which, if any, of my sources have been wrong. People remember different things. Sometimes their memories of the same event are quite different, even contradictory. Greg himself was constantly polishing up his life and often had several versions of the same story, using whichever one seemed most suitable at the moment.

In my many conversations with Greg he nearly always got in the last word. I would not deny him that privilege in this preface.

It's about his advice to me on writing this book. His advice was very simple. Looking back on it from this point in time, I think it was deceptively simple.

"Don't be too serious in the writing of it," said Greg. "Have fun with it."

> Jock Carroll
> *December 31, 1980*
> *Toronto, Ontario*

THE LIFE & TIMES OF GREG CLARK

1

All stories, if continued far enough, end in death, and he is no true story-teller who would keep that from you.

—*Ernest Hemingway*

Humorists have their dark days, too. On this particular day Greg looked tired and unhappy.

"I have a great ending for this biography," he said. "You come in here some afternoon and find me in the bathtub with the top of my head blown off."

"Thanks a lot," I said, "but no thanks."

"It's my life," barked Greg. "If I want to put a gun to my head, that's my prerogative."

"Prerogative?" I said. "What's that mean?"

"My privilege," explained Greg. "My right. I've laid my life on the line in two wars and a hundred other times. I've *earned* the right to shoot myself when I want."

"Well, all right," I agreed reluctantly. "But not just yet. Going back over your life, I've discovered a whole lot of contradictions, glaring inconsistencies and outright lies that have got to be straightened up."

Greg went right on talking about suicide. He'd lost his hearing in one ear in World War I and he seemed able to flick the other ear off when there was something he didn't want to hear.

"Now take Hemingway," said Greg. "He killed himself with a double-barreled Boss shotgun, with a full choke."

"No, he didn't," I said. "He used a twelve-gauge Angelini and Bernardon, made for him in London."

Greg glared at me. "I have just finished the Carlos Baker biography of Hemingway and I know what I'm talking about."

"I have just finished the Milt Machlin biography," I said, "and Machlin says it was an Angelini and Bernardon."

Greg paused for a drink of scotch. "That's biographers for you," he said. "They never get *anything* right. In any case, I think I'd use one of my Webley naval pistols. Shoots a slug the size of your thumb, four-fifty-five caliber."

I took out my notebook. "I'll just write that down," I said, "so there won't be any arguments about it later."

"You don't seem very damn sympathetic," said Greg.

"Malcolm Muggeridge wasn't very sympathetic about Hemingway," I said. "He said it was the only time Hemingway had ever hit his target."

"That's a bit too clever, isn't it?" said Greg.

"Yes," I said. "While we're on guns, how many have you owned?"

Greg brightened up. "Damn near everything," he said. "From a twenty-two to a cannon."

"A *cannon?*" I said.

"Yes. A bronze cannon from an old Hudson's Bay Company fort. But I couldn't get ammunition for it, so I donated it to Fort York, here in Toronto. Then I had a nine-millimeter Schmeisser machine gun from World War Two, but the police made a fuss when I tried to register it. I had to give it away to the Forty-eighth Highlanders museum."

I had a drink of scotch.

"Then," said Greg, "there were the two Colt Frontier single-action forty-fives—one with a long barrel, the other with a short barrel—the nine-millimeter Luger, the thirty-two caliber Walther automatic, the three-eighty caliber Beretta and that lovely, brand-new Browning nine-millimeter automatic presented to me by Major Hahn, made at his plant here in Toronto. But there was no serial number on it and the R.C.M.P. came and took it away from me."

I was coming to the end of a page in my notebook. "Is this going to be a long list?" I asked.

"That's just some of the pistols," said Greg. "I also had a very handy four-ten Harrington-Richardson shotgun pistol. When Jim Frise and I were out fishing, we'd go down side roads and knock crows off the fenceposts with it. Now they argue that kind of a gun is illegal. People are funny."

"What are your views on gun control?" I asked.

"Up at the cottage," said Greg, "I had a couple of twenty-gauge shotguns and a little four-ten for shooting porcupines. Then there was the Lee Enfield three-oh-three, the Number Four Mark One, the short jungle gun we were going to use in the Far East—if we'd gotten there in time. Then the bolt-action Savage two fifty-three hundred that was discontinued. And the Springfield thirty-oh-six I bought from Ted Smith up at Midland. Ted's brother Oliver was mayor of Midland then. Ted's arthritis was bothering him, so he sold me the Springfield. I meant to give it to young Greg, but every time I saw Ted he started talking about his gun and I felt so bad I gave it back to him."

I was getting tired writing down all these guns. "Is that it?" I asked.

"Oh, no," said Greg. "There's the Winchesters. I had three of the eighteen eighty-six models alone. The thirty-three, the forty-five ninety, the forty-sixty-five—now *there* was a slug! The Winchester forty-four-forty—that was an eighteen ninety-two model, I think." After a brief pause, Greg continued, "My wife, Helen, had a Winchester twenty-five-thirty-five. My son Murray had a Winchester thirty-thirty. My personal gun was a seven-millimeter Mauser, a beautiful thing."

"It sounds like a nice little arsenal," I said. "But you can't shoot yourself right now. All these lies you've been telling me—you'll have to stay around and help sort out the facts from the fiction."

"I suppose it would upset young Greg and Doreen," said Greg, mentioning his son and his daughter-in-law.

"Another thing—" I began.

Greg just went on talking to himself. "There's also my daughter Elizabeth and her husband to consider . . . although they do live in New York."

"Besides," I said, "even though I've been listening to your stories for twenty years, I still haven't heard them all."

"Twenty years!" snorted Greg. "The speed you work at, it'll take another twenty years to write the book. I can't stay around that long."

"You'll live to be a hundred," I said confidently. "You're too miserable to die."

"Heh, heh, heh," chuckled Greg. "It's true I am a mean little son-of-a-bitch. Did I tell you what my niece Barbara did? Just after I got the Service Medal of the Order of Canada, she forwarded a letter someone had sent to me, addressed Mr. Gregory Clark, S.M.O.C., O.B.E., M.C. and all that. Across the envelope Barbara wrote, 'They left off the S.O.B.' Heh, heh, heh."

"Getting back to your biography," I said, "it's true I've heard you described as a mean little son-of-a-bitch. Also as Canada's Eddie Guest. Also as a newspaperman, a fisherman, a hunter, a soldier, a war correspondent, a romantic, a cynic, a sob sister of the press, a lovely old gentleman, a charlatan, a funny man, a sad man, a loner, a man with a thousand friends."

I poised my pencil over my notebook. "Now, as briefly as possible, what's the truth?"

"I'm just a myth," Greg confessed. "After some fifty years of scallywaggery I managed to create this myth, a kind of puppet which I hold up in front of me and wiggle with my fingers. Did I tell you the joke my sister Mabel came in with the other day? It was on a plane and against the window was this dear old lady, working away at a crossword puzzle. She was wearing a black bonnet and a black dress with white lace, a sweet old thing. Seated next to her was one of those big, fat businessmen, reading the financial section. After a while the old lady says to him, 'Pardon me, sir, but are you a member of a service club?' 'Yes,' he says, 'as a matter of fact I'm in the Rotary Club.' 'Wonderful!' says the old lady. 'Then could you give me a four-letter word, ending in I-T, meaning what Rotarians are full of?' 'Grit,' says the businessman. 'G-R-I-T.' 'Oh,' says the old lady, looking down at her puzzle. 'Have you got a pencil with an eraser on it?' "

Greg laughed so hard he began to choke. He paused for a sip of whiskey.

"Getting back to your biography," I said, "there's Gil Purcell, the head of Canadian Press and one of your best friends. He says he thinks of you more as a philosopher than a writer. True or false?"

Greg ignored the question.

I tried again. "Now, your good friend Bruce West has another theory. He—"

"Getting back to Barbara," said Greg, "she's one you've got to meet."

I was confused. "Barbara? Barbara *who?*"

"Mabel's daughter," said Greg impatiently. "Of all my nieces and nephews, she's the most spectacular. Barbara *Harris,* now. Married to Doctor Robert Harris, son of a famous bone surgeon, Dr. R. I. Harris, M.C., C.M.G. A very severe, very distinguished, very important doctor. You know what they're like."

"No," I said. "I only know cheap doctors."

"Anyway," said Greg, "what I'm talking about is not Dr. R. I. Harris. At Toronto General he walked the corridors like a general, never seeing anybody or speaking to anybody. The interns knew his C.M.G. stood for 'Commander of Michael and George,' but they pretended it stood for 'Call Me God.' "

"If you are *not* talking about Dr. R. I. Harris, M.C., C.M.G.," I said, "may I ask what you *are* talking about?"

Greg glared at me. "One thing I can't stand," he said, "is someone who is always interrupting me. I don't see how we can do this book if you're going to keep asking me questions."

I fell silent.

After a significant pause, Greg continued. "What I'm talking about is Barbara. She knows all the best jokes and she tells them with a great big belly laugh. One day someone said to her, 'You're always talking about your father, Tommy Drew-Brook, but you hardly ever mention your mother. Why is that?' Barbara said, 'If you mean to suggest there's something incestuous about it —you're damn right there is.' She's a throwback, but she has the family puzzled. Way back in the Drew-Brook family tree there was an English lord who had the most extensive collection of erotica of his day. Maybe she dates back to him."

"Greg," I said, "you certainly have the gift of the gab. I suppose you inherited that from Joseph T. Clark, your late father, the famous editor-in-chief of the *Toronto Daily Star* for so many years?"

"No," countered Greg. "I think I absorbed all these words through my ass. Perhaps you had better make that 'through the seat of my pants.' In my high-chair days, you see, my chin barely came up to the edge of the table." Greg lifted up his hands and peered at me over the edge of an imaginary table. "So my parents put this big dictionary under me. It was a giant Webster's dictionary, as big as the family Bible. Did I ever tell you about the time I was discussing farts in the trenches in World War One?"

"Farts?" I repeated, not believing my ears.

"Yes, farts," said Greg. "F-A-R-T-S. If you have a spelling problem, better get yourself a good dictionary. Get the new Webster's that's just out. It has all the four-letter words in it. Bill Oille and I looked them up the other day."

"Bill Oille?"

"My doctor. But I'm talking about farts, on which I am somewhat of an authority. As a matter of fact, I founded the Epsom Dart & Fart Club in England during World War Two, and I must tell you the story of that some time. But this other time, we were sitting around in the trenches, discussing farts. There is a fine line, as you must know, between letting go a good fart and shitting yourself. I suppose everyone has miscalculated at least once. I said to these soldiers, 'Now, we all fart during our waking hours, but isn't it true we also fart in our sleep?' They agreed that they also farted in their sleep. 'Now!' I said. 'Has any one of you ever shit himself while farting in his sleep?' No, they agreed, none of them ever had. 'Then,' I said triumphantly, 'that just goes to prove one thing. Man has more brains in his ass than he has in his head!'"

"Greg," I said, "I can't use this kind of stuff in your biography! Nobody will believe me!"

"I suppose not," admitted Greg. "Ralph Allen was always saying I had a shithouse sense of humor. Although I prefer the term outhouse humor, myself."

"The worst thing about you," I said, "is I can't tell when you're telling the truth and when you're just telling stories. If you'd just stay in character—"

"Oh, well," said Greg, "there may be a few tiny little things you'll have to sort of skate around. But that's your job. After all, I've done all the work."

I got up and picked Carlos Baker's book on Hemingway out of Greg's bookcase. I found the part where Hemingway described Greg and I began reading it aloud.

"'Greg Clark loves his wife and his baby. He loves guns and books about guns. He also loves to think. He thinks very well but never strains himself. Greg is very romantic . . . You cannot dismiss him or classify him because he is always acting and you cannot tell how much of it is acting. He also acts inside himself. He does things for people. There is too

much India rubber in him. I have never seen him angry. . . .
If he has a weakness it is having too much sense. He writes
the best of anyone on the paper. I have known him a long
time but I do not know much about him. Greg is my friend
and I know less about him than I do about Hindmarsh.
Hindmarsh is a son of a bitch and a liar and they are easy to
understand. A good man is hard to understand.' "

Greg interrupted me. "Did you notice," he asked, "that I was
mentioned eight times in the book and Morley Callaghan was
mentioned only four times?"

"No," I said, "but that seems highly irrelevant to me—"

"Not to me, it isn't," chuckled Greg wickedly. *"Not to me, it
isn't!"*

"Anyway," I said, "what's interesting is Hemingway's analysis
of you. He's known you a long time but he doesn't know much
about you. He says you're a good man. He—"

"Did I ever tell you about meeting Hemmy in London during
the war?"

"No," I said, "but—"

"Or about his room at the Ritz at the liberation of Paris?"

"No," I replied, getting impatient. "Look, Greg, this isn't a
book about Hemingway. It's a book about you. What I'm trying
to get at here is Hemingway's opinion of you as a good man, if
indeed that was his opinion."

"Oh well," said Greg. "Hemingway was always a bit of a liar—
like all good writers."

"I'm beginning to see that," I said. "But the truth about you
must be around somewhere. And I intend to discover it, even if I
have to make it up."

"I'll help you with that," said Greg, chuckling. "Now, let's have
another drink."

Which we did.

2 _____

Nobody ever says a nice word about you in this business until after you're dead.

—*Anon.*

While discussing his biography with me some years earlier, Greg had said, "First get the facts out of the way. Go over to Gil Purcell at Canadian Press and get a copy of my obituary. That will have all the facts in it. Then you can get on with the book."

Canadian Press, known as CP, was certainly the right place to get Greg's obit. CP was full of newsmen who'd known Greg for years, and the general manager was Gil Purcell, one of Greg's closest friends. Here is a portion of Greg's CP obit as of May 29, 1961, written by Greg's fellow war correspondent Doug Amaron.

CP BIOGRAPHICAL SERVICE   *GREGORY CLARK*
Sketch 1161 (29-5-61)   *Newspaper Man*
                                             Born Sept. 25, 1892

EDITORS: This sketch is for your reference library. It provides material about the subject for use in connection with current activities, but is primarily for use in event of death.

By The Canadian Press

When the moulds were cast from which pixies were created one must have been left over for Gregory Clark.

Perch a pork-pie hat atop fuzzy white sideburns; match twinkling grey eyes with a cherubic smile; clothe a five-two frame in a rainbow of colors; add a gnarled cane and an almost cocky jauntiness and you have Greg Clark.

Here was a man of many talents, the greatest of which was to make people smile. He was unsurpassed as a storyteller, written and spoken, and his flow of words was matched only by his pranks of dress.

He favored tweeds, the more colorful the better, and shirts of primary hues. A red vest often was added to the mixture and trousers were hitched with broad, eye-piercing suspenders. His footwear might be elastic-sided boots of a kind usually found only in a museum.

Greg Clark was a show-off, but no one would have had him otherwise. For all his lack of size he was a big man, with a personality as warm as the colors of his dress. His friends were legion.

Won Army Commission Because of His Size

Greg Clark received his commission within a few days of joining the army in the First World War.

His commanding officer, the late Victor Sifton, explained it this way:

"The story is told that the sergeant-major in charge of the awkward squad, noticing the almost insurmountable difficulties the diminutive man was having in handling the rather heavy Ross rifle, reported to the officer in charge as follows: 'Sir, that little so-and-so will never make a soldier. You will have to make him an officer.'"

"King-Size Leprechaun"

The newspaper profession claimed him as its own and with justification. His writing career, begun at the *Toronto Star* in 1911, was broken only by two years of First World War service.

His homey full-page feature story, illustrated by his pal Jimmy Frise, who died in 1948, was one of the forces that built up the *Star Weekly*.

In 1947, he and Frise left to join the weekly Montreal *Standard,* which developed into *Weekend Magazine.* He was *Weekend*'s associate editor and his regular full-page "shortie" —as he called it—and his daily brief Packsack in a score of newspapers made him by far the most widely read Canadian.

Tribute to Greg was paid by University of Western Ontario in the form of an honorary Doctor of Laws degree, conferred in 1960. Presenting him for his degree, Western's president, Dr. Edward Hall, said:

"We honor Gregory Clark for the sheer pleasure which he gives to people. We honor him, too, as an interpreter of people. We pay tribute to him as a people's philosopher. . . . Truly a king-size leprechaun."

Collected Canes

Two collections of Greg's stories—"So What?" and "Which We Did"—were published before the Second World War with Frise illustrations. They sold well, but some of Greg's friends accused him of using his royalties to buy a batch of each so they would be out of print.

Years later, publishers tried to get him to put together a new collection of his yarns. His invariable reply: "What is all right for an *hors d'oeuvre* is no good piled up in a basket for supper."

He had a change of heart in 1959 and "The Best of Gregory Clark" appeared, followed in 1961 by "Greg's Choice"—two volumes of "shorties" chock full of the humor and philosophy of their author.

But Greg was more than a writer. Fishermen and hunters, bird-watchers and program chairmen who seek the best speakers for their club meetings also called him friend.

He collected trout flies by the thousands; his cane collection was one of the finest in Canada; he was an authority on how game and fish should be cooked; he was a gadget man, with an assortment of odds and ends from tump lines to wading sticks.

Won Military Cross

Military circles, too, had a place for him in their ranks, as the soldier who won the Military Cross in 1917 and as the war correspondent who was awarded the OBE for his writings in the Second World War.

Gregory Clark was born in Toronto Sept. 25, 1892. His father was Thomas Joseph Clark, for many years editor of the *Toronto Star,* and his mother was the former Sarah Louisa Greig.

[AUTHOR'S NOTE: *Greg's mother was Sarah Louise Greig. Louisa Greig was his grandmother. His father's name was Joseph Thomas Clark.*]

After education at Harbord Collegiate and University of Toronto, he joined the editorial staff of the *Star* at 19. He used to say he entered the newspaper profession through the side door, because his father was editor, but he won his way to the top on his own merits.

Known in later years for feature writing, in his long career at the *Star* he was also a senior reporter and shared the bylines on major stories of his day with such men as the late Fred Griffin and the late Matthew Halton.

Greg's spot-news assignments, under the pressure of able competition and ever-present deadlines, took him virtually to every part of this continent and abroad.

Greg's Humor Lived After Pundits Gone

In 1957 at 64 Greg Clark became the first active newspaper man to be honored by the Toronto Men's Press Club with a life membership. On that occasion a colleague expressed the philosophy on which most of Greg's writing was based.

Bruce West of the Toronto *Globe and Mail* recalled that Greg had told him he was appalled, when entering the newspaper profession, by the number of heavy thinkers, writing on the problems of the world and other matters of profound import.

"I decided," Clark told West, "that someone would have to sit in a corner of the newspaper and play marbles, just to help the reader keep his balance."

West commented that "some of the delicious facets of this marble game can still be quoted word for word by thankful newspaper readers long after the pundits have been forgotten."

Covered Hauptmann Trial

He talked to kings and commoners, to field marshals and privates, to the pillars of the professional world and to the derelicts along Skid Road. And his heart went out first to those at the bottom of the ladder.

"In the great campaigns of war and peace it is the privates, corporals and sergeants who eventually have to carry out the hard work—not the generals," he said. "If you cultivate their respect and friendship they won't let you down."

He was in Paterson, N.J. for the trial in 1935 of Bruno Hauptmann, the kidnap-slayer of Charles Lindbergh's son. He went to Nova Scotia in 1937 to report the Moose River mine disaster.

[AUTHOR'S NOTE: *To my knowledge, Canadian Press has never made a mistake. Therefore I quote this reference to Greg's appearance at the Moose River mine disaster in 1937 exactly as it appears in the CP obituary. Other sources indicate the event took place a year earlier, in 1936.*]

Three months after war began in 1939 he accompanied the 1st Canadian Division overseas as a war correspondent and shared the perils of a war reporter in the field in the Mediterranean and on the Western Front until September, 1944, when his younger son, Lieut. Murray Clark, was killed in action near Calais.

[AUTHOR'S NOTE: *Murray Clark was Greg's older son. This is the last author's note which will appear in this book. From here on let the facts fall where they may.*]

Then, at 52, after nearly five years of writing of the triumphs and tragedies of war, of the great events such as Dunkerque and the silent patrols of the Moro Valley, he returned to Canada.

Had Amazing Memory

Greg had an amazing memory and a facile imagination that could create a cameo of writing from the simplest incident. He was accused often of letting imagination run wild with fact but usually even the most fanciful story, when traced to its source, was true.

Alex Forbes of Hespeler, Ontario, a hunting pal, could vouch from personal knowledge for Greg's acquaintance with the mighty. The two were shopping in New York one day and across the store Forbes saw Greg shaking hands, chuckling and chatting with another man. Suddenly Greg shouted:

"Hey, Alex! Come over here a minute. I want to introduce you to a friend of mine."

Forbes crossed the floor and met for the first time Edward, Duke of Windsor, a man Greg had interviewed at least three times.

Hemingway Story Typical of Greg

Greg Clark was a colleague for three years in the 1920's of author Ernest Hemingway, then starting his career as a *Toronto Star* reporter. He showed Greg much of his fiction and Greg recalled later:

"If I said it was too jerky, too queer, too lean, Hemmy would set it aside and mail it next day to Ezra Pound in Paris who would publish it in the *Transatlantic Review*. But if I cried: 'Ah, now you've got it, Hemmy! This is swell! Anybody can read this,' he would wait until I had gone home and then quietly drop it in the waste basket. I may thus claim to have had some effect on the early literary style of Hemingway."

Butt of Own Humour

He liked to tell stories against himself, one of his favorites being his unhappy experience when he entered a ladies washroom by mistake. It was too late to escape when he learned his error—women were coming in—and he sat for 10 minutes with his feet raised in the air, fearful that the sight of his shoes and trouser cuffs might reveal his sex.

His fishing tales were his finest and he would have been a wealthy man had he received a dollar every time he told about the jade-green monster—a 30-minute account of the muskie that leaped into his canoe and tore off his sweater.

A close family man, Greg often wove the experiences of his relations into his stories. In his immediate family were his wife, two sons, Murray, killed in 1944, and Gregory Clark, Jr., and one daughter, Elizabeth, Mrs. Hiro Wakabayashi.

-30-

Well, so much for the facts.

3

You can't go home again.

—*Thomas Wolfe*

It was September 21, 1970—a warm autumn day just four days before Greg's seventy-eighth birthday. Greg and I were about to begin a photographic tour of the houses he had lived in over the years. Our first scheduled stop was 52 McKenzie Crescent, the house in which he had been born in 1892. Although misspelled, McKenzie Crescent was named after William Lyon Mackenzie, fiery newspaperman, rebel and Toronto's first elected mayor.

"Drive along Queen Street and turn up Dovercourt," said Greg. "McKenzie Crescent is just a short street running from Dovercourt up to Dundas."

As we drove, I said, "I've been casting about for advice on how to put your life back together again for this book."

"It is together," said Greg. "Just don't take it apart."

"Do you remember Jacqueline Sirois?" I asked. "Back in the early days of *Weekend?*"

"Yes," said Greg. "What about her?"

"In those days," I said, "she was married to Brian Moore."

"He writes novels about Catholics," said Greg.

"He does now," I said. "But in those days he was grinding out thrillers for Harlequin Books. One was called *Wreath for a Redhead,* another, *The Executioners.* He told me at the time that every book should have a flagellation scene on page fifty, and another one in greater detail on page three-fifty."

"My first and only flagellation scene took place at Fifty-two McKenzie Crescent," said Greg. "Right where we're headed for."

"Oh, good," I said. "Is there a blonde in it?"

"Yes," said Greg. "A little blond girl the same age as I was—about four years old. We were playing together in the backyard

when it happened. She dropped her drawers to have a pee. I
didn't know anything about girls or sex, but I was puzzled by her
lack of exterior plumbing. I bent over for a better look and the
next thing I knew my mother had me by the scruff of the neck
and I was being dragged into the house."

Greg continued, "There was a little whisk used to hang in the
hall—I can see it right now. My mother grabbed this whisk and
she whaled the bejesus out of me. I think she got hysterical.
Eventually her sisters had to pull her away from me. That was the
end of my sexual curiosity for years."

"I don't think that's the kind of flagellation Brian had in
mind," I said.

"I suppose not," said Greg, "not with the way the world is
going."

He waved a hand toward the sidewalk. "Look at that."

The sidewalk was crowded with youthful members of the coun-
terculture, aggressively eccentric in their strange hats, bizarre costumes, long hair and beards. They were not Greg's favorite people.

"The hairy fairies," he said. "You know, Mother Nature grows
tired of a species and gradually phases it out. Man will be surprised when he learns that he, too, can go the way of the dinosaurs."

"I wish you wouldn't be so hard on homosexuals," I said.
"You're going to antagonize half the literary critics in the world.
We have to think of the book reviews, you know."

"That's your problem," said Greg. "I won't be around for the
reviews. As for me, I have never met a homosexual, of either sex,
whom Nature hadn't obviously decided to discontinue."

We passed Givens Street and Greg said, "That's where I first
went to school—Givens Street Public School. I had long curls at
the time and a bully picked me out right away. Waited for me
every day after school. He'd put me down and hold his fist up
against my nose. He didn't hit me, he just enjoyed the idea of
what he *could* do to me."

"What did you do about it?"

"I tried coming home different ways every day," said Greg.
"Down back alleys and over fences. That just made the game
more interesting for him. Eventually Dad took me to the barber

shop and had my curls cut off. But that didn't help much. I was a shrimp, no good at games, the natural prey of bullies."

We drove north on Dovercourt and found McKenzie Crescent, but found we couldn't turn into it.

"They've made it a one-way street," said Greg. "We'll have to go along Dundas and come down from there."

We cruised slowly down McKenzie Crescent, looking for number 52.

"There it is," said Greg. "That's the house."

"That's number fifty-six," I said.

"They must have changed the number," said Greg.

We got out and looked at the house from the sidewalk. As we stood there, a gray-haired lady wearing a blue-and-white checked dress came along the sidewalk.

She stopped, stared at Greg, then hurried up to him.

"Oh, Mr. Clark," she cried, "it's so wonderful to see you, after knowing you from your stories all these years!"

Her name was Mrs. W. J. Gilfillan. She had a son, Gary Gilfillan, who worked for the Canadian Broadcasting Company. She'd read nearly everything Greg had written and owned many of his books.

"I live just down the street," she said. "Number nine McKenzie Crescent."

"Number nine," said Greg. "That would be the old Alexander Muir home."

"Yes," said Mrs. Gilfillan. "We've lived there since nineteen twenty-nine."

"Poor old Alexander Muir," said Greg. "He wrote 'The Maple Leaf Forever.' It became our national hymn—but he never made a penny from it. He wrote it for a contest, back in eighteen-sixty-seven, the year of Confederation."

"That's right," said Mrs. Gilfillan.

"It was Muir who got my brother, Joe, his first spanking," said Greg. "That was about the turn of the century. He followed Muir down the street, chanting *'Old Daddy Man-ure! Old Daddy Man-ure!'*"

Greg chuckled. "All the kids did it, but Joe was too young to know you were supposed to do it from a safe distance—where you couldn't be recognized. Muir reported Joe to Mother—and Joe was sent to his room to wait for a spanking."

Mrs. Gilfillan said good-bye to Greg and went on her way.

Greg returned to the contemplation of the house where he'd been born. The birth had taken place in the front upstairs bedroom on a sunlit Sunday morning, September 25, 1892.

Greg was the firstborn child of Sarah Louise Clark, age nineteen, and Joseph Thomas Clark, age twenty-five. Greg was to be followed by a brother, Joe, born on January 31, 1896; by a sister, Mabel, born on May 11, 1899, and a final brother, Arthur, born on December 5, 1909.

As the hour of Greg's birth approached, the small house bustled with people. Upstairs was Greg's mother, the attending physician, Dr. Rae, and Greg's maternal grandmother, Louisa Greig, whom Greg came to know and love as "Grandma Greig." Up- and downstairs were his mother's three sisters, soon to be his aunts. Also in attendance were Mrs. Taylor, a next-door neighbor; a maid named Bella; and Mamie Armour, a friend of the Greig sisters who was an amateur astrologer.

Pacing downstairs and puffing on a cigar was Joseph Thomas Clark, as frightened as any first-time father.

Shortly before the birth Mamie Armour announced, "The child that is born at this hour will have long life, prosperity and countless friends."

Greg, a healthy ten-pound baby, was born soon afterward. Downstairs, an agitated Joe Clark heard the welcome cry, "It's a boy!"

The happy father rushed upstairs and held out his hands to take his newborn son from Grandma Greig. Unfortunately, he had forgotten the still-smoking cigar in his hand and, as he slid his hands under Greg, he managed to burn Greg on the behind, producing a yowl from the infant.

"Well," said Dr. Rae, "what a way to welcome a fellow into the world."

However, according to Greg, the incident had a happy result. Greg's blistered butt left him with no lasting trauma and Greg's father felt so guilty about the incident that it produced a bond of affection that lasted for life. According to Greg, anyway.

The year 1892 was not a particularly auspicious one in which to be born. In fact, a business recession was developing into what would be called the Great Panic of 1893. The Clarks lived modestly but comfortably. Joe Clark was a promising young editorial writer and was slated to become a famous editor, but he was in the newspaper profession—one not noted for making rich men of its reporters, photographers, writers or editors. When he died, after fifty-seven years in the newspaper business, he left an estate of twelve thousand dollars.

According to Mabel, Greg's sister, their father only once expressed regret about his career as a newspaperman. She had just become engaged to Thomas Drew-Brook and had spent several weeks looking for a house in which they might live. They had been unable to discover one they could afford.

Joseph Clark paced the family living room while she discussed the problem. He said, "You know, this is the first time in my life I've regretted not having money, so that I could buy my daughter a house. Other men do that."

Mabel was shattered to think she had brought on this self-reproach. She threw her arms around him and wept. "Dad, if you could, you wouldn't be the father I love."

However, on November 3, 1892, something happened that was to shape Greg's life. A group of locked-out printers started a newspaper, the *Evening Star,* announced as "A Paper of the People." This was destined to become the *Toronto Star,* the largest and most controversial paper in Canada. Both Joseph T. Clark and his son, Greg, would spend more than thirty years of their working lives on that paper.

The man most responsible for the growth of the *Star,* and its eventual owner, was a remarkable man named Joseph Atkinson. At the time of Greg's birth, Atkinson was twenty-seven years old and had just married Elmina Elliott, a pretty young female journalist at the *Globe.*

Atkinson, born in Newcastle, Ontario, had been left fatherless when he was six months old. His mother died when he was thirteen and at that time he went to work in a woolen mill. By 1892 Atkinson had worked himself up through the newspaper business to where he was one of the best reporters on the best newspaper in Canada, the *Globe.*

During the first few years of Greg's life, Atkinson was covering Parliament for the *Globe* and ranging across Canada and the United States on important feature assignments. On one of these assignments in Kitchener, Ontario, he met a young high school student named William Lyon Mackenzie King, destined to be-

come the prime minister of Canada. Their mutual interest in social problems led to a lifelong friendship. After graduating from
the University of Toronto, King also went to work for the *Globe*.
At one time Atkinson and King shared a desk and collaborated
on election stories.

Obviously, even before Greg was born, the groundwork had
been laid for much of his life. With the *Toronto Star* he was to
have a long career, almost a love affair. Like some love affairs, it
was to end with feelings of disillusionment and betrayal, with love
turned to hate and with the final ugliness of divorce.

Meanwhile he was to begin the discovery of himself and of the
family situation into which he had been born. His ancestors on
both sides were Scots. As well as the Clarks and the Greigs, there
were the Mathewsons and the McConkeys and the MacMurrays,
just to name a few. True or not, Greg claimed he grew up to hate
the English, the landlord race that forced the Celts off the farms
of Ireland and Scotland.

Reminiscing with sportswriter Ted Reeve one day, Greg said,
"We hated the English in our family because the Duchess of
Sutherland had come up into Sutherlandshire with her English
soldiers and burned our crops. We found our way down to the
sea and eventually we got over to Canada. This led to a special
toast in our family. I'm not allowed to propose it, because the
Clarks are not Scottish, we're Hebridean, from the island of
Lewis in the Hebrides. But my sons—my son, Greg, who is a
Murray of Sutherlandshire, he's a great, big bugger, Ted, as big as
you are—I'm only a little shrimp—my son Greg says, 'Gentlemen, raise your glasses!' So we raise our glasses and he says,
'God damn the Duchess of Sutherland!' And we drink to that.

"Of course," said Greg, "if it weren't for her, we wouldn't be
here."

"No," said Reeve. "You should send her a Christmas card
every year."

"Yes, we should," said Greg. "If it weren't for her, we'd still be
somewhere up in the goddamn mountains!"

4

It is a good thing, being born the son of an editor, although not as good as being the son of a publisher, or the son-in-law of a publisher, or a son-of-a-bitch.

—Greg Clark

Greg's father, Joseph Thomas Clark, was one of many great old-time newspaper editors who flourished in Toronto at the turn of the century.

These famous editors included John Ross Robertson and "Black Jack" Robinson of the Toronto *Telegram;* John R. Bone and J. H. Cranston of the *Toronto Star;* M. H. Hammond and John Lewis of the *Globe;* W. F. Maclean of the *World;* E. E. "Don" Sheppard of *Saturday Night*—and many others.

Joe Clark became perhaps the best-known and most-loved of all. When he died in 1937 the newspapers of Canada, large and small, daily and weekly, mourned him and praised him in extravagant terms. A GREAT EDITOR PASSES. A DEAN OF CANADIAN JOURNALISM. LITTLE JOE DIES. A LIGHT HAS GONE OUT IN THE WINDOWS OF MEN.

Joe Clark was not only known in the city where he made his reputation, but in Pincher Creek, Alberta, in Timmins and in Medicine Hat. He was known in cities and hamlets and from British Columbia to Prince Edward Island. He was a most famous newspaperman for nearly half a century. Back in 1907, when he was making a fact-finding trip across Canada, the Edmonton *Bulletin* announced his arrival in that city as follows:

The newspaperman in Canada who does not know him is a very lonely person, and the newspaperman who does not know him by reputation is a very ignorant person—and the same may be said of persons other than newspaper people.

What was Joe Clark like?

He was, like his son, a small man. Like him, he had twinkling blue eyes and a very large head, almost too large for his body. It was compared to the head of a Roman senator.

His lack of size was very real. As a young man he answered an advertisement for a printer on the Collingwood *Bulletin*. He entered the newspaper office and met a tough, gruff editor of the old school.

Joe Clark said, "I'm the chap you hired."

The editor looked at him and spat on the floor. "I hired a man, not a boy." He returned to his work.

Joe Clark took off his bowler hat and jammed it down over the editor's head until the brim came off in his hands.

"When you can wear this boy's hat," said Joe Clark, "let me know." He stomped out.

Even as a boy, Joe Clark was quick to resent remarks about his size. One of his Grey County school chums described him as "the most pugnacious pacifist" in town.

He was born in Flesherton, Ontario, on September 4, 1866, the year before Confederation. He was the son of William Mathewson Clark and Phyllis McConkey Clark. He was an active youth, playing lacrosse and hockey as well as other school sports. In later years he became an excellent bowler, cricketer and golfer, as well as a fine billiards player.

It would seem he had more natural aptitude for sports than his son Greg, who was to claim that he had spent his life avoiding games of all kinds. Certainly they shared the same sense of mischief and fun. As a schoolboy, Joe Clark and some friends once nearly drove a local teacher out of his mind. They hid the teacher's cow, but placed the cowbell in a tree, attached to a long string. For a whole evening they kept the distracted teacher running in and out of his house. He could hear the bell announcing the return of his beast, but each time he rushed out the animal was nowhere to be seen.

Joe Clark's mother died when he was still a boy. At the age of thirteen he was apprenticed to the printing trade and began work in the office of the *Grey County News*. Soon he moved on to

Wiarton to work for the Wiarton *Echo*. He slept in a small room, little more than a cupboard, in the newspaper office. His spending money was fifty cents a week. One of the few pleasures he could afford was reading. He was befriended by a young Catholic priest in Wiarton and given the run of his library. In later years he was to claim that it was because of this priest that he spoke French with an Irish accent.

When he'd learned the printing trade, Joe Clark set out to see Canada and the United States. He was a "tramp printer"—a man who used his trade to see the world. In the year 1882, when he was still only sixteen, he worked briefly in Toronto, setting type in C. Blackett Robinson's printery on Jordan Street. His salary was six dollars a week; his board bill was three twenty-five. The balance, he said, was "sheer velvet."

He was traveling in the United States before he was twenty years old. At some point in this period of his life he is known to have traveled with a theatrical troupe, but the details of his stage career have not come down to us.

Meanwhile, Joe Clark's sister, Mabel R. Clark, and his brother, James Clark, also became involved in the newspaper business. Mabel became a reporter with the Clinton *Record*. For the last fifteen years of her life she was editor of that paper. His brother, Jim Clark, went to work for the Pickering *News*. In the year 1888, that paper was put up for sale, with an asking price of five hundred dollars. Jim had two hundred and fifty in savings and he phoned Joe, in the United States, to suggest a partnership.

"Have you got two hundred and fifty dollars?" he asked.

Joe raised his share and the two brothers bought the paper in 1888. At the time Joe Clark was only twenty-one years of age. While Jim ran the business end, Joe drove around the countryside picking up bits of local news and began his career as a writer.

There were no Linotype machines available then and papers like the Pickering *News* were printed from hand-set type. Joe Clark's early stories were written in reverse, as he composed them directly in type, at the case. An example of the hand-cranked flatbed press on which the Clarks produced the Pickering *News* is now on exhibit at Metropolitan Toronto's Pioneer Village.

Gathering the news, writing it and printing it must have left Joe Clark with little spare time—but enough for him to begin courting the daughter of a pioneer Pickering family named Sarah Louise Greig. They were married in 1891.

Joe Clark's editorials in the Pickering *News* were beginning to attract attention in Toronto publishing circles, but at the same time it was becoming apparent to the Clark brothers that the Pickering paper could not produce enough money to support both of them.

Joe Clark moved to Toronto and got a job with A. B. Rice, a veteran Toronto newspaperman who was then publishing a West York paper called the *Tribune,* with an office and printing plant at Dundas and Keele streets, then known as Toronto Junction. Rice had noted Clark's writings for the Pickering paper and, indeed, had often quoted his work.

Rice wrote later, "My first meeting with Joe Clark is one of my most cherished memories. He was short and slight, and appeared about eighteen, although really nearing his middle twenties. He had bright blue eyes, a wealth of fair hair and a countenance of unusual charm. My face must have registered some surprise, for Clark said, ruefully, 'I seem to be queered again by my ridiculous appearance.'" Rice simply said he had expected an older man and put Clark to work. His editorials were soon the best things appearing in the *Tribune.*

Rice was an unusual publisher in that he saw and felt that Clark's talent deserved a better showcase. One of Rice's friends was W. F. Maclean, then editor of the *World.* Rice mentioned Clark to him and Maclean immediately said, "Is he the little fellow who used to write those bright things on the Pickering paper?" Joe Clark was soon working for Maclean as an editorial writer. By the time he had been there a year, he attracted the attention of E. E. Sheppard, the man who founded *Saturday Night.*

Sheppard, a flamboyant character who affected a Buffalo Bill hat, was a brilliant, bombastic writer who hated French-Canadians, Catholics, Yankees and the British monarchy. The early popularity of *Saturday Night* was attributed to his free-swinging "Front Page" editorials, which he signed "Don." He was about to embark on a three-month business trip and needed a first-class editorial writer to replace him on *Saturday Night*'s "Front Page." The man he chose was Joe Clark. For a time Clark continued with his job at the *World* while writing *Saturday Night*

editorials under the pen name of "Mack." Soon Sheppard hired
him as assistant editor of *Saturday Night*.

Some other things were happening on the Toronto publishing
scene during that year of 1892. These events were to have an important bearing on Joe Clark's future. The printers at the *News*, a
Toronto daily, were battling with the owners of the paper over
the introduction of mechanical typesetters. Locked out, the
printers began their own newspaper, the *Evening Star*, on November 3, 1892. By July of 1893 the paper foundered for lack of capital. It was then bought by William J. Gage, a publisher of school
textbooks. In fact, until now, he'd enjoyed a virtual monopoly in
this field in Ontario. Unfortunately, Mr. Gage was a Conservative
—and the Liberal government of Ontario had handed over the lu-
crative textbook contracts to another publisher, who happened to
be a Liberal supporter.

Gage now bought the *Star*. His enemies felt he was simply buying a weapon with which to attack the Liberal government until
he got back his contracts for schoolbooks. However, Gage was
not all business. He was also a member of the Lord's Day Alliance. Another of the purposes to which he lent, or bent, his new
newspaper was to fight a stirring and successful campaign against
the use of streetcars on Sunday.

Fate continued to bring Joe Clark and the *Toronto Star* closer
to each other. Gage sold the *Star*. The new buyer was ostensibly
E. E. Sheppard, Joe Clark's boss at *Saturday Night,* but in fact,
the secret purchaser of the *Star* was Frederick B. Nicholls, president of the Canadian General Electric Company and a man holding interests in various utility and street railway companies. His
hidden purpose in buying the paper was to upset the decision
against Sunday streetcars and increase the market for electricity.

For the next year Sheppard operated as front man for Nicholls.
During this time he used Joe Clark to write editorials for the *Star*.
The *Star* presses were moved to the *Saturday Night* premises and
the newspaper was edited and printed there.

On December 13, 1899, the ailing *Star* was sold by Nicholls to
a group of wealthy Liberals who wanted to support the policies of
Sir Wilfrid Laurier. The man they hired to run the paper was
Joseph Atkinson. Atkinson hired Joe Clark as editorial writer. He
was to remain with the *Star* for the next thirty-seven years, except

for one brief period in 1906 and 1907 when he left to serve as editor of *Saturday Night*. Atkinson was dismayed when Clark left and was not happy until he had him back on the *Star* staff. Although another writer, John Lewis, had become editor during Clark's absence, Atkinson used to say, "Lewis thinks he is editor, but I pay Clark more."

Much has been written of the somewhat strange attachment between Joseph Atkinson and Joseph Clark. Some regarded Clark as Atkinson's conscience. When the two disagreed on editorial policy, it was not always Atkinson's opinion that prevailed. They stood on opposite sides of the liquor question. Atkinson was a teetotaler and a prohibitionist. Clark liked a drink, or two drinks, as well as anyone. When Joe Clark was once asked to write an editorial in favor of prohibition, he politely declined. "I don't believe in it," he said, "and I could never write in favor of it." Although prohibition remained the policy of the paper, Clark was not asked again to write in favor of it.

The two men were also far apart on the matter of religion. Atkinson, who became known as "Holy Joe" Atkinson, had a strong religious background and he had his newspaper give full coverage to religious matters. During the 1920s there was a movement for a union of Protestant churches, a movement to which Atkinson wished to give full support. In his biography of Atkinson, Ross Harkness wrote:

> When at last it became evident that a considerable element within the Presbyterian Church was unwilling to unite with Methodists on the basis that had earlier been agreed upon, he [Atkinson] could scarcely be restrained by editor Clark from hurling the *Star* into the fight on behalf of Church union.
>
> One morning he burst into Clark's office.
>
> "Mr. Clark," he declared, "we've got to have an editorial tomorrow on church union."

Patiently Clark repeated what he had said so many times before—that a dispute over doctrinal matters was not something a secular newspaper should deal with; that no good end would be served by an editorial along the lines Atkinson wanted; that it would only inflame still further tempers al-

ready too hot; and that much of the anger would be turned
upon the *Star*.

"But, Mr. Clark," the Chief protested, "Church Union is
so important we can't keep silent any longer."

[It is interesting to note that, despite a work relationship extending over nearly forty years, Atkinson and Clark never addressed
one another on a first-name basis.]

"Mr. Atkinson, in spite of you I shall prevent the *Star*
from doing something that can only harm it," Clark said with
determination. "I will not write such an editorial myself, nor
will I instruct any of my staff to write it."

Mr. Atkinson glared at his editor for a moment, then
turned on his heel and left. The editorial was not written.

Within ten years of the time Joseph Atkinson took over the direction of the *Star,* it had risen to first place among Toronto
newspapers. Atkinson kept it a workingman's paper and made it
more. It became the newspaper of the common man: the champion of reform, mothers' allowances, workmen's compensation
and old-age pensions, the enemy of privilege. It also supported
the Liberal Party and the policies of Sir Wilfrid Laurier. The
phrase, "The twentieth century belongs to Canada" was used often
by Laurier and usually credited to him. Actually, it came from
one of Joe Clark's editorials in the *Star*.

Joe Clark was a kind man and this was apparent in the many
editorials he wrote for the paper. His personality became fused
with that of the paper, to the paper's benefit. In 1936, *The Globe
& Mail* columnist, J. V. McAree, wrote this about him: "He has
been one of the chief reasons for the remarkable success of the
Star. He has given it not only direction, but character. He has
made few enemies for the paper and has not in the world, we
think, a personal enemy." Joe Clark did not regard the editorial
page as some lofty pulpit from which he could dispatch fire-and-
brimstone sermons to the world. Even on serious issues, he
leaned to the light and ironic.

When Joseph Thomas Clark died on July 23, 1937, the newspapers of Canada were filled with tributes, many of which explained the man and the esteem he had earned. The *Toronto Star*
wrote: "He was a self-made, self-taught man, learning from life

and experience, though few men read more widely. Mr. Clark was a democrat to his finger-tips. He was a firm believer in democracy. In life and politics he was a Liberal; in faith and outlook he was a reformer. A student of history and a tolerant interpreter of human affairs, he could smile at most of the world's lunacies while calmly following an editorial course that sought always to make the world a somewhat better place in which to live."

His obituary in the Winnipeg *Free Press* had this to say about him:

Joe Clark was a happy warrior, commenting lightly and brightly on the greatnesses and weaknesses of mankind in general and on the daily affairs of the world in which he worked and loved to live. Possessed of a piquant sense of humor, he did not take life too seriously. He stood resolutely on the side of right against might and against wrong, but he labored under no delusions as to his ability to re-make or reform the world. He was not a crusading editor. Yet through the more gentle and more subtle art of irony, wit and good humor, he left an imprint none the less deep and lasting.

J. H. Cranston, the longtime editor of the *Star Weekly,* outlined Joe Clark in action as an editor:

We recall most vividly the leader he wrote the day after the famous reciprocity election of 1911. The *Star* had thrown itself wholeheartedly into support of Laurier's reciprocity treaty. It had campaigned vigorously for a trade arrangement with the United States, even going to the extent of filling its King Street windows with exhibits of meat which could be bought at lower prices across the line than in Canada. The Toronto *Telegram* shouted "Buffalo Bologna" at the *Star,* and U. S. President Taft helped the Tories by a speech in which he stated that Canada was "at the parting of the ways." The electors refused to take the *Star*'s advice, and everyone wondered what the *Star* would have to say about the verdict.

We on the paper turned just as anxiously to the editorial page as anyone else and there to our amazement we saw a learned discourse on "The Decline of Ping Pong," and not a word about the election. Joe went into great detail as to the rise of the game, its effect upon those who played it, and its gradual falling off in public favour in sentences as solemn and portentuous as if he had been discussing the rise and fall of the Roman Empire.

After all the scream and the roar of the reciprocity battle it was a most unexpected and amusing anti-climax which no one but Joe Clark could have sprung on the curious public. He showed that he not only had the ability to absorb defeat without rancour but even to get fun out of it.

Joe Clark did get fun out of life. As a boy he was an active hockey and lacrosse player and in later years a cricketer, a billiards player, a golfer and fisherman. He was one of the early members of Lambton Golf Club and later switched to Lakeview. He was one of the founders of the Canadian Club and a president of the Toronto Playgrounds Association.

He kept up a correspondence with many: William Jennings Bryan; Goldwin Smith, the wealthy Toronto intellectual whose Grange became the Art Gallery; Howard Greenwood, a cricket companion at Pickering, who later became Parliamentary Secretary to Winston Churchill; B. K. Sandwell, a famous Toronto editor; and many others.

A sense of fun, an enjoyment of life, seemed always to be bubbling within Joe Clark. Here is a letter written to a friend a few years before his death:

Mr. W. H. Plant,
Toronto.

Dear Sir:

For some time I have felt that it would be necessary for me to caution you against a growing tendency on your part to allow your domestic affections to interfere with your true interests as a golf player.

Today I learn on phoning your office that you have gone off on a motor trip to Quebec with your wife and daughter and have not taken your golf clubs with you—not even your putter with which you might have practiced on the carpet in the rooms of the hotels where you tarried overnight. To succeed in golf, you ought to know, for I have impressed this on you often enough, you must take life seriously. This year you encouraged me greatly by the fact that, except for one game, you played all season in the eighties. Just as I was hoping to see you finish the year with the prospect of playing in the seventies next season, you yield to weakness of your domestic affections and jaunt off to Quebec with your family without letting me or the pro know you were going.

Well, it's your affair. If you prefer your wife and children to golf, that is your privilege. It is for you to say. You are at the crossroads, the turning point in your career. You are free, as far as I am concerned, to make your choice. You know golf and you know your family and I, a stranger, cannot intervene in any way.

Bert, I sympathize with you no matter what your problems are. It is a fine day. I dictate this just before I leave for the Club. Imagine that first tee on a day like this and the sun overhead like a cup in the vast putting green of the sky!

Yours sincerely,
Jos. T. Clark.

5

"DAISY BELL" ("A BICYCLE BUILT FOR TWO")

—Hit song of 1892

The year in which both Greg and the *Toronto Star* were born was an interesting one. People were singing about a bicycle, but it was also the year in which the United States' first motor car was built —the forerunner of millions. The Coca-Cola company was formed in Atlanta, Georgia, by a pharmacist named Asa Candler, who had acquired control of the beverage for twenty-three hundred dollars. The first Fig Newton bars were produced by the New York Biscuit Company. "Gentleman Jim" Corbett knocked out the famous John L. Sullivan in the first championship fight in which the boxers wore padded gloves. In Italy the minimum age at which Italian girls could marry was raised—to the age of twelve. In New Zealand, women gained the right to vote. Theirs was the first country in the world to institute female suffrage.

The Toronto newspapers reflected the world of the 1890s somewhat sketchily. A lengthy report on a gathering of local Presbyterians would be followed by a short item on a cholera epidemic sweeping Europe or the deepening economic depression in the United States.

There was no satellite system, no television, no radio, no wire services as we know them today. In one way readers benefited from the situation. There were few, if any, one-newspaper cities. Even the small town of Port Hope, Ontario, with a population of six thousand, supported three different newspapers, with different points of view.

Because of communication and transportation costs, the big stories were local stories. The local fair or a local bicycle race received extensive coverage. Crime, then as now, was a news staple.

In 1893 newspaper circulations reached new heights as they reported on the famous Lizzie Borden murder trial at Fall River, Massachusetts, from which sprang the popular rhyme:

> Lizzie Borden took an ax
> And gave her mother forty whacks;
> When she saw what she had done
> She gave her father forty-one.

Crime also played a part in the early reporting career of Joseph Atkinson, Greg's future employer. The top news event of 1890 in Ontario was the arrest, trial and hanging of J. R. Birchall. Hangings were often bungled and the hanging of Birchall at the Woodstock jail was a dreadful one, witnessed by some two hundred prominent citizens and reporters.

Atkinson's detailed report of the brutal execution was a classic and occupied virtually the entire front page of the *Globe,* for which he then worked. His story included a vivid description of the scene, the audience, the doomed man's last hours with his wife and an interview with the hangman, who showed Atkinson how to fashion a noose, on the eve of the execution. It foreshadowed the kind of detailed, human-interest reporting that would become a feature of Atkinson's *Toronto Star.* It also set Atkinson against capital punishment; he was to argue for its abolition.

The newspapers of that day sold for a cent a copy. For ten dollars, at that time, you could buy a suit of clothes, an overcoat or a round-trip rail ticket to Chicago. For a comparatively modest sum, you could buy a whole newspaper—plant, presses and all— or start up one of your own. This was common practice on the part of political parties or businessmen with an ax to grind.

While Greg's father was establishing himself in the Toronto newspaper field, Greg had more immediate problems. Shortly after his birth he acquired a severe case of eczema. His whole body became a red, itchy mass. His hands had to be bound in flannel mittens to prevent him from scratching away his skin. Treatment of eczema in those days was mostly mechanical and not very successful. Babies were dusted with white and gray powders, smeared with ointments, daubed with the juices of plants. If the cause was dietary or the result of an allergy, the treatments frequently made the condition worse.

Greg's mother may have been somewhat ashamed of his appearance. She did not take him to church for baptism, even though she was an active churchgoer. Late in life, Greg used to speculate on the lifelong desire for affection and approval that motivated him in many areas. Looking back, he felt that this was rooted in his unattractiveness as a baby. Deep in his subconscious, he felt, there were glimpses of adults turning away from him in distaste—of strangers peering into his carriage, gulping and then struggling for a few polite words. Today's studies of infant psychology lend weight to his theory. Babies need to be fondled and handled and they are aware of adult reactions at much earlier ages than we used to believe.

Greg inherited his father's large head and small body. Unfortunately, while Greg's head was large, it lacked the classic proportions of his father's and was marred by an overly large nose. Greg felt worse on the arrival of his younger brother, Joseph Clark. Not only was the new arrival given his father's name; he turned out to be a handsome, blond child and became the center of attention.

When young Joe turned two, he was stricken with pneumonia, a circumstance that cast a pall over the house. There were no antibiotics and, in the case of small children, the disease was frequently fatal. Greg's father stayed home from work. His mother, having been given the beautiful baby she wanted, was now almost speechless with terror at the prospect of losing him. Dr. John Malloch, the family doctor, called in two well-known specialists who examined the boy, shook their heads, and said there was nothing more that could be done. He was too far gone.

Dr. Malloch did not give up, though. He packed Joseph in ice to reduce his temperature and continued his efforts. Eventually he turned the tide. When young Joe recovered, he became more than ever the family pet.

Greg found the newcomer difficult to combat, although doubtless he tried as best he could. A family anecdote has come down through the years about the day Greg, age eight, and Joe, age four, were sent to the corner store for some groceries. Their mother told them the three or four items she wanted and the two of them set off together under a large umbrella in a slight drizzle.

When they returned ten minutes later, Greg was marching grimly along under the umbrella and Joe was trailing along behind, not only wet but crying as loudly as he could. Neither had any of the groceries.

"We didn't get them," announced Greg disgustedly.

"Why not?"

"We made an arrangement when we left," said Greg. "*I* was to carry the umbrella—and *he* was to remember the groceries!"

Many of Greg's early memories were not of his mother or his father, but of his mother's mother, Grandma Greig. She was Louisa McMurray Greig, the widowed mother of six children. Her husband, William Greig, had emigrated with his father, John Greig, from Scotland early in the nineteenth century and settled near Lake Ontario east of Toronto. On the family farm there, the Greigs continued many of the old-country crafts, doing their own weaving, making their own bricks.

On her husband's death, Louisa Greig moved into Pickering with her children. It was here that Joseph Clark, then part owner of the Pickering *News,* met the family. At first he had taken out another of her daughters, but he shifted his affections to Sarah Louise and married her in November of 1891.

With her children married, Grandma Greig divided her time between their houses, as was customary in those days. She was not only a welcome but a sought-after visitor to all her children. She was a great cook and her children quarreled about which house she should visit, particularly in the fall, at pickling time. A deep, dark mystery still lives in the Clark family about the disappearance of her recipe book. Here, copied out in her neat longhand, were all her famous family recipes. At her death, this book disappeared and, although accusations have flown back and forth, the book has never been found.

Grandma Greig was often at Joseph Clark's home, because Greg's father was fond of his mother-in-law. He made sure that they had delicacies she liked when she was there, and he brought home from the office the country papers she liked to read.

From his earliest days, young Greg saw her not only as a wonderful cook, but as a kind of magic visitor. Perhaps he was looking elsewhere for the attention his parents were giving to his brother Joe. Also, Grandma Greig was a storyteller. Greg sat on a footstool covered with red carpeting, with Grandma Greig's elastic-sided shoes clasped between his knees, as she told him stories of romance and horror. She recalled the day a rabid dog had killed her young brother in front of her eyes. At other times, she spoke of the runaway Negro slaves who had been sheltered at her father's pioneer farm near Markham. She was not an educated woman (Greg did not remember ever seeing Grandma Greig, or his mother, reading a book), but Grandma Greig was a great teller of tales and a great believer in her own intuitions.

"Always trust your first impressions," she told Greg. "Nature has put a description of the contents on every package. A bull is a bull. A wolf is a wolf. A crow is a crow. They look that way because that is what they are."

It then followed, "Don't trust men who toe in or toe out. Those who toe in are selfish. Those who toe out are not to be trusted. Trust a man who walks with his feet straight ahead."

One of her stories was about a man who found a lucky stone, a stone with a hole through it. She told young Greg, "Now, if you find one, put it on a piece of string around your neck and it will protect you from the arrow that flies by day and the pestilence that stalks by night."

Greg began an immediate search, combing all the neighboring driveways. He did not find one until twenty years later, on the beach at Brighton, England, where he was on leave from the war in France in 1917. Having found his lucky stone, he never again parted from it. It hung high around his neck on a piece of string. When the string was worn out, he would carefully thread a new string through the stone and around his neck before removing the old one.

Grandma Greig obviously meant much to Greg as a boy. She was a warm mother image who quickened his imagination and was perhaps the first to demonstrate to him the power of the storyteller. However, one thing she passed on to him that was to his disadvantage was a family defect known as the familial intention tremor. This is a tremor of the hand that begins with the formation of an intent to pick up a glass of water or a cup of tea or another object. Greg's mother inherited it from Grandma Greig. Oddly enough, Greg was the only one to inherit the tremor; it did not appear in either of his brothers or in his sister. He passed the tremor on to two of his own three children, the eldest and the youngest.

The affliction caused Greg some embarrassment on at least a few occasions in his life. When he arrived overseas in World War

I, his platoon noticed the trembling of his fingers when he attempted to pick up a pencil to make notes, and for a while thought they had acquired the most frightened lieutenant in the Canadian Army. It took a few wire raids to convince them that Greg's nerves were at fault—not his nerve. In later years, when given a glass by a bartender that was filled right to the rim, Greg would take the first sip bent over the glass on the bar, so that his trembling hand would not spill it on the way to his lips. Strangers, seeing this and Greg's trembling hand, doubtless thought they were watching a man in the last desperate stages of alcoholism. One helpful imbiber showed Greg how to loop his tie around the back of his neck, grasp the end of the tie and the drink in one hand, and hoist it to his lips by pulling on the other end of the tie.

This was a long way in the future.

First, Greg's horizons widened to include Givens Street Public School. His academic career did not begin well. He had inherited his father's size, or lack of it, but not his father's eagerness for combat.

Greg described himself differently. "I was a small boy who couldn't run without tripping, who couldn't jump without falling on his rump, who couldn't throw a ball either far or straight, who didn't dare rassle, who, in short, was the kind of boy you can see every day walking to or from school a few polite paces in the rear of a knot of other boys and looking very wishful, very eager and very much out of it."

In 1899 the Clark family moved from McKenzie Crescent to 66 Howland Avenue, which ran north from Bloor Street, two blocks east of Bathurst. Greg's school was now Huron Street Public School. The move followed the birth of Mabel, Greg's sister, on May 11, 1899. With three children and a maid, the McKenzie Crescent home was somewhat crowded. Fortunately, Joseph Clark's fortunes as a newspaper editor were prospering.

The new Clark home on Howland Avenue provided a new lease on life for young Greg, now age seven. He began to acquire friends for the first time—boys named Billy Milne, Bob Jenkins and Cecil Perry. By the age of ten, Greg had met two other neighborhood boys who were to have a marked influence on his development. These were Stuart Thompson, a relative of the famous naturalist Ernest Thompson Seton, and Hoyes Lloyd. These two were enthusiastic young naturalists. Although they were older than Greg and his friends, they did not mind the small fry tagging along on their field trips. From them Greg got his first inkling of the fascinating world of nature.

Hoyes Lloyd grew up to become a distinguished ornithologist and a director of the International Wild Fowl Migratory Bird Convention. Stuart Thompson became a well-known amateur naturalist in Toronto, where he conducted nature tours of High Park for many years and wrote books about Canadian animal and plant life.

At Huron Street Public School Greg did not distinguish himself. He had an almost comic inability to grasp mathematics. However, he had some pleasant memories of his classrooms. Nearly seventy years later he wrote a story for *Weekend Magazine* called "Miss L. Bruce—A Love Story," based upon one, or perhaps more than one, of his public school teachers.

6

MISS L. BRUCE
A LOVE STORY

by Greg Clark

I never even knew her first name.

Yet for three years of my life, she dominated every day, every hour. I was putty in her hands.

She was a tall, dark, spare woman. I imagine she was in her mid-thirties when I first met her. She had firm cheek bones, the skin tight over them. Her eyes, not large behind shining steel-rimmed spectacles, were intensely dark, and always simmering or smouldering with either anger or humour. It took us several weeks to be sure that it was humour.

Carrying her pointer, as big, in our eyes, as a billiard cue, she would walk slowly up and down the aisles as we bent to our desks. We were not afraid of her. Her skirts, usually maroon, swept the school room floor.

We had her for three years, Junior Third, Senior Third, Junior Fourth. These are now generally called Grades 5, 6 and 7. In the country schools in these days, it was not uncommon to have the same teacher for four or five years. But in city schools it was most unusual to have the same teacher from one grade to the next. We had Miss Bruce three years. She was promoted with us.

I was never higher than No. 26 in a class of thirty-four. Arithmetic was my ruin. I just couldn't get it through my head. To this day, when I have to add up a column of figures, my left hand creeps out of sight, under the desk, to carry. Carry three. Carry five.

And fractions. Or percentages! Let us say it is the arithmetic period. The problem before us is as follows:

Farmer Jones took twenty dozen eggs to market. He sold twelve dozen at fifteen cents a dozen. He sold six dozen at twelve cents a dozen. He sold the remainder at ten cents. What was the average price Farmer Jones received for his eggs?

We bent to our exercise books. All would be silence, except for sniffling and scraping.

"Gregory?" Miss Bruce would say.

Now, all this problem had done for me so far was to conjure up the picture of Farmer Jones's farm. It would be early morning. Over the fields the mist would be lying. The roosters crowing. The cows mooing at the gate. The horses stamping in the stable. And out the farmhouse door would be coming Farmer Jones and a boy about my age, ten, with baskets on his arms to collect twenty dozen eggs.

As I scrambled to my feet the classroom would erupt with snorts and snickers. Everybody knew I was the dunce in arithmetic. With a wave of her dark slim hand, Miss Bruce would quell the snickers.

"Tell us, Gregory," she would say, "what signs and wonders you beheld on your way to school today."

So I would tell them, for instance, that at the mansion of Mrs. Timothy Eaton, at the corner of Lowther Avenue and Spadina, the gardeners were putting in the spring annuals.

"How many gardeners?"

"Three."

"What flowers were they planting?"

"Geraniums . . . uh . . ."

"On your way home, Gregory," Miss Bruce would say, "stop and see what other plants they are putting in. You may sit down."

She was not making fun of me. For in the next breath, she might ask, perhaps, whichever of my seatmates had snorted loudest; or even one of the clever, bland-faced No. 1 girls up at the front of the class, to stand and report what they had seen on their way to school. Stage-struck, they would stand embarrassed. Apparently they had seen nothing on their way to school. Whereupon, it being arithmetic period after all, she would ask one of the tongue-tied clever ones to read the solution of Farmer Jones's problem.

What she was doing, of course, was getting me into the act. I was only one of the backward pupils at the rear of the classroom. She got us all into the act, according to our bents. The next worst arithmetic boy to me could read swiftly, accurately and with style. Miss Bruce would ask him to read to us. Stanley, a boy two or three years older than the rest of us at the back of the class (he wore long pants, that's how old he was!) was a hero in the whole school because he was the champion pitcher of one of the sandlot baseball teams that flourished in every few city blocks. One day Stanley put up his hand eagerly in response to one of Miss Bruce's questions. To his horror, Miss Bruce selected him from the forest of hands. Big Stanley rose and stood confused and blushing. He didn't know the answer. He sat down.

In a few minutes, Miss Bruce called on Stanley to stand up.

"Stanley, I believe you have a baseball in your desk?"

"Yes."

"Would you take it, please, and from where you are, show us how you hit the doorknob."

And Miss Bruce pointed to the doorknob up at the far corner of the classroom. Stanley eagerly took the ball, wound up dramatically and hit the doorknob square on the nose. The whole class, even the clever-faced No. 1 girls up front, scrambled to retrieve the ball clattering around our feet, and hand it to Miss Bruce.

As she gave the ball back to Stanley, she said:

"You have something called perfect co-ordination, Stanley. It is something to be proud of."

Before we were half way through Junior Third, or Grade 5, we all knew Miss Bruce was far more interested in us backward ones at the back of the class than in her bright pupils. Often, she would bring her chair down from the little platform on which her desk stood and sit with us.

They have more interesting titles for us nowadays; but we backward children were mostly kept in until four o'clock, three days out of five, for special coaching. But it was fun. For the next stupidest arithmetician to me would be asked to read from the Third Reader; Stanley would be asked to show how to hold the ball, with the fingers just so; and I would be told to tell how the roofers put the tar and gravel on a roof—a procedure I had just witnessed that noon. And the small dark shy girl who stammered so badly would be asked to go to the blackboard and copy out a sentence Miss Bruce had written above. That little girl, age nine, I suppose, could write with the flowing ease of Miss Bruce herself.

"That is beautiful!" Miss Bruce would say, as the girl resumed her seat among us. (There were more fights in the school yard and on the way home over that little chubby girl than over any other cause. Let anyone, boy or girl, mock her, and it was a bloody nose. In Grade 5, in those days, you could sock a girl for cause.)

When the summer came and we felt we were all parting company to move to the next grade, Miss Bruce held a little court. She had a small speech for each of us. For me it was:

"Gregory, don't be afraid! There is more to life than arithmetic."

And she lent me Chester A. Reed's *Bird Guide,* a small brown pocket book illustrating in colour all the birds of this country.

"You can bring it back," she said, "in September. You like seeing things, Gregory. See if you might like to know the wild birds."

This was the instant birth of the love of nature that has been the joy of my life for the sixty-five years since.

On my return to enter Senior Third, Grade 6, imagine my feelings on finding Miss Bruce sitting smiling at the desk in the room to which our class was directed. She was promoted too. Soon the fog deepened for me. I met grammar. And grammar was more incomprehensible to me than arithmetic. With simple, lovely things like words, how can you fit them into pickle jars of laws? It became, in my 10th year, a question whether I should spend my time, kept in each day, on arithmetic or grammar. But still Miss Bruce brought her chair down to the back of the class, and still Big Stanley and the rest of us showed off our non-academic talents, and when summer came again, Miss Bruce lent me, at our farewell party in the classroom, Rudyard Kipling's *Just So Stories,* recently published.

"You will learn more grammar from this," she said, "than from anything I can teach you. You can bring it back to me in September."

Yes, we had her for the third year, in which year she lent me Kipling's *Kim* and took me to show me how to join the Public Library which was away downtown. And all our gang, clever and backward, stayed together until we were at last promoted into Senior Fourth, or Grade 8, the fatal Entrance Year.

Sam Richardson, assistant principal, was our new teacher.

"I understand Gregory," he said to me in front of all, "you have the gift of the gab. I am afraid that will not help you with me. I see by your report that you are very poor in arithmetic and grammar. So we will spend the coming year on those two subjects, principally. Understand?"

I understood.

That was a bare, toilsome, forgotten year out of my life. All I remember of it were the schemes and stratagems I devised for dropping into Miss Bruce's classroom at recess and after hours. And I even braved the dangers inherent in teacher's pet by walking with her after school down to the street-car line on her way home. And being allowed to carry her satchel of books and papers. We talked of India and the wide world.

"I dream," she said, "of saving money enough to visit India some day."

Well, we passed our entrance, under the strong hand of Sam Richardson, every one of us, including Stanley. And I entered the fabled world of high school, where there was Latin and Greek, both with grammars a backward child could understand, not a hodge-podge Chinese puzzle like English grammar. And a debating society, and a literary society, and a school library, quiet and stately, where you could visit after four until the caretaker threw you out at five thirty. The ogres of algebra and geometry I met and conquered with the aid of special coaching. And when I got my matriculation, I wrote my first love letter to Miss Bruce.

It was a letter in which I told her I now knew what she had been teaching us in those three years now long behind me. She was teaching us courage.

She was telling us we were good for something. Even the gift of the gab. I never posted that letter. It sounded mushy to me. And sixty years ago, to be mushy was the same as being square today. My second love letter I never posted to her was written when I was thrown out of the university for failing my first year twice due to the time I spent hanging around the office of the undergraduate newspaper, *The Varsity;* and endless hours in the great university library, when I should have been at lectures.

In that letter, I told her I knew where I was going now and that was to be a newspaper reporter, and I thanked her for the three years in which she had excited me to look, look, look at the beautiful strange world. I didn't post it, because it sounded a little highfalutin' for a cub reporter.

My last unposted letter to Miss Bruce was written in a dugout north of Arras, France. In that war, we always carried an unposted letter to our mother and father, and one to our wife or sweetheart. These were to be found in our paybook if we were killed, to say goodbye. My third letter was to Miss Bruce, thanking her for telling me something I thought of as I led my platoon in the winter night up the line for a tour of eighteen days' duty.

I imagined I saw the tall, serene, maroon figure of Miss Bruce.

"Gregory, don't be afraid," I thought she said. "There is more to life than death."

Well, I wasn't killed. And when the ship that brought me home came into Halifax harbour, I stood in the stern and one by one tore up the three farewell letters and threw them into the wind.

Now, how do you explain that never in all these years did I walk the few blocks to the old school to see Miss Bruce? You explain it. I cannot. Is it shyness? Is it fear of losing something precious, tying you to childhood?

In the early 1930s I got on the Bloor Street car.

There, ten feet from me sat Miss Bruce. She was much older than I held her in memory. But she was as straight as ever. On her head a little maroon hat. Her black-gloved hands folded in her lap. It was, as you can believe, the moment of truth for me. I had only to go to Christie Street, a few blocks. I had little time. Less time than a man with a sword.

I got up and walked from strap to strap until I stood before her. I reached down and took one of her black-gloved hands.

"Miss Bruce?" I said.

She raised her eyes, dark and simmering still, behind the steel-rimmed spectacles.

"Yes?"

"I'm Gregory," I said.

"Yes?"

"Gregory Clark," I said. "You had me in Junior Third, Senior Third, Junior Fourth, remember?"

Miss Bruce studied me with an intense expression.

"You lent me *Kim,*" I said. "And *Just So Stories.*"

"Yes?"

"You remember," I said, "about not being afraid? Not being afraid of arithmetic? Or grammar?"

All right, reader. Stop reading here. This is the way half the love stories of the world end.

Miss Bruce was trying to remember.

"There were so many," she said.

I let go her hand.

"Did you ever go to India?" I asked.

"India?" she replied. "Oh, you must be mistaken."

Christie Street was only five blocks away now. She looked away, puzzling. She looked up at me, trying to recollect.

Christie Street was coming up. I rang the bell cord. I reached down and took her hand again. I got off the car and had a little trouble seeing the curb.

Whatever you do, if you have a teacher who put you on the path, who showed you the way, who taught you not to be afraid, go find her, or him, go find them before it is too late.

Before they forget you.

7

LUNCH AT LA SCALA

It could be said that this biography began in 1947, but that wouldn't be wholly accurate. In any case, that was the year I first tried to write about Greg Clark.

I was trying to make a living as a free-lance writer. *Maclean's* magazine was then Canada's most prestigious market and, on the assumption that it was best to begin at the top, I began bombarding them with a series of suggestions and ideas.

The trouble with most of my suggestions was that they had already been done, somebody else was already doing them, they were subjects I knew nothing about or they were the kind of assignment no editor in his right mind would give to an unknown free-lance writer.

On this occasion I suggested to *Maclean's* that I be assigned to do stories on Yousuf Karsh, the famous Canadian photographer, or Guy Lombardo and his Royal Canadians. Failing that, I wondered whether they would care to send me out West to examine the mechanization of agriculture or to the North Pole to see if the Russians were getting too close.

I also suggested a story on Greg Clark and Jimmie Frise. It had just been announced that they were ending long careers at the *Star Weekly* and going to work for the Montreal *Standard*.

Ralph Allen, then assistant editor at *Maclean's,* wrote me as follows:

Dear Mr. Carroll:

Thanks for your letter of January 18.

I'm sorry to say that your affinity for unfortunate coincidence is still downright sensational.

We have carried profiles on Lombardo and Karsh within

the last two years, and don't think either of them warrants a repeat.

We consider Clark and Frise direct competitors, and can't afford to publicize them.

You probably saw that *Life* is just out with a preview of your "Who Owns The Top of The World?" piece.

And we have a story on farm industrialization on assignment right now.

Therefore, all of your proposed subjects are out with us for the time being at least.

Many thanks for letting us know about them anyway.

Yours sincerely,
Ralph Allen
Assistant Editor.

This letter may not seem wildly enthusiastic, but it was better than most of the rejection slips and letters I was getting in those days. Allen was at least kind enough not to make the point that there were dozens of more experienced newspapermen around who had worked with Greg on stories and had worked beside him as a war correspondent, including Allen himself.

In any case, I began selling stories to *Maclean's* in a few years and, more importantly, to the Montreal *Standard,* where Greg had gone to work. This led to a staff job with the *Standard* in 1949 and my first meetings with Greg.

At the time the Montreal *Standard* was a national weekly publication, much like the *Star Weekly,* which it had been trying to catch up with for years. It contained a first-class photo-news section, a condensed novel, a color comic section and a magazine section containing short stories, feature articles and well-known columnists. Greg's work was to continue producing the humorous adventures which had made him famous in the *Star Weekly*. He did this from his home in Toronto.

I was doing photo-stories and features that took me out of town much of the time and occasionally out of the country. Nevertheless, we were assigned to work together on a few occasions: for the stories Greg wrote on Marilyn Bell after her famous swim across Lake Ontario; for an interview with Premier Leslie Frost; and the time we chased Prince Philip across the Arctic, along with a score of other newsmen, on one of his Royal Tours. On these occasions I functioned only as a photographer; Greg did the writing. Perhaps the editors were hoping I would learn something.

For a long time Greg's stories in the *Standard* called for a new photograph of him every week. He would don a different costume for each one, change hats, clean a gun, play with a fishing rod, read a book—so that the editors had a huge file of photos on hand, from which they could choose one to illustrate whatever story he came up with that week.

Most of these were taken by Louis Jaques, the *Standard*'s senior photographer, who would do a score or more at one sitting, at the head office in Montreal or at Greg's home in Toronto. Occasionally, when Jaques was busy, I would be sent over to Greg's home to replenish the supply. In this way I met Greg's wife, Helen; his daughter, Elizabeth, then a young art student; and Greg, Jr., a high school principal, and his wife, Doreen.

In 1951, after a brief stint as a correspondent in the Korean War, I was invited to join the Canadian War Correspondents Association. Greg was the favorite of this hard-bitten, hard-drinking crew, and at their get-togethers I came to meet many of Greg's special friends: Gil Purcell, the one-legged tyrant who was general manager of Canadian Press; Bruce West, columnist for *The Globe & Mail;* Ralph Allen, by then editor of *Maclean's* magazine, and many others who had served overseas with Greg in World War II.

The difference in Greg's behavior in his separate worlds was startling. At home he was a prim, docile husband and father who was not allowed to have liquor in the house. With the war correspondents or his hunting and fishing friends, he was the life of the party, a roistering old sweat.

At the press club ceremony where Greg was made an honorary life member, he was pulled up to the bar by Ted Reeve, a former football star, a former lacrosse star, a famous sportswriter and a man who loved his rum.

"Greg!" said Reeve. "Let me buy you a drink!"

"Oh, no," said Greg. "I'm going home and I mustn't come in with liquor on my breath."

Reeve towered over Greg by at least a foot and their attitudes were farther apart.

"Good God!" roared Reeve. "If I didn't come home smelling of rum my wife wouldn't know me!"

At first I found this behavior of Greg's hypocritical, but I was to learn he had his reasons.

Because we were, for a long time, the only two Montreal *Standard* employees living in and working out of Toronto, we had other occasions to get together. We would make trips to the Montreal head office together to discuss our work and, in Toronto, Greg would often drop into the Toronto bureau office for information, sometimes to take me to lunch. He would appear unannounced, like the magical gnome he resembled, one of his famous gnarled walking sticks in his hand, a tweed jacket over a bright-yellow turtleneck sweater, a porkpie hat tipped jauntily to one side, blue eyes glinting from under shaggy white eyebrows.

This day he said, "I have come to take you to lunch."

"Where?" I asked.

"To La Scala, which is a fine Italian restaurant, run by Greeks. It has a wonderful golden chair in front where an old man can sit down if he needs a rest."

On the walk to the restaurant Greg was stopped by a senator, two old ladies, a young man and a veteran of World War I. Some knew Greg as a person, some knew him only through his stories.

One of the old ladies said, "Are you *the* Gregory Clark?"

"No," said Greg, "I'm the *other* Gregory Clark."

The old lady came closer and peered into his face. "Ah, yes," she said, "*now* I can see the difference."

We were bowed into La Scala with the warmth and respect due a gentleman of Greg's reputation.

"First," said Greg, "we will have a drink. I will have a J&B and water."

When the drinks came he picked his up and held it lovingly in his hands, with respect. Still looking at it, he said, "You know when I had my heart attack, Bill Oille, my doctor, said I was to be allowed only one drink at lunch, and two drinks before dinner. But I had to use a measuring cup—a thing called a jigger, I believe. So I went down to Eaton's and inquired around and finally came home with this strange little thing. I measured out one drink into it and poured it into my glass. I stared at it, not quite believing. Then it dawned on me—what a wonderful life I'd had! I was so excited I had to phone up Gil Purcell. 'Gil,' I said, 'I've just made the most wonderful discovery! I've just poured myself a drink with that little jigger Bill Oille made me get. You know what? *All my life I've been drinking doubles!'* "

We toasted this and consulted the elaborate La Scala menu brought by a young Italian waiter named Ottavio. "What a beautiful Italian menu," said Greg. "Imagine all this Italian food being cooked by Greeks."

He looked at the waiter over the top of his glasses. "That's right, isn't it? You're the only Italian in the place?"

"No, no, no, sir," protested Ottavio. "Here we are all Italians! There is only one Greek."

Greg turned back to the menu with a sigh. "Ah, well. It made a better story the other way. I am just what my son said. James Murray Clark. The one who was killed with the Regina Rifles."

"What was that?"

"He read one of my stories in the old *Star* and he said, 'Dad, you're not a *reporter,* you're a *troubadour!'* " Greg went on, "Of course, I wasn't supposed to be the *reporter.* Fred Griffin was the great *Star* reporter. He supplied the facts—I supplied the human interest."

"Were you sent on the same stories?"

"All the time. Old Hindmarsh of the *Star* was under the misapprehension Griffin and I were enemies—instead of great friends. He thought sending us on the same story would make us work twice as hard. It was one of those clumsy ideas editors get. But we writers should try to be kind to editors. They have a terrible job."

I put my notebook on the table and began making notes of Greg's conversation.

"What are you doing?" he asked.

"I am making notes about you," I said. "Since you have failed to put the real Greg Clark in your own books, I am going to use him in one of mine."

"Hmmm," said Greg. "A lot of people have been interviewing me lately—updating my obituary, I guess. They ask me things like, 'What is your favorite book?' I have no favorites. I read a book the way I launch a canoe. I just jump into it and take off, enjoying the rapids, enjoying the calm places. Sometimes I think I have no critical faculty whatsoever. I just like everything and everybody."

He went on, "I lost my religion at sixteen, you know, from

reading over my head. Then the war finished it off completely. But even afterward, I remained a bit of a Puritan. I couldn't go out chasing women, the way some of the men did during the war. I used to say, 'No son of mine is going to have a whore for a mother.' A kind of Presbyterian pride, I guess."

Greg laughed at this self-analysis. "But I do have a religion. It's love of earth, rock and sky."

"What kind of religion is that?"

"It was an expression used by George Russell," said Greg.

"Who is George Russell?" I said.

"An Irish poet," said Greg. "He wrote under the pen name of A.E.—and he was part of the Irish Revival. He was called upon to say a eulogy on the death of an artist. So he said, 'Love of earth, rock and sky is a form of worship.' That is my religion. Life is so wonderful. I love all of it."

He studied the menu again. "There's my favorite—*linguine a la vongole*—baby clams. But I must force myself to experiment. As I get older I find myself only ordering proven things—things I know are good."

Greg broke off abruptly and began to laugh at himself, loudly and with great enjoyment. "Did you hear that?" he said. "And I've just finished telling you, at great length, that I have no favorites! What nonsense men talk!"

Ottavio stood by respectfully with his order pad and pencil. Greg ordered the Ravioli a La Scala, and I ordered the Veal Scallopine Marsala.

"And the *minestrone*," added Greg. "We should have that. I don't know what it'll be—the thick kind, or the thin kind they make in the south of Italy. I think they just throw in a few vegetables at the last minute."

He turned to Ottavio, the waiter. "Do you know the famous restaurant in Naples? Auntie Teressa's? Zia Teressa's?"

"I have heard of it, sir."

Greg said, "It was a world-famous restaurant in Naples—built out over the water. The finest seafood in the world. Auntie Teressa presided at a cash register in the middle, but every now and then she would go to an open window—shouting and haggling with the fishermen below, bringing in their catch."

Ottavio, the waiter, said, "I have heard of it, sir. But of course during the war, I was just a child in a village near Calabria. It

Greg Clark begins his life as an entertainer.

Joseph Thomas Clark,
Greg's father, in the year
of Greg's birth.

Greg's mother, Sarah
Louise Greig, at the time
of her engagement to
Greg's father.

(Above) Greg was learning to fish while still wearing the long curls and dresses his mother liked.

(Left) Greg's brother and rival, Joseph William Greig Clark.

A studio portrait of Greg's mother and father; in the foreground is his aunt, Mabel Clark, who became editor of the Clinton, Ontario, *News-Record.*

Greg's mother and three of her four children: Greg, 8 (standing); young Joe, 5 (sitting); sister Mabel, 2.

Greg's one love, Helen Scott Murray.

Greg at Go Home Bay with the ukulele he used in his courtship of Helen Scott Murray, right. With them is Greg's youngest brother, Arthur.

Helen with the Clark family. Left to right: Arthur Clark, the youngest; young Joe Clark; Mabel Clark; Greg's mother; Helen and Greg; Greg's father, Joseph Thomas Clark.

In 1905 Greg's father had become editor of the *Toronto Daily Star,* which was to become Canada's largest newspaper. He is third from the left in the center row, at the right of publisher Joseph E. Atkinson. Many of these men left their mark on Canadian journalism. Back row: James Simpson, R. K. Mearns, Charles Fortier, C. W. Jeffreys, Charles F. Raymond, John R. Bone, Herbert Cranston, Thomas McGillicuddy, Arthur Roebuck. Middle: W. A. Hewitt, Harry F. Gadsby, Joseph T. Clark, Joseph E. Atkinson, Colin C. Campbell, Wm. R. Plewman, H. Dean Carman. Front: W. A. Clark, Lou E. Marsh, Harold Adamson, W. F. Wiggins. *(Toronto Star)*

A fellow reporter of Atkinson's was William Lyon Mackenzie King, right, who became Prime Minister of Canada and had great influence on Atkinson. This photo of King with his parents was taken in 1910, a few years before Greg joined the *Toronto Star. (Toronto Archives)*

The remarkable Joseph E. Atkinson, who rose from poverty to ownership of the *Toronto Star.* This photo was taken in 1892, the year Greg was born. At this time Atkinson was one of Canada's best reporters. He would have a major influence on Greg's career. *(Toronto Archives)*

Greg's *bête noire* at the *Toronto Star* was managing editor Harry Comfort Hindmarsh, the publisher's son-in-law. This is how he looked when Greg joined the paper. *(Toronto Archives)*

Helen and Greg were married on August 14, 1916, a few days before Greg went overseas.

Greg in France in 1917.

(Left) Greg with the late Victor Sifton, of the publishing family. In 1917 Sifton was adjutant of the 4th Canadian Mounted Rifles and Greg his assistant. *(Below, left)* The officers of D Company, 4th Canadian Mounted Rifles, before the battle of Vimy Ridge. Three died in the battle. Back row: Lt. Edwin Austin Abbey, Lt. J. A. B. Cheney, Lt. William G. Butson, Lt. L. C. Johnston. Front row: Capt. William Muirhead; Major A. A. MacKenzie, D Company commander; Lt. Greg Clark.

(Below, right) Greg and brother Joe in World War I. Joe succeeded in transferring to the Air Force overseas and won his Observer Wing and D.F.C.

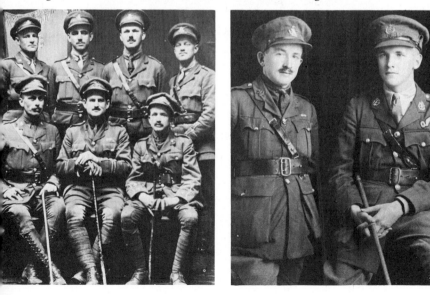

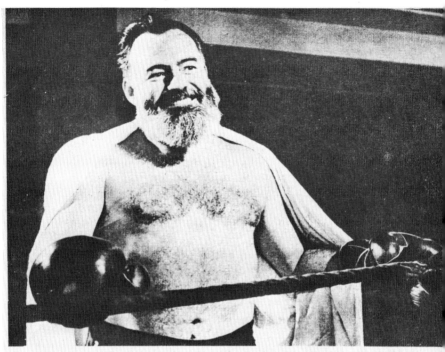

Behind the bush is Ernest Hemingway, getting in shape to write about World War II.

Hemingway
Slept Here

How two Toronto newspapermen helped the world's greatest writer to get a start in life

By Gregory Clark

Illustrated by Duncan MacPherson

Now, Ralph Connable was head of the Woolworth chain in Canada, a wealthy and witty American. And the Kansas City Star happened to be, in those years, the beau ideal of every newspaperman in America. And this tall young squirt whom Donaldson was wishing on us was wearing a short leather coat and a peaked cap and was carrying a walking stick! He walked, I noted, with a slight limp as he went over eagerly and took the radiator.

THERE IS no business in the world in which there are so many hangers-on as the newspaper business. Eager, hopeful hangers-on. This, I figured was one of them. He was a large, rather heavy, loose jointed youth with a flushed face dark

Ernest Hemingway was a fellow reporter of Greg and Morley Callaghan in the early Twenties. *(Toronto Archives)*

Greg's fishing career began in earnest after World War I.

Greg's sons, Murray and Greg, Jr., learned to fish early.

At times Helen was a quiet, introspective wife.

Margaret Trowern, now married to Greg's friend Billy Milne, and Helen dress up for a masquerade.

(Above, left) Bathing suits of the Twenties. From left to right: Margaret Trowern, Helen's best friend; Helen; Greg. *(Below)* Greg's wife with their children on an outing in the mid-Thirties. From left to right: Murray, Elizabeth and Greg, Jr. *(Above, right)* Greg's youngest child, Elizabeth, tempts the family dog.

(Above) Greg's nephew, Jeff Drew-Brook, with Greg, Jr., and Murray. The boys shared a love of the Go Home country. *(Below, left)* Greg's formidable mother-in-law, widow of the Reverend James Murray. Known affectionately as "Dodo," she lived with Helen and Greg for most of their married life. *(Below, right)* Greg's brother-in-law, Thomas Drew-Brook, was a World War I flier and later worked for Canadian intelligence.

was a terrible time—we lived on chocolate bars, whatever we could get—before the Germans began using them for booby traps. Once, I remember, I found a whole carton of cigarettes—I was the richest man in the village."

"War is a terrible thing," said Greg as the waiter walked away. "I have seen enough. The last one I was kicked out of France twice. I landed in Arras on the tenth of May, just when the roof fell in. We correspondents got out with the British G.H.Q. at Boulogne. Then I went back in again with the Canadians who were going to try to save the Fifty-first Highland Division, who were encircled at St. Valerie. That failed, and we got out of Brest this time, on the seventeenth of June."

"Your war diaries must be interesting."

"No," said Greg. "They're not the stuff of literature. Even at a time like Dunkirk—of world-moving events—all you find is observations about a couple of strange birds I happened to see at the time. The inconsequentials. To keep up this role of mine, I wrote only the commonplace things."

"What was it Hemingway said about you?"

Greg smiled. "He said, 'Greg, you're going to peter out your life on some warm hearthstone.' But I was wrong about him, too. When he was hanging around Jimmie Frise and me at the old *Star Weekly,* he used to bring me these little pieces he'd written. Hard, flat, ugly little stories. I thought they were terrible. Occasionally, he would do something about fishing or hunting which I'd like. If I said I liked it, I think he took it home and tore it up. It couldn't be any good!

"When I saw him in London during the war, he'd bashed himself up in a car accident in a blackout. When I came into his hospital room, the first thing he said was, 'Well, Greg how have I done?' Not how are you or anything like that, but *'How have I done!'* He was a great egotist.

"I said, 'The best thing you ever wrote was *The Green Hills of Africa.'* Hemingway turned to the table beside his bed and poured himself a half-tumbler of straight whiskey. Without a word, he drank it down. Then he turned back to me and said, 'Greg, *you always were a damn fool!'* "

Greg waited till my scribbling caught up with his story. "Look," he said, "what are you going to do with all these notes you're making?"

"I told you. You'll make a great character in my next novel."

"Well," said Greg, "if you're going to go to all this trouble, you might as well write my biography."

I didn't say anything because I was quite taken aback. A biography meant a dead person. Greg seemed too bright, too cheerful, too much fun, too full of life for that.

"If it's an official biography," said Greg, "I can help you out. Let you look through my notebooks and things."

"Notebooks," I said. "That'll be those dull diaries you were talking about. Full of observations about bird-watching and other inconsequentials."

Greg smiled. "Yes, those are the ones."

"I don't know," I said. "You're such a great fictional character. I don't like the idea of losing you in the pages of a biography."

Greg laughed. "You do say something funny once in a while," he said. "Then it's agreed about the book."

We finished our meal and Ottavio brought the bill.

It took a while to settle up because Greg would not accept a two-dollar bill in his change and because Mr. John Grieco, the owner of La Scala, came to say good-bye.

Outside, finally, we walked along a sunlit street lined with old houses. One had been torn down to make way for a parking lot. This exposed the wall of the old house next to it. There, painted on the bricks, was an ancient billboard, which had been hand-painted there a hundred years before. The old-fashioned lettering advertised a sign-painting company, long out of existence.

"Look at that," said Greg. "As good as the day it was painted. Almost worth coming back to take a picture of, isn't it?"

Greg knew I photographed old houses slated for the wreckers, as well as old walls like this, which were coming into view all over Toronto.

After admiring the old sign, we walked on.

"You know," said Greg, "I've made a very interesting discovery. You don't change when you grow old. You remain just the same. But everything else changes. Your home. Your friends. Your city. The things you are used to just disappear, one by one. And you are left alone."

On reaching Yonge Street, we parted company.

"I am going this way," said Greg, "to buy a mobile in Kresge's. My housekeeper, Mrs. Armstrong, tells me you can buy them there for only twenty-five cents. I have a lot in the house now, including a wonderful Japanese one my son-in-law, Hiro, brought me. But two more will be useful. I love the sound of them when there is a little breeze."

He turned away, with a slight, half courtly, half mocking bow.

An hour later, back in my office, the phone rang. It was Greg, his voice cheery again.

"That next story of mine," he said. "When is it scheduled?"

I found out the scheduling date of his next *Weekend* story and gave it to him.

"Good. That's fine," he said, "because I have another story ready that should go soon."

I thanked him again, for the lunch and the conversation.

"Yes," said Greg. "We must do it again soon. However," he said, "the next time *you* can pay for it. *Arrivederci.*" He hung up, chuckling.

"*Arrivederci,*" I said.

8

I should have been a guide in Algonquin Park.
—*Greg Clark*

About twenty miles north of Penetang, on the eastern side of Georgian Bay, is a rocky island, known locally as High Rock. At the turn of the century it was shown on maps as Island 127 and for a few centuries before that it was known to the Ojibway Indians as Qwawbikong, "the place from which we go home." For the Ojibway it was a favorite meeting place and camping ground, after the hunt or other sorties. From here they dispersed to their homes. At the turn of the century, the stone ruins of fireplaces they had built could still be seen there. Eventually, the bay sheltered by the island became known as Go Home Bay, the river emptying into the bay as Go Home River and the lake which fed the river as Go Home Lake.

For more than eighty years the Go Home shoreline and approximately one thousand acres of the surrounding wilderness has been the site of an organization called the Madawaska Club. This is the place where Greg Clark spent his summer holidays, first as a freckle-faced boy, later as a man with his own family. In a way, it is a place where he did much of his growing up.

The idea for the Madawaska Club was born one day in 1896 in a conversation between two professors at the University of Toronto. The two professors were W. J. Loudon and Charles Wright. Loudon was involved with preparations for a visit that year by the British Association for the Advancement of Science. A stopover for an outdoor luncheon was being arranged for the British party at Rock Lake, near Algonquin Park, to break their train trip from Ottawa to Toronto.

Loudon knew the Rock Lake area well. It was unspoiled wilderness. The lake was filled with speckled trout and the surrounding woods abounded in game, ducks and geese. He mentioned to Wright that it would be an ideal area for the establishment of a hunting club for members of the university interested in outdoor life. Wright was enthusiastic. They named their projected club the Madawaska Club, because Rock Lake was near the headwaters of the Madawaska River.

They soon found more supporters for the project at the university, but they were unsuccessful in obtaining a grant of land at Rock Lake. They shifted their attention to Georgian Bay and were successful in obtaining a grant from the Ontario government at Go Home Bay a year or two later. Although they retained the Madawaska name, the club was now seen not strictly as a hunting camp or a sporting club, but as a summer retreat where university members would build summer homes for their families.

It was also decided not to limit membership to graduates of the University of Toronto, as originally planned, but to open it to undergraduates, officials of the university and a few friends of the organization, who were enrolled as charter members. One such friend was Joseph T. Clark, Greg's father.

Shares in the club were sold for twenty-five dollars each. The first funds were used in 1898 for the building of a cookhouse and a clubhouse where members stayed while choosing a site to build their own cottages. On his first trip to Go Home, Joe Clark caught a half dozen bass, up to five pounds; a pickerel that weighed nearly ten; and lost a huge muskie, which were numerous in the area. Excited at the prospect of such good fishing, he immediately made plans for his own cottage, which was built in 1899.

Like most of the other Go Home cottages, it was of frame construction, with cedar-shingle siding. It was built by Joe Nault, the original caretaker of the Go Home property, at a cost of three hundred and fifty dollars. In those days, for this amount of money, it was possible to build quite a substantial home. The Clark cottage consisted of a large family room, three bedrooms, a large dining room and a kitchen with a small adjoining bedroom for the maid. It was located near a point on the inner bay. Professor George Anderson, of the university, built his house on a small island to the west of the Clarks. To the east, some two hundred yards away, was the cottage of Professor C.H.C. Wright.

The Clark cottage was named "Edgewater." Here, in 1899,

young Greg Clark stepped ashore at what was to be his summer home for the next sixty years. There were, of course, no roads reaching to Go Home at the turn of the century. The families arrived by a small steamer which ran daily from Penetang. The Go Homers used scows, fishing boats and the Georgian Bay shoal boats for moving goods and furniture to the bay. There were no motorboats in the colony for the first ten years, and it was not unusual for cottagers to sail or row the twenty miles to Penetang for supplies.

The Clark family, which now consisted of Greg, age eight, and Joe Clark, Jr., age four, moved in for the months of July and August. Greg's father came up for weekends and stayed for his two-week holiday during the summer, a pattern familiar to families across Canada. Mabel, Greg's sister, was not born until the following year.

For Mrs. Clark, with only her two small boys and a young maid for company, the cottage must have been somewhat lonely at times, despite the presence of other Go Homers nearby. Greg's situation as the oldest male member of the family for most of the summer doubtless hastened his maturity. By the time Greg was fourteen he had acquired his own canoe and rifle and was exploring the waters and woods of the area like a young Indian brave.

Greg was already fascinated by nature; the unspoiled wilderness of Go Home was a paradise to him. Like Paradise, Go Home had its serpent. The shores of Georgian Bay and the Bruce Peninsula are the home of *Sistrurus catenatus catenatus,* the Massasauga rattlesnake. The Massasauga is a relatively small rattlesnake, generally less than three feet in length. Because its fangs are small, it usually manages to inject only a small amount of venom in a bite. However, ounce for ounce, the Massasauga venom is one of the deadliest in the world.

There is only one recorded death in Ontario directly attributable to the snake. It is not aggressive and its rattle is merely a request to be left alone. However, it has some very dangerous aspects. It is nocturnal and is able to strike accurately in darkness because of its heat-sensing organs. It also curls up behind fallen logs and in rocky crevices, where its gray-brown protective coloring makes it difficult to spot. Its natural reaction to being stepped on or disturbed is to strike. Contrary to popular opinion, it does not always rattle first. The bite can be doubly dangerous in the case of a small child, because there is much less body tissue to absorb the venom.

One of Greg's chores at the cottage was to make an early-morning tour of the property, checking the beach, the cottage and the path back to the family outhouse, to ensure that no night-ranging rattlers had curled up on the premises. The family dog, which would bark loudly when it discovered a snake, was his faithful ally. Greg probably killed a hundred rattlers in his years at Go Home. Typically, he said, "I always felt sorry for the little creatures. All they wanted was to be left alone."

The snake population ebbed and flowed over the years, depending on the prey available and other natural factors. In cold weather the snakes coil together in huge underground masses. Workmen building a cottage on *Qwawbikong* once unearthed a huge ball of torpid snakes. They counted more than a hundred before giving up. To dispose of them, they scraped the reptiles into two nail kegs, built a large bonfire around them and set fire to it.

Greg killed his first rattler when he was ten, in an area that Go Home people referred to as the Pittsburgh Camp. This was a beautiful pine grove leased by a group of Pittsburgh sportsmen as a fishing camp. This group had lost their camping privileges, partly due to the ramblings of Greg and his young chums. Exploring the Pittsburgh Camp one day, after the fishing group had left, they found a deep pit filled with hundreds of rotting fish. They reported this to their parents, who reported it to the game warden. Investigation revealed that the Pittsburgh sportsmen had been running a pool every day, the prize going to the fisherman who brought back the largest number of bass. As a result of the contest, they were bringing back more fish than they could eat and so were dumping the surplus in a pit.

The Pittsburgh group lost their camping privileges because of this, and the area became a favorite picnic ground for those at Go Home. The children played baseball and filled pillowcases with cranberries from a nearby sphagnum bog, to take home for Thanksgiving dinners. Ten-year-old Greg was leading a cranberry party back along the trail when he encountered a rattler coiled in the path. While Grandma Greig and his mother kept the other children out of harm's way, Greg beat the snake to death with a stick.

Even in death, the rattlesnake can present a danger. The striking action is a highly persistent reflex action that lasts for some time after the snake is dead. In one laboratory test the head of a rattlesnake was completely severed from its body, yet, an hour later, the head of the snake would bite objects placed within reach. This peculiarity has resulted in some people being bitten by dead rattlesnakes.

Rattlesnakes were just one form of the wildlife abounding at Go Home. There were skunks, raccoons, foxes, deer, even the occasional wolf and black bear. In the early days of the colony a pair of eagles nested in a pine on Qwawbikong.

It may have been that Mrs. Clark conveyed some concern to Greg's father about danger from predators. In any case, he said to Greg one day in 1906, "How would you like to have a rifle?" Greg gave the answer any fourteen-year-old boy would give, and sent away to Marlin, Winchester and Remington for their gun catalogs. The gun he settled on was a Winchester 38.55 carbine, the 1894 model. This rifle fired a huge slug, backed by a .255-grain bullet, larger even than the normal military load. It was a rather monstrous weapon for a fourteen-year-old boy and one that some fathers might have hesitated to buy. It was perhaps because Greg's father was not a hunter, and scarcely knew one end of a gun from the other, that the purchase was made.

There was some questioning by the other cottagers about the wisdom of the purchase when the proud owner showed up with the gun at Go Home. However, Greg was smart enough to stay away from the cottages with his weapon and to range far afield for his target practice.

The first victim of the carbine was a huge snapping turtle. It was early, on a misty morning, and Greg was perched on a high rock overlooking Clark's Bay. He was waiting for a glimpse of a black duck family he had discovered that summer, already "the quiet watcher" described by Ernest Thompson Seton. His trusty carbine was by his side.

The mother duck, followed by six black, fluffy ducklings, came down from the marsh, out through the water lilies and into the shallow water at the edge of the bay. Suddenly there was a commotion in the water. One of the ducklings disappeared, leaving only an ominous circle of widening ripples. The mother fluttered and splashed back into the reeds, followed by the remaining

ducklings. Greg jumped up and saw the dark shape of a huge turtle gliding away under the water. He followed it along the shore
and when it surfaced in the bay, he blasted its shell with a shot
from the carbine.

He paddled out in his canoe, tied a rope to the still-struggling
reptile and towed it back to the cottage. It was so large he needed
help from his brother Joe to drag it up on the beach and back
into the woods behind the cottage. Here they threw the rope over
the branch of a tree and hoisted the snapping turtle into the air.
Another shot from the carbine ended the creature's agonies.

For Greg the carbine was the beginning of a lifelong love affair
with guns, of which he was to own many. He liked to shoot much
more than he liked to hunt. Hunting was, for him, simply another
chance to escape to the great outdoors. Overseas, when the troops
were out of the line, there was daily rifle practice. Greg always
volunteered for Musketry Officer duty, because it gave him a
chance to shoot.

The carbine was probably an example of the trust Greg's father
had in him, and of the relationship that existed between them.
Greg was never spanked by his father. In fact, the idea of corporal punishment from this source had apparently never entered his
head. When his younger brother Joe once came in for a spanking,
Greg was quite shocked by the incident, and upset for several
days afterward.

Joe Clark was a gentle man and his guidance of his family was
also gentle. He rarely laid down arbitrary rules.

One day Greg asked him, "Dad, what is character?"

"Character," said his father, "is something you're born with.
Let's imagine it's a silver chalice of some kind. When your father
gives it to you, it's battered and banged up. You can simply accept it as you receive it, or you can clean it up, polish it, repair it,
improve on the character you were given in the hope you can
pass it on to your son."

One day at Go Home Greg was paddling back from a very successful fishing expedition with a fine catch of bass. He passed
close to the cottage of Dr. Alexander McPhedran, a distinguished
physician from the university and a religious man. Dr. McPhedran hailed Greg and when he came to shore he said, "Gregory,
have you been fishing?"

"Yes, sir," said Greg.

"Don't you realize you're not allowed to fish on the Sabbath?"

"No, sir," said Greg, taken aback.

"Well, go on your way," said Dr. McPhedran. "But remember next time."

There were many rifts and disagreements at Go Home and this incident might well have led to another, except for the diplomatic way in which Joseph Clark handled it. When Greg told him about it, he said, "All right. When you go fishing next Sunday, put a few good bass on a string and take them in and present them to Dr. McPhedran." Greg did that. This time it was the doctor's turn to be taken aback. However, he accepted the fish and stammered out his thanks. That was the end of the controversy about fishing on Sunday at Go Home Bay.

Although Joseph Clark was opposed to walloping his children, he had no trouble making his feelings known. He spanked Greg's younger sister Mabel only once during her childhood, but one evening at Go Home he addressed a few words to her that she remembered for the rest of her life. Mabel was not yet in her teens at the time. She was in the kitchen at the cottage and was rudely bawling out the maid. Her father walked into the kitchen and overheard part of the conversation, although Mabel broke off as soon as she noticed him. He did not say anything at the time, but after dinner he said to her, "Let's go for our row."

It was one of her childhood treats to row him around the bay on quiet evenings before sunset. She rowed awkwardly, her legs up on the sides of the boat for purchase, and lifted the oars high in the air to let the water drip off the oars. It was less rowing than playing.

When they were well out on the water, her father said, "What I'm going to say to you now is probably the most important thing I'll ever say to you. *A woman who is not kind would be better never to have been born.*"

Fifty years later, recounting the story, Mabel said, "You know, those words sank into my mind like a knife. I knew exactly what he was talking about. And to this day, when I think of it, I can still see those drops of water, colored by sunshine, dripping slowly off the ends of the oars."

One of the early aims of the Go Home founders was the establishment of some kind of summer school of science. Such a school, it was hoped, would provide useful summer work for university students. It would also be in a position to make helpful studies of fish and wildlife in the area. A grant was obtained from the Minister of Marine and Fisheries shortly after the turn of the century. A biological station was built at Go Home with the funds; it operated until 1914.

Greg already had a keen interest in nature. He eagerly sought to make friends with the university students and to discuss the work they were doing. However, he was regarded by those at the biological station as just one more pesky teenager and his attempts at friendship were somewhat cruelly rebuffed.

One day he heard that the students were to begin a study of rattlesnakes and were looking for specimens. Greg set out in his canoe, found a suitably large rattler, pinned it with a stick and dropped the creature into a large potato sack. He put the sack in the front of his canoe and headed for the biological station to make his contribution to science.

Halfway to the station, the snake wriggled free of the sack and announced its freedom with a loud, whirring rattle. Greg pushed the snake back into the bow of the canoe with his paddle. At frequent intervals he had to stop paddling and repeat this maneuver, as the snake was not happy at his end of the canoe and kept slithering toward Greg.

By the time Greg reached the dock at the biological station it was nearly dusk. However, he could see a group of students on the veranda of the station and he shouted up proudly, "I've got a rattlesnake for you!"

Somebody muttered, "It's that Clark kid." There was some argument about who would have the chore of seeing what Greg had. Finally one student came down the dock toward the canoe, a lantern in his hand.

"Where's the snake?"

"Up there, in the front," said Greg, indicating with his paddle.

The student put down the lantern and bent over the front of the canoe, looking for what he assumed was a dead snake. The vicious rattle that greeted him sent him sprawling backward, knocking over the lantern.

"Good God!" he cried. "He's got a *live* one!"

The others came running down the dock. The snake was recaptured and lifted, writhing, from the canoe. The Clark kid was now treated with more respect, although he was not encouraged to deliver any more live rattlesnakes by canoe.

The canoe, that typically Canadian vessel, played a large part in Greg's life at Go Home. One day he encountered two Indians from the Christian Island Reservation. In their fishing boat they had a young Indian girl who had been bitten by a rattlesnake two days previously. Her leg had swollen badly and they were taking her for medical treatment. Their fishing boat was slow and clumsy, so Greg volunteered his canoe, which was accepted gladly. The two Indians took the paddles and Greg, along with the girl, enjoyed the swiftest canoe ride of his life to a doctor down the bay.

Strangely, at a later date, two other Indians were to save his life. His canoe was blown offshore by a brisk wind and Greg made the mistake of swimming after it. The wind, of course, carried the canoe farther away every minute. By the time Greg realized what was happening, he was far out in the channel and completely exhausted. The wind grew stronger, the water grew rougher.

There was no chance of regaining the shore and he was about to drown when a miracle occurred. A Mackinaw boat appeared around a distant point. This was a twenty-foot boat with a pointed prow and a square stern, equipped with a jib and mainsail, once common on the Great Lakes. It was named after Mackinaw City, Michigan, once an Indian trading post. In the boat this day were two other Indians from the Christian Island Reservation. They saw the empty canoe and had the good sense to look for, and find, Greg before he disappeared beneath the water. It was a tale such as might have been told by Grandma Greig and doubtless reinforced Greg's belief in the supernatural.

One summer, with two other young boys, Greg planned an overnight canoe trip that was to take them up to Go Home Lake, to Musquash, down to Bala, then down the Moon River to Georgian Bay. The return trip up the open shore of Georgian Bay would bring them up around Moose Point, a place notorious for gales and rough water. When word of this proposed trip passed around Go Home it was regarded as folly by many parents.

One lady of this opinion was the wife of Professor George Anderson, who lived on a small island west of the Clark cottage. The Andersons were childless. Professor Anderson was known to

Greg as "Uncle George," but Greg felt little affection for Mrs. Anderson, whom he regarded as a busybody and a gossip.

He said, "She had a lower jaw like a ventriloquist's dummy, always going flap, flap, flap."

Mrs. Anderson took it upon herself to row over to the Clark cottage, where the boys were packing for the canoe trip. Greg's mother was on the cottage veranda. Resting on her oars, Mrs. Anderson called up, "Sadie! I think you're insane, letting that boy go on this trip!" Her high, piercing voice carried well across the water.

Before his mother could answer, Greg walked to the edge of the veranda, cupped his hands around his mouth and gave his impression of Mrs. Anderson: "Myah, myah, myah, myah!"

Greg said later, "It was the first time in my long life of fourteen years that I had ever suddenly taken charge. My mother was too shocked to speak. Mrs. Anderson turned red and rowed furiously back to her island."

Greg's mother retreated to the kitchen. Greg wondered if he had gone too far, but when he went to the kitchen a few moments later he found his mother doubled over with silent laughter. He realized that he had chosen the right moment to assert himself and that his mother, at least, shared his feelings about Mrs. Anderson.

Those years of growing up at Go Home were happy years. There were long, lazy days of sunshine, days of lightning and summer storms. Greg's school friends—Billy Milne, Woody McKeown, Frank Ryan and others—were frequent guests during the holidays. Greg played the mandolin; his friends played guitars or banjos. His sister Mabel spoke of wonderful moonlit nights when the boys would lie offshore in canoes, singing and playing, the music carrying softly across the bay.

By the time he was seventeen, young Greg was the acknowledged summer patriarch of the Clark cottage. His youngest brother, Arthur, was born that year and Greg behaved more like a father than a brother. He fell in love with the new baby and for the next few years looked after him constantly. He took him to the beach, took him for rides in his canoe, even packed him through the woods as a papoose on his back.

In later years, Greg's constant fishing and hunting trips, his love of nature and the outdoors, could almost be viewed as a return to those lost, happy days at Go Home Bay.

9

I don't want to be a soldier,
I don't want to go to war

—Popular song

From 1899 until he left for World War I, Greg Clark lived in his father's house at 66 Howland Avenue, a street two blocks east of Bathurst, running north from Bloor Street.

It was an area into which Toronto was only beginning to expand. West of Bathurst Street, there were still great open areas, known as "goose pasture," where Greg and his playmates built forts and dug caves. One summer they "smoked" an entire baby carriage, an abandoned wicker affair which they converted into cigarettes, piece by piece.

East of Bathurst, a thickly populated district had grown up close by the University of Toronto. A wealthy district, known as the Annex, running from Avenue Road to Bathurst, just north of Bloor Street, was rapidly filling up with large homes, as were Madison, Huron and St. George.

In 1892, the year Greg was born, a high school was built to serve these new areas. It was known as Harbord Collegiate and it was here that Greg was to spend the years from 1905 to 1909. There were only three such collegiate institutes serving the whole of Toronto. Jarvis Collegiate served the eastern section of the city; Harbord, the western section as far as Dufferin Street; and Parkdale Collegiate, the remainder.

One of the original Harbord teachers was E. W. Hagarty, who became principal during Greg's time at Harbord. Hagarty had founded the Harbord Cadet Corps in 1898. His own son, D. Galer Hagarty, destined to die at the Battle of Sanctuary Wood in 1916, was already an excellent marksman who had represented Canada at the Boys' Bisley shooting competition in London, England.

Ironically, for a youth who was to distinguish himself as a soldier and a war correspondent, Greg came into almost immediate conflict with the military-minded Hagarty. Greg turned out for two or three sessions of marching and drilling in the cadet training program and then decided this was not for him. Hagarty, a large, grim man whom Greg disliked on sight, promptly reported this insubordination to Greg's father, Joseph Clark.

Joseph Clark sided with his son. He sent a note back to school saying that his son did not wish to continue with the cadet training and, so far as he knew, there was nothing in the Education Act that made such training compulsory. Greg's cadet training was dropped, but Greg felt that Hagarty did not forget the incident, or forgive it.

A few years later, while Greg was at the University of Toronto, student reporters on the university newspaper ran a major article that severely criticized Hagarty as a military martinet. Greg was one of the Harbord graduates who contributed to this attack, so it may be assumed that he did not forget the incident either.

Hagarty, in addition to being the founder of the cadet program, was head of the Classics Department and had published a Latin grammar which was highly regarded. Later, Greg could say, "For all his faults, it was Hagarty to whom I owed my delight in Latin and Greek. Even if he was more interested in the grammar than the story."

Hagarty's assistant was a man named David Alexander Glassey. "Glassey was a beautiful man," said Greg. "Holy doodle, could he teach! With him you felt the beauty of the language, you became aware of the philosophy of the Greeks, you got a dramatic picture of what the Greeks meant to civilization. There was a whole bunch of us at Harbord who simply loved his guts."

Greg had other favorite teachers at Harbord. One was Herbert Irwin, who taught history and who was surprised to learn how much Greg had already read from the shelves of his father's library. Greg was also fond of Gertrude Lawler, a highly regarded English teacher. Another teacher, Eliza M. Balmer, had been the first woman graduate of the University of Toronto.

Greg was not above the normal cruelties of schoolboys. The

caretaker at Harbord was a man named Charles Vine and Greg
chanted along with the others:

> "Old Vines, old Vines,
>   He's full of crimes,
>   He's rotten to the core.
>   He thinks he owns old Harbord School,
>   But he only sweeps the floor."

Greg's adolescent years saw a gradual change in his attitude toward religion. His home was a religious one, mainly because of
his mother. While the family lived at 52 McKenzie Crescent, all
attended Chalmers' Presbyterian Church at Dovercourt and
Dundas. When they moved to Howland Avenue, they began to attend a small frame church known as St. Paul's. The minister there
was the Reverend George Fasken, who called on the Clarks when
they moved into their Howland Avenue home. The Reverend Mr.
Fasken made an indelible impression on Greg, for he chewed tobacco. This was the first sign of humanity Greg had seen in the
preachers to whom he'd been exposed so far.

Greg began attendance at Bible class at St. Paul's, where his
first teacher was a Dr. Abbot, a professor of psychology at the
University of Toronto. It was not long until Dr. Abbot visited the
Clark home and announced, "Greg is destined to be a Presbyterian minister. He's got the words, the rhetoric, everything."

Greg's father remarked dryly, "And I suppose we'll have to get
him a soapbox to stand on behind the pulpit?"

Greg's father was not a man of formal religion. When he did
attend church, in the interests of domestic harmony, he carried a
small pebble in his waistcoat pocket. When the sermon began he
slipped the pebble into his mouth as an aid in keeping awake.
Greg and his younger brother Joe knew about the pebble and
during the service they watched and waited for the inevitable.
Sooner or later, their father's head would drop forward and the
pebble would fall from his mouth to roll along the floor of the
church.

For Greg's mother, as for many women of that era, the church
was the center of her social life. She now switched to the more
fashionable Bloor Street Presbyterian Church at Bloor and
Huron, taking the family with her. Greg dutifully attended, the
thought of the ministry still in his mind, but other factors were

now at work. He was doing an immense amount of reading, with the encouragement of his father—and his father now introduced him to the worlds of theater and music. As editor of the *Toronto Daily Star,* Joseph Clark had free passes to all the theaters in town. He now made these available to Greg, exposing him to a world with far wider horizons than those of the Bloor Street Presbyterian Church.

In 1907, when he was in Second Form at Harbord Collegiate, Greg began his first diary. It was one of many such personal journals in which he was to record his experiences and reflections over the years.

The first entry, made on January 1, 1907, read, "I am writing this diary so that at the end of the year I may sum up and see how little I have done. Then I may do better later." The Presbyterian ethic of self-improvement was obviously strong within him. At this time he was attending Sunday School regularly and also was attending regular church services at least once every Sunday, sometimes twice. In his diary he commented on and analyzed the sermons he heard. He also began trying out sermons of his own on school chums who came to his house.

On September 25, 1907, Greg turned fifteen years of age. He described his birthday:

Fine and *cold!* Windy. Presents:—$2.50 from Mater, Pater and Gross Mutter. Tie from Mabel. Note paper from Joe. "Voyage of Beagle" from Lill. I made Joe a poison bottle. Will McMurray and Bob in tonight. Sent to Bausch and Lomb for 200 insect pins.

His fifteenth year was not a year of great change. His diary reflects his all-consuming interest in the things of nature—the sight of a downy woodpecker in Queen's Park, the collecting of butterfly and plant specimens on walks to the Humber River. He was constantly picking up books in secondhand bookstores, books such as *How to Know the Butterflies* or *A Field Guide to the Stars*. His diary recorded great excitement when he got his very own copy of a government bulletin called *Farm Weeds of Ontario*.

Greg was still a small, shy, freckle-faced boy. He diligently attended church and Sunday School. He shoveled the snow in front of his house and raked the leaves from the lawn with such

eagerness that other parents pointed him out as a model child, a
fact that did not add to his popularity. At fifteen his worlds were
those of his parents, school, church, the summer cottage and the
world of nature.

However, in the books he was beginning to read were the seeds
of change. These books were of all kinds, by Ralph Connor,
Dickens, Sheridan, Huxley, Darwin. Gradually Greg's feeling for
formal religion began to die. His diary tells the story:

February 10, 1907.
Got up late and went to church. Mr. Fasken being in
Guelph, a Mr. Hall, city missionary, preached a very good
sermon on city missionary work. After dinner I wrote out my
diary and read some French, but fooled for some time.
After tea, I went to church again and heard a fine sermon
on missionary work in British Columbia by Mr. Kerr of
Knox College, with many fine anecdotes. Got home and announced that I was going to be a minister.

November 24, 1908.
A man, the Rev. Mr. Waters, from India, spoke to us on
some missionary topic after school. But he made a speech to
a lot of kids that should have been delivered to a grown-up
audience. So I arose and departed.

January 3, 1909.
Today being Sunday I began the new year by attending
church in both morning and evening. I was greatly struck by
the richness of Hymn Number 507. It approaches my idea of
a hymn, a triumphal paean.
I heard the music played by the bands of several regiments,
united, at the Ex. I was greatly roused, at the time, by it. I
should like to hear this piece played by a good organist and
sung by a choir if that is possible. Our choir, with few excep-
tions, is a lot of frog-mouths. They have as much enthusiasm
as a frog, too.

February 21, 1909.
Also slushy. At church I heard a very solemn sermon
preached. He opens the sermon by admonishing us not to be
passive, not to toss it all up because we imagine we are
finished, it's all up with us! Then he spends half an hour of

rambling argification. Then he thunders to let all be as it is:
—don't worry; Providence will look after you!
Now, I didn't listen to his dry, irrelevant, middle-period of
reasoning. Therefore, it appears strange to me. And I am
only one of many youths that are in a similar stew.

Despite his gradual disenchantment with formal religion, Greg
retained a certain ambivalence about it throughout his life, as he
did about many things. For instance, his disenchantment did not
prevent him from marrying a minister's daughter. Nor did it prevent him from being baptized by his father-in-law when he returned from World War I, at twenty-eight years of age.

Greg's feelings about religion were occasionally tempered by
his audience of the moment. In irreligious company he would
announce, almost boastfully, "I was saved from religion—by
books." To a different audience he would say, almost regretfully,
"I lost my religion—from reading over my head." And he would
go on, "As an older reporter who'd reached the age of discretion,
I still found myself going into all kinds of churches. I was spell-
bound by the ritual of the mass. And those Baptist, Anglican,
Methodist cathedrals in England, those marvelous English choirs.
Particularly the Anglican—there's a peculiar, floating quality, a
soaring built into it for the resonance of the ritual. Boy, can they
pick you right up by the seat of your pants and throw you toward
heaven!"

Over his adult years, this ambivalence was expressed in many
little conceits. At one time, he would say, "Until sixteen or seventeen, I was going to be a minister. For fifty-five years now, I have
been preaching—but nobody has tumbled to it. All in the shape
of stories!" Again, he would announce, "I am not a Christian. I
am a Jeson."

In the year 1972 he was eighty years old and he was saddened
by the savage fighting then going on in the world, between Jew
and Arab in Palestine, between Catholic and Protestant in Ireland. He took a more bitter view of religion then. "Religion," he
said, "has been the source of our troubles for centuries. It should
be obvious by now that religion should be banned."

But 1972 was still a long way in the future. Greg was still a
small, shy boy, trying to find his place in his third year of high
school. He wrote in his diary, "Got a new suit with Long Pants!
My first!" He was fifteen years old.

10

THE CITY OF BOOKS

The year 1909, in which Greg was to enter his final year of high school, was the year he almost disappeared into books.

Physically, his life was much the same. It was ten years now since the Clark family had moved to 66 Howland Avenue. He still had a large circle of male friends his own age. Some of them were destined to remain friends for life. Others would drop from his life, and some were to die shortly in the great World War soon to come.

One of these friends was Cecil Perry, a companion on many hikes to High Park and the Humber, who was to become an artillery captain and be killed in 1917. Another friend was "Woody" McKeown, son of a famous St. Michael's Hospital surgeon, who would become a Toronto magistrate. There was Billy Moyle, a shy, musical boy who later went to live in Switzerland and was to die there. And there was Billy Milne, a boy who would marry the best friend of Greg's future wife and who was to be a friend of Greg's for life. But Greg had not yet learned to feel at home with the opposite sex.

At Harbord Collegiate, his academic career continued in a familiar pattern. He was good at languages and literature, but terrible in mathematics or any subject that required preciseness. Socially, he varied from taking an active part in theatrical and literary groups to withdrawing from these groups when he felt slighted or not appreciated. He had a few short-lived enthusiasms for particular sports, including skating and snowshoeing, but was not a great team athlete as was his friend Billy Milne, who was both a hockey and a football star.

The end of the school term in June would be signaled in his notebook by some gleeful exclamation like, "O frabjous days!"

and at the end of the holidays his notebook would resume, "The frabjous days are over."

Greg's summer holidays, of course, were spent at Go Home Bay. The Christmas holidays were also a highlight of his life and frequently were spent at Aunt Lib's house in Clinton, Ontario.

Aunt Lib was a sister of Greg's mother. She was married to Thomas Jackson, who owned three clothing factories in Clinton. The Jackson home was a large, warm place, always overrun with visiting nephews and nieces, filled with the aroma of good food, and a scene of happy confusion during the Christmas holidays. Visitors like Greg would be met at the station and driven to the Jackson home in a huge sleigh with straw on the floor and jingling sleigh bells on the horses.

In January of 1909 Greg was mostly occupied at school with meetings of the Reading Club and the Senior Literary Society. The first was devoted to a discussion of Dickens' *A Christmas Carol* and Poe's "The Gold Bug." Greg returned home from the second meeting feeling downcast. He confided to his diary, "I became convinced of Artie Singer's genius; of Dagmar Printz's attractions; of my own utter damfoolishness."

He gave up reading *A Christmas Carol* (his second attempt at it) because he felt it rambled too much. He turned instead to an old book he had found on the Spanish Inquisition and was properly horrified by the descriptions of torture he found in it, but noted that Poe had drawn on Inquisition methods for his story, "The Pit and the Pendulum." From the Spanish Inquisition Greg dived into Palgrave's *Golden Treasury of Songs and Lyrics* and into Homer's *Iliad,* following which some of his notebook entries were made in Latin.

A particular friend at this time was Bob Jenkins. Using passes provided by Greg's father, Greg and he would attend concerts of the Mendelssohn Choir, where they would catch glimpses of such important figures as the Governor-General. On one occasion, after the singing of "God Save the King," Greg noticed that the Governor-General hauled out a huge pair of field glasses to stare at people in the audience.

Bob Jenkins and Greg were at a stage where they picked up ideas of all kinds and spent evenings wrangling about everything —Byron, religion, philosophy, Shelley, Coleridge, and their own position as deep thinkers. Even while thus engaged, Greg's mind

was busy making observations. For instance, he thought that the
Jenkins family would make an excellent subject for a humorous
novel, one which would provide him with great opportunity for
satire.

By February of 1909, the two boys were arguing about thrift,
Lord Roseberry, Rockefeller, parliament, journalism, Greg's father, a viaduct that was a local political issue, actresses, morals
and why Greg should resign as secretary of the Senior Literary
Society. At the next meeting one of his friends held him in his
seat so he could not carry out his intention.

In April of 1909 he reported in his diary, "Perry and I went to
the Princess theatre. 'The Soul Kiss' was on. There was a deuce of
a lot of leg-show and tights in this, from pony to leading 'lady'
[sic]. At the Library, I got a book by Israel Zangwill."

Bad spring weather kept him indoors for a few days and he
read H. G. Wells' speculations on the future and part of *The
Celibates Club* by Zangwill, and also had his first look at Omar
Khayyam's *Rubaiyat*. He made a note to read the *Rubaiyat* again,
to single out some of the more delicate sentiments that he'd
passed over in his first hasty reading. He found H. G. Wells
highly interesting and felt that he had had several new lines of
thought opened up to him. Zangwill's book he found delightful.
"My opinion of Jews is certainly not bad, for I know Art Singer
and Sam Cohen. This book strengthens my prejudice towards
anti-Jewists."

Books. Books. On a rainy day, Greg counted the clothbound
books he had acquired so far as his very own. It was 160 at the
time. He was reading at such a pace that it was a wonder he
passed any subjects at school. And, in fact, he would make
heavyhearted resolutions at the end of the Christmas and Easter
holidays to cut down his reading. He would trudge to the Central
Library to turn in his books—and end up by taking more out.

He read Chesterfield, Dickens, Wells, Hubbard, Whitman,
Maeterlinck, Nietzsche. He delved into anarchy, cooperative
movements, the Inquisition, the French Revolution, the religions
of India. He had an overwhelming curiosity about ideas, men and
events.

Throughout his reading are woven several skeins of his developing personality. Sports played a part, but a small one. There

would be small temporary enthusiasms—a day when he nearly bowled his arm off playing cricket, a few weeks of shooting frequently at the rifle range, a weekend of skating—but the enthusiasms for sport were usually short-lived. Of them all, probably only his interest in guns and shooting was to remain with him through life.

In his sixteenth year he did discover girls and he made a careful note of it. It was May 16, 1909. He wrote:

I read an essay by Maeterlinck and one by Nordau from a book I borrowed from Hume. I observed two females, vulgarly spoken of as girls, at whom I enjoyed myself by looking. I have never seen a girl before. They appear, as a class, very fussy and brainless. But looks seemed to count with me today. Perhaps I am a natural being after all.

It was not until September of the same year that the subject arose again. This time Greg and a bunch of his friends had gone to the Canadian National Exhibition and were enjoying the carnival atmosphere of the midway. "Perry and I alone are harmless," wrote Greg, "but with Jeff Smith and Ben added, we are a riotous crew. Especially on the midway. But the other boys picked up girls, so I beat it. The one minute I was as riotous as the riotousest; the next I was moodily beating it for the exit and in a sneery, pessimistic figure of mind. It must have been the hot dog I ate."

Perhaps Greg really believed it was the hot dog . . . but more likely he was quite aware that a new element had appeared in the life of himself and his male friends—an element that would eventually end the idyllic days.

A few days later he was observing:

I must take a pill! I feel gloomy; the Sword of Damocles and general presentiment. I guess I am turning into a man and the change brings a glimpse of the open sea of life with its breakers ahead. I see some shoals. I wonder what kind of a navigator I am. Here goes!

At school his attempts to navigate seemed frequently to end up on the shoals. In his final year at Harbord, he makes only a few references to members of the school staff—unhappy references in the main. The principal of Harbord, E. W. Hagarty, remained

Greg's *bête noire* throughout his high school years. In his final year, Greg worked night and day to make the commencement evening a success. After the commencement Greg wrote bitterly:

> And after all that, Hagarty walks into our room and says, "Now, I wish to thank D—— especially. Miss S—— of Senior Four has also worked a great deal and has done much to make it a success. Clark also helped."
>
> Now, Miss S—— certainly did the most. But D—— did hardly anything. That's the thanks I get. And then the teachers all think against me, because I had to skip some classes. Now, all expect me to take charge of the school magazine and when I get mad and refuse, they look astounded and say in a hurt tone of voice, "Well, I'd like to know who's going to do it!"
>
> I am going to let the social part go hang. I am going to drop into oblivion.

Miss Lawler, his English teacher, was one who took an interest in his reading and his fledgling attempts at writing. Of her Greg wrote:

> She no longer tries in vain to raise my compositions to several pages of academic damfoolishness, but descends to my level, enters the spirit of the thing and, remodelling my sentences, helps to eradicate all unnecessary lengths; and is giving me the benefit of her knowledge of the impressionistic style. I understand mine is such; but imperfectly such.

Whatever social or school disasters, Greg now had a perfect retreat. His attic room at Howland Avenue he referred to as The City of Books, a private place which he guarded jealously. School holidays, such as those of Christmas in 1909, were welcomed not only because of the relief from school, but for the opportunity to retreat to this domain.

> Here are the holidays! Yes, and they shall be hallowed! Hallowed by thoughtful reading and silence. I have heaped about mine elbows many books: Carlyle, Maeterlinck, Emerson, Macaulay, Spencer, Huxley and many peculiar books, *outré* books, which it would not be polite to mention in conventional society.

Despite his many withdrawals, Greg kept coming back into "Society," as he called it, at Harbord Collegiate. In his final year he worked on the school magazine, helped plan the commencement exercises, and became president of the literary society. Additionally, a small group of his friends gathered regularly at each others' homes to read learned papers to each other and to praise or damn great writers of the past. This group referred to itself as "The Côterie."

Greg's career as president of the literary society came to an end with a semipolitical argument at the school over the society's constitution. The members split into the "Constitutionalists" and the "anti-Constitutionalists." The argument was whether Fourth and Fifth Form students could occupy senior positions in the society as well as Sixth Form members. Principal Hagarty and Greg were, as usual, on opposing sides.

Greg resigned in a huff and once again he vowed to devote his life henceforth to reading, reading, reading, *ad infinitum*. He was now able to make these declarations in French and he said, *"Je vais dans l'obscurité; je vais accompagner les ombres."*

However, within a month, he was regretting, it seemed, his latest withdrawal from the world. He wrote:

I am passing the portals, into the Obscurity. Heretofore, I was a figure; I won a certain general respect, and a pleased smile, when I turned around. But now, I walk the corridors as one of the crowd. The leaders are busily flitting about, winning respect and honour, and to them I must scrape and smile. I am the Man Who Was!

Once one has tasted fame, it is hard to reconcile oneself to lesser things.

At home, Greg conducted a small war with his mother. He was already growing away from her religious view of life. She complained, from time to time, about Greg's friends as being wild, immoral, even sinners. As Greg observed, at least they were cheerful sinners. To escape argument, Greg retreated to his attic study, The City of Books.

11

American cities with competing newspapers will soon be as rare as those with two telephone systems.

—*A. J. Liebling*
May 14, 1960

News is the stuff that goes between the ads.

—*Lord Thomson of Fleet*

A half-century later, Greg and I paid a visit to 66 Howland Avenue, which had contained his City of Books. "In those days," said Greg, "the great new homes of the rich were going up more to the east, on Madison, Huron and Spadina—pronounced 'Spadeena,' in the *refeened* way." En route, we drove past Brunswick House. "My mother hated that place," said Greg. "My father would stop there for a beer on his way home."

Driving up Howland, Greg held out his hand and showed me a small horseshoe-shaped scar on his finger.

"That's the only scar I've got," he said, "after all these years and a couple of wars. I got it right here on Howland Avenue—from a bear, if you can believe it."

"A bear?"

"A bear," said Greg. "One of our neighbors on Howland, a Mr. Southworth, somehow got hold of a black bear cub. So he drove a cedar log into his lawn and chained the cub to it. It wasn't an unusual thing to do in those years. The bear was quite tame and I used to play with it. It weighed about the same as I did—about fifty pounds. But we were wrestling one day and it gave me a playful clout that cut my finger open. I stopped wrestling with it after that."

We stopped in front of 66 Howland, where Greg had lived so many years before. By coincidence, the house was up for sale, with a sign saying, "Inspection by Appointment Only." We got out of the car and took pictures of the house while Greg reminisced. "I remember one Christmas Eve here, there was a drunk on the street with a cornet. He would play, 'Hark, the Herald Angels Sing,' collect a dime from the nearest house and then rush down to the Brunswick House for a beer."

Greg smiled at the memory. "When he got to our house, my father gave him a dollar to play the carol ten times. My father had probably been drinking himself. The drunk kept playing the carol over and over—it was probably the only tune he knew. Pretty soon all the neighbors were at their windows, wondering what the hell was going on. Especially the Misses Rounthwaites, who were very important maiden ladies in St. Alban's Cathedral up the street."

Back in the car, Greg said, "You know, I may have misled you a little about why I lost my religion. I said it was from reading over my head as a boy. But it may have been even simpler. It may have been the lousy music in church. My mother had a beautiful voice and I have a vivid memory of the sound of her lovely voice beside me in church, amid all the howling, whooping and bellowing of the Presbyterian hymns."

"Yes," Greg said, "it may well have been the lousy music and unctuous blather of the sermons. If the others had sung like my mother and the parsons had sermonized as moderately, as wisely and as humorously as my father did, I might well have retained some religious sense. My father had a terrible ear for music. The only way he knew they were playing 'God Save the King' was because everyone stood up."

Greg looked at his watch with an expression of mock horror. *"It's twelve o'clock!* Do you know this is the first time in five years I haven't had a drink by noon?"

Greg's drinking these days was strictly therapeutic, he claimed. After his first heart attack he'd been examined by Dr. William Oille, the heart specialist.

"Well, Greg," said Oille, "I can treat you in two different ways: with pills, or with scotch. Which would you prefer?"

Greg laughed. *"Which would you prefer?* What a question!"

In search of Greg's therapy we drove down to the lakefront and ended up at the Seaway Hotel, where we seated ourselves in the Anchor Lounge. The waiter poured Greg's J&B from the jigger, added soda and was about to remove the jigger when Greg stopped him.

"Haven't you ever noticed how a Scotchman drinks?" Greg asked. He took the empty jigger, poured a little soda water into it, rinsed it around and poured it into his glass.

"Never waste a drop," said Greg.

The waiter had not recognized Greg and he was not particularly amused by this performance. However, he followed us to the door wearing a big smile when we left. Greg had left him a five-dollar tip.

"You've made my day," said the waiter.

We repaired to the adjoining Marine Room, a dining room overlooking the lakefront. Greg was fond of Italian food and ordered the meat ravioli with cheese. While waiting for the food we caught up on families, friends and the newspaper business.

As I had just been pushed into the ranks of the unemployed for the second time in three years, publishers were very much on my mind. After nineteen years on *Weekend* with Greg, I had become the victim of an economy wave, along with others who'd been there even longer. We were dis-employed, de-hired or given the golden handshake. Whatever the semantics, it was a shock. After that I had joined the Toronto *Telegram* for a short ride which ended with John Bassett's announcement that he was folding the paper.

"I understand it was the union's fault," said Greg.

"Oh, *balls!*" I said. "The union did all it could to save the paper. The crux of the matter was the impending capital gains tax. Bassett sold the *Tely* just in time to avoid it. And the *Star* paid him ten million dollars for the *Tely* subscription list, which they knew they could deduct from their income tax. In essence, Bassett was bailed out with a large chunk of taxpayers' money."

"You're too abrasive," said Greg.

"Roy Thomson said a television license was a license to print money," I said. "Bassett used the *Tely* to get his television station —now he doesn't need the paper any more."

Opinions about John Bassett were always sharply divided. In

the federal election of 1962, when he ran for parliament in the riding of Spadina and was defeated, Montreal *Star* managing editor Walter O'Hearn dashed off a poem celebrating Bassett's defeat. The last verse was:

> Oh, some men seek money, and some men seek fame,
> And some the elusive vagina.
> And some seek adventure—but what's in a name?
> John Bassett was screwed in Spadina!

Greg and I had different backgrounds. Greg got his start at the *Star* because his father was the editor and a friend of the publisher. When the Newspaper Guild first tried to organize the paper Greg was immediately given the title of Associate Editor to remove him from union eligibility, along with a thousand-dollar raise. It bothered Greg's conscience somewhat, but as he was in debt as usual he accepted the situation.

My first union experience was similar but different. I began working in factories and arrived at one factory in the middle of a three-way union battle involving a company-led union, a communist-led union and the United Steelworkers union. As I was neither a communist nor a part of management I joined the Steelworkers union and encouraged others to do the same. This annoyed the factory management and after a time they offered me a promotion if I would drop my union activities. When I turned down this proposition I was fired. I had no particular objection to being promoted, but in these circumstances it sounded too much like the old ditty, sung to the tune of *O Tannenbaum:*

> The working class
> Can kiss my ass,
> I've got the foreman's job
> At last!

After some months, E. B. Jolliffe, then lawyer for the Steelworkers, succeeded in having me reinstated, but I think it's fair to say that this early experience colored my view of the labor-management relationship. Later I saw little difference between factory owners and newspaper owners, although the latter did seem to be more intoxicated by the sound of their own voices. Like many Canadian newspapermen, I regarded Roy Thomson, later Lord Thomson of Fleet, as the ultimate publisher and the

ultimate horror story. With miser-like monomania he acquired
the most newspapers, made the greatest profits, provided the least
news and paid the lowest wages.

Greg, however, could not be held to long-drawn-out arguments
about vanishing newspapers, chain ownership and the role of
newspapers in society. Perhaps he had been down that road too
many times.

Drinks arrived at our table and I proposed the toast of old
Hearst reporters:

> "Here's to William Randolph Hearst!
> He wants to see the U.S. first,
> First in armies,
> First in navies,
> First in castles for Marion Davies!"

Greg laughed. He preferred humorists to deep thinkers.

"Atkinson did only one humorous thing I remember," said
Greg. "I'd been told to drop into his office from time to time to
pick up material for his obituary—stories of his childhood and
that sort of thing. He had this huge oriental jar in his office and
every time I went in I would go over to it, lift the lid and look inside. Then I would replace the lid and carry on with the interview. Finally one day Atkinson broke down and asked why I always looked in the jar, I said I was looking to see if there were
any cookies in it. The next time I came in and lifted the lid—it
was half full of cookies!"

Greg's views of editors and publishers rarely went beyond his
personal experience. He remembered Atkinson almost fondly, yet
came to hate Harry Hindmarsh, who was, by and large, simply
carrying out Atkinson's orders.

A man's lack of business ethics or social responsibility did not
interest Greg a great deal, but he could get quite exercised about
behavior that affronted his personal ideal of sexual morality. One
publisher we had heard about considered himself a great
swordsman and boasted about it. "Just look at that son-of-a-
bitch," said Greg angrily, "wandering around with his cock in his
hand all the time. He doesn't realize that human beings have
grown up past the animal stage."

On the other hand, Greg was not nearly so affronted by the

same promiscuity on the part of newspaper or fishing companions. Only a few minutes later Greg was reminiscing about one sportsman in particular whose pursuit of women left the publisher far down the track. "Yes," said Greg, chuckling wickedly, "he was a terrible man. They used to say he'd tackle anything hot and hollow—from a lamp chimney to a bull's asshole."

Our weighty deliberations were brought to an end by the arrival of our lunch. When Greg's ravioli was set in front of him he stared at it in utter dismay. Finally he said, "This is the goddamndest ravioli I have ever seen." He pushed it around with his fork. "Look at it. Did you ever see ravioli served in tomato soup? The cook must be a Ukrainian. Or perhaps a Chinaman."

I took a look at his ravioli. It was not very appetizing—little pastry envelopes floating around in what appeared to be a kind of tomato soup.

"For our next lunch," said Greg, "we'll go to a real Italian restaurant, run by Italians. But I'd like to know who runs this place, just out of curiosity."

"As it happens," I said, "I can tell you. It's Seaway Multi-Corp, which owns Levy Industries, which used to be Levy Auto Parts."

"That explains it," said Greg. "These damn conglomerations are ruining things. These take-overs and mergers are mainly tax dodges, so you and I end up paying all the taxes. In the old days companies were run by families, who knew what they were making, whether it was pianos or whiskey. The Heintzmanns made pianos. The Gooderhams made whiskey. Nowadays companies are ending up in the hands of people who don't know how to make anything—except make money."

"And newspapers too?" I asked.

Greg looked at me over the top of his glasses.

"Well, now," he said. "There's no use both of us being unemployed, is there?"

When we had struggled through the meal Greg called for the check. The waitress stood by and looked horrified when Greg dipped his fingers into his glass of drinking water and wiped them on his napkin.

Greg explained to her, "Never drink Toronto water. Gordon Sinclair says it's full of fluoride, which is a rat poison. It's only good for rinsing your fingers."

Greg paid, adding an overly generous tip, and we said good-bye to the Multi-Corp Marine Room.

I drove to the front door of the King Edward Hotel. Greg got out, closed the car door and then leaned in the open window.

He said something that sounded like, *"Megaach, megaach, ming wan gudie kowish meshong."*

"What the hell is that?" I asked.

"It's Ojibway Indian talk," said Greg. "As near as I can get to it. It means, 'Thank you, thank you, may we eat again.'"

He stood back and waved good-bye as I drove away.

12 _____

A newspaper writer is one who has failed in his calling.

—Otto von Bismarck

The *bête noire* of Greg's life at the *Toronto Star* was Harry Comfort Hindmarsh, who married the publisher's daughter.

Hindmarsh graduated from the University of Toronto in 1909, the year before Greg entered it. Had their university years overlapped they might well have become friends instead of enemies. For one thing, both of them, in their time, worked for *The Varsity,* the undergraduate paper. For another, Hindmarsh seemed a much warmer person as a student than he was as a newspaper editor.

Hindmarsh took objection to the sometimes savage hazing to which freshmen were subjected. He campaigned against this practice so actively that at one point he was suspended from school for a two-week period.

Next, he tried to have college fraternities abolished as snobbish and undemocratic. To this end, he formed the Democratic League. In the next student elections his league managed to defeat every fraternity candidate. This would have endeared him to Greg, who took part in a somewhat similar battle at Harbord Collegiate.

Hindmarsh did join the University Masonic Lodge, of which he became Master, and he later went on to become a 32nd-degree Scottish Rite Mason. He considered the Masonic Order democratic because it was open to men from all levels of society, regardless of race, religion or color.

During his university career Hindmarsh took a year off to work as a reporter on the Detroit *News,* where he became enamored of the newspaper business. In *The Varsity,* of which he was editor in his final year, he wrote that every day in the life of a reporter was full of surprises and every day was an education. He urged his readers, "Let the university men of the continent take hold of its great newspapers." He certainly took his own advice.

When Greg entered the university in the fall of 1910 he was only seventeen years of age. He was still plagued with self-doubts and terrible anxieties. When his mood changed he would be filled with great hope and enormous ambition. One day he would dream of himself as a famous man of letters. The next day he would burn with self-contempt for the pettiness of his thoughts and actions.

While growing up Greg had enjoyed the friendship of two young cousins, Irene and Lillian Jackson, who lived at Flesherton, Ontario. Both sisters were musically talented; one played the violin, the other the piano. They were also very well read and they encouraged Greg in both literature and music. Lillian suffered from tuberculosis and in those days it was simply accepted that she had only a few years to live. Knowing this, Greg took pains to write to her often during his high school years, sometimes letters of ten or fifteen pages in length.

In due course, Lillian did die and Greg had occasion to reread the letters he had sent her. Anyone else would have seen the letters as an act of kindness or friendship—especially from a teenager—but Greg was embarrassed and upset when he read them again. He thought, What a prig I am!

One cause of his unhappiness, if not the main one, continued to be his lack of size. Later, with some accomplishments behind him, he could deal with the situation, even joke about it—but not at age seventeen.

In his efforts to seem grown up, Greg had taken to smoking cigarettes and, imitating his father, also affecting a pipe. This was mostly in secret and certainly never at home in front of his mother.

Greg's mother was not a worldly woman, nor an imaginative one like Grandma Greig. The newspapers, journals, magazines and books that filled the house were read by Greg and his father and later by his brother, Joe, and his sister, Mabel. His mother's interests lay with relatives, her husband and children, her house and the church.

While at the university Greg was still very possessive of his

City of Books at 66 Howland Avenue. His mother, a good housekeeper, would enter the attic room when he was out to straighten up his books and possessions. On finding evidence of these invasions of his privacy he would note to himself, "The Despoiler has been at it again."

On September 25, 1910, when he turned eighteen, his mother gave him a present. Unwrapping it, Greg discovered it to be a pipe.

Somewhat guiltily, Greg said, "Mother—what's this?"

"Oh Greg," she said, "I've known you've been smoking for two years now."

With the addition of the pipe, Greg was now almost identical to Joseph Clark. A few nights later Greg and his father attended a play, a production of Somerset Maugham's *Smith*. Waiting for a streetcar after the theater, Greg and his father both puffed on their pipes. A couple standing nearby watched them. Greg heard the woman say, "I think they must be brothers."

Prior to his graduation from Harbord, Greg had been active in literary and debating societies and on the school magazine. At the university, a new boy among hundreds of new boys, he was a small frog in a very big puddle. He was repelled by the cold stone buildings and his lack of friends. When he attempted to take part in social activities, he felt that people were whispering that he was officious. When he attempted to discuss his ideas about the importance of existence, he found himself called a four-flusher.

One day he was in such a discussion in the main room of the student union and left to find a magazine in another room. On his return he overheard someone saying, "Clark is a remarkable little feller—but mad as a damn dingo dog." Greg skulked away, unseen.

Once again he returned to being a bookworm and a hermit. It is a common complaint today that students arrive at college almost unable to read or write. In such company, Greg would have been a giant.

As summer approached he jotted down a list of poems he meant to copy out in order to have his own private anthology to read on canoe trips or to refer to on long, solitary walks. The list included: Kipling's "Recessional," Longfellow's "Challenge of Thor," the *Rubaiyat,* Charles Lamb's "The Old Familiar Faces,"

Moore's "The Light of Other Days," Tennyson's "Crossing The Bar," Poe's "The Raven," Wilde's "Salome," the *Jubilate Deo* and Goethe's "Wanderers Nachtlied."

Rebuffed at the university, he took to wandering the streets at night, seeing himself as "The Observer" or "The Onlooker." In his second year at the university he wrote a column for *The Varsity* which was called "The Onlooker's Corner."

His view of Toronto was romantic, to say the least. He saw Yonge Street as *"Le Boulevard des Femmes Damnée"* and the citizens who strolled there as members of the Under World, with capital letters.

He observed:

> This promenade furnishes me with voluminous material for moralizing; and moralizing is one of my vices. The men quietly wandering along and aping Happiness, here on the crumbling edge of things; the women and girls grinning and leering; Italians with large, out-spread feet, squat bodies and chattering mouths; and Jews, many Jews—short, fat, corpulent Jews, with pig eyes, broad mouths, flat noses, and dough, freckled faces; gaunt Oriental Jews, with dark faces, long noses, and burning eyes; and beautiful, Christlike Jews, with soft, gentle eyes, purely curved noses, strong, full-lipped mouths and the carriage of kings. It is a strange procession that files along and is not in any way detracted from in interest by the men of a different class, who swagger along in fine clothes, manly bodies and an air of superiority—but who leer opportunely at the women and girls.

It was pretty frightening out there, on the street of the damned. One night a horseless carriage crashed into a pedestrian, killing him and spilling his brains on the pavement. Greg observed it, but kept on walking.

As the end of his first university year approached, Greg felt he was at the crossroads of life. He wrote, "This coming month shall decide my career! If I succeed in studying, I continue my university course, and become a lawyer and man of the world. If I fail this month, I become a dreamer of dreams, a poet, an artist. *Allons!"*

Instead of studying his weak subjects, Greg again disappeared into his books. He noted that his nerves were bad because he jumped at an unexpected sound or grew irritable when he found that the arrangement of books in his room had been disturbed. He urged himself to take more walks.

In his reading—Brandes, Maeterlinck, Anatole France, Edmund Gosse, Huysman—Greg now began to have the courage of his convictions. His criticism of Brandes' biography of Ibsen was one he held against all biographies at the time. He felt that biographers gave opinions of their subjects in broken sections, written at different periods of the subject's development. He felt this burdened the reader in order to ease the author. He liked a critical biography written from one unshifting viewpoint.

What Greg was saying here is not clear, at least to this biographer. Greg may have believed that a man's character was something frozen in time, persisting unchanged through his life, but this was not true of Greg's own character. Perhaps he was still looking for absolutes.

He thought Maeterlinck's play, *The Bluebird,* was a delightful allegory, but did not approach his prose works. At the time, he was reading Maeterlinck's *Treasure of the Humble* as if it were gospel.

He seemed drawn in all directions. On one single day he recorded in his notebook that he had enjoyed a great mixture of languages: studied Greek; bought a Hebrew Bible; spoke a few words with a Chinaman, a German and an Italian, each in his own language; attended a university lecture in French on the contemporary art of Belgium; and learned some Arabic.

The inevitable happened. He failed his first year at the university.

13

FROM GREG CLARK'S DIARY
OF 1912

(NOTE: Greg's spelling and grammar were sometimes erratic and he occasionally made up his own words. In this chapter his prose is presented intact.)

New Year's Eve

No resolutions, bless your soul!

The dying year can die in peace. It has had a short life and a gay one. It has been no sad dirge, nor has it been a sweet song: it has been a full-toned symphony, with Rose Motifs, Stein Songs, barcaroles, and even discords—but a full symphony!

I have read monstrously: C. Lamb, Hazlitt, Rabelais, Chesterton, Belloc, Shakespeare, Ibsen, Wedekind, Shaw, Arnold Bennet, Mathew Arnold, John Earle, Maeterlinck, Baudelaire, Oscar Wilde, Sterne, Thoreau, Thackeray, et al.

The first half of the year was spent in loafing and culminated in failure to pass my examinations. The second half, in reading extensively on the drama, and writing for the "Varsity." Lately, I am the "Onlooker" therein.

The only recommendations are—that I eradicate the last remnants of aimless loafing, and—study Algebra.

Monday, January 1

This day, I ate Brobdinagiously and acted Lilliputianly. Jewell, Mosher, Bill Gregory and I met in the little office of the Union and played at Five Hundred.

Bill Gregory intends to enter the Church of England ministry, and this fact always hangs over him,—a cloud shadowing his youth. He is twenty-two years, large, red-faced, flinty-eyed and pipe-smoking. The average sensual man with no great points.

Mosher, twenty-one, ugly, deep-eyed and rhetorical, finishing off all his remarks with a parliamentary "Sir!" has considerable argumentative ability, is very observant, and has a fair heart.

Jewell, handsome, cynical, witty, well read, has a vast sense of humour, hates mankind, loves a woman for a day, demands your most serious attention while he speaks and sets off a string of repartee and firecracker wit, when you speak; is supremely jealous, revengeful, and sensitive; has a deep artistic appreciation, has artistic talents himself of no mean order, but is shackled by a vagabond's fickleness, lack of purpose, lack of nerve; but who must come out well to satisfy his Epicure's taste for comfort.

Tuesday, January 2

I have the same good intentions towards my academic work that has distinguished January the seconds for four years. But I cannot afford a mistake this year. One would cost me my course at College. And I have begun to see just how essential that course, with its four years of study, reading, and contemplation, is to my life, as planned.

I went to Shea's [theater] to-day, and was struck by my lack of critical powers. It was a poor bill, but I was not able to judge a thing by merit—I either liked or disliked. The main fault with the vaudeville theatre is, that there is too much nigger-accent and rag-time. Then there are not enough pretty women. Those that there are hide any beauty of form under ugly clothes.

Music is abominable. They got onto one good piece and killed it by over-doing it: Finck's "In the Shadows."

"For each man kills the thing he loves." Pish!

The theatre in America needs some strong hand to wave about and let in a little current of air. But, hélas, this country, too, is as much a nation of shop-keepers as the U. S.

Wednesday, January 3

I bought to-day a copy of Maeterlinck's three plays, "Alladine and Palomides," "Interior," and "The Death of Tintagiles."

Maeterlinck still holds for me the attraction he always did. In fact, with the years, the attraction grows; although much of that mystic hero-worship that I had for him is dead. For instance, I saw the new year in reading "The Seven Princesses." I forgot to mention it.

Maeterlinck is in New York with his wife, who is playing in something, and as his "Blue Bird" is to be here for a fortnight, next Monday, it may be that he will come up to see the production. I should like tremendously to meet him.

Thursday, January 4

Jewell has been ill, threatened with typhoid fever, but he only stayed down a couple of days, and was at the Union to-day, cleaning us up on Five Hundred.

He and I went to the theatre in the evening. There was a remarkably pretty girl in the chorus, surrounded by others that were fair—but Jewell and I both spotted this one. Wouldn't it be the deyvil if our tastes ran clash like that all the time. It would spoil what promises to be a friendship.—We are already planning bachelor quarters.

We had a talk on the way home. He said that he bet me a case of beer (beer—because literary men were born and not paid,) that he would write a greater work than mine. I took him on.

His strength, so said he, lay in the knowledge of abstract things. He said I was no philosopher, no observer, and had no analytic critical mind.

I was calm. I replied merely that among writers there were philosophers of life, observers of life and—lovers of life. I am of the last mentioned.

Friday, January 5

I went to the theatre again this evening—"Doctor de Luxe"— musical comedy. There were some very pretty girls.

Nietzsche has said that one must have chaos, before one can bring forth a dancing star. I certainly have the chaos. Rubbing noses in deep conversation with Jewell, as I do each day, I see how unformed, uncollected, and unrelated are my ideas. This is leading up to say that with regard to girls, I don't know what I like and don't like. I have a predilection for dark-eyed blondes—

yet my heart is warm towards bright-eyed brunettes. I like tall, athletic, buxom girls—and yet I like dainty, demure ones.

I know very little about girls. I don't know what they like or what they are like. My acquaintance with them so far has been a "How are ye." Or "D'lighted 'm sure." I know more about bookgirls. But they are a strange, nervous, neurotic, irresponsible crew,—dear to the mind, but to the heart—pouf!

Monday, January 8

I am keeping all T.P.'s Weeklies. I have a stack of over a hundred, and I find them very useful for reference whenever I need a subject for an Onlooker, or an opinion on some recent literary event.

It would be good stuff to write up the English papers for "Varsity": T.P.'s, "Eye-Witness," (which by the way, is not on the book-stands,) "Spectator," and "The Illustrated News."

I am growing Tory.

Tuesday, January 9

College opened, and I was on the spot. The weather is abdomenally cold, just now. The oriflamme is percolated with patines of bright gold,—at the acme of its power.

Friday, January 12

Jewell and I saw the "Passers-By" at the Princess.

The play was well constructed, except for the climaxes; and it was well acted. But Jewell, sitting huddled in his seat, was shaking with laughter most of the time. Entre-actes, while smoking, he made puns and satirical witty remarks—and he can make a grandiose sentence into the most scathing criticism. He is a master of playing on words, on bathos,—and he uses all to good advantage.

This is his custom. He rarely sits through anything, without covering his smile apologetically with his hand. There is always some character that convulses him with mirth. He is always spying out humour and pathos—He says he has a sense for both— but both make him laugh.

Unless he is happy in criticizing, he cannot enjoy a play as much as I do. I *live* in the action of a play, and every emotion, however crudely exprest, flits through my sympathetic being.

Saturday, January 13

I took in a lecture on "Music and Shakespeare."

In the evening, I heard Stephen Leacock on "University and Citizenship." I think Stephie had a couple of quarts of whiskey in him. But he gave a great speech. His versatility won the day.

I have had a couple of fights lately—street brawls. Victorious. I glare around. My sentiments are shockingly savage. And—I have seen about seven dozen girls who appeared to me attractive. Unusual, because outside my familiar circle, there isn't a damn for anybody else. I am afraid I am growing up. Heaven forbid. I am the happiest man of my acquaintance, and it is just because I am not growed up. Jewell says I am a child. I feel like a child—I am fond of children—so I must be a child. Hence—Heaven forbid.

Sunday, January 14

I read Chesterton's "The Man Who Was Thursday."

I wrote up yesterday's lecture.

I wished I had gone to church, abends.

So here I sit with the two guardian candles, reading Elia, smoking cigarettes, and scratching my hair.

I often think what a great man I shall be someday. Author, playwright, bachelor, conservative, smoker. It looks lovely from here, that life. And, I feel that it would be impossible for me to fail in winning it. I feel as if I were just as good as living it now; only I like to sit outside a while, and contemplate it.

With mother's cooking, realization is better than expectation.

Monday, January 15

Remarkable fact, that some days, there is nothing to record. It is a shame, too, that it falls out so, on this page. This is the nice flat page I like to write upon. The page opposite is curved and humpy and does not amiably offer itself to my pen. I look forward all day to this scripture, when the day falls on the fat side of the book.

I shall extinguish my candles with the little saffron assay-pot I use for a snuffer, and go to bed.

Thursday, January 18

Nothing. (See preceding page)

Sunday, January 21

I went up to the house of an Artie Windsor.

He is a queer little dapper chap, who says few words. He plays the piano with lively ability.

I am reading E. V. Lucas's life of Chas. Lamb, in two vols.

It is an idea biography—congenial, full of human interest, and *anecdotal.*

Tuesday, January 30

Everyone had such an amused grin on their faces for the last week, when I was in sight, that I became sensitive of it and had my hair cut.

Damn the people. I do not grin at their stupidity, mediocrity and complacency; nor mock their ugly faces and crude, gawky manners. Why don't they leave me alone? I'll get even with them, the witless log-heads. Talking rot, with grand opinions of everything, and oracular speeches on anything. The merchants, bankers, shop-keepers.

Wednesday, February 7

I have to get to work. A careful scientific eradication of all idle moments will give me plenty of time to study extensively, read quite a bit for pleasure, and perform such duties as writing letters and "Onlookers" and attending the theatres.

I wish I could remember some of Jewell's puns and word-plays to record. He sits in a corner and keeps up a running fire of comments, additions and corrections. His manner, presence and wit are sufficient to guarantee the attention of all in the room, and his words banish absolutely the faintest gravity or seriousness of subject. One feels like a fool, the minute one has made a sensible or serious remark, when J. is in the room. And he is merciless.

Jim Pedley said in regard to his articles on the "Highbrow": "I hitched my waggon to a star."

"Oh no, Jim!" says Jewell. "No waggon. Nothing of the waggon left but the tongue and it has been a-waggin' ever since. A regular go-cart, like Ethel Barrymore's—there's a case of hitching a wagon to a star. . . ." And so on, until somebody stops him.

Thursday, February 8

I took in the concert of the Theodore Thomas Orchestra in the afternoon, and of the Mendelssohn Choir at night. I like the instrumental more than the vocal music. Lhevinne, pianist, played a Liszt concerto.

Monday, February 19

J's "Quackiad" appeared in to-day's issue and caused quite a sensation.

I read the "Smart Set" [magazine] all afternoon.

Tuesday, February 20

We have been the subjects for a colossal hoax. Here we, who have been advocating broader reading, especially of the moderns, have been neatly satirized in Jewell's "Quackiad," but, worse than that, made unutterably foolish, because the poem which we printed as an original piece, is taken almost word for word, simile for simile, out of Byron's "English Bards and Scotch Reviewers."

Gad, how J. must have laughed when I innocently carried half a dozen copies of the paper away out to him at his office!

Saturday, February 24

J., Bob and I played bridge with Fowlds all afternoon.

Fowlds always insists that we drink tea. He puts a little pot on a thin gas flame and about the sixth rubber, it boils; then F. rustles up four drinking troughs—a shaving mug, a couple of assorted glasses, and a tin can. He then cuts two holes in a tin of condensed milk and blows through one to force a merry stream out the other into our cups.

Jewell's face during these proceedings is a study.

Wednesday, March 6

Perhaps an hour. Art is long.

Thursday, March 7

Some. Time is fleeting.

Friday, March 15

Theatres to-day. It is hard to get down to labor. I have been reading essays by Francis Grierson lately. He believes in the medium of the short essay. He certainly is a master of its use. He advocates some sort of a practical mysticism, which is hard to understand.

The last issue of "Varsity" came out Wednesday. My little Onlooker hobby is gone and I miss it. I hope to be at College next year so that I can continue the good work.

Sunday, March 17

I am Fate's jest. Perhaps she creates a lot of 'em. Here is the month half gone, and I am wofully behind in my work.

Fate's jest. In exterior, an out-and-out clown—laughed at, scorned. Internally, sensitive to insanity, soft, child-souled, and sad.

"I, too, have tried to be a philosopher. But cheerfulness was always breaking in."

I would give my soul to be taken seriously. I made a good speech last Thursday at the Freshmen's supper to the sophs., and that may help some. I am going to utilize every gift and every talent to show these empty kegs around me that I am no girl.

Wednesday, March 20

I have not seen Jewell for several weeks. I imagine he is peeved because I have not called him up often, gone to see him, and expressed more delight over his success with Neilson's [a chocolate manufacturer]. He has likely found out my shallowness of nature, and the extent to which I can bluff an interest. When he was around the college, I could spend plenty of time with him, because he was the most interesting man there. But he is away now, and I have to find others.

I am rather lonesome without the Onlooker to write.

I am reading a good deal outside academics. Gerhart Hauptmann's Plays. Henley's views and reviews. Etc.

Saturday, March 30

I was out walking, and came to a narrow walk. Ahead of me was a very important-looking gentleman, strolling at an easy, sight-seeing pace, whom I attempted to pass repeatedly. Finally I jumped down on the mud and went in front of him, and said, à la Theodore Hook: "Pardon me, but are you anybody in particular?" "What!" says he, in an English accent. "Are you anybody in particular, that you should maintain the whole sidewalk?" says I, who look strangely like a brick-layer. He flushed and said: "What do I look like, Sir?" trying to give me the idea that he was an English noble, travelling incog. "Why, like a fairly successful undertaker" says I turning away. He was one of those much-shaved, dark faced empty men, that foolishly dress in black.

Tuesday, April 2

I saw a robin and felt a blizzard.

On my way to College, this morning, I was overtaken by a certain S.P.S. professor, who knows me only by seeing me in his daily passage to and fro. He slackened his pace, and on seeing my pipe, he began in a fatherly air: "Mr. Clark do you realize what smoking will do for you?" I removed my pipe and said in an oracular tone: "I realize, Sir, that it will do for me what it did for Thomas Carlyle, for J. M. Barrie, for my father. I realize that it will do for me what it has done for the vast majority of men, when it has left a minority of religious fanatics, women suffragists, and others mentally deficient." He gave me a glare, and hastened his pace. I laughed comfortably at his uncomfortable back.

You see, I'm beginning to cast the lamb's woolly exterior.

1921: Sic!

Wednesday, April 10

> To-morrow, and to-morrow, and to-morrow,
> Creeps in this petty pace from day to day,
> To the last syllable of recorded time;
> And all our yesterdays have lighted fools
> Their way to dusty death.

Wednesday, April 24

Just look at all the paper I have wasted in the last two weeks. I have been so deep in dreams and sudden despairful awakenings, that I have not been able to do much actual work. But I have sailed many a possible sea of the future. I have been over many scenes of the triumphs coming in my life. Like all other boys under twenty, I have been imagining myself a great man.

Thursday, April 25

I was down to hear Arthur Nikisch with the London Symphony Orchestra, and that audience so raised my critical standard that I doubt if ever again I can listen to the usual concerts I have been in the habit of attending.

They played Symphony Pathétique of Tchaikowski and I was carried, I realize it, for the first time in my life into the realm of pure music. The second and third movements were absolutely nothing else but the result of creative and executive genius meeting each other half-way.

The little, stiff-mannered conductor, with his subdued methods, perfect command of the orchestra, without a sheet of music for his direction, who gazed with his slumbering Hungarian eyes at the instrument he wished to call forth, and who seemed to feel every wave of emotion, who experienced every thrill of passion in his music, was the leading spirit that made last night what it was —the concert of the generation.

Sunday, May 5

Exams since Thursday. Two Greeks on Saturday that nearly killed me. I was not in any condition to write them. I should have filed aegrogat.

Robert Browning's centenary. I read the "Pied Piper" and then howled in memory, and beckoned Edith Wynne Matthison to come back with her New Theatre company.

Let me amuse me with an entry of pocket contents: two pipes, pouch, a packet of cig papers, a packet of cigarets, key ring, knife (one half blade,) seventeen matches, a nickel, a watch, (stopped, indicating 11.20. I wound it last the day I put on this present suit,) seven pencils (two pointed,) a pen (whose nib stuck into me and caused the search that resulted in this index,) a wallet, meaningless papers and notes, a smutty postcard, two notes from Dr. Colquhoun, a library card, a long empty coin-wallet, a rosary, a composition of Jessie Robinson's that a careful friend stole from the professor and brought me to read, some exam papers, a piece of string and a stamp stuck to a burnt match.

Thursday, May 23

I have passed a week with Woody McKeown and Billie Milne at the former's farm at Erindale. It rained all the time and by the grate fire, I got in much reading. Austin Dobson's "Eighteenth Century Vignettes," Leslie Stephens' "Eighteenth Century Literature and Society," a goodly amount of Spectator, and odds and ends.

I met a very attractive little girl,—Beatrice Schreiber, granddaughter of Collingwood Schreiber, Dom. engineer.

Sunday, June 9

Since my last entry, I have been away canoozing in Algonquin Park. I had a splendid time. It is a bit early in the spring, as the portages are wet, the water high, the streams swollen, the flies bad, and the fish not in their natural habitat. We went from Joe Lake to Ragged Lake south; and north, to La Muir.

I was struck by the wasted timber, the number of deer, and the number of signs of civilization, old shanties, camps etc.

One ranger took two hundred and forty four beaver from one marsh. The Govt. is holding a sale of pelts.

A French-Canadian fire-ranger says he caught barrels of gray trout last fall to feed a lumber camp. The fish were spawning and out of season.

I learned two extra facts about canoozing. Carry blanket in bottom of turkey so as to be able to see that your change outfit is always dry and handy. Take high shoe pacs.

Sid Howard, the head of our trio is almost a first rate bushman.

Friday, June 21

I have been out another week at McKeown's. It was fine, warm weather, and as a grate-fire was superfluous, I should say, not needed, I did very little reading: Grierson's "Modern Mysticism," which is a better book of essays than his "Humour of the Underman" which I read some time ago.

I refailed in my year—a double first without honour. I do not regret the two years at "Varsity," nor do I consider them misspent. I have read prodidgiously, and acquired an intimate knowledge of useful things, with which, had I been studious at College, I would have had at most a shallow acquaintance. The mass of other subjects on the curriculum would have crowded my beloved literature and biography into a mean margin. On the whole, I consider those past two years of book-wormy stagnation, fermentation, and leisure, as god-sent; and as a far-sighted manipulation of the fates—bookish leisure without academism.

Tuesday, September 3

Yesterday, I arrived home after a very pleasant vacation. I had plenty of camping, canoeing and shooting. I think I put myself in final good form for the coming years of labor.

I begin my life sentence in a few days.

I have the ideas and sketches for some story writing. I hope I can give them birth this winter.

Jewell is gone to B. C., chasing his old phantom, the little better job. He will be writing yet, I wager, in spite of his love of business life.

I bought a big tin of John Cotton's mixture, immediately on my arrival in town. The second thing I did was to visit the Library—Grierson's "Parisian Portraits."

14

On the sweat of newspaper writers thrive publishers, editors, sub-editors, copy readers, copy boys, advertising salesmen, circulation agents, librarians, secretaries, stenographers, pressmen, engravers, mailers, accountants, truck drivers, delivery boys and at least a dozen other serfs.

The newspaper writer presents to society a skeletal frame, ragged clothing, holes in his shoes and cavity-ridden teeth simply because he is leeched of cash, blood and ideas by hordes of parasites.

No other craftsman is so like a Cairo streetcar as the writer. He groans, shrieks and totters ever forward under a load so crippling that the last hangers-on to his efforts must drag their toes in the dung of passing camels.

—*McKenzie Porter*
Newspaper columnist

Greg went to work for the *Toronto Daily Star* on Thursday, September 5, 1912, shortly before his twentieth birthday. This newspaper and Greg were born in the same year, 1892. It had first appeared as the *Evening Star,* put together by a group of locked-out printers, and announced as "A Paper for the People." The paper changed hands a number of times until it was bought in 1899 by a group of wealthy Liberals who wanted to support the policies of Sir Wilfrid Laurier.

In that year a remarkable man named Joseph Atkinson became thirty-four years of age. He had spent eight years as a first-rate reporter on the *Globe* in Toronto. He had become managing editor of the Montreal *Herald* and had just been offered the job of managing editor on the Montreal *Star,* then Canada's largest English-language newspaper. It was a magnificent opportunity for a young man, but Atkinson hesitated to accept because the Montreal *Star* was an organ of the Conservative Party and he felt that his ideas of social reform would be in conflict with the paper's policy.

When the new owners of the *Evening Star* asked him to become editor and manager of that paper he accepted, even though it was then the sickliest of all Toronto papers, struggling along with a circulation of only seven thousand. This was certainly an idealistic decision for a man later charged with lack of principle. Atkinson also persuaded his new employers to agree that he should run the paper not as a Liberal Party organ but in the best interests of the newspaper itself, as decided by him personally.

He also showed a lot of financial foresight. He made an agreement that, of his $5,000 annual salary, he would take $2,000 in shares of the paper. Also, he would be permitted to buy out the other owners' shares as they became available. He also asked for and got a ten-year contract.

During the first dozen years of his stewardship, Atkinson carefully nursed along the paper's circulation and revenues. Just as carefully, he acquired more and more shares. Shortly after Greg went to work for the paper, Atkinson acquired a further small block of shares, which gave him more than 50 percent and total control of the paper. He was now free to launch the *Star* on a controversial career which would make it the largest, richest newspaper property in Canada.

Greg was to have a part in that success story, but at the moment he was a very small cog in the *Star* machine. To him Atkinson was a remote figure, rarely seen in the newsroom, whose appearance was usually associated with warnings about no smoking or turning out unnecessary lights. Greg noted that the staff called Atkinson tight and grasping. Greg's father said that this might be so, but that Atkinson was a business genius.

Atkinson was a business genius, but he was also lucky in some of the newspapermen he inherited with the paper or managed to acquire. Not the least of these was Greg's father, Joseph Thomas Clark. Another was one of the most famous city editors of his day, Colin C. Campbell. He was the hard-fisted, hard-drinking newspaperman made famous on stage and screen. Stories that did not meet his standards were ripped to shreds in front of the unfortunate reporter's eyes—and the reporter was told to get the hell out and stay out until he had the story right. Reporters endured this treatment because they respected Campbell's news judgment and because, when the final edition went to press, he would be transformed from an ogre to an ordinary human being headed for the nearest bar.

Atkinson's right-hand man was another outstanding Scot, John R. Bone, a scholar and a lacrosse player who took over the managing editor's job which Atkinson had originally handled. Bone patterned himself on "the Chief," even to the extent of picking up some of Atkinson's mannerisms—the thoughtful frown and the pursed lips when confronted with a decision. He even moved his home to the same Lorne Park neighborhood where "Holy Joe" lived. Greg saw this as sycophancy and he did not like Bone as much as he liked Cranston, editor of the *Star Weekly*.

James Herbert Cranston was a sternly religious man and a great admirer of Greg's father. His coverage of religious stories had greatly impressed Atkinson. In 1905 Cranston had uncovered a combine of plumbing firms which was rigging the bids on major plumbing contracts in Toronto. Many prominent Toronto businessmen were involved and other Toronto papers avoided the story when threatened with an advertising boycott. The *Star* published the story in full, an act which led to the conviction of the guilty parties and Canada's first anti-combines legislation. Before being assigned to the *Star Weekly*, Cranston had served a year as Atkinson's personal secretary. During his years as editor of the *Star Weekly* its circulation grew from 16,000 to more than 250,000, surpassing that of the daily.

There were many other long-term employees destined to play important parts in the success of the paper. George Maitland functioned as city editor, news editor, telegraph editor, editorial writer, feature writer or in any other capacity needed. Bill Argue remained with the paper for forty-five years and was recognized as one of the top circulation men in North America.

At this point Greg was the lowliest of cub reporters. His salary was $12 a week, of which he turned $5 over to his mother for room and board. He reported for work at seven in the morning, occasionally working until late at night, depending on his assignments.

He was sensitive about being the editor's son, although he realized this had some advantages. Outside, on his first minor assignments, his father's name helped to open doors and begin conversations. But even then he felt that people were making comparisons and thinking he would never be the man his father was. His lack of height bothered him most. Sometimes he was mistaken for an office boy. As he was leaving one office he overheard a clerk saying, "A nice, dignified height." Greg seethed inside. Some day, he resolved, he would show people the relationship between height and dignity.

He covered minor accidents, did the usual checking and scalping of morning paper stories and began covering council meetings and police courts. These areas were a training ground for young reporters and a burial ground for old ones. Some police courts dispensed a rough-and-ready justice. Greg was somewhat shocked to hear judges making rude jokes in the course of serious trials. But he laughed along with the other reporters when a lawyer, returning to court from a long, liquid lunch, summoned a witness to the stand and then demanded: "All right, now, my boy, what's your name? Answer me yes or no!"

At a York township council meeting Greg noted the appearance of William Maclean, member of parliament, resplendent in a loud checked suit and wearing a Maclean clan tie. Mr. Maclean was appearing on behalf of a proposal to create a diagonal road from Sudan Avenue to O'Sullivan's Corners. Just a coincidence, Greg noted to himself, that the road would pass through a farm owned by Mr. Maclean.

Greg was beginning to absorb more of his father's sense of humor. His father told him a funny story about E. E. "Don" Sheppard, the eccentric founder and owner of the weekly newsmagazine, *Saturday Night*. Greg carefully wrote down the whole story in his personal journal. It seems that during a visit to Winnipeg with other Toronto newspapermen, Sheppard made arrangements for a regular nightly poker session in his hotel room.

One of the poker players was a man named Kane, a man who had a desperate fear of rats.

Just before one of the games Sheppard bumped into a hotel porter with a large trap in which he had captured a half-dozen live rats. Sheppard bought the trap, rats and all, and took it to his room where he placed it out of sight under the card table. Prior to Kane's arrival he informed the others of his plan and gave them their instructions.

The game began and the liquor flowed freely. In the course of play Sheppard opened the rat trap with his foot and the rats poured out and began running around the room. When Kane saw them he leaped up on his chair in terror.

"Jesus Christ!" he cried. "Look at the rats! Six of them!"

The others looked carefully around, but affected to see nothing. "There aren't any rats here. You're seeing things."

They went on dealing the cards.

Kane's mind was reeling. Still standing on his chair, he tried valiantly to pull himself together. He squeezed his eyes shut and then slowly opened them again. The rats were still running around. With a trembling hand he reached down and tried to grab the bottle of whiskey from the table.

Sheppard pulled it out of his reach. "No, no, you don't," he said. "You're too far gone. You've had enough."

"Just one drink, for God's sake!" cried Kane.

Sheppard was adamant. The game continued.

Kane remained on his chair for a few more minutes. Then, with a tremendous effort of will, he stepped down, pulled his chair back to the table and sat down. Again he reached for the bottle.

When Sheppard once more moved to stop him, Kane said hoarsely, "It's all right, Ned. I don't see any rats now."

Greg was not only absorbing his father's sense of humor, but his attitude toward liquor. Sent to cover a temperance meeting, he noted that the temperance advocates were all queer-looking, almost fanatical. "They look," he wrote, "as if a glass of booze would relieve the inner tensions warping their souls." One minister at the meeting struck him as having the touch of a maniac about him. In later years Greg would joke about his own drinking. "I am a teetotaler," he would announce. "But not a *bigoted* one."

Not long after he joined the *Star* Greg discovered there was a market for light humorous pieces such as those he liked to write. The market was the *Star Weekly,* then the poor stepsister of the daily.

Atkinson had long wanted a weekly companion paper for the *Star,* but had not been able to bring it into being until 1910. The first edition of the *Star Weekly* was published on April 9 of that year, with Greg's father, Joseph Clark, as editor. Joseph Clark's idea was to produce a kind of weekly literary journal featuring theater, music and book reviews.

This sold poorly. Over the first year it was revamped to an entertainment package with comic strips, syndicate features and a photo section. Greg's father was not happy with this kind of publication and he returned to the editorial page of the daily. James Herbert Cranston became editor.

At the end of the first year the *Star Weekly* had reached a circulation high of only 16,000 copies and was losing money. At first Cranston had only one assistant and little or no budget. He encouraged reporters from the daily to contribute to the weekly, but there was no payment, just the satisfaction of seeing their by-line over the work.

This appealed to Greg and in his first four months at the *Star* he had two items in the weekly—one a short feature article, the other a short story. As a by-line "Greg Clark" seemed simple enough, but he had trouble with it. At the university, on the masthead of *The Varsity,* they had listed him as Greg Clarke—adding an "e." On his first stories in the *Star Weekly* they billed him as "Gregg Clark."

Not all the *Star* reporters looked kindly on the idea of writing for the *Star Weekly* for no pay. One day, in the washroom, Greg found himself standing alongside one of the senior reporters.

The man said, "You the Clark writing those things for the weekly?"

"Yes, I am," said Greg, pleased that someone had noticed.

"You don't get paid for them, do you?"

"Well, no," said Greg, "but—"

"Better cut it out," said the man, zipping up. "Some of the boys don't like it."

Greg was deflated, but he ignored the warning. It might have caused him to miss a very interesting life.

Harry Comfort Hindmarsh had preceded Greg to the *Star* and

was already making his mark. The *Titanic* sank on April 14, 1912, the year that Greg joined the staff. In the days following the disaster an ugly rumor sprang up that crew members had jumped into the lifeboats, leaving women passengers on the deck of the sinking ship. Interviewing survivors in New York City, Hindmarsh established the falsity of these rumors and buttressed his story to the *Star* with affidavits from eyewitnesses. Atkinson was pleased, made Hindmarsh assistant city editor and took him home for dinner to meet his young daughter, Ruth Atkinson. It was not long before they were engaged to be married.

Hindmarsh was a good newspaperman and, as he had stated at the university, he had an eye for power. He was a big man, weighing 230 pounds and standing six feet, three inches. He wore his hair close-cropped and this, with his somewhat square skull, gave him the look of a Prussian officer. He did not put himself on a first-name basis with the staff, but addressed everyone by their last names, as Mr. Smith, Mr. Jones or Mr. Clark. He was not well liked.

Over the years, Hindmarsh, as Atkinson's son-in-law, became the voice of authority, and gave the *Star* a reputation for callous treatment of its employees. There was some evidence he was not always happy with Atkinson's commands, but he carried them out to the letter.

Ernest Hemingway was one of many who were fired or forced to leave by Hindmarsh. When the Newspaper Guild first attempted to organize the *Star*'s editorial employees, Hemingway, by now a successful novelist, wrote a letter: "I am sending a cheque for $100 to beat Hindmarsh. On second thought I am making it $200." Hemingway also said that working for Hindmarsh was like being in the German army under a poor commander.

The *Star* was a champion of organized labor on its editorial pages. Despite this, it ruthlessly crushed this first union attempt to organize and got rid of the union leaders one by one. The last one to go committed suicide.

Greg could see storm clouds ahead. Not long after joining the paper he wrote in his notebook: "Had a big row with Hindmarsh today in spite of the fact that he is going to marry the paper. It is great to see Maitland and others sucking his big toe therefore."

15

MAY YOUR FIRST LOVE
BE YOUR LAST

Greg Clark

When Greg got around to writing a story about his one and only
love affair he gave it the above title. It was a very romantic story
and near the beginning of it he wrote:

> But now I come to the point where I must tell the truth,
> the whole truth, and nothing but the truth, so help me!
> I had fallen in love at the age of thirteen.
> She was eleven.

Greg goes on to say that he saw this dark-haired, eleven-year-
old beauty strolling on the sidewalk with her older sister and that
he fell instantly, permanently in love on the spot. Trailing the
pair, he discovered they were the daughters of a local minister.
The name of the sister he had fallen in love with was Helen.
Then, according to Greg's story, he attended her father's church
every Sunday for years, just so he could catch a glimpse of Helen
from afar.

Greg did fall in love with Helen Scott Murray, daughter of the
Reverend James Murray, and perhaps Greg's description of the
event is the way it should have happened. However, she does not
appear in his journals until he was twenty years old and working
at the *Star*. Up until that time he had never kissed a girl, held a
girl's hand or even had a date.

His main preoccupations were dreaming about becoming a famous writer and trying to make seven dollars last through the
week. In January of 1913 he promised himself:

> I shall go to Holland and live beside a windmill and write
> stories that will make people laugh and cry and laugh. And

when the white hair comes, still living beside the windmill, I shall write stories that will make people laugh and cry and laugh. And when at last I am forever laid beside the windmill, my stories will still be making people laugh and cry and laugh.

On January 15, 1913, he wrote: "I can never make my salary last out over Tuesday or Wednesday. Friday evening, on payday, I feel rich and comfortable. Sunday I am careful. Tuesday I am broke."

On that same day he went to a small party at the home of Russell Baker, a friend of his. Baker's girl friend was named Helen Murray. Greg remembered her as one of two or three girls who had appeared in his daydreams at Harbord. That same week he went to a burlesque show called "Whirl of Society," starring Gaby Deslys. Greg noted that she was "a little flat-breasted," but among the other girls she sparkled like a diamond among pearls. Among those other girls was a comedienne named Fanny Brice. Greg's friend, Art Windsor, played the piano for the troupe at a cast party and introduced Greg to Fanny Brice. She made little impression on Greg and showed little interest in him.

Greg met Helen again shortly thereafter, mainly because his friend Billy Milne was courting a girl named Margaret Trowern, who was Helen Murray's best friend. At this gathering Greg annoyed his friend Billy by monopolizing Margaret's attention.

The Boston Symphony appeared in Toronto at this time and Greg reviewed the performance for the *Star*. His friend Art Windsor read the review and pointed out Greg's lack of musical knowledge in that he had confused the roles of the orchestra and the soloist in the playing of a concerto. Greg was not daunted. He toyed with the idea of becoming a drama and music critic, but his ambitions were somewhat confused. In his spare time he was trying to write short stories, without much success. He had a talent for sketching and he made tentative plans for attending art classes, but did not follow through.

At the next gathering of friends he succeeded in antagonizing Russell Baker by paying too much attention to Helen. Greg proposed that he and Helen should become a reporting team, working together on big stories. Baker was very obviously peeved. Although he had once admired Baker, Greg now began to feel that he was not good enough for Helen.

Within a month Greg took up half a page of his journal with
the dramatically spaced words:

> Tonight, I was at Helen Murray's
> with the bunch.
> And,
> I think I fell deeply in.

He was only half in. Soon, as his hopes alternately soared and
collapsed, he would be filling a whole page with the single, woeful
cry:

> Helen!

Of the next gathering, he wrote:

> The gang was at Margaret's again. Helen was feeling
> queer, she said, and acted queerly. After the festivities, she
> rose to go, and Russ at once prepared to accompany her,
> which he did, but with chest-busting objections from me—
> silently.
> Silly! Where do I come in. It may be only a sentimental
> softening of my brain that lets me believe I have a chance,
> and to think Russ not good enough for her.
> Back up, me boy! You are getting precocious.

In his hopelessness he compared himself to Cyrano de Ber-
gerac. "A little soul bears up for a little this corpse which is a
man." Barely twenty, and a victim of love. People told him he
would get over it, but he knew better. All the faces, forms and
personalities that he saw were insipid compared with Helen's.

Then a miracle happened. She accepted his invitation to see
Raymond Hitchcock in "The Red Widow." That evening he drew
from her an admission that she was not especially in love with
Russell; what she liked was the camaraderie of the whole group.
Greg's spirits soared.

But the very next night, he learned, she and Baker and Margaret and Billy were paired off on a date. He could not understand it.

His press passes came to the rescue again. She went with him to
a Toronto Symphony concert to hear Tchaikovsky's *Pathetique*
and Liszt's *Second Hungarian Rhapsody*.

But the very next day, when he phoned, she said no, she was

staying in that day. She would be engaged the next afternoon. She would not see him, she thought, for a little while.

Greg's love for Helen turned into hate for Baker. He saw now that he had been deceived by this man. Baker was actually a lout, a lecher, totally unworthy of the incomparable Helen. He fantasized a fitting end for this monster. The setting, of course, would be the world which Greg knew best, the north country. He would worm his way back into Baker's confidence. Casually he would invite Baker on a canoe trip in Algonquin Park. Three days into the wilderness, beyond human call, on some stretch of raging white water, with Greg steering from the stern, there would be an inexplicable accident—from which neither man would return.

On reflection, though, Greg thought it might be better if Helen received a secret note explaining he had sacrificed his own life to save her from Baker. He could leave the note with her friend Margaret, to be opened only if he did not return.

Greg was saved from this murderous scheme by a stroke of luck. Baker and Helen and Billy Milne and Margaret Trowern went on a Sunday outing to Georgetown. Baker, during the course of the day, said or did something the girls found unforgivable. He was banished and the other three returned without him. Billy phoned Greg with the good news—perhaps now he could become the fourth in the group.

Greg rushed to fill the vacancy, but there was something wrong. Helen was still moody, preoccupied, distant. Greg did a bit of investigating. Before Baker, Helen had gone out for two years with a boy named Staff Rice. Could it be that Helen was still pining for him? With clever casualness Greg talked to Helen about her seeming melancholy, her listlessness. He brought up the name of Staff Rice. Was there . . . ? Did she . . . ? Helen was noncommittal.

Then, quite unexpectedly, Billy Milne confirmed the worst. Helen was still thinking about Staff Rice. On March 10, Greg wrote in his journal:

> Life is finished!
> So damn short! Like a hanging!
> There is nothing left but work.

He tried to work, but with little success. He got a few dates with Helen and took her to hear the New York Philharmonic and

John McCormack at Massey Hall. But she was noticeably cool. At a later party she danced with two other boys! He made another date, but when he phoned to confirm, she told him she couldn't go—she was having Staff Rice in that night. Greg spent the night in hell.

Eventually Staff Rice followed Baker into oblivion. Greg was favored with a few more dates. Helen was distant. In his misery Greg concocted a romantic plan. On parting, he explained, he would light a match. If she wanted to see him again, she would do nothing. If she wished to be rid of him, she was to blow it out. He lit a match. Helen blew it out with a laugh.

This, thought Greg, was really the end. He wrote: "I should like to go to Russia and write symphonies. I should like to go to Holland and write gray poems. I should like to go to Ireland and walk on the roads with the tinkers. Go to hell!"

He relieved his frustrations by punching a startled fellow named Robertson in the mouth. In Greg's presence, he had associated Helen's name in a nasty way with that of another young man named "Boob" Batten. Then Greg sought out "Boob" Batten and gave him hell for giving rise to the story.

There was little humor for Greg in the year of 1913. The only funny thing in his journal was an anecdote told him by his father. A friend of Joseph Clark's, named George Ham, had called him at the paper.

"Joe! Come and have a drink with me. I'm under doctor's orders this past week and I'm only allowed one drink a day. So I choose who I'll drink with."

Joseph Clark joined Ham at a place called the Chop House. When the drinks appeared Ham pointed at his. "See that drink? This is June seventh. Well, that's my drink for November eighteenth!"

Greg could not stay away from Helen. In June he persuaded her to accompany him while he made the rounds of the police stations. With cruel honesty she told him she had no feelings for him. The words wounded Greg but he prattled on. Perhaps their friendship would grow into love. Perhaps they could get married so they could go about together without scandal, but if she wished, they could live separately. Helen shrugged off this foolishness, but continued to go out with him.

That summer he persuaded his parents to invite Billy Milne

and Margaret Trowern and Helen to Go Home for the summer vacation. It turned out to be a stroke of genius. Helen loved the Georgian Bay retreat. She liked fishing, the wild animals they saw, the carefree days of sunshine. The magic of summer nights with ukulele music sounding across the moonlit waters did its work. That August, seven months after his headlong tumble, Greg kissed Helen for the first time. He was in ecstasy.

Back in Toronto that fall, he doubled and redoubled his attempts to fan friendship into love. It was slow going. At times Helen felt smothered by his constant attention and withdrew into herself, but on Christmas Eve of 1913 he persuaded her to accept his engagement ring. Marriage, because of his financial position, was still very much in the future.

People had different reactions to the engagement. Some time after the event Greg was riding a local train with Billy Milne when they were joined by a young man named Trebilcock. He had known Helen earlier and he now said to Milne, "I hear Helen is engaged."

"Yes," said Milne, glancing at Greg.

Trebilcock caught the glance, looked at Greg in amazement and blurted out, "Not to you, surely!"

He turned red with embarrassment and made a quick departure.

Greg's family was pleased. Helen had impressed them that summer at Go Home. Speaking about it later, Greg's sister Mabel said, "I'll never forget Helen that summer. She was so beautiful to look at and so beautiful in herself. I never heard her say a mean or unkind thing. Greg followed her everywhere. He was so *damned lucky* to get her. They're exactly the same height, you know."

It was not a point Greg had ever mentioned in his journals.

16 _____

But on Saturday I'm willing
If you'll only take the shilling,
To make a man of any one of you!

Song of World War I

Greg saw Helen virtually every day for the next year. If he could not see her in the evening because of an assignment, he asked her downtown to join him for lunch. Occasionally he was invited for dinner at her home. Her father, the Reverend James Murray, was a stern man and not overly impressed with Greg, whom he saw as a failed minister.

Even though they were now engaged, Helen was subject to strange moods and periods of withdrawal. Possibly at times she was overwhelmed by Greg's possessiveness and his expectations of her. Her mother warned Greg, "You will never find anything spontaneous in the daughter of the Reverend James Murray. You'll spend a lifetime of energy trying to call something out of her that isn't there."

Greg nevertheless worked at the problem. He and Helen were both aware that something was wrong. On occasion she would try to tell him that she cared and for him to be patient. Once, a little wearied by her lack of affection, he suggested that he should act cool and distant until warmed by her approach. The result was two days and evenings in which they met and sat together like total strangers. The silence was broken by a lovers' quarrel.

In the meantime, they were enjoying a continual round of plays and concerts, as well as *Madame Butterfly,* their favorite opera. A German program at the symphony included Strauss's "Death and Transfiguration," a work that amazed Helen. She wondered if the orchestra librarian had made a mistake, giving the drum score to the violins and the violin score to the bassoon. Greg found it

definitely "cubist," a new word he had adopted to describe anything new or impressionistic. Both Greg and Helen wallowed in
the *Tannhäuser* overture, which he felt indicated their simple,
unintellectual taste in music. They went to a matinee of *Twelfth
Night,* presented by the Stratford-on-Avon Players, which Greg
said was the first Shakespeare he had ever enjoyed, as it was
staged with none of the usual affectation.

Gradually he began to take more of an interest in his work at
the *Star,* which he had been neglecting. He wrote to "Woody"
McKeown, a longtime friend, who was on a trip to Europe and
who shared an interest in writing. Greg urged him to try a travel
piece for the *Star Weekly,* because he felt Woody had the humor
and the erratic mental processes necessary for yeasty writing.

Mentioning this to Helen, Greg opened the lid on yet another
horror. When Woody was a member of their little group, he had
paid so little attention to Helen that she was piqued. She had, she
confessed, tried to egg him on and let him know she was a bit
"soft" on him. Greg was hurt, furious and jealous, all at once.
How many other such betrayals lay in Helen's past? How could
they now meet socially? They would have to at least be cordial,
but Greg knew that if he saw Helen being cordial to Woody, his
suspicions would run riot.

In Greg's private world the beginning of World War I had been
almost unnoticed. For two years now, Helen had consumed his
thoughts, lessened his performance at the *Star* and almost elimi-
nated his attempts to do any creative magazine work. He had
completed one short story, which had so far collected only a
standard rejection slip from Newton MacTavish, editor of *The
Canadian Magazine.*

It is regretted that this offer for publication does not come
quite within the requirements of *The Canadian Magazine.*

The author's courtesy in sending it is acknowledged with
thanks.

The editor is always glad to receive tenders of either suggestions or manuscripts.

Greg's courtship was prim, prudish by later standards, but not
inconsistent with his early religious training or with the Victorian
standards of Toronto at this time. A few years earlier a small
child had fallen into the Don River and disappeared beneath the

water. A small crowd gathered at the scene, including a police officer and a young man who was an expert swimmer. The would-be rescuer began to take off his clothes, but was halted by the policeman. After all, it was daylight and there were people around.

"Have you a swimming suit?" asked the policeman.

"No, I haven't."

"Then you cannot strip naked and go in here," he was told.

The child's body was later recovered by somebody properly garbed according to the city bylaw governing swimming within the city limits. The incident was the subject of an indignant editorial in *Saturday Night,* but doubtless many proper Torontonians saw nothing untoward about it.

To express some of his feelings about Helen, Greg began a new, intimate diary, a secret diary, where forbidden longings might presumably be hidden even from himself. He wrote:

> The sexual part of my affection for Helen is by far the lesser. When I hold her in my arms, I feel as if I did not want that part of her love at all. And I am confessing this with violent protests from my "manhood" which I believe is an artificial part of me, instilled by the yarns and boastings of my cronies in school days.
>
> Or it may be the hard shell remaining from old ideas because I always frowned sex down as a conquerable thing and preached to the boys against it.
>
> I want her. Everything in me writhes with that thought. But it is far down in me, in an unexplored region.
>
> I am intensely jealous of her. I hate her, when she talks of boy friends of the past. A dream, in which she appeared as a liar, sent me into the sulks and to asking her about the past. She sulked, because of my suspicions.

Their love affair continued, always an ecstasy or an agony. Sometimes Greg thought wistfully of the uncomplicated earlier years of reading, planning, dreaming.

Meanwhile, back at the *Star,* his work revived somewhat. Some days he managed to get two or three items in the daily—a small feature on orphan asylums, a report on the first cab in early Toronto. Occasionally one of his own sketches accompanied the stories.

The hierarchy at the *Star* was slowly changing. Greg was a favorite of Cranston at the *Weekly,* but less liked by Bone, managing editor of the daily. Greg found Bone officious and very put out if the smallest voucher or bill did not come to him for his signature.

When Greg reported to work at 7:30 A.M., he found Hindmarsh and Maitland already at their desks. Both were vying for advancement and found visits to Atkinson, over Bone's head, to be good strategy. Greg found Maitland a keen and diplomatic editor who would occasionally permit a bit of fancy writing. Hindmarsh was gruff and bullying. Greg thought he might be kindhearted underneath, if his ambition would only permit it, but he remained always on his dignity and everyone under him had to remain a cub.

For the *Weekly* Greg wrote a piece on the problems of the unemployed, their problems worsened by too much bureaucratic deliberation. He received a number of compliments, the most welcome of all from his father, who said it was the best he'd done yet. Greg enjoyed the feeling of something done well, a feeling of strength.

For a time after the outbreak of the war, life in Toronto seemed little affected. Greg noted that people continued to smile, to go about their work, even though terrible events were taking shape in Europe. He understood his own vagueness and lack of interest—he was still obsessed with Helen—but he speculated on the nation at large. Was it that Britain had so long been regarded as invincible, a bulwark that protected Canada from any possibility of harm?

However, more and more of his contemporaries began to enlist. Many were boys he had considered triflers and lightweights. They were going off to fight, leaving him to his lovemaking. That was something he must not forget.

Billy Greig, Greg's cousin, visited the Clarks in uniform. He was with the Queen's Own Rifles, third contingent. In 1915 the war came even closer to home when Greg's younger brother, Joe, applied for a commission in the King's Own. Shortly afterward Mrs. Clark saw the second contingent march past on Albany Avenue and she came home crying, thinking of Joe's application and his coming life in barracks. She had heard about an outbreak of meningitis at Exhibition Camp, where recruits were assembled.

Greg's brother Joe was four years younger than Greg and had

developed quite differently. He was more athletic, was much more outgoing and took life in his stride. At eighteen, he had already worked as a reporter, both at the *Star* and at the *Globe*. Greg watched this progress with some envy. Joe was dapper, witty, wore the latest clothes, was welcomed everywhere. Greg could not understand this. He knew for a fact that Joe seldom read books, if ever. Furthermore, people talked of them as though Joe were the older brother.

Greg restated his lack of interest in the war, but with less conviction. Helen had always opposed the idea of his enlistment, but now she said she would not wish to stand in his way if he wanted to go.

By 1916 Greg's father was writing editorials in the *Star* urging enlistment. As always, he wrote convincingly: "You may have a dozen reasons now for staying at home. But the day will come when all these reasons strung together will not make one good reason."

When Greg raised the question at home, his father explained that his editorials did not apply to Greg. After all, they had one son, Joe, already in the army and that was sufficient contribution for one family. Joe was now a gay dog when he came home from camp, resplendent in his new uniform. Greg's friend Billy Milne soon left for overseas.

At the *Star,* Greg added the military beat to his coverage. He covered regimental doings and training. Then, to his surprise, he discovered that there were already veterans returning home and having problems with rehabilitation. The government and the public had not yet really awakened to the magnitude of the problem of helping veterans—some of them disabled—back into the social fabric. Greg had to fight to get his copy in the paper, but when he did, it hit a nerve. As was his style and the *Star*'s he wrote of individuals with compassion and sympathy, and the other Toronto papers were quick to follow suit.

Greg stood five feet, two inches and weighed only 110 pounds. His chest measurements were 31–34. He was below the army's minimum standards and might well be turned down. But he knew from his work on the military beat that regulations weren't always followed to the letter.

Early in 1916 he began looking for a commission. Lieut. Col. Legrand Reed, officer commanding the 170th Overseas Battalion, Mississauga Horse, promised his favorable consideration, but first

Greg would have to enlist as a private. This he did on March 27, 1916, becoming Private Gregory Clark, ✕681565. After being sworn in, he was given a temporary pass and told to report in on April 10.

His enlistment created little excitement at the *Star*. Greg announced his departure to managing editor Bone and added, "I understand that the *Star,* after the fashion of the numerous firms we have written up, does something for those of its employees who enlist?"

Bone stroked his chin. "In what way?" he asked guardedly.

"You keep the job open," said Greg.

"Ah, yes!" said Bone enthusiastically. "Certainly, absolutely! In fact we regard you as only being on leave of absence. You are another of the *Star*'s representatives at the war."

Greg recorded Friday, April 7, 1916, in his journal:

My last day at The Star! Only half a day at that, it being my half-day off. So I went to J. R. Bone and asked him quite frankly if there was any extra money coming to me. He has had a week to think it over. He asked me what I would be prepared to do for The Star. I said I could do nothing. That seemed to end the matter.

I consulted Dad. Dad said, "If you had delayed enlisting thirty days longer, you would have had your draw for holidays, with two week's pay."

I at once took the matter back to Bone. He referred me to Mr. Atkinson. "Why, of course," said they both. In fact, Bone was greatly upset over not having thought of that. So I drew in all $87.50 from The Star office today. The largest lump sum I have ever possessed. Helen and I were jubilant. We had a grand old spree to celebrate our departure from journalism for a time.

In barracks, Greg was stunned to discover that the commonest words were the vilest words in the English language. He was shocked to learn that women and liquor were the chief interests of soldiers and that both were pursued with a filthy frankness.

On one of his first marches his platoon mates whistled at women on the street and issued lewd invitations. Greg was outraged at these insults to womanhood. He shouted, "I warn you fellows once and for all! If any girls of my acquaintance pass by and I hear insults like that—I'll swing my rifle butt on the head of the man who does it! I'll kill him, I tell you!" This tirade, from the smallest man in the squad, provoked hoots of laughter and more rude invitations. This little squirt must be from some other world.

Men were now being funneled overseas quickly. Greg began his service as a red-coated cadet officer on April 10. He was commissioned on May 31. He entered barracks as a supernumerary subaltern with the 170th Battalion on June 5. During June and July he received training at Jesse Ketchum School and Camp Borden.

On August 11, 1916, he was warned for overseas. He wangled a short leave and arrived at Norway Point, Lake of Bays, where Helen was staying with her parents. They were married on Monday, August 14. On August 18, a married man, but still a virgin, he entrained for Halifax and the slaughter in the trenches.

Greg arrived in Liverpool on September 1 and spent that month and part of October at Napier Barracks, Shorncliffe, with three hundred other officers. He was posted to the 4th Canadian Mounted Rifles at Etrun, in France, and arrived there on November 23. He was assigned to D Company, which was in the line when he arrived, and he was led there, under shellfire, in the dark. Occasional flares and shells lit up the trenches they sloshed along. They arrived at the entrance to the dugout which was headquarters for D Company and Greg was feeling his way down the muddy steps when a shell exploded nearby. He skidded down the steps and rolled through the burlap curtain that covered the doorway. He took the curtain with him and rolled into the room, knocking over the candles and plunging the dugout into darkness.

From the darkness a voice cried, "What the hell was that?"

A match was struck, a candle was lighted and the company officers uncovered the struggling bundle on the floor.

"Good God," said Captain MacKenzie, commander of D Company, "It's half a man!"

Greg untangled his equipment, struggled to his feet and saluted.

"Lieutenant Clark, reporting for duty, sir."

MacKenzie and the others surveyed the newest, youngest, smallest officer, then burst out laughing.

"Have a drink," said MacKenzie. A tot of rum was poured into a tin cup and given to Greg. He got it down with difficulty. It was his first taste of liquor.

17

IN FLANDERS FIELDS

We are the Dead. Short days ago
We lived, felt dawn, saw sunset glow,
  Loved and were loved, and now we lie
    In Flanders fields.

—*Colonel John McCrae*
Canadian doctor, soldier, poet

The shell that blew Greg down the dugout steps on his arrival in France damaged his right eardrum and led to total deafness on that side. He noticed it almost immediately, but did not report it, he said, for fear of appearing to be a total non-hero, a man shipped back as soon as he arrived.

He compensated by tilting his good ear slightly forward. In later years he was to claim it was really a blessing in disguise. "I could sleep through anything," he said. "A battle, a noisy party in the next room, anything. All I had to do was turn on my left side, with my good ear on the pillow, and I was cut off from the world." It was just another example of the good luck he felt attended him all his life. To make sure of it, Greg brought along his own supply of good luck. The pockets of his officer's tunic bulged with lucky charms, well-rubbed coins and a collection of small brass matchboxes that contained souvenirs of the past few years with Helen. The whole collection grew throughout the war. He added a pocket copy of the New Testament, a nail from a horseshoe found in France, the stone with a hole in it.

His charms worked, right from the beginning. He was walking on the bathmats—wooden boardwalks along the bottom of the trenches—soon after his arrival with one of his men when a German sniper's bullet spanged on a piece of angle iron supporting the barbed wire in front. One half of the bullet ricocheted away; the other half buried itself in the wall of the trench above Greg, exactly where his head would have been had he been of normal height. The soldier looked at the hole and observed, "Mr. Clark, you're built exactly the right size for trench warfare."

Greg's first tour of duty was a fairly uneventful one. The normal tour consisted of six days in the front line, six days in support from two hundred to four hundred yards back of the trenches and then reserve duty, some eight hundred to a thousand yards in the rear. After that followed an indeterminate period in rest billets, perhaps in some ruined village or town several miles from the front.

Frontline duty was the worst, with patrols and attacks, constant sniping and shellfire. However, the support and reserve units, occupied in digging trenches, laying wire and carrying ammunition, also suffered many casualties, as these activities were the target for some of the heaviest shelling. In January of 1917 Greg was sent out of the lines with an 8th Brigade Training Unit, to make up for training he had missed in his abbreviated military career.

The coarse, bitter humor that helped keep soldiers sane began to relieve Greg's deadly seriousness. It was one comfort that could be retained in the mud and filth and the stench of death. His size, about which he'd been so abnormally sensitive, for the first time became something with which to have fun, to create laughter, instead of being laughed at.

In one of Greg's refresher courses, a husky instructor was demonstrating how to carry boxes of Stokes shells, with the use of a tump line around the forehead. The sergeant instructor loaded himself up with five boxes, a considerable weight when filled with shells. Behind a nearby hut, Greg and a Lance Corporal Jackson had noticed a large pile of empty Stokes boxes. They skipped out of sight and the corporal succeeded in piling up seven Stokes boxes on Greg's back, held on by the tump line. Then he tucked another empty box under each of Greg's arms and suspended a tenth empty box from a string, which Greg clenched in his teeth.

Greg was now almost buried under Stokes boxes and the corporal led him from behind the hut to the demonstration area, with Greg staggering as though he were under a tremendous load. The corporal danced about in front of him, shouting, "Keep your

Murray knocked down this brace of partridge, an event etched in his brother's memory.

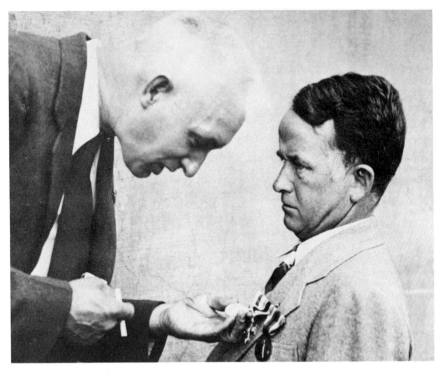

Jim Frise, famous *Star Weekly* cartoonist and himself a veteran of World War I, pays mocking admiration to Greg's medals.

Greg and his friend Jim Frise would fish anytime, anywhere. *(Ack Forbes)*

Famous "Birdseye Center" cartoon of Jim Frise. *(Courtesy of John Frise)*

Jim Frise grew up in the Lake Scugog area of Ontario and drew on his small-town background for the "Birdseye Center" cartoon. *(Courtesy of John Frise)*

Cowboy Keane, famous *Star Weekly* contributor, tempts Greg with canned rattlesnake meat.

Three big-name *Toronto Star* writers: Gordon Sinclair, world traveler; Fred Griffin, ace reporter; Greg Clark.

(Left) Greg's first collaborator, Charles Vining. *(Above)* The *Star's* famous sports columnist and athlete, Lou Marsh. *(Toronto Archives)*

A friend of Greg and Hemingway was Canadian novelist and short story writer Morley Callaghan.

Morley Callaghan writes of life only as he sees it, a habit which has brought him literary kudos.

"I Never Knocked Out Hemingway"

DIOGENES was an ancient philosopher who wandered through life with a lantern in his hand. He said he was looking for an honest man. Diogenes was born 2,000 years too soon. The man he was looking for is Morley Callaghan, the Canadian novelist and short story writer.

Callaghan is recognized as one of the greatest short story writers in the world. His stories have been reprinted in all languages and, in textbooks for writers, used as models of literary perfection. They have appeared in virtually every worthwhile magazine, and for 12 years in a row there was a story of his in the

Canadian novelist Morley Callaghan insists that the truth be told, even though it spoils a good story

By Jock Carroll
Standard Toronto Bureau

we're all joined together — and we're all, well —

1920s, he was reported to have knocked out another writer, a man by the name of Ernest Hemingway.

Hemingway, Callaghan and F. Scott Fitzgerald were good friends during their Left Bank periods. Callaghan had returned to Toronto when the Hemingway knockout story appeared in the New York Herald Tribune.

"I had never knocked Hem out," says Callaghan, "and all our boxing was by way of a healthy lark. For instance, after going a few rounds one day, I remember Hem throwing his arm around my shoulder in a Paris bar and telling the bartender I would al-

Greg interviewed Mary Pick-
ford—and took her fishing.

A mess of trout caught by Greg
and Sir William Mulock.

Jim Frise's New Year's card featured "Birdseye Center" characters. *(Courtesy of John Frise)*

A Frise Christmas card featured himself and Greg in character. *(Courtesy of John Frise)*

People lined up for the latest news of the Moose River
Mine disaster in 1936.

Greg describes his wish to be buried in a favorite fishing hole in a story
collaboration with Charles Vining. *(Toronto Star)*

(Left) Greg's birthplace at 56 McKenzie Crescent, Toronto. *(Jock Carroll)*

(Below) Attic room at 66 Howland Avenue was Greg's "City of Books" in his youth. *(Jock Carroll)*

After Greg married, his first home was a third-floor
flat at 147 Indian Road. *(Jock Carroll)*

Greg's first rented house was this one at 90 Woodside Avenue, where he
lived in the Twenties.

Greg's daughter, Elizabeth, was born while the Clarks lived in this house at 3 Baby Point Road. *(Jock Carroll)*

Greg's sixth Toronto home, at 47 Baby Point Road, was virtually next door to the home of his friend and collaborator Jim Frise. *(Jock Carroll)*

In the spring of 1938 Greg rented this large, rambling house at 19 Indian Grove. *(Jock Carroll)*

From April 1954 to July 1966, Greg lived in this home, owned by his daughter, at 119 Crescent Road. For the last ten years of his life, Greg occupied Suite 683 at the King Edward Hotel. *(Alexandra Studio)*

Greg wrote daily stories about the rise of the famous *Toronto Star* building at 80 King Street West. *(Norm James)*

Jim Frise and Greg at the time of their move to *The Montreal Standard.*
(Charlie King)

Greg's father died in 1937. (Greg and his brother Joe are the two leading
pallbearers.)

Helen and Greg with Pelee Island pheasants.

distance, gentlemen, in case he drops one!" The class laughed, even the instructor.

Once, Greg's sense of humor nearly did him in. One dark night he was with a soldier named Wolf when they saw a sentry approaching. "Let's hide and give him a start," suggested Greg.

Somewhat doubtfully, Wolf joined Greg in the shadows of a trench. However, when the sentry was still some distance off, Wolf stepped out of their hiding place, pulling Greg with him, and loudly called out "Brandon!" which was the password of the day.

The sentry acknowledged them and passed on. Greg was disgusted at the failure of the joke and said, "What's the idea?"

"Didn't you see who it was?" said Wolf. "It was Findlay."

He explained that it was Findlay's habit to carry a Mills bomb in his hand when on patrol alone. He threw first and asked questions afterward.

In February of 1917, Greg rejoined his battalion at Burburre, where the unit was in training for the upcoming battle of Vimy Ridge. Some historians feel it was here, on Easter Monday, April 9, 1917, that Canada became a nation.

Greg saw his brother Joe shortly before the battle. Joe had served with distinction with the 75th Battalion during the latter half of 1916, having arrived overseas some six months before Greg. However, Joe's heart was set on joining the Royal Flying Corps and, in January of 1917, after several attempts, he managed to wangle a transfer to the 13th Squadron as an observer. Up until this point he had not met Greg overseas, but had kept in touch with him by letter. Joe, much more than Greg, was a voluminous letter writer and his letters home to his family were later bound into several volumes by his father. Throughout the war he wrote home several times a week, telling what he could of his experiences.

On November 14, 1916, he wrote:

Dear Dad, Mother and Gang:

I don't know how you ever got the idea that Greg and I weren't in correspondence. I've been writing Greg for weeks and weeks, have sent him my Colt automatic, and a lot of first hand dope about kit, luggage, etc. As a matter of fact I've written him nearly as frequently as I've written you— you silly old gang.

Do you think I'd let that untutored, unsophisticated little

brother of mine wander all alone over England without writing him what to do, where to go, etc? Say !!! . . .

Greg, in Joe's eyes at least, was the younger brother. It was not until the week before Vimy that the two brothers were united. By then Joe was attached to the 13th Squadron of the R.F.C. and found time to look up Greg with the 4th C.M.R. They wrote a mutual letter home on April 3, 1917.

Dear Old Family:

JOE—I dropped in to see a chap I know in the C.M.R.'s to have a bite of breakfast, really, however. He's standing beside me now, and I believe he's reading what I write. He also has put on my helmet and goggles.

GREGORY—Well, at last. I was just in the act of shaving when he walked serenely in the door. Now, before we go any further, let me say that he is looking 100% better than he ever looked before. Red cheeks!

JOE—Greg always had a good deal of the blarney about him. As for *his* good looks, he has a moustache patterned after that worn by Pete Laforge Sr., only there are no chewing tobacco stains on it. He looks "top hole" as they would say in the Squadron mess. He hasn't grown much though.

GREGORY—The lad is still the Senior, I'm afraid. He speaks from a vast height of experience in regard to the blinkin' infantry, and the way he gloats and brags about the upper regions is enough to make an infantryman resign. And, anyway, he rides up to the door of our 'umble 'ome in the side car of a motorcycle.

JOE—I'm smoking a huge cigar, "one of the famous ones", a gift from my brudder. Golly, it's good to see him again. Unfortunately I have to rush back to the Squadron as I have a special shoot on at 2 p.m. and it's 11.30 now.

GREGORY—Good news arrived with little Joey. He has got his wing! *A* wing, the badge of the observer, in two months, which is some record.

JOE—We are now once more quite close together and now that the old hoodoo has been vanquished, we'll probably see a good deal of each other. Greg's Company appears to be a very happy little family with Daddy MacKenzie at the head of the table.

GREGORY—Now, we'd like to have written more, but as you can understand, we are excited. But we are united at last, Family dear, so we are jake.

JOE—Write to us both soon, fambly dear,

Your loving,
Joey and Greg.

As it happened, they would not see each other until that summer, when Joe was in England recovering from a plane crash and when Greg received his first leave. Meanwhile, the battle for Vimy Ridge, Greg's first great baptism of fire, was only a week away.

For almost three years the Western Front had changed little. It was a terrible moonscape of shell holes, mud, barbed wire, trenches and blasted trees. Until now, the Canadian divisions had been sent into action individually. For Vimy it was decided that all four Canadian divisions would go into action as an army for the first time, as the spearhead of an attack that would mark the first great breakthrough of the war. They suffered over ten thousand casualties in three bitter days of fighting.

At first, Greg was scheduled to be left out of battle, as the newest lieutenant and the only married one. His argument was that he deserved the chance to get a nice Blighty and be shipped home to his bride. After much argument he and Johnston tossed and Greg won command of 15 Platoon for the battle.

The battalion's training included a five-day stint in the trenches at Vimy, which were to be their jumping-off point. Behind the lines one day, at Lillers, the officers of D Company had a group photograph taken. Writing home, one of the enlisted men remarked that all the officers except Clark viewed the coming battle with foreboding. Their fears were well founded, for, of the seven officers, three died on the ridge. Greg was to survive the battle and win the Military Cross.

Greg's company, D Company, assembled in the Vimy trenches at midnight on Sunday, April 8. A, B and C companies were assembled in shell holes in no-man's-land. D Company was to jump off last, at zero plus three. At zero hour, which was 5:30 A.M., the tremendous barrage behind which the troops advanced was begun. The sky filled with a vast, whispering murmur of thousands of shells, which blossomed into a great sheet of yellow-and-red flames on the German lines and moved slowly forward. The earth spouted from great potholes. Phosphorous shells burst overhead in a golden cascade.

At zero plus three Greg gave the command and 15 Platoon went over the top into what seemed like the edge of hell. Greg noted later that it was so terrible, it was almost beautiful. They stumbled ahead through and around shell holes and dead bodies, while Germans ran past them to the rear, their hands in the air. Here and there men crumpled quietly, like a suit of clothes from which the body had been miraculously snatched.

At 0600 hours, Greg's platoon halted while the barrage rolled on ahead to pound the German reserve units. Greg took cover in a shell hole with Bertrand, his batman; Macpherson, a stretcher bearer; Sergeant Windsor; and two runners. A German shell entered the wall of the shell hole below them and tossed the entire group in all directions, miraculously without wounding one of them.

When the platoon made the crest of the ridge, the German troops could be seen running about below and trying to reorganize. Lieutenant William Butson ordered Greg's platoon to dig in on the crest—then he collapsed, both his eyes shot out by a bullet which entered the side of his head.

On Tuesday the platoon came under return artillery fire from the Germans and was also harassed by short rounds from their own rear. They were now dug in near the Cable House—a former German communications pillbox—and Lieutenant Johnston invited Greg to come with him to eat their rations in the Cable House itself. As the Cable House was a logical target for German artillery, Greg argued with Johnston, but to no avail. Johnston climbed out of the trench and headed for the Cable House. He had gone no more than fifteen feet when a shell landed nearby, blowing him to pieces. One of his legs flew back into the trench, thudding against Greg's feet and Sergeant Mackie's helmet. For Greg it was the most sickening moment in the attack. After a while someone picked up the leg and threw it over the parapet.

The C.M.R. held its position until Wednesday night, under constant shelling and with heavy losses. At that time they were relieved by the 58th and 116th battalions. Back at the Dumbell Camp at Mount St. Eloi, along roads lined with dead horses, there was some celebration—but not in D Company. The commanding officer, Captain MacKenzie, and the company sergeant major were both wounded. Dead were three sergeants and three lieutenants. For his composure under fire, Greg was recommended for the Military Cross, which he received in June. Later, he used to say it was because he was one of the few officers to survive the battle.

After a short rest period behind the lines, the C.M.R. went back into the old Vimy front line as reserves. By April 20, 1917, they were in the new line at the Mont Forêt quarries. Through the rest of April, May and June they did several tours on the Mericourt front. In July the battalion was at Avion, with rest billets back at Château de la Haie, and shortly afterward it was shifted to the Hill 70 front, where the 1st and 2nd divisions were in battle.

In August of 1917 Greg was appointed assistant adjutant to Major Victor Sifton and also in that month he received his first leave since his arrival in France more than eight months before. When he returned from the leave in London, his battalion was moved to Neuville St. Vaast, the old Vimy front. Here C Company was practically wiped out with the first use of poison gas.

Greg was promoted to acting captain in March of 1918 and confirmed as captain at the end of that month. In April he became adjutant. By August of 1918 he had spent a full year as assistant adjutant and adjutant and had become restless in the job.

Most days it was much safer than frontline duty, although on a couple of occasions he came closer to being killed by artillery fire than he had in the lines. His time was taken up with supplies, transport, billets and other administrative work, for which he was hardly suited. He was also not on the best personal terms with Colonel William Patterson, the colonel of the regiment. Greg had become overly zealous about defending enlisted men charged with various breaches of military discipline.

As he told the story later, he had fallen into this in a strange way:

I arrived in London, the last guy in the world who should have been going to war. There I was, a collector of butterflies, a bookworm—so the first thing I did in London, of course, was to head for the bookstores on Charing Cross Road. In a bin of books I found an old, dog-eared copy of the Manual of Military Law. It was on sale for thruppence. On looking inside it I saw that it had been carefully cross-indexed and annotated in the most beautiful handwriting—with defense advice for almost every military offense you could think of—from insubordination to buggery—something I didn't even know the meaning of. Obviously it had been done by some regimental sergeant major who made a life work of defending his men. So with this book in my bag, I was the best barrack room lawyer in France.

Greg now had been in France for two years. He dreamed of Helen, but failed in his application for a Canadian leave. However, back in Canada, other things were working in his favor. The *Star,* along with other newspapers, was running short of trained reporters and had met with some success in getting former reporters transferred from military service to service as war correspondents. The *Star* put through a request on Greg's behalf and it began moving through the proper military channels.

By the time approval reached France, Greg's unit was about to embark on the advance on Cambrai. Greg was in charge of B Company for the attack. The colonel gave Greg the battle plan and then told him that his promotion to major had come through —and his posting to Canada to become a war correspondent.

Greg felt reluctant to leave on the eve of battle and decided to take part in the attack. His men and fellow officers protested profanely. Dozens of times, they had seen men killed or wounded just when due for a leave or posting. It was madness to tempt fate. He should leave immediately. Greg stayed with the company that night, but when the attack was called off for twenty-four hours, he decided to take the good advice: he departed.

Back in Canada, Greg's family did not know what was happening and anxiously awaited word. "It was terrible for everyone," said Greg's sister Mabel, "always expecting that cable from the government. It was especially ghastly on Sundays at our house. Being a newspaper family, we knew that the wires were quiet on Sundays and that was the day the casualty lists were put through. We all just used to sit around on Sundays, waiting for the phone to ring. When it did ring this Sunday, I answered it and a voice said there was a cable for Mr. Joseph Clark.

"I was petrified," said Mabel. "I said to Dad, 'It's for you.'

"He turned away from me and walked over to the window. He stood there with his back to me for several seconds, wondering if it was a 'killed in action' cable, and whether it would be Greg or Joe.

"Finally he came and took the phone from me. He listened— and I watched his face. Gradually the most incredible expression of relief spread over his face. The cable was from Greg. He was on his way home to retrain as a war correspondent."

Greg arrived back in Toronto with two other soldiers, Bill Wallace and "Pink" Goudy, also former Toronto newsmen being reassigned to war reporting. However, Armistice Day intervened. It would be another twenty years before Greg became a war correspondent.

18

The sole of the average human foot contains 387,000 sweat glands.

—Filler contributed by Clyde Gilmour, television singer, film and music critic, composer of Smoe Enschnanted Evenig, a love song dedicated to the printers of the world.

Fifty years later, sitting in his suite at the King Edward Hotel, Greg talked about his return from World War I.

"When I was a cub reporter," said Greg, "Hindmarsh was a big, solemn guy coming down from Osgoode Hall—he was a court reporter. And when I came home from the bloody war, by God, there he was, assistant city editor. With George Maitland as city editor—and signs all over the newsroom—No SMOKING!"

"No smoking!" repeated Greg. "This was Maitland, you see, the Baptist. And there was Hindmarsh. Well, by this time, I was having no part of journalism. My dad said, 'Oh, come now.' I said, 'Listen, Dad, I've been up in my conning tower, bossing eight hundred men. You think I'm going to come back for forty-five dollars a week to run errands for these guys, with their No Smoking signs? No smoking in the newsroom? What the hell's going on?"

The ban was as inconceivable to Greg in the newsroom as it would have been in the trenches. Still in uniform, Greg encountered managing editor John Bone, who expressed regret that Greg was thinking of another career. Bone asked if Greg would consider going on to the staff of the *Star Weekly*.

"As a cub," said Greg, "I wrote little pieces for the *Weekly*—which didn't pay you because you were a member of the daily staff—but I loved to see my by-line on these little pieces. Well, there was nobody on the *Star Weekly,* except Cranston, the editor, and Harry Jakeway, his assistant, and an old Englishman named Mr. Jones.

"So," said Greg, "I became the first staff writer. Up till then everything was bought from syndicates, or clipped, except the odd bit from a daily man. So that's how I got back into the newspaper business, which I had no intention of doing when I got home from the war. I was a major, for God's sake, I was a big shot, in my own opinion. Faced with No Smoking signs! And I never did like Maitland very much, although he was a pleasant guy—and an absolute wizard at handling the annual Hydro statement or government white papers, that sort of thing. After he left the news staff he became one of the editorial writers and ended up editor-in-chief, after my dad died. Pleasant enough, but not my kind of guy. Imagine, no smoking!"

During one black period in the war, Greg's company had gone without cigarettes for several days. Things were desperate. The only box of comforts from home was a small wooden packing case which had come from a group of religious ladies in Toronto. They invariably sent toothpaste and toothbrushes in one shipment, and soap and facecloths the next. As the men were in no humor for an issue of soap, the box had not even been opened and Greg had been using it as a stool in the headquarters dugout.

In boredom one day Greg broke it open and discovered that it contained several hundred plugs of chewing tobacco. Also inside was a note from a member of the committee, imploring the recipients to keep silent about the contents. She and her husband had become exasperated with sending washcloths and soap and had brazenly deceived the religious committee by sending along a case of chewing tobacco. The unknown lady was cheered. The plugs were cut up for cigars and cigarettes or stuffed into pipes. The tobacco lasted the company for a week, until the cigarette famine was over.

There were other adjustments for Greg to make when he returned to Toronto after the war. Helen had lived with her family during his time overseas and Greg moved in with them on his return, partly because of Dr. Murray's failing health. He died on December 18, 1919, as a result of a car accident. Helen and Greg took a six-room apartment on Indian Road, with room for

Helen's mother. The cost of the apartment was seventy dollars a month and Greg's salary was now seventy dollars a week.

Out of concern for Helen and the family he hoped was coming, Greg began loading himself up with life insurance. By the end of his first year home he had five policies in force, totaling $10,000, with premiums totaling about $300—more than a month's salary.

Other things had changed during the war years. The Little Blue Tea Room had been a romantic rendezvous for Greg and Helen. "We gave it up," said Greg, "when I found a cockroach in the chocolate sauce. On the way out I complained to the lady at the cash box. What she said was the clincher. 'My, that's strange,' she said. 'Why, we're so careful to strain everything.' "

Before going overseas Greg had written a series of articles on the problems of returned men. His own return was to add to his knowledge on the subject. As well as having his first experience of living with a wife—and a mother-in-law—he found himself looking back at the comfortable discipline of army life, the friendships forged then, which were now dissolving—and the dead.

Greg's elaborate diaries had become a victim of war, despite his good intentions. Before he'd gone overseas, Joseph Atkinson had told Greg's father, "I know of no one better equipped than Greg to go into the war game and bring out of it a life's work in writing alone." But infantry life did not lend itself to making notes—not during attacks and counterattacks or night patrols or constant shellfire. Out of the line, Greg noted, the men were emotionally and physically exhausted, almost in shock. They sat around eating, sleeping and smoking—including Greg himself.

At one point during the war Greg's unit had been supported on the left for several days by an outfit containing Cecil Perry, one of Greg's oldest boyhood chums. Neither learned of the other's presence and Perry was killed soon after. At times Greg's notes consisted solely of the men lost on a particular day.

His brother Joe, in the air force, was not a diarist, but managed to put down much material in the shape of letters home. Members of the air force had the advantage of a daily return—if they survived the day—to a reasonably comfortable billet, equipped with pen and paper.

Joe's almost daily lengthy letters to the home front were kept by the family and later collected into several bound volumes. It was Joe's intention to create a book from his experiences; he did produce a few hundred pages of a book on his return to Toronto. "Then he sat down one day and read it over," said Greg, "and tore the whole thing up."

Greg and Joe were not the only writers or storytellers in the Clark family. His sister Mabel was considered by many to be Greg's equal as an entertainer and she was also beginning to write short stories in her second year at the university in 1919.

The war, its aftermath and the ideas of the time were to give her life a different direction. In 1919 a smallpox epidemic hit Toronto and there was a rush for vaccinations. For some reason Mabel's vaccination became severely infected. She was in bed for several months and was unable to catch up on her lectures.

Greg's father, despite the fact that Mabel was his only daughter and a favorite, had never encouraged her in a journalistic or literary career, as he had both Joe and Greg. He saw his daughter's illness as fortuitous. "I've never been really keen on your going to university," he said. "You know all you need to know now. You stay home and learn how to run a house."

Fortunately, it worked out well for Mabel. "It's an old-fashioned idea now," she later said, "but I've always enjoyed keeping house more than anything else I've ever done."

As there was a seven-year difference in age between Greg and his sister, they had not been close as children. Greg felt little sisters were more a nuisance than anything. A number of Mabel's early romances were finished off by Greg in early stages. "That Bill is a nice chap—whatever happened to his teeth?" Or, "He seems nice—despite that limp handshake."

When Greg came back from World War I, Mabel found her brother much changed. He was more forceful, more self-confident, even slightly obstreperous now.

Thomas Drew-Brook, the man Mabel married and lived a long, happy life with, came back from the war in terrible shape. Serving as a fighter pilot, he was shot down and came near death. He weighed eighty-six pounds when released from a German prison camp and came home wearing a large body brace. While in prison camp, Drew-Brook had met another prisoner—William Stephenson—the undercover agent who was to become famous as Intrepid in World War II. In the next war, Drew-Brook also worked with British security, coordinating Canadian operations.

Greg and Helen became good friends with Mabel and Drew-Brook, spending much time with them, both in Toronto and at the family cottage at Go Home Bay. Later, their children would bring them closer together.

The artist who had illustrated some of Greg's prewar pieces, Jimmie Frise, had returned from the war to his work on the daily paper. He had fought at Vimy, with the artillery, where he was hit by shrapnel, losing one of the fingers of his left hand.

As part of the artists' pool at the daily, Frise was wasted much of the time, retouching photographs, drawing diagrams with an X to mark the spot of an accident or a crime, or doing paste-ups. He had a raw, untutored talent for humorous drawings and cartoons, and he was restless. Both Cranston, editor of the *Star Weekly,* and Greg wanted him on the *Star Weekly* staff and were successful in getting him transferred there in 1919.

By the end of another year, they were successful in getting Fred Griffin on the weekly. They had tried earlier, but without success. Griffin was unhappy with work on the daily. Greg noted, "Our editorial page screams 'industrial democracy' and 'getting together', but our own local room is run as a pure autocracy where liberty and personal pride are as naught."

The manager of the York Press asked Greg if he knew a good man he could hire as assistant. Greg suggested Griffin, then quickly told Griffin of the upcoming offer. When it came, Griffin went to Hindmarsh and used the offer to wangle a transfer to the weekly. Greg was pleased with the result of his activity, but warned himself, "I must keep clear of internal politics. Unhealthy."

His thoughts were still not yet clear of the war. He had filled a notebook with reminiscences, at his father's urging, but none of this had jelled into the short stories he was hoping to write. Around this time, Cranston lunched with an editor at *Maclean's* magazine, who stated that Greg was one of the few new writers around with a narrative style that would lend itself to a future literary career. Thomas B. Costain, the *Maclean's* editor, went shortly afterward to *The Saturday Evening Post,* and Greg wondered if perhaps he might try to sell to that famous market.

Still he didn't write. He bought a beautiful black cape for Helen—and charged it. She accepted it only on the condition that he would write two short stories to pay for it. Despite his salary of $3,600 a year, he was now over $600 in debt—$100 owed at the office, $130 to the tailor, $75 to the dentist, $125 for the cape and various sums owed on other household bills. His father, as editor-in-chief, was now making $7,000 a year, after twenty years with the paper, and Greg felt he was going to have to find some outside income.

Still he idled. Some weeks he had only three or four short articles in the weekly. He felt that the war had upset nearly all his preconceived ideas of men and life—and yet had given him no opportunity to replace what he had lost. He still felt unbalanced.

Meanwhile, Atkinson's pet project, the *Toronto Star Weekly,* was poised on the brink of great success. The weekly's circulation had hovered between 10,000 and 20,000 in its early years and the paper had failed to attract advertising. Despite the losses, Atkinson persisted and began adding comic strips, which were an essential for a weekend paper. At war's end the circulation had climbed to 67,000 and the *Star Weekly* was actually showing a profit of a few hundred dollars a month. In the first year after the war, the circulation jumped to more than 120,000 as the paper gradually added new comic strips, a picture section, syndicated fiction and—important to Greg—more humorous material.

The main opposition was the *Toronto Sunday World*—owned by the *Mail and Empire*—but it faltered in the race with the *Star Weekly* and was soon bought out by Atkinson. This cleared the way for the *Star Weekly*'s rise during the next thirty years until it became the first publication in Canada to reach a circulation of 1,000,000 copies—a circulation four times that of the parent daily, extending right across Canada and even southward into the United States.

Greg, along with Jimmie Frise and a large number of other talented writers, photographers and artists, was to share in this success, but for the first few years after the war his career marked time.

At home, Helen was suffering minor sicknesses and ailments, perhaps brought on by her first pregnancy. Greg could not yet find his way clear to tackling the kind of creative work he felt he should be doing. He was still trying to come to grips with the changes the war had made in him. At times he was more aggressive, at others more humble.

At high school, when he was about thirteen or fourteen years old, Greg had created a bit of a stir among the teachers by an essay in which he had stated, "After thorough investigation and serious consideration, I am of the opinion that Shakespeare has been greatly overrated." Greg's father had never let him forget this grand observation. Now, on rereading Shakespeare's plays, Greg found himself doing penance. "However, pleasure is not really penance. But it does make a writer feel so small. In that, I am punished."

He still awoke to nightmare scenes of the war: the time Butson's eyes were shot out—and the horror of guiding him back down from the ridge at Vimy; Johnston being blown apart and his leg landing at Greg's feet; the soldier with his jaw shot away who tried to communicate with Greg with his eyes as his life gushed away.

One of the longest scenes which replayed itself in his mind was the bombing run of a German plane over their lines. He and Victor Sifton were crouched in a shell hole, watching the bombing run. The bombs were dropped at regular intervals and as the first three or four exploded they could see the bombs following a perfectly straight line, coming directly toward them. The bombs continued to drop. It was simply a question of whether the two would be bracketed or obliterated. The eighth and last bomb fell fifty feet short. Greg and Sifton were shaken, but unharmed.

Greg's restless nights did not disturb Helen, for they had slept in separate bedrooms ever since their war-delayed honeymoon, when Helen had discovered that Greg was a monumental snorer.

19

Hindmarsh is a son of a bitch and a liar and they are easy to understand.

—*Ernest Hemingway*

Greg was sitting in his suite at the King Edward, chuckling at Gordon Sinclair's radio version of the news and sipping his noon-time scotch. Both Sinclair and the scotch were daily rituals. When the news was finished, I brought out my surprise: a bottle of Glenlivet, a Highland malt whiskey.

"Your favorite," I said.

Greg broke out laughing.

"What's so funny?" I said. "I had to go to three liquor stores to find this—and it costs twice as much."

"I know," said Greg. "It's so good hardly anybody can drink it."

"I have it on the best authority," I said, "that on your last trip to the hospital, you kept a bottle of Glenlivet beside the bed—"

"I started off keeping a bottle of Hudson's Bay scotch," said Greg. "A nice, gentle scotch, which is what I drink these days. But there were so many friends dropping in, having a drink, then another one, that I kept running out of scotch. Especially Bruce West. So I asked Bill Oille what to do and he said to get a bottle of Glenlivet or Glenfiddich. And it worked perfectly! One drink of that malt whiskey and people would look at their watches and say they had to be running along. Some didn't even finish the first drink. It really cheered me up to watch the expression on their faces, and I would tell them how I had discovered this wonderful real Highland whiskey."

I poured myself a drink of Glenlivet. "Well," I said, "I'll drink it. I can't afford to waste all that money."

"The ice is there," said Greg.

"What shall we talk about today?"

"About Hemingway," I said.

"I was out walking the other day," said Greg, "and I found a little backshop where you can get croissants. It reminded me of Paris, when you get up in the morning and then walk all over looking for a place to get some ham and eggs."

"Not ham and eggs," I said. "Hemingway. Your hearing must be getting worse."

"And out in front of the cafés," said Greg, "you see these melancholy Parisian gentlemen having their breakfast. They have a bowl—not a cup—but a great big damn bowl of black coffee. And hanging on the edge of the bowl is a croissant, which they dip into the black coffee. And that is their breakfast. They are sitting there, watching all the girls go by."

"I know that Hemingway began hanging around you and Jimmie Frise," I said. "And you got him his first assignments. And you and Helen helped find an apartment when they came back from Paris . . ."

"I am talking about Hemingway," said Greg. "If you would just stop interrupting."

Greg sipped at his scotch. "Those Parisian gentlemen," said Greg, "are dunking their croissants in the coffee. *Dunking!* We've always thought of dunking as an American habit, but the French have been dunking for centuries."

"What's that got to do with Hemingway?"

"When Hemingway came back from Paris," said Greg, "he showed us the only way to drink red wine. We went up to that restaurant—the old Old Angelo's—and he ordered red wine and French bread. Then he showed us how to break off a piece of bread and dip it in the wine, meanwhile looking very intellectual. That was the mark of the in group—those who really knew!"

"He was an instant expert on everything," I said. "He even told Morley Callaghan how to box."

"Morley got to know Hemmy when he came back to the *Star* for the second time," said Greg. "And, of course, later on in Paris. But I must have been one of the first people ever to see the manuscript of *The Sun Also Rises,* written in his own handwriting, not even typed. The great Hemingway style, which was going to revolutionize writing. And I saw it and I thought it was *lousy!*

"I said, 'Hemmy, what more do you want than to be a feature writer on the *Toronto Star*?' He just looked at me. He sent Jimmie and me both copies of *The Sun Also Rises* when it came out, both autographed. In mine he saluted me as 'that great intuitive critic of the art of writing.'

"I can still remember the look of those handwritten pages," said Greg. "Crabbed handwriting. And he was a lousy speller. I remember that famous chapter where he was fishing in Spain and arguing with someone about William Jennings Bryan. They had a couple of bottles of wine chilling in the stream and the more they drank the worse the argument got."

Greg laughed. "I was looking at history years before it appeared—and I didn't know it! No wonder he thought I was the stupidest guy about writing. That description of me in his notebook is devastating. He eviscerates me. But I liked him in those days. Helen and I helped find him an apartment when he came back with Hadley. When the baby was born—that was Bumby—Helen went over to show Hadley how to bathe a baby. We always liked Hadley."

"Tell me more," I said. "Morley also said Hemingway could be pretty ruthless. He seemed to have some need to turn on people who had helped him. He satirized Sherwood Anderson, who introduced him to Paris. He turned on the man who published his first stories—and his first book publisher—and on F. Scott Fitzgerald . . ."

Greg did not wish to examine this side of Hemingway. He said nothing.

"It was only a few years after Bumby was born that he left Hadley," I said. "That was for wife number two, Pauline Pfeiffer, the rich one. Her wealthy relatives were able to provide him with an apartment in Paris, a house in Key West, money for his first African safari and more important, time to write."

Greg would not be drawn out. "We always liked Hadley," he said again.

Hemingway became the most famous writer to have labored for the *Toronto Star*. His conflict with Hindmarsh became a legend.

Hemingway arrived in Toronto in January 1920. He had been born in Oak Park, Illinois, on July 21, 1899, the son of a doctor and a music-minded mother. The doctor was a keen outdoorsman and hunter and had built a family cottage at Bear Lake, in Michigan, where the family summered. As a boy Hemingway enjoyed much the same outdoor life as Greg had at Go Home Bay.

During his high school years he did not excel at team sports but learned to box and wrote short stories and articles for the school magazine. By the time he graduated he was rebelling at the strictness of family life and was beginning to get seriously interested in writing. With the help of an uncle in Kansas City, he got an introduction at the paper and landed a reporter's job at fifteen dollars a week.

The Kansas City *Star* was a legendary newspaper. Hemingway quickly fitted in with the worldly reporters and atmosphere, but he was more attracted to the war in Europe, which the United States had now entered. Unfortunately he had inherited a bad left eye, which disqualified him for enlistment. Through chance he learned that the eye would not affect joining the Red Cross as an ambulance driver. He and another young friend on the *Star* did that in the spring of 1918. They were shipped quickly to France in May and on to the Austrian-Italian front north of Venice.

Hemingway was eager to see the actual fighting and volunteered for work in the mobile canteens that brought cigarettes, chocolate and other comforts to the frontline troops. On July 8, a little more than a month since he'd left the States, he was very nearly killed.

While he was delivering cigarettes to a forward trench, at night, a huge antipersonnel canister containing steel-rod fragments and metal scrap exploded nearby, killing one soldier Hemingway had been talking to, and badly wounding another. Hemingway's legs were punctured with hundreds of tiny pieces of shrapnel. When he came to, he threw the wounded Italian over his shoulder and carried him back to the nearest command post. En route he picked up a machine gun bullet in the knee.

For the next six months he was hospitalized in Milan and underwent a series of operations to remove the shrapnel. He also fell in love with a pretty nurse seven years his senior. He was still desperately, romantically in love when he arrived home in 1919, but her letters cooled and eventually she wrote that she was marrying another man.

In his hometown young Hemingway was a war hero—but had trouble readjusting to civilian and family life. A chance visitor to town was the wife of Ralph Connable, head of the Woolworth stores in Canada. They had a lame son about Ernest's age and invited Ernest to Toronto for the winter months as a companion for him. Once in Toronto, Hemingway found his way to the *Star*.

The office occupied by Greg Clark and Jimmie Frise was a gathering place for young reporters and writers in the Twenties and Thirties. Hemingway found his way there too, and was introduced to *Star Weekly* editor Cranston by Greg. On a free-lance basis, he began selling small features to the *Weekly* and did some work for the daily, after his work caught the attention of managing editor John Bone.

He returned to the States in the summer of 1920, worked briefly for a trade magazine, then met and married a redheaded woman named Hadley Richardson, who was seven years his senior and had a trust fund which provided an income of two to three thousand dollars a year. With this income and the knowledge that he could send back free-lance articles to the *Star,* he and Hadley sailed for Paris in the fall of 1921. There he produced a few poems and a few short stories; he also met famous literary figures of the age, such as James Joyce, Ezra Pound, Gertrude Stein and F. Scott Fitzgerald. Some of them helped his career.

In the fall of 1923, when the first Hemingway child was about to arrive, Hemingway accepted an offer to return to the *Star* as a full-time reporter, at a salary of seventy-five dollars a week. The job was to last only four months, in part because of the Hindmarsh policy of cutting prima donnas down to size.

Hemingway was ignored or told to cover labor meetings, attend hotel conventions or chase fires. His first major assignment, deliberately or not, was to New York, a few days before the birth of his first child. On his return, he was given a bawling out by Hindmarsh for checking on Hadley at the hospital before reporting in to the *Star* office. By the end of the year Hemingway had had enough. His resignation became one of the *Star*'s legends, allegedly a sixteen-foot letter which he pasted to the *Star*'s bulletin board, outlining Hindmarsh's deficiencies. Although often described, this does not seem to have survived. The Hemingways set out again for Paris in early January.

On this second short stay in Toronto Hemingway had made new friends interested in serious literature. These included Jimmy

Cowan and Mary Lowery of the *Star* and a twenty-year-old law student who was working on a part-time basis. This was Morley Callaghan, now one of Canada's major authors. In those days he was in his second year at the University of Toronto and he was interested in serious writing.

Hemingway began talking to Callaghan in the *Star* library one day. They quickly discovered their mutual interest in writing and in the literary ferment of Paris. The two men showed each other samples of their work. Hemingway gave Callaghan an autographed copy of *Three Stories and Ten Poems,* his first published book: "To Callaghan with best luck and predictions." On his first reading of Callaghan's work he announced, "You're a real writer." Departing for Paris, he told Morley to send along his stories to him and he would show them around.

Within a few years Callaghan's career would take off in the same spectacular fashion as Hemingway's, and also would become tangled up with it. Riding that first wave of success, Morley took his bride, Loretto, to Paris for their honeymoon in 1929. There they met Hemingway and his new wife; Ezra Pound; F. Scott Fitzgerald; James Joyce; and other literary greats of the period.

Morley has written vividly of the experience and of his relationship with Hemingway in his reminiscence, *That Summer in Paris*—including the storm that developed when a columnist reported that Callaghan had knocked Hemingway out during a friendly boxing match and what that storm did to his friendships with Hemingway and Fitzgerald. Greg's friendship with Hemingway apparently changed little over the years. When Hemingway's third son was born in 1931 he was named Gregory. Partly, said Ernest, for several historic popes and partly for Greg Clark.

Shortly after my talk with Greg about the Hemingway period, I was called by Duncan Macpherson, the artist and political cartoonist at the *Star*. He was going to Morley Callaghan's house the next evening to make some sketches of Morley for a book. Macpherson invited me to come along and get Morley to talk about Hemingway and Greg during those early years at the *Star*.

20

If Greg Clark spent two weeks with Jesus Christ, he'd come back with a Greg Clark story.

—*Morley Callaghan*
Novelist and short story writer

Morley Callaghan greeted Duncan Macpherson and me in friendly fashion at the door of his large, rambling house at 20 Dale Avenue in Toronto's Rosedale district. His wife, Loretto, was with him. She fixed us drinks while Morley apologized for the piles of typewritten manuscript that were everywhere.

"It's always like this when I'm working on a book," said Morley. "And it's just as bad upstairs."

He showed us a page of manuscript which was so scrawled with corrections as to be almost indecipherable. There was handwriting in between the lines, across the top of the page, down the sides and along the bottom.

"It's the way I've always worked," said Morley, "but I think I'm getting worse. When it gets so I can't read it myself, it goes off to the typist."

Duncan sat down near Morley where he could make quick sketches of him and I set up a tape recorder. Greg and Morley had been good friends in the early *Star* years, but time had seen them drift apart. In the Twenties Morley had enjoyed meteoric literary success. His novels were published by the prestigious house of Scribner's. His short stories appeared in the best magazines. For thirteen years in a row there was a short story of Morley's in the prestigious O'Brien anthology, *Best Short Stories*. This success in a field to which Greg had once aspired may well have made Greg envious.

In the Thirties, the Depression years, people were not buying books and magazines as freely. Morley went through some hard times. So did other serious writers. The 1930 royalty statement of his friend F. Scott Fitzgerald for his novel *The Great Gatsby* was $17.09. Ironically, Greg's *Star Weekly* humor pieces met with great popular success during the Depression. His *Star Weekly* salary protected him from hard times and he had lots of leisure to go fishing.

"The great thing about Greg," said Morley, "is that he knows how to get along with men. He can get along with the most extraordinary mixed bag of men and they can all like him. He was probably a splendid officer in the first war, y'know."

Morley always examined all sides of a question. "On the other hand," he said thoughtfully, "Greg is nice to women. You worked with him, Duncan—don't you think he has a courtly manner with women?"

"Oh, yes," said Macpherson, sketching away. "Very much so."

"Now," said Morley, "whether Greg likes all these fellows, really likes them, I don't know. But he can make the average man feel he is quite interested in him. That is an extraordinary quality. Greg would have made a wonderful mayor."

For an artist, Macpherson is quite sensitive to words. He broke out laughing at this putdown.

"That's not Greg's opinion," I said. "He claims he should have been a guide in Algonquin Park."

"No," said Morley, again qualifying his own remark, "in politics Greg would be utterly out of place. I wouldn't bet a nickel on Greg's judgment. For instance, he was fond of Hemingway, but oddly enough he was not fond of Hemingway's writing. This is a very strange business, this of Greg and writing. Greg's story is that if he said he liked a Hemingway piece, Hemingway would throw it in the wastebasket. If Greg didn't like it, Hemingway would send it off to some magazine in Paris and sell it."

"It's a good story," Morley went on. "It just doesn't have any truth in it. Hemingway wasn't writing stories when he was here. What Greg remembers were early stories of mine which sold to *Transition* and *This Quarter,* in Paris.

"Gordon Sinclair is even more incorrigible than Greg about the Hemingway period. Gordon wrote a book about his early years and I saw him on television, promoting the book, saying with an air of *utter conviction* that he sat with Hemingway in Child's restaurant, watching him correct the proofs of *The Sun Also Rises*. Afterward, I ran into Gordon on Bloor Street. 'Gordon,' I said, 'don't mind me telling you this, but if you look at a copy of *The Sun Also Rises,* you'll see it was published in nineteen twenty-seven—four years after Hemingway left here—so you couldn't have seen Hemingway correcting proofs in Child's restaurant. What you may have seen were those first poems and vignettes— *In Our Time*—which were privately printed in Paris about nineteen twenty-three.' 'Oh,' said Gordon, 'well, my memory gets fuzzy.' But not long after, he had *another* article published in which he said he had watched Hemingway correcting the proofs of *The Sun Also Rises* in Child's restaurant!"

Morley laughed. "I guess it's a shame to have a factual memory! After all, part of the charm of life is what *might* have happened! But the important thing is Greg was fond of Hemingway. The changes that took place in Hemingway's character would have been a profound shock to Greg."

Morley sipped his drink. "I remember running into Greg at the press club one day. He thought Scribner's was putting Hemingway down—tearing him apart—in their official biography. Well, you know Scribner's wasn't dragging Hemingway down—they adored Hemingway—but they were trying to do an honest biography.

"But Greg was romantic about him. But still, no fool. He told me about running into Hemingway in Paris near the end of the war. Old Ernest was surrounded by twenty adoring officers, being very drunk and hearty and masculine. It was a different Hemingway. There was also a possibility Hemingway was going off his rocker. Greg was sensitive enough to size the situation up. He didn't join the party. He knew it wouldn't be like the old days. Hemingway would undoubtedly make a big fuss over him, but Greg knew there would be an unreality about it. It wasn't his boy."

Morley grew more thoughtful. "Here's where Greg was wonderful. I was a twenty-year-old university student when I went to the *Star*. I didn't know the big names like Greg Clark, Fred Griffin, Charles Vining. My only friend there was Jimmy Cowan. I'd met Hemingway and Jimmy Cowan told me Greg was Hemingway's friend, so I wandered into Greg's office, talked to him, and we became quite friendly.

"I spent a lot of time sitting in Child's with Greg. I genuinely liked him. He looked at my writings—and he didn't like them. But he always left open the possibility that *someone* might find them wonderful. *He* could be very, very wrong. Those were encouraging words from an established writer like Greg, to someone like myself who was very young."

"Do you remember any of the early stories you showed him?"

"Let me see. I think Greg saw *The Girl With Ambition,* which was the first published by *This Quarter* in Paris. And I think he saw another called *The Wedding Dress.* But let me tell you a story that brings out that open quality of Greg's. I had struck up a friendship with some people in Paris who were reading my stories. But I was now back in Toronto at law school. One day a book arrived in the mail—a magazine really, but it was *this* thick. It was a copy of *This Quarter,* an orange cover with great big black letters on the cover: JAMES JOYCE, EZRA POUND, ERNEST HEMINGWAY, CARL SANDBURG, MORLEY CALLAGHAN! I was astounded. So next day—at this time I was still dropping in on Greg—I walked down to the *Star* and showed it to him.

"Greg looked at it. Now, the very first thing he did—he didn't say, 'Oh, Jesus, they published *that* story?'—he just walked right into Hindmarsh's office, put it down on his desk and said, 'Look! Did we miss something in this guy?' Hindmarsh just mumbled.

"Now, the wonderful thing was Greg didn't take this as a rebuke to his judgment. Or grumble that he still thought it was a lousy story. Or say 'Who reads *This Quarter?*' Not at all. He welcomed it with open arms, not like an old hard-boiled newspaperman. In the same way he applauded Hemingway's successes, even though lots of the guys were saying they still didn't see anything in his writing."

Without interrupting his sketching, Macpherson asked, "How much encouragement would you get in Toronto in those days?"

Morley laughed. *"None whatever!* But if you want to be a writer, or a poet, or a painter, you have to have a passion for the thing. And you pick your league. If you decide you're a minor league ballplayer, you play minor league ball all your life."

Macpherson said, "Don't you think, from time to time, the right atmosphere can play a part?"

"Well," said Morley, "an atmosphere can mean something in a peculiar way—engendering excitement in you. A city like Paris is always exciting in that something exciting is probably going on there—even if you can't find it, even if you are quite outside of it. I was lucky in a way. There was an article in *Esquire* some time ago which said I was one of fashion's favorites. There was a time there when Scribner's seemed to have all the favorites—Hemingway, Scott Fitzgerald, James T. Farrell, John Dos Passos, Morley Callaghan. And things happened for me. Ring Lardner got the *New Yorker* after me. I wrote a little story and they liked it. But if I had done a lousy one, which I was perfectly capable of doing, it might all have ended right there. It's a strange life. Sometimes you come through, other times you fall flat on your face."

Macpherson said, "Did Greg have the same drive to be a writer?"

"I have never known," said Morley. "To this day I have never known what Greg thought of himself as a writer."

Morley's wife, Loretto, said, "I do remember some talk once about him hoping to make some stories out of his war experiences."

"He did win the Leacock Award," said Macpherson, "for a book of war stories. But that was a collection of his columns."

"I never knew how ambitious he was," said Morley. "Once I remember him saying that the *real* writing was being done in newspapers. They were the writers who were being read every day. I thought this was utter garbage, but I didn't say so, realizing Greg was serious. I guess as a writer Greg felt he had the common touch and it was better to have readers.

"Today, people come out with the statement that television has displaced everything. If you want to be in touch with your time you have to work in television. Personally I think television is the great meathead audience. Remember the early pulp magazines? That's what television has displaced."

The conversation was interrupted by the arrival of Morley's two sons, Barry and Michael. With them was Alan Fleming, designer of the CN logo and award-winning books. They all knew Greg and the conversation continued about him.

Barry Callaghan said, "I never heard anyone around the university discussing Greg as a serious writer."

"No," said Morley, "but Greg is a Toronto fixture. He probably has more readers today than he ever had."

Barry said, "You must be talking about people over fifty."

"Not entirely," said Morley. "I had a young plumber in the house the other day. He had a vague idea that I was a writer of some kind or another. But what he wanted to know was whether I had ever met Greg Clark."

Barry began to say something, but Morley interrupted. "I know what you're going to say. Avant garde literary groups are not talking about Greg. Greg knows that. He knew it forty years ago. His point is, who reads them?"

Macpherson finished the sketches, which he would later combine for his portrait of Morley for his book, *Macpherson's Canada.*

Morley examined the sketches. "Look at this one," he said. "Makes me look like Richard Nixon. That kind of frightens me."

Morley's wife said, "All kinds of people have tried to paint Morley—and just given up on him."

Macpherson laughed. "I was one of those. About ten years ago. But I was overwhelmed just because he was Morley Callaghan. I'll get him this time."

Macpherson *did* catch him, too. The portrait is on page 155 of *Macpherson's Canada.* Morley, in his conversation that evening, also did a perceptive sketch of Greg and of Greg's relationship with Hemingway. Greg wrote one short article about Hemingway's early years at the *Star,* called "Hemingway Slept Here." It appeared in the Montreal *Standard* on November 4, 1950.

A short time earlier, Hemingway had published a novel called *Across the River and into the Trees,* which caused a literary furor. John O'Hara wrote a lead review for the New York *Times,* praising the book and declaring Hemingway to be the greatest writer since Shakespeare. O'Hara's opinion was not widely shared and many critics savaged the book. Greg wrote:

Now that Ernest Hemingway has been rated by the *New York Times Book Review* critics as the greatest writer of English since Shakespeare, it is about time those of us who have anything to put on record about him do so before we drop dead of astonishment.

Hemingway has a Canadian angle. It is not very important. He didn't learn anything here. He was cooking, so to speak. His genius was already in the oven; only, of course, nobody here could even smell it. Here is my two bits' worth.

The late Jimmie Frise, cartoonist, and I had come home from World War I and been given the dignity of a private office around 1920. Our job was to enliven, with cartoons and light stories, the sober little *Star Weekly,* which was a black-and-white journal of something under 70,000 circulation.

It was not much of an office: just room for Jim's drawing board and my typewriter, plus a rusty old radiator. The window looked out on a brick wall and a lane. Of these features, of course, we were unaware, being young men with a future.

One autumn afternoon—I think it was in 1921—our office door opened and Arthur Donaldson stuck his head in. Arthur was head of the *Toronto Star*'s local display advertising, the best dressed man in Toronto in his time, and the friend of everybody. Behind Arthur loomed a large, gangly young man, perspiring.

"Are you busy, boys?" inquired Arthur, ushering in the youth. "This is Ernest Hemingway. He's an American newspaperman. Worked on the Kansas City *Star*. He's up here visiting Ralph Connable."

I sized the young gentleman up, instantly. Kansas City *Star,* eh? Ralph Connable, eh? Jimmie Frise got up and offered the young fellow our only other seat, which was the radiator.

Now, Ralph Connable was head of the Woolworth chain in Canada, a wealthy and witty American. And the Kansas City *Star* happened to be, in those years, the beau ideal of every newspaperman in America. And this tall young squirt whom Donaldson was wishing on us was wearing a short leather coat and a peaked cap and was carrying a walking stick! He walked, I noted, with a slight limp as he went over eagerly and took the radiator.

There is no business in the world in which there are so many hangers-on as the newspaper business. Eager, hopeful hangers-on. This, I figured, was one of them. He was a large, rather heavy, loose-jointed youth, with a flushed face, dark loose hair and a big red mouth. He perspired easily along under his hair on the forehead and under his lower lip. He appeared to be shy, anxious and restless. When he spoke, he could not pronounce the L. He did not have much to say that first afternoon. He just sat on the radiator and answered Jimmie's amiable questions as Jim scratched away at his drawing board. I was busy at the typewriter.

The young fellow hung around till closing time.

Next day he was back, about noon. He went and sat on the radiator. We took him to lunch. He came back with us and sat on the radiator until dusk. It seems he had been in the war, too. That's where he got the stiff leg; not, as I had supposed, because of the leather coat, in a motorcycle collision. He seemed pretty young and inarticulate to have been in our war—Jim's and my war.

I cross-questioned him. How long had he worked on the Kansas City *Star?* Oh, only a little while. Because he had gone overseas with some characters on that paper who had volunteered as ambulance drivers with the Italian Army.

Ah, ambulance drivers! But, it seems, he had transferred, in Italy, to the army, and had been with the Arditi. The Arditi were the toughest of the Italian divisions.

When he left us that evening, I warned Jim. "Jim," I said, "don't get too chummy with this kid. He'll stick you for ten bucks, and that will be the last of him. He's one of those yearning youngsters, those imaginary guys. Kansas City *Star,* for Pete's sake! Maybe he was an office boy. And Italian Army? Pawff! Him in the Arditi?"

The next day, while Jim squirmed at his drawing board, I further cross-questioned the lad on the rusty radiator about his connection with the wealthy Connables in town. It seems Hemmy's father was a Chicago doctor whose summer cottage was near the Connables' cottage on Lake Michigan.

So that evening, as we went home from work, I was thus able further to caution Jim about this hanger-on in our office. Just a problem child, I explained, sponging on the friends of his father up here, and trying to get a job on the newspaper. Probably never worked on the Kansas City *Star,* probably never was at the war.

All Jimmie said was that I had a very suspicious nature. The kid was a nice young guy.

Next day, I pursued my inquiries by asking the youth about the war. But he had little to say about it. He wanted to hear me tell about my experiences.

Now, in 1921, you could hardly get anybody to listen to your war stories. It was quite a treat to find a young fellow on the radiator whom you could make sweat with tales of war. And while Jim sat with a sly grin, at his board, scratching, I entertained the hanger-on with my experiences of battle. He apparently had had none. All he did was nod. And perspire.

But Jim took him skiing that winter. And in the spring, I took him fly fishing up the Credit river about 40 miles from town. He told me many interesting things about fishing in Spain. But I did not listen very attentively, because I wanted to tell war stories. And anyway, what he had to say about fly fishing in Spain did not sound articulate. He had a queer, explosive way of describing things. He agitated himself easily. I supposed his fishing in Spain was like his working for the Kansas City *Star,* or his war with the Arditi. Probably mythical. But he hung around. And he stayed with the Connables.

One day he informed me, with an air of agitation, that he had to go back to Chicago for a few days. But he would be back.

"Good," I assured him heartily. "Good! See you later."

A few days later he was back on the radiator. After the usual exchange of disjointed generalities with Jim, he limped over to my desk and interrupted my typewriter. He produced a cardboard box from his pocket. It was full of medals.

"Mmmmmm," I said as I examined them. They were very pretty.

"Itaw-yan," explained Hemmy, without his L's.

One was a silver cross.

"Croce de Guerra," said Hemmy.

"Ah, like the Military Cross!" I exclaimed.

"This," said Hemmy, a little thickly, showing me a gold one, "is the Medaglia d'Oro per Valore."

The highest Italian award, the gold medal for valor.

"Oh, boy!" I automatically turned it on edge.

And as long as I live, I shall never forget the cold chill that leaped out, radiating, from my back and over my shoulders and into my cheeks. For on the edge was inscribed:

"*Tenente Ernesto Hemingway.*"

It took me some minutes to get control. I examined the other service medals. I fumbled through some press clippings that were stuffed in with the medals. Lieut. Ernest Hemingway, who had served with the Arditi in the Italian army with great distinction, had been decorated in Chicago by General Diaz, who was touring America, Hemingway being one of two Americans who had got the gold medal for valor.

Etcetera, etcetera. Jimmie was up on his feet, exclaiming over the beautiful medals, reading the clippings and giving me kicks in the ankle. Hemmy was back on his radiator, flushed, embarrassed—for me, possibly.

Well, I asked him about fishing in Spain, and about the war in Italy; and we took him fishing and went and saw the managing editor to see if Hemmy might do some little reporting jobs. And we took him over to Childs each morning about 10:30, where a random gathering of newspapermen used to meet daily for a bull session.

And Hemmy wrote some things. One of them was a brief description of Mayor Tommy Church at the boxing matches. It was good. Maybe we did not know how good. At all events he was taken on as a reporter. He went away for a while and came back with Hadley Richardson, of St. Louis, as his bride. They lived in an apartment house on Bathurst street north of St. Clair avenue.

And when John Hadley Nicanor Hemingway was born here (called Nicanor after Hemmy's bull fighter friend in Spain) my wife and I went up and showed Hadley how to hold a new baby in a bath. And Jim took Hemmy skiing; and I hunted around for somebody else to listen to my war stories, because I had kind of lost my pep at telling them to Hemmy.

In his article Greg went on to describe the creative writing Hemingway had been attempting while in Toronto, with all the inaccuracy that Morley Callaghan deplored. Greg, after all, was an entertainer, not a historian.

There was a postcript to that evening at Morley's home. It was a dozen years later, some years after Greg had died, and I was talking to Morley on the phone.

Morley said, "I didn't see a lot of Greg, y'know, over the years. He would call and ask me to lunch with him at the King Edward, but I just didn't go. It was those stories Greg told—and wrote—confusing me and Hemingway. I felt they negated the closeness Greg and I had enjoyed in the old days. I just didn't feel the same about him."

Morley continued. "A funny thing happened just a few months before Greg died. I happened to be lunching at the King Edward when the headwaiter whispered in my ear, 'There's a man here says you're looking much older.'

"The headwaiter pointed across the room and it was Greg, of course. He was in a wheelchair, lunching with another man. I walked over to his table and this is how Greg introduced me. 'I want you to meet Morley Callaghan, who *used to be a famous novelist*.' Now, why would Greg say a thing like that? It was on the tip of my tongue to say, 'Yes, and this is Greg Clark, who used to be a friend of mine,' but I managed to catch myself. I just laughed, patted him on the back and went back to my own table. But I've thought about our friendship since. I should have been more generous, y'know. I should have been more loyal to the days of my youth."

But youth passes and people change. On Hemingway's death Morley wrote that Hemingway had become a man trapped in his own legend. To say that Morley and Greg also became prisoners of their own success is perhaps overly dramatic, but has a bit of truth in it.

21 _____

If you see my mother, don't tell her I'm working on a newspaper . . . she thinks I'm playing the piano in a whorehouse.

—Old newspaper joke

In the ten years following World War I Greg was trying to juggle many things. He was disentangling himself from the war, beginning his own family, establishing himself as a feature writer on the *Star Weekly* and still bothered by his failure to find time for creative writing. The appearance of Hemingway and Morley Callaghan at the paper in the early Twenties renewed his ambitions, but he still couldn't find or make the time to accomplish much.

His position on the *Star Weekly* meant that Hindmarsh could not bury him on the court beat or leave him dangling without an assignment, as he did with others he wished to bring to heel, but he was allowed to commandeer Greg, Fred Griffin, Charles Vining and others from the weekly for major news events and disasters such as the Great Haileybury Fire of 1922. These were all-out, exhausting efforts. The *Star* did not recognize overtime, in terms of extra pay or time off, except on the editorial page.

It did not take Hemingway long to realize the impossibility of creative work under Hindmarsh, but Greg was in no position to take off for Paris. As Joseph Clark's son he had some security, but it also made him aware of some of the paper's problems.

Timothy Eaton, the department store magnate, had been one of the original group that purchased the *Star*. Later he invested another twenty thousand dollars for plant expansion. For nearly twenty years, Eaton's had run a full-page daily advertisement. Timothy Eaton is also said to have engendered the parsimonious streak in Atkinson which led to the infamous *Star* economy waves.

Once, while the Atkinsons were visiting the Eaton home, a slip of paper was delivered to Eaton.

"That," he said to Atkinson, "is what the boys took in at the store on Saturday. Do you know what the *Star* took in yesterday?"

"No, I don't," said Atkinson.

"Then you should," said Eaton.

Atkinson often repeated that this was the greatest business lesson he ever had. It was one he learned well. Soon he had daily reports of advertising revenue, broken down by companies and geographically and matched with earnings of the same day the previous year. Cranston, the *Star Weekly* editor, who had put in a year as Atkinson's secretary, said he became dizzy with addition, multiplication and subtraction of business figures.

As Atkinson acquired control of the paper, his views became too radical for some businessmen, including John Craig Eaton, who succeeded his father. Eaton sold back the *Star* shares he had inherited and he precipitated a panic at the *Star* in 1921 by canceling the regular full-page Eaton's advertisement.

Atkinson's reaction was one of the infamous *Star* economy waves. Copy boys were fired. Reporters were refused streetcar tickets and told to buy their own to cover stories. A new pencil could only be obtained by turning in the stub of the old one.

Atkinson held a conference with his chief executives, to review the paper as a whole. Present were John Bone, Walter Harris, George Macdonald and Greg's dad. Atkinson wanted to cut the news from sixty columns of space to fifty columns. This would save paper and make possible further staff cuts. Joe Clark took the opposite position. "A temporary loss of Eaton money can be made up later—but let the public know we are cutting back and things will get more serious."

As often happened, Joe Clark's views were the ones that impressed Atkinson. The *Daily* began running special features and added a serial story. The circulation increased. The *Star*'s official biography of Atkinson reports this as another indication of Atkinson's foresight. Sir John Craig Eaton died in the following year; shortly afterward, Eaton's advertising was resumed.

Before the war, Greg had adjured himself to stay out of office politics, but now he was finding it easier said than done. Over at the *Star Weekly* Greg had gotten Cranston to institute a Friday luncheon for staff members to bring them closer together. He also

156 THE LIFE & TIMES OF GREG CLARK

approached Atkinson about Jim Frise. Although attached to the *Weekly,* he was still being used to excess by the *Daily* for routine work. A born comic artist, Frise was impatient to do that kind of work and had received job offers elsewhere.

Soon afterward, Atkinson attended one of the *Star Weekly* luncheons, was impressed with the quality of the staff and, Greg felt, learned that the phenomenal growth of the *Weekly* was due to more than machine methods. "The *Star*'s personnel problems," Greg wrote, "are because Atkinson is surrounded by men who click their heels and carry out his orders without imagination or comprehension." And the circle of men surrounding Atkinson was growing smaller.

The success of the *Star Weekly* as a money-maker also fortified Atkinson's editorial independence at the *Star.* It sold on the newsstands and made money, almost entirely without the benefit of advertising. Atkinson could see the day when he could say what he liked in the *Daily,* regardless of advertisers. If they dropped their ads, he could still make money at the *Star Weekly.*

John R. Bone, then managing editor of both the *Daily* and the *Weekly,* secured Atkinson's permission to add to his income in a novel way. He secured a contract with a group of British and American newspapers, had his secretary type out stories appearing in the *Star,* and mailed them off under his own by-line. His efforts foreshadowed the Toronto Star Syndicate, which became a highly profitable enterprise in later years. Legally, there was nothing wrong with this, as the Canadian copyright law had been designed to protect publishers, not writers. However, to writers who had not been paid for their work in the first place, or to writers like Hemingway, Robert C. Reade, Charles Vining and others, it must have been galling to see their editor collecting money for what they had written.

At one time there was a gathering of the writers who wanted this stopped. Greg talked to his father about the situation. Joseph Clark put the best possible face upon it. "Atkinson is not paying Bone what he might command at some other paper," he said. "This is his way of making up for it. And tell the boys they will be best advised not to make a fuss about it. It will look like a union—and they will just get themselves fired." On Greg's advice, the palace revolt died.

On August 1, 1921, Greg wrote in his journal: "I have not yet written my stories for the magazines. And on the eve of important domestic events I am looking to borrow $600. to pay accounts outstanding." The impending domestic event was the birth of his first son, James Murray Clark, on September 1, 1921. He weighed 8 pounds, 12 ounces. People remarked that he looked like Greg and, for the next six months, the proud father kept a careful record of Murray's weight as it increased to 15 pounds, 15½ ounces.

Murray's arrival just preceded Greg's own birthday, which was September 25. On that day, Greg wrote:

Twenty-nine years old today! In eleven years I shall be forty. Well, thank goodness I have a son to perpetuate youth. But I don't feel oldish. Gad! Ten years ago, when I thought of this day—and the unbelievable things that have happened between! Well, who knows, what will befall in these 11 years between now and 40.

Greg and Fred Griffin talked about leaving the *Star* someday and writing novels. Greg "committed" himself to writing a play on William Lyon Mackenzie and the rebellion of 1837. His "commitment" consisted of writing a letter to Bertram Forsyth, the director of Hart House Theatre, announcing his intentions. Before he could follow through he was sent to Washington for twelve days to cover an armament conference.

On his return he found himself still dealing with the war, but on a more practical level. Unemployment was very high and many soldiers he'd known overseas contacted him for help in finding work. Greg excoriated himself for his treatment of one old comrade, a Lieutenant Wyatt who'd served with Greg in the 4th C.M.R.

Wyatt called to see me at 11:30 A.M. today. We talked for an hour, he being only in the city a few hours on his way to Stratford to visit his sister who is ill. We talked about old times very hearty and then I saw him on his way.

Why the devil didn't I invite him to lunch with me?

This did not occur to me until tonight. But it is a streak of stupidity, selfishness and neglect in me which is often apparent. I wish I could get over it. What a dub he must think me! Imagine me calling on him in North Bay and being turned loose in the town!

Fat-head!

In 1922 he managed to get himself a raise to $77 a week, which he correctly figured out as $4,004 a year. For his son's benefit, he noted that he owed the bank $250, the garage and the grocer $100 each. He determined to teach Murray the folly of living beyond his income. "How," he wrote, "I don't know yet. But I will train him."

Murray continued to delight him and Helen, and to demonstrate an amazing memory. When he was less than a year old Greg and Helen drove with him from Muskoka to Toronto, stopping overnight at a hotel in Orillia. After tea, they carried him over to the fairgrounds in Orillia, where a carnival was in progress. Later, when he was three years old, Murray asked them if they remembered the chicken on the merry-go-round. They didn't. Murray became impatient and said, "It's up at the hotel and the chicken went round and round!" At that both Greg and Helen remembered. There had been a large rooster on the merry-go-round at Orillia. Murray continued to surprise them with memories of scenes and incidents from his brief past.

Suddenly it was 1925 and Greg was a father once again. Gregory Joseph Clark, to be known as Greg, Jr., was born on April 28, arriving quickly after a great rush to the hospital. He was a quiet baby, good-natured and placid. With his dark complexion, he resembled the Murrays more than the Clarks, Greg noted.

In that year the city of Toronto erected a cenotaph in front of City Hall. Greg saw the dedication in advance of the unveiling. It read, "To All Who Served—1914–1918." This dedication enraged Greg. He went to see Atkinson, who at first defended the wording, but came to agree with Greg that it should be dedicated to those who had died. "Pink" Goudy, a reporter on the Toronto *Telegram,* had raised the same question earlier, but the issue had died out. Greg persuaded Goudy to reopen the question and they wrote passionate attacks on the "served" inscription in both papers. Hundreds of supporting letters poured in. Veterans' organizations jammed the next City Council meeting and the inscription was changed to "TO OUR GLORIOUS DEAD," the old wording being removed in time for the official unveiling.

Even after the birth of Greg, Jr., Murray, the firstborn and therefore the more articulate, attracted most of Greg's attention.

When Murray was five years old he sat nearby while Greg and his brother-in-law, Tommy Drew-Brook, a fighter pilot who had been shot down in flames during the war, exchanged war stories.

Murray suddenly interrupted. "Why do men go to war? First they are little babies, then they are boys, then they are men and go to war and get killed. But there is still a little baby in them!"

Murray was also showing Greg's appreciation of nature. "A robin sings as if something were dropping in its mouth," said Murray. "It sounds like rain dropping."

Greg's daughter, Elizabeth, born on April 9, 1931, also added to Greg's collection of cute sayings. After she had recited a short poem by an anonymous author, Greg asked, "And who wrote the poem?"

"Arthur Unknown!" said Elizabeth triumphantly. Arthur was a word she knew well as the name of Greg's brother Arthur. When she saw him arriving at the house with his shotgun in a gun case, she would run to report, "Here comes Uncle Arthur and his violin!"

Greg was a normal, dutiful father when his children were young. He collected their funny sayings. He gave them nicknames. Murray was Baba; Greg, Jr., was Babe; Elizabeth was Dids. But it was an age when children and housework were considered a woman's responsibility. Greg left even household repairs to Helen. The idea that a man should share in cooking or changing diapers was surfacing only in the minds of a few advanced thinkers.

Hunting and fishing were normal activities for the male. Greg had a real need to prove himself here, by boating the most fish or coming back as high gun on the hunt. If he fell down in one area in his handling of the children, it was where one least would have expected it. All his life Greg had suffered painfully from the feeling that his brother Joe was his father's favorite. When it came to raising his own children, one would have expected him to carefully avoid this situation. Instead, seemingly unaware of what he was doing, he made it plain that Murray was his favorite child.

But now, as the decade following the war ended, Greg began to run short of time, even for Murray. He was about to begin the busiest, most important part of his career at the paper.

22

When I was young my father and I were not very close. If someone had said, "Now, will the real Greg Clark stand up?" I would have been looking around just as eagerly as anyone else to see who it was.

—*Greg Clark, Jr.*

A talented writer who shared Greg's early days at the *Star Weekly* was Charles Arthur McLaren Vining. Vining was born in Winnipeg on September 4, 1897. His father was the Reverend Andrew J. Vining and his mother was the former Agnes McLaren.

Vining, unlike Greg, was a successful scholar and athlete. He entered Woodstock College in the fall of 1911, at the age of fourteen. At the end of his first term his average in twelve subjects was 92 percent. He was also quarterback and manager of the undefeated football team.

He went overseas in 1916, the same year as Greg, and was seriously wounded in 1917. He returned to the University of Toronto, where he graduated at the top of his class in political science. In 1921 he went to work for the *Toronto Star* at twenty dollars a week.

Almost immediately he took a place alongside the *Star*'s top reporters—Fred Griffin, Roy Greenaway, Athol Gow and Cliff Wallace. He covered disasters, science stories such as the discovery of insulin and the announcement of Eastman's new Kodak color film, and interviews with top political figures. He could reproduce hour-long interviews from memory, without notes. He could be witty, serious, satiric—whatever the assignment required.

Within a year of his arrival he was helping to organize CFCA, the *Star*'s radio station. This was one of the first radio stations in Canada and a pioneer station in Toronto. Dropping it later on was regarded as one of Atkinson's great mistakes in judgment.

In 1922 Atkinson made a very real mistake. He bought the London *Advertiser,* an ailing competitor of the London *Free Press*. It may have been a spur-of-the-moment decision or he may have been looking ahead to building a chain of newspapers. Atkinson's original investment was in the vicinity of $250,000. His first intention was to send his son-in-law, Harry Hindmarsh, to run the paper, and indeed the Hindmarsh family was preparing to go when Atkinson changed his mind and decided to send managing editor John R. Bone. This move would have cleared the way to make Hindmarsh managing editor at the *Star*.

Perhaps sensing this, Bone declined to go. His next choice, George Maitland, was also reluctant. The job fell to Charles Vining, obviously a rising star, even though he had little more than a year's experience as a reporter. "I was too inexperienced to have any misgivings about the *Advertiser,*" said Vining later.

He threw himself into the job, working from 7 A.M. until after midnight to put out the paper's morning and evening editions. Over the next three years the editorial product improved, but the paper failed to gain against the entrenched London *Free Press*— and in fact lost ground.

"I can't understand it," said Atkinson. "Everything I do in Toronto is right, yet when I do the same thing in London it is wrong." London did not yield to give-away premiums and promotions, which had worked in Toronto. In 1926 Atkinson made a quick about-face and sold the *Advertiser* to the London *Free Press,* which eventually killed it. He lost an estimated $500,000 on the project.

Charles Vining, who was on the spot in London, did not see it as an editorial defeat. He felt that the leading Liberals in London resented the Toronto ownership. London was an ingrown city. The *Advertiser* did not receive the local store advertising it needed. "The most hostile Liberal," said Vining, "was Ray Lawson, later Lieutenant-Governor of Ontario. He became even more so when I refused to keep his name out of the paper in a tax evasion story."

When Vining told Atkinson about this event, Atkinson said, "I would like to think, Mr. Vining, that I would have had the strength of character to do what you did."

Vining suspected that this was Atkinson's way of telling him he had been too idealistic and inexpedient. Nevertheless, Vining was given the chance to return to the *Star Weekly* as Associate Editor. He would, of course, have to take a drop in salary to be on a par with Greg and Griffin—from $125 a week back to $90.

Vining had a highly developed sense of humor and got along well with Greg and Jim Frise, whose famous Birdseye Center cartoon was now an established part of the *Weekly*. In addition, Vining was eager to write for other markets.

At that time in Toronto, a young man named Joseph McDougall was publishing a little magazine called *The Goblin*. Many of the *Star* family used to repair to the old Child's restaurant opposite the *Star* for coffee and conversation. Here McDougall suggested that Vining do a series for *The Goblin*. The items would be short, pithy profiles, made up of great generalities and minute trivialities. To avoid complications with the *Star*, these would be published under the anonymous initials of "R.T.L."

Here is how Vining handled W. L. Mackenzie King:

"Mr. W. L. Mackenzie King went to school for twenty years and then became a statesman, which shows the futility of higher learning.

He does not enjoy being grateful to people.

He has a hearty laugh but hardly a proportionate sense of humour.

He has a genius for detecting the approach of trouble and an equal talent for avoiding it."

Vining not only did these profiles for *The Goblin*, he later did others for *Maclean's* magazine and published a collection of them called "Bigwigs." Vining did not claim to have invented this staccato journalistic form. It was being used at the time by Charles G. Shaw in the pages of *Vanity Fair*. Shaw is believed to have derived it from work done earlier by the biographer Owen Hatteras.

Vining was astute enough to see that being a newspaperman was a young man's game, especially at the *Star*. If there was to be a financial future for the players, there had to be some way of getting a financial stake in the paper. From the paper's point of view, he reasoned, it would be good business to hang on to the various talents it was developing.

One Sunday afternoon in the winter of 1926, in his lower duplex at 8 Crescent Road, he gathered a group for tea. It included Fred Griffin and Greg Clark; Bill Wallace, the assistant advertising manager; and Fred Tate, the assistant business manager. Vining proposed that the group ask Atkinson for some form of participation or face their departure. The group heartily approved on Sunday afternoon, but on Monday morning at the office Vining found he was the only rebel left. The matter was not pursued. In view of the wholesale firings which attended the Newspaper Guild's attempt to organize the *Star* some ten years later, this was probably just as well.

Greg, Vining, Fred Griffin, Jim Frise and others shared one small office at the *Star Weekly*. It was a difficult place to work, but it also bubbled with ideas. In 1927 Greg and Vining undertook to produce a magazine called *Sporting,* along the lines of that bright new magazine called the *New Yorker,* but one which would focus on the foibles of Toronto. The energetic Vining put together a 32-page dummy and one of their business partners, Victor Sifton of the publishing family, secured enough promises of advertising to ensure publication for at least a year. The partners lost their collective nerve and dropped the project, however. With the Great Crash of 1929 just around the corner, it was probably a good decision.

Greg's and Vining's humor found outlet in the *Weekly*. With Cranston's blessing, they began contriving a series of "stunt" stories, which they did in tandem and took turns in writing. One of their earliest and most successful was called "The Thousand Dollar Bill." Arming themselves with a thousand-dollar bill from the business office, they set out in downtown Toronto to buy a 95-cent tie.

After carefully selecting the tie they wanted, they would nonchalantly drop the bill on the counter and wait for the reaction. Jaws dropped open. Clerks stared at it. Managers were hastily summoned. None of the smaller shops, of course, had enough money on hand to make change—and the banks were closed.

"Have you anything smaller?"

Greg and Vining insisted it was the smallest bill they had with them. Reactions were varied. Some shops turned them away as though they were gangsters or perhaps counterfeiters. Others fawned on them and urged them to open charge accounts instead. The story was pure fun, for which Cranston was always looking.

The thousand-dollar bill story ran in the *Star Weekly* on October 22, 1927, under Greg's by-line. This Charles-Greg story was the prototype for the Jim-Greg stories to come later, and in fact became confused with them.

Vining and Greg did one of these stunt stories every few weeks. Working as a pair enabled them to tell the story in light, breezy dialogue—and to manufacture funny dialogue when the story didn't produce any. On dull days they could even get away with interviewing each other.

In one, called "Everybody's Happy," Vining was the author and Greg started it off by saying, "If you're going to interview somebody, why not me for a change?"

Vining says he doesn't think this would work, but says that, to begin with, he would have to describe Greg's appearance.

"What would you say?" asked Greg.

Vining said, "I would just tell what you look like. Five feet, two inches tall, tousled iron grey hair, large head, small face, green shirt, red tie, big clothes, shoes not shining, pockets always bulging with old letters which are never answered, hat over one ear, small glittering blue eyes behind a screen of long straight lashes, humorous terrier brows, acquisitive nose, hard mouth if you take off that straggly moustache, loud voice, big stride, cold hand, fine telephone manner, ready promise but—"

"That's a libel!" protested Greg. "That's my character, not my appearance!"

Vining went on, unperturbed. "There would have to be something about your habit of procrastination, your fixed rule never to be any place on time no matter how important it is, the way you mismanage your money, and your artfulness in bluffing about things you don't know anything about—"

Greg's protests grow, and in the end he is begging Vining *not* to interview him—but by then, of course, they have another light, humorous feature for the *Weekly*.

Vining was too ambitious and able a man to remain at the *Star* indefinitely. Soon after the series began he went to an advertising agency at twice his *Star* salary. From here he was appointed president of the Newsprint Export Manufacturers Association of Canada and on the outbreak of war he was loaned to the government. He became chairman of the Wartime Information Board and was deeply involved in wartime intelligence operations, including work for Sir William Stephenson, the Quiet Canadian, whose undercover work was outlined in *Intrepid*.

With Vining gone, Greg did a few stunt stories with Merrill Denison, another *Star* writer. Denison, who went on to become a well-known playwright and author, was not at home with the somewhat undignified stunts and soon bowed out.

Greg's good friend Jimmie Frise had been illustrating the stunt stories and in 1930 Greg hit on the idea of using Jim as his partner, real or imaginary. This worked even better.

The Frise half-page cartoon feature, Birdseye Center, was already an established success at the *Star Weekly*. Back in 1921 the *Weekly* had been using a somewhat similar cartoon called "Among Us Mortals," by W. E. Hill, purchased from the United States. Cranston encouraged Frise to try something along the same lines, but more distinctively Canadian. At first Frise, a very modest man, said he couldn't do it—certainly not on a weekly deadline. Eventually he was persuaded to produce one, called "Life's Little Comedies." Over time this evolved into Birdseye Center, based on Frise's experiences as a youth growing up in Port Perry, Ontario. It was fantastically popular even before the Jim-Greg stories began. In the next twenty-five years the cartoon and the stories became the *Star Weekly*'s best-known features.

Frise liked people. "He was," said Greg, "totally incapable of discriminating. He made no distinction between the useful and the useless, the good and the bad, the worthy and the unworthy." The office he shared with Greg became a magnet for writers, advertising men, country editors, pool sharks, horseplayers, bums looking for a handout. Jim and Greg were known as soft touches. In addition, Jim had a weakness for cards, horses and dice.

In Birdseye Center Frise developed famous characters like Pigskin Peters, a kind of village fool; Archie and his tame moose; and Eli Doolittle, the laziest man in town. They became familiars in homes across Canada. Thousands of city dwellers had grown up in small towns and villages; Birdseye Center took them home again every week.

Jim Frise was a tall, lanky man and Greg was short and plump. In his illustrations for the Jim-Greg stories Frise exaggerated their differences, as he exaggerated Greg's clothing—the porkpie hats, the long scarves, the suspenders, the bulging pockets. Comic couples have a long tradition—from Don Quixote and his squire to Laurel and Hardy, Abbott and Costello and many others. Jim and Greg were instantly popular.

As time went on, the stories leaned less on stunts and became more the kind of adventure that might happen to Canadians anywhere. Sometimes they sprang from Greg's imagination, sometimes they grew out of actual incidents on fishing trips or weekends at the cottage.

One of the early Jim-Greg stories is "Rejuvenation Pills," which follows.

23

REJUVENATION PILLS

A Story by Greg Clark

"I wish," said Jimmie, "we were living a hundred years from now."

"A hundred years ago would be better," I disagreed.

"Ah!" said Jim, "a hundred years from now, all this bewilderment we are living amidst will be over. All the problems solved. We'd know how communism turned out. And what became of Germany and Italy."

"If we'd lived a hundred years ago," I debated, "we would know now what had happened. I would feel a lot safer, if I had lived a hundred years ago."

"Think of the miracles," cried Jim, "that are certain to come to pass in the next hundred years. Do you realize that in our lifetime, more miracles have happened than in the rest of the entire history of the world?"

"I guess we have lived in a thrilling time," I admitted.

"Thrilling?" said Jim. "Listen. Human history is divided into two parts. The past hundred years is one half. The other half are all the millions of years before."

"Maybe it's over," I suggested.

"When we were born," said Jim, "the telegraph was the last supreme wonder of the world—the telegraph. Since we were born, recollect the miracles that have come to pass. The telephone, the phonograph, the electric light, the gas engine, the motor car, the paved highway, radio, the aeroplane, television, the X-ray, a million per cent development of electrical and mechanical understanding, several thousand per cent increase in medical science, so now they can take your gizzard out and show it to you and put it back without you feeling anything."

"Why?" I asked.

"Previous to our birth," continued Jim, "the greatest event they could tell us about in the school books was that Columbus sailed across the ocean. Now people fly the ocean in a few hours."

"A hundred years from now, I suppose," I supposed, "all we will need to do is go up to community stratosphere platforms overnight, and wait for the earth to revolve underneath us, and then come down for breakfast in London or Calcutta."

"Boy," said Jim, "how I would love to live a hundred years from now. What will we look like? What will we be doing? Will there be newspapers or only news broadcasts with television? For example, the news agencies all over the world will be television reporters with their outfits to rush from place to place. All you will have to do is tune in on a world news centre, say, in London. There you will learn from an announcer what is going on. A revolution in Spain. A big parade in Moscow. A murder in Chicago. You just twist the dials and get the local station, and there, instead of X marks the spot where the body lay, you can see the police carrying the body out and the suspect being grilled like a pork chop."

"In which case," I explained, "you and I would be out of jobs. They won't need cartoonists and writers."

*   *   *   *   *

"In a hundred years," said Jim, "I doubt if many people will have to work. We are just about now beginning to discover that work is the bunk. Despite the million discoveries of how to do things easily and painlessly, we still have the silly idea that we all have to toil and labor the way we did back in the days of wooden plows and Magna Charta. It's that early training stuff. It is hard for mankind to forget what it learned in its infancy. But in a hundred years, I bet nobody will have to work except those that want to work."

"Will anybody want to work?" I protested.

"Don't be absurd," said Jim. "Mankind is divided into two classes: those who don't want to work, a very large class, and those who can't help working, a small class, but easily able to support all the rest of us. This interesting division into classes has been staring us in the face now for nearly a hundred years. But we haven't tumbled to it yet. We still think it is a political division. It's nothing of the sort. It's purely a biological distinction.

Some men are born to like work. To be unhappy unless they are working. They get as much kick out of work as we get out of fishing."

"For heaven's sake," I cried, "it's true."

"Of course it's true," said Jim. "Take one of these people away from their work and they actually pine, grow ill and die. It's like liquor to them. They are work addicts. Yet, from time immemorial, we have foolishly allowed these people, these addicts, to possess the earth and the fullness thereof. With their energy and pep, they have bossed us and bullied us and made life miserable for countless generations of mankind."

"How simple it all is," I mused.

"A hundred years from now," went on Jimmie, "with the aid of medical science, advanced psychology and that sort of thing, we will have all work addicts classified. We will put them in a special uniform. We will supply them with all the machinery they, in their folly, have invented. And we will permit them to work to their hearts' content, the poor addicts, while the rest of us, the natural man, the human, lazy, happy multitude, will be amply supported in glorious leisure."

"Jim," I confessed, "I too would like to be living a hundred years from now."

"It will be a great time," declaimed Jimmie. "The workers will be honored by us all, instead of hated for their wealth and industry."

"I would feel kind of sorry for them," I confessed.

"They would likely be very snobbish about it all," said Jim thoughtfully, "and as the years went by, we might behold the comic spectacle of our own children aspiring to be workers."

"Like now," I offered, "young people wanting to be movie stars and aviators."

"As a matter of fact," said Jim, "there is in all human hearts a faint desire to want to do something. When it is no longer necessary, a hundred years from now, to do anything unless you want to, I wouldn't be surprised to see a most extraordinary development. We might get those cathedral builders we used to have centuries ago. We might get poets again. People might actually get to like living so much that they would just naturally want to make their lives beautiful."

*　　*　　*　　*　　*

"A minute ago, Jim," I said, "I was happy to be alive in this exciting age. But now, you make it all seem kind of drab. As if we were here standing in the dawn, in the cold, and fog, and greyness, waiting for the day we will never see."

"You never can tell," declared Jim. "Sometimes I get the feeling we are on the very edge of the secret of life. As if we were hovering on the very rim of immense revelations, when all our troubles and misunderstandings will vanish away like mist, and we'll stand in the clear, all over the world, understanding, comprehending and realizing. Almost any day now, some scientist will discover the very essence of life. Maybe before we die, we can take a pill or drink a liquid that will restore our youth and allow us to live indefinitely."

"Come on, science," I cheered.

"Oh, it's partly done already," said Jim. "What do you suppose those monkey gland experiments were for? And all these gland pills and rejuvenation pills?"

"I hadn't paid much attention to that stuff," I said. "I guess I still feel pretty peppy."

"You can buy pills now," said Jim, "that make you twenty years younger. For as long as they last, they restore to your system the worn out essences of life itself. To all intents and purposes you are twenty years younger."

"That would be a nice feeling," I admitted, trying to remember what twenty years ago felt like.

"The way I understand it," said Jim, "we are all lit up inside by our glands, as if they were a string of those little lights you put on a Christmas tree. Some are bright and some are dim, according to the way we are born. Sometimes one of them burns too bright and all the rest go dim. Sometimes one goes out, and then they all go out. Our glands are all hooked up on a sort of circuit."

"Taking pills then," I said, "is like putting in a fresh bulb."

"Sort of," agreed Jim. "We have glands in our head and neck and all over our bodies. Some of them are so small, they haven't been discovered yet. Others are so newly found, the doctors don't know what they are for, but they all work together to make us what we are. One gland makes us lazy and another makes us work. One makes us bad tempered and another makes us have dry skin or bushy hair. In a few years, they will be able to give a gland pill so you can see a joke. Or to improve your ear for music."

"Character won't be worth having," I protested, "if you can buy it at the drug store."

"You see what I am getting at?" said Jim. "A few more steps in this game, and they'll find a gland preservative and then we can live to be five hundred years old."

"Are any of these pills to be had?" I asked.

"Doctors use them all the time," said Jim. "You've heard of thyroid pills and adrenalin pills?"

"As journalists, Jim," I declared, "we ought to have been looking into this long ago. We should even have been taking some of these pills."

"You can't take them without a doctor's orders," Jim said. "If your glands are good and you took a pill, goodness knows what it might do to you. But of course these rejuvenation pills you can get anywhere. They're on sale like any patent medicine."

"I'm not particularly anxious to be twenty years younger," I mused. "Twenty years ago, I was in the war. I'm not very sure I would like to be as I was then."

"Even ten years ago," agreed Jim. "I wouldn't like to go back ten. I used to be so anxious and working and worrying and full of trouble."

"Ten years ago," I said, "I had the eczema."

"Even five years," said Jim. "Five years ago, I thought I would never get my house paid for. It used to keep me awake at night. Now I don't care."

"It would probably," I said, "be only a physical feeling. It would only last a couple of hours. Let's try it. We owe it to humanity."

"On an empty stomach," said Jim. "We'll take a couple of hours for lunch."

Our favorite druggist spoke very highly of four or five brands of rejuvenation pills. He told us of an elderly gentleman amongst his clients who had taken off thirty years on one brand of pill. There were Chinese pills, big jelly looking objects; and tiny pinhead pills made in Europe by societies with long names, that were the secret, the druggist told us, of the fact that all the fashion styles come from Paris. Some of the pills were in old-fashioned packages with pen drawings of virile looking gentlemen with long black beards. Others were done up very discreetly in vivid modernistic style; others in a plain envelope, as the saying is.

"This here," said the druggist, "is one of the newest. It comes from Europe. They say the German army is fed on them, daily."

We bought that one. Fifty pills—two dollars and seventy-five cents. They were small white flat pills with a curious pallid expression. We read the instructions:—"The effect of this prescription is cumulative. Take one tablet the first time, two tablets the second time, and so on until a maximum of five pills at a time are taken; by which time, a permanent sense of rejuvenation and well-being will permeate the whole system."

"Well," laughed Jimmie, "let's take the first one here at the soda fountain to begin with."

Which we did and then went forth to stroll in the crisp noon air, amidst all the hurrying throng of luncheoners.

"It does not say," said Jim, "at what intervals to take them. But I suppose we ought to give them at least time to dissolve."

"I feel a slight sense of well-being already, Jim," I submitted, squaring my shoulders.

"They have a minty flavor," said Jim. "Not at all bad to take."

"Pop us out a couple," I suggested, and Jim produced the bottle and we each palmed and swallowed two.

We mingled with the crowds up towards the big department store corners.

"Jim," I said, "do you notice anything?"

"I certainly feel light on my feet," said Jim. "But the best part of it is, how nice everything looks. And everybody."

"Ah, this is a great old town," I agreed. "Anybody that couldn't be happy here couldn't be happy anywhere."

"Wheeeeee," said Jimmie. So we went through the revolving doors of one of the big stores and stood in the lobby while we took the next course; three pills each this time.

"They dissolve quick," said Jim.

We stood in the lobby for a little while, letting them dissolve and watching all the lovely people hurrying through. There were a lot of other people, mostly young men, standing in the lobby. It felt good to be there with them, standing and watching everybody passing.

"Where to?" asked Jim.

"Let's go through the gent's furnishings," I said. "I've got the idea I'd like to look at some ties and shirts and things."

We spent a happy twenty minutes looking at the haberdashery. I had no idea haberdashery had developed so interestingly of late. Snappy, we used to call it when I was younger. Jim and I both agreed that the youth's and young gent's was away ahead of the rest of the department, and we told the salesmen so. Jim finally bought a club stripe tie and I got two blue shirts with nifty fall-over collars that expose the throat.

"How do you feel?" I asked Jim.

"Hungry," said Jim. I observed that he had his hat on the back of his head and his hair was sticking out in front. It looked nice. So I put my hat the same way. Jim began picking things up off the counter and putting them down again. I followed him and did the same. It was fun.

*   *   *   *   *

We saw the escalator at the same time, and raced for it. We rode up three floors on it and then came down four. Then Jimmie invented the trick of going down the up escalators and up the down ones. A man came over and told us not to do that.

"Let's go to the toy department," said Jim.

Did we ever have a swell time in the toy department! We tried all the things, the pop-guns and the mechanical automobiles. We blew the horns and beat the drums. We pushed dolls off the counters and spent a long time at the magic counter. It was when we got to the wagon and tricycle department that the difficulties began.

There was one lovely wagon like an automobile. It was blue and had shining metal headlights and disc wheels. I got it first.

"Get off it," said Jim, pushing me.

"I got it first," I retorted.

"Get off it," hissed Jimmie, giving me a dirty pinch.

"I won't," I yelled.

Jim put his shoulder against me and sent me flying to the floor. Weeping with rage, I rushed him and we clinched and punched and pinched and shoved all over the department, stumbling over carts and tricycles, while girls tried to separate us and managers came dashing up. They got us apart, and Jimmie leaned sobbing bitterly against the counter.

"Aw, Jimmie," I said. "I'm sorry."

"Now," sobbed Jimmie, his fists in his eyes, "we'll be late for school."

24

THE MOST INTERESTING PEOPLE

Having given up the idea of becoming a minister, Greg certainly did the next best thing in joining the *Toronto Daily Star*. The *Star* had more ministers, ex-ministers and would-be ministers than a Sunday School paper.

Even after Holy Joe Atkinson's death, the *Star* chose a reformed evangelist, Charles B. Templeton, as managing editor. Before hitting the trail in search of God, Templeton had worked as a sports cartoonist at *The Globe & Mail*. He finally caught religion from his mother and swept into the city room crying, "I've got it. I've got it!"

Sportswriter Jack Marks was there at the time and was momentarily bewildered. "For a few minutes," said Marks, "I didn't know whether he'd got religion or got the clap."

Marks had a face like Buster Keaton and a dry, incisive way of making a point. I once asked his opinion of the scion of a publisher, with whom Marks had served in the army. "He was a real nice guy," said Marks. There was a significant pause. Then Marks deadpanned, "When he got a box of cookies from home he ate them with his head in his locker."

Long before Templeton's time, the *Star* had been graced by another outstanding servant of God, the Reverend Robert E. Knowles. As a minister at Galt, Ontario, Knowles electrified his congregation with fiery sermons in which he strode about the platform, thumped the Bible and tore off his collar. As too often happens, this excessive energy led to the writing of novels. He turned out six and they brought him fame and fortune. But God was unkind to him. Knowles was in a serious train accident. The man sitting next to him was killed outright and Knowles was hospitalized. When he recovered, he could not face up to writing novels or delivering sermons.

After psychiatric treatment, Knowles began writing for the *Star Weekly* and then for the *Daily Star,* where he became Canada's most famous interviewer. He interviewed celebrities, movie stars, and every prime minister of Canada and Britain of his day. He invented a technique that has only lately been rediscovered by practitioners of the new journalism. Before his subjects could overwhelm him, Knowles overwhelmed them. "Just answer my questions," said Knowles. "And keep your answers as brief as possible. I find that I generally know more about the subject than the people I talk to."

Before the victim recovered, the interview was over. Now Knowles took flight. His brief encounters were draped in purple prose and were padded with mixed metaphors and literary quotations, often inaccurate. Describing an actual airplane flight from London to Paris, he wrote: "It was wonderful! Simply wonderful! Next to falling in love for the first time flying is the greatest experience in life."

There was a nervous woman passenger on the plane, worried about the safety of some Venetian glass she had in her luggage. Knowles admonished her: "Madam, it ill becomes you, or any of us, to be concerned at such an hour as this with these petty baubles, for we are pilgrims of the skies—and it would better become us to think of our latter end."

For weeks on end Knowles had interviews on the front page of the *Star*. Other papers ridiculed this star of the *Star* as "the man who interviews himself." Literate readers cringed, yet read him in fascination. The man in the street and Joseph E. Atkinson read him with admiration.

Quite sensibly, he refused to go on salary and asked to be paid at space rates. He earned more money by sheer verbosity. He explained to another reporter why he larded his interviews with quotations. "I enjoy getting paid for something Shakespeare wrote."

Another minister who contributed to the *Weekly* and the daily for thirty years was the Reverend William A. Cameron. He was a Baptist singing preacher and he became Canada's first radio preacher on the *Star*'s pioneer radio station, CFCA.

The *Star*'s library was organized by another unusual part-time minister, the Reverend Adam Fordyce (Biddy) Barr. He was a former football and lacrosse player who gave up his first parish after a doctrinal disagreement with his bishop.

Another famous *Star* minister was Dr. Salem Bland. He was a Methodist who had lost a number of church positions for championing labor unions and arguing for better food for the troops overseas. He found refuge writing a daily column called "The Observer." In the Twenties and Thirties he saw hope for the working man in the Russian experiment, as did Atkinson. Both eventually became disillusioned.

Atkinson's evangelists were not always suffered gladly by the regular newspapermen. Frank Chamberlain was a gentle soul who had been hired to write touching stories for the *Star* Fresh Air Fund, the Santa Claus appeals and religious features. During his first few days on staff he was rushed off to Quebec city to interview a boatload of preachers arriving from Britain—an assignment that probably came down from Atkinson via Hindmarsh.

Chamberlain got back to the *Star* on a Sunday morning. He spent the whole day typing out his interviews and by evening he had about eight columns—nearly a whole newspaper page—of copy. Griffin was doing a short stint as news editor that Sunday night and Chamberlain placed his epic on his desk. "I'll never forget the look that came over Griffin's face," said Chamberlain. "Griffin was not a very religious man."

Griffin thumbed through the pages with disbelief. "What the hell is all this crap?" he finally exploded. He dumped it in the wastebasket. Next morning it was resurrected from the basket and ran word for word through all editions. Hindmarsh was a great news editor. He knew what Holy Joe Atkinson wanted.

Griffin was to die in harness at the *Star*. So was another longtime *Star* employee, Bill Argue, the circulation manager, whom Atkinson had inherited when he took over the paper in 1899. Argue fought the *Star*'s circulation battles expertly for nearly fifty years. As he grew older he several times raised the question of a retirement pension with Atkinson, who kept telling him it was "under consideration." Atkinson was still considering it when Argue, still at work, died at the age of seventy-five.

Atkinson explained his policy as a kindness. The enforced idleness of retirement was often too great a shock for older men. He had another ingenious rationalization for the *Star*'s lack of a pension plan. On its editorial pages the *Star* was arguing for government old-age pensions, not then in existence. The institution of a *Star* pension plan, said Atkinson, might weaken the paper's editorial position.

Another old-timer inherited by Atkinson was Walter C. R. Harris, the business manager. He was a good bowler, football player and lacrosse player and had excellent financial sense. When sixty shares of *Star* stock came on the market in 1914, he and John Bone, the managing editor, bought them before Atkinson heard they were available. They were the only *Star* employees ever to hold stock. Even though he had a majority and controlling interest, Atkinson badgered them to sell their sixty shares to him, but they held out until they died—still on the job, naturally. Atkinson was then able to buy the shares from their widows.

Bill Hewitt also came with the paper. He'd been a friend of Atkinson's when they were both young reporters. Hewitt stayed with the paper as sports editor until he and his son Foster Hewitt left to take charge of hockey at Maple Leaf Gardens.

Hewitt's successor as sports editor was the legendary Lou Marsh, a sports columnist also inherited with the paper. Marsh could play nearly every game he wrote about. He boxed, swam, played football with the Argonauts, sailed sloops and iceboats, raced motorboats and drank life to the full. In his spare time he refereed hockey games and boxing matches throughout Ontario, sometimes fighting his way out of arenas through angry fans who didn't agree with his decisions. His "Pick & Shovel" sports column was one of the *Star*'s great circulation builders. He is still honored by the Lou Marsh Trophy, awarded to Canada's outstanding athlete of the year.

On this amazing ship where Greg made his living for thirty years, women were slow to make an appearance. Mary Lowery Ross, at that time Mary Lowery, contributed fiction to the *Star Weekly,* as did other female writers. Claire Wallace made a name for herself as a stunt reporter and as the columnist of "Over The Teacups" before going on to radio fame. Alexandrine Gibb, an outstanding athlete, wrote a column called the "No Man's Land of Sport." At somebody's whim she was sent on a tour of Russia in 1935. Her reports were not too illuminating.

Next Atkinson bought a series of articles from a social worker named Margaret Gould who had gone on a welfare study tour of Britain, Scandinavia and the Soviet Union. Margaret Gould had been born in Russia of Jewish parents and spoke Russian. Her articles were played up in the *Star*. After her return she was hired as a *Star* editorial writer. Some saw her as a Russian sympathizer and blamed her for the *Star*'s soft attitude toward Russia.

By 1937 Atkinson was seventy-two years old. His wife had died some years earlier. Some felt that Margaret Gould was an evil influence on the aging publisher. It was true that he spent a lot of time with her. Perhaps it was because he shared her social concerns. Again, he had grown quite hard of hearing and perhaps it was because he could hear her loud, shrill voice quite easily.

A mysterious figure at the *Star* for many years was Claude Pascoe. He had been a major in the White Army force which fought in Russia in 1919. He'd also served with the Black and Tans in Ireland. Under Hindmarsh's instructions, he worked to sabotage the Newspaper Guild's first attempt to organize the *Star*. This and other odd jobs convinced the staff that he was a Hindmarsh informer. Unlike so many *Star* employees, he was given a retirement allowance.

It is a sad irony that Joseph Atkinson, who began as a young idealist, came to be regarded by some as an evil hypocrite. Rival publishers played a large part in creating this image. McCullagh's *Globe & Mail* once editorialized about the *Star:* "It puts on a face of sanctity, filling its columns with benevolent platitudes, and observes the opposite in practice."

Some of this criticism was sour grapes. Some of it was class interest. Atkinson became a millionaire, but refused to act like one. He didn't join the cozy club of gentleman publishers. His paper was an early champion of labor rights, social reform, public ownership of utilities, oil, gas and water-power resources. On these and other issues it dragged other newspapers unwillingly into the twentieth century. His success in taking a tiny newspaper and building it into the most widely read and most successful publication in Canada indicates that his policies expressed the hopes and ideas of the average man.

Atkinson did not use his wealth for personal aggrandizement or lavish living, but to put the *Star* on an unassailable financial base, free from the business and political pressures he had experienced early in his career. He sought to perpetuate this beyond his death, writing a will which left the paper in control of a charitable trust. This attempt to create a truly free newspaper was regarded by many as a final great act in the public interest. It was frustrated by the Ontario Charitable Gifts Act, passed by the provincial conservative government, aimed directly at his will and, unbelievably, made retroactive.

The *Star* had incurred the wrath of many prominent Conservative politicians over the years. This vengeful piece of retroactive legislation had the effect of forcing the paper into private enterprise operation. In the light of recent Canadian newspaper concentration in the hands of a few publishers with other business interests, Atkinson's intent seems today to have been even more farsighted and in the public interest. The legacy of an independent newspaper, not subject to political or business pressures, would have partially justified some of the Atkinson-Hindmarsh excesses in the development of the *Star*.

Much of the ammunition for attacks on the *Star* came from its treatment of its own employees. In concentrating on the success of the paper, Atkinson seemed to lose touch with those making that success possible. Many were alienated—even Greg, the most loyal of employees. Greg came to feel that Atkinson was moved by the misfortunes of humanity in the mass but not by those of individuals.

During the Depression the paper bought circulation with huge promotion contests and lengthy serializations such as *The Life of Christ, The Life of Edith Cavell* and *Dickens' Love Letters*. These inspired two Toronto writers, Dan McArthur and J. L. Charlesworth, to write a song that was sung lustily at newspaper bottle parties to the tune of "Bonnie Dundee."

AD ASTRA

To Hindmarsh and Knowles Mr. Atkinson spoke—
"If we don't sell more papers The Star will go broke;
I've got three super-salesmen who say they can sell—
They're Jesus and Dickens and Edith Cavell."

So fill up the columns with sob-stuff and sex,
Shed tears by the bucket and sobs by the pecks,
Let the presses revolve like the mill-tails of Hell
For Jesus and Dickens and Edith Cavell!

"This Jesus is gentle, surround him with tots,
The Mayor and his kiddies should make some good shots—
Get letters from Cody and Joey Flavelle
On Jesus and Dickens and Edith Cavell.

"As a lover this Dickens is really the bunk,
  His letters are long and his technique is punk,
  But he looks kinda sexy, his whiskers are swell;
  Besides, we've got Jesus and Edith Cavell.

"Edith Cavell is the best of the lot,
  It's always hot news when a woman gets shot,
  Get plenty of pictures for those that can't spell
  Of Jesus and Dickens and Edith Cavell."

So hey for the paper that strives for the best,
  If Jesus makes good we'll put over Mae West,
  With cuties and comics and corpses and smell
  And Jesus and Dickens and Edith Cavell!

25

I, the captain of a Legion of Rome,
have learnt and pondered this truth, that
there are in life but two things, love and power,
and no man can have both.

—a stone tablet unearthed in Africa

With the Jim-Greg stories underway Greg should have been heading toward the happiest period of his life. He was teamed up with his good friend, Jimmie Frise. His work had taken a line which afforded him some creative freedom, and the Jim-Greg series was about to become the most popular feature on the *Star Weekly,* which was on the way to becoming national in scope and Canada's largest publication. He had a reasonably happy marriage and three young children. There was ample time for hunting and fishing trips and summers at Go Home Bay. But, on October 24, 1929, the first of several disastrous trading days hit the New York Stock Exchange. The Great Depression was about to begin.

Joseph Atkinson had just completed his twenty-three-story skyscraper at 80 King Street West and both his newspapers were leaders in their fields. He was in a good position to weather the storm, although he did lose some money in South American government securities, then considered one of the most conservative of investments—but he panicked. He called in Hindmarsh a few days before Christmas and gave him a figure by which his budget must be reduced—*by the end of the year*. Hindmarsh drew up a list of fourteen reporters who were to be fired.

Out of this situation grew the legend about wholesale *Star* firings which took place on every Christmas Eve . . . a bitter contradiction of the *Star*'s charitable promotions and its position as self-proclaimed champion of the workingman. In his book, *J. E. Atkinson of The Star*, Ross Harkness tries to track down the facts behind the legend, with mixed results. Thirty-year-old personnel records can be read in different ways and thirty-year-old memories are often confused and contradictory.

Whatever the details, it is apparent that, from the time of Hemingway, *Star* editorial people were handled in a sometimes benign, sometimes dictatorial manner. Periodic economy waves decimated the staff. The older and richer Atkinson became, the more he seemed concerned with *Star* profits and penny-pinching. His instructions to Hindmarsh were carried out literally and insensitively. Hindmarsh also seemed intent on building up his own personal power.

One of his first individual firings on the *Star Weekly* was reported by J. H. Cranston in his book, *Ink on My Fingers*. Hindmarsh told Cranston to get rid of the *Star Weekly* makeup man. Cranston sent a memo arguing that the man was suffering from eye trouble and had just had to pay for an expensive operation on his child. Hindmarsh's reply pointed out that the man's mother ran a grocery store and could support her son's family. Cranston said the store was a small one and could hardly support them all. Hindmarsh's final memo read: "As Mr. ——— and his family will not be reduced to actual privation, the order will stand."

Cranston himself was the next to go. Hindmarsh got rid of Cranston in stages. Cranston must have all purchases approved. Cranston must submit all manuscripts to Hindmarsh for final approval. Next, a new editor of the *Star Weekly* was appointed and Cranston was demoted to associate editor with a salary cut of one-third. Two months later Hindmarsh told Cranston he could accept a further demotion to handling copy on the *Daily,* with an additional 50-percent cut in salary—or he could resign. If he resigned he would receive a year's salary as a going-away present.

Cranston had little choice. The *Star* had no pension fund and doubtless even more humiliating demotions could force him into quitting later, with no going-away present. Cranston resigned. He had been with the *Star* for thirty years, had even served as Atkinson's private secretary. Under his editorship he had seen the *Star Weekly* grow from a circulation of 16,000 to a peak of 250,000, to where it was showing a profit of half a million dollars a year.

Along with the economy-wave firings, and the firings of those who stood in Hindmarsh's way, there were others which seemed mysterious but may have reflected Atkinson's desire for complete control of policy, and his sometimes abrupt switches in policy. J. A. Stevenson, the *Star*'s Ottawa bureau chief, was fired ostensibly for writing for outside publications on his own time— but his Conservative connections were suspect and his appointment had been vigorously opposed by Atkinson's good friend Mackenzie King. Stevenson remained in Ottawa as Ottawa representative of the London *Times*.

The longtime London correspondent of the *Star* was Henry Somerville. His dismissal came to him as a bolt from the blue. He had just returned from a personal Hindmarsh assignment to track down some Atkinson ancestors in the English countryside. Waiting for him in his London office was an abrupt note of dismissal from Hindmarsh which stated that Somerville was "not in sympathy with the type of journalism which the *Star* is trying to develop." Somerville had been one of the organizers of the Catholic Social Guild at Oxford University and it may be that his Catholicism struck a wrong note with Atkinson or Hindmarsh at the time.

Somerville did carry on as a Catholic writer, becoming an editor with the *Catholic Register* in Toronto. Sometimes these strange firings produced strange results. Somerville, from his position at the *Catholic Register,* attacked the *Star* later for its anti-Catholic coverage of the war in Spain by its famous foreign correspondent, Pierre van Paassen. This attack was to result in the firing of Van Paassen by Hindmarsh, which has itself become another *Star* legend embellished over the years.

I asked Greg about the Pierre van Paassen legend.

"Oh, yes," said Greg. "That's true all right. You must understand, of course, I took no interest in politics—international, federal or local. I was preserving my innocence so I could write the kind of things Jimmie and I had to produce."

"You've told me that before," I said. "But you've also told me the paper wouldn't trust you with politics."

"Yes, that's true," said Greg.

"On the other hand you told me you were covering Mitch Hepburn at a political dinner, and you became enraged when you saw Hepburn slide his hand up the skirt of a young waitress. Didn't you?"

"Well, yes, I did tell you that," said Greg.

"His aides tried to calm you down," I said, "saying it was just one of those things—that Hepburn had had too much to drink—but you wouldn't listen. You not only left the dinner, but you went right back to the *Star* and reported the incident to Atkinson. He was as shocked as you were. And this may have had something to do with the liberal *Star* abandoning Hepburn, the Liberal leader, in provincial politics?"

"Y'see, that's why they couldn't trust me with politics," said Greg.

"But when the *Star* lost Catholic support, they sent you to cover a papal election and bring the Catholics back into the fold. Isn't that about as political as you can get?"

"Well," said Greg, "in a way all those things are true. But let's get back to Van Paassen. Now he was reporting the war in Spain, with the Loyalist government on one side and Franco's Catholic forces on the other. The Catholics in Toronto became incensed at his reports, which were datelined Spain. Two priests showed up at the *Star*. They said, 'Mr. Hindmarsh, we have absolute proof that Mr. Pierre van Paassen has never left his apartment in Paris.' Hindmarsh studied their reports. He was a great newspaperman, you know. Then, without a word to anyone, he booked passage on an ocean liner, found Van Paassen sitting at some sidewalk café. Hindmarsh walked up to him, looked him in the eye and said just two words. 'You're fired!' Then he turned around, got back on the boat and returned to Toronto."

Greg chuckled. "All the way across the ocean! Just to say 'You're fired!' "

In his biography of Atkinson, Ross Harkness examines the Pierre van Paassen dismissal in much more detail. Hindmarsh did go to Paris, but did not find Van Paassen at home. Hindmarsh talked to the servants, neighbors and the milkman. On his return to Toronto, he sent Van Paassen his notice and a parting check for a thousand dollars.

It was a strange end for a distinguished foreign correspondent. Pierre van Paassen had gone to Russia for *The Globe & Mail* at the same time the *Star* sent Fred Griffin. Their first reportage was similar, but *The Globe & Mail,* expecting more violently anti-communist coverage, had criticized Van Paassen. Amazed, he switched his dispatches to the *Star*. Not long afterward, he was expelled from Russia for some of the opinions he expressed, and became the *Star*'s roving European correspondent. His assessment of events remained uncannily accurate. He predicted Hitler's seizure of power in Germany, the persecution of the Jews and even Hitler's eventual attack on Russia.

Pierre van Paassen's firing seems to have been a placation of Catholics. The *Star* was under attack as a "Red Rag" and the "King Street *Pravda*." In an attempt to mollify Toronto Catholics, Greg Clark was dispatched to Rome in 1939 to cover the election of a new pope. His fulsome stories were given heavy-handed treatment by Hindmarsh and may have repelled those Catholics still reading the *Star*. The paper even found it necessary to run a denial of the rumor that Greg was a Catholic.

According to the *Star* reporter Frank Chamberlain, Pierre van Paassen was the innocent cause of other firings at the *Star*. Chamberlain referred to the event as Van Paassen's "Last Supper."

On Van Paassen's first visit to Toronto after joining the *Star*, Chamberlain was asked to buy a keg of beer and organize a party at the apartment of reporter Eric Gibbs over the Ward-Price auction rooms on College Street. Among those present were reporters Art Wells, Keith Munro, Claude Pascoe, sportswriter Alexandrine Gibb, Tim Reid, columnist Claire Wallace, *Maclean's* magazine writer Eric Hutton and Rhodes scholar Hugh Whitney Morrison. "It was a successful party," said Chamberlain later. "We were all dazzled by our famous foreign correspondent and sat around on the floor listening to his stories. The beer slowly disappeared. Nobody became drunk. At midnight the party quietly broke up and I drove Van Paassen back to the King Edward."

The next day, all hell broke loose at the *Star*. One by one, the partygoers were summoned by managing editor Vernon Knowles. According to Mr. Hindmarsh, the quiet party had actually been "a drunken orgy with reporters sprawled on the floor dead drunk." This report had been phoned in to Atkinson in the middle of the night by the father of one of the women at the party. Tim Reid was fired on the spot. Frank Chamberlain was fired on the spot. All efforts to describe the actual event were brushed aside.

An exasperated Eric Gibbs shouted, "What the hell is it to the *Star* if my apartment had been afloat in beer and we were all

doing the Australian crawl across the carpet?" Gibbs was fired—
and went on to become *Time* correspondent in London and Paris.

Frank Chamberlain's dismissal was not immediately enforced,
apparently because a replacement wasn't available for his work
on the *Star* Santa Claus fund. Later, when he resigned on his
own, news editor John B. Drylie said, "I'm glad you're going,
Frank. I was told to make it so rough for you, you'd quit." Orgy
organizer Chamberlain went on to become publicist for the
United Church, the Y.M.C.A., the Boy Scouts and the Temperance Federation.

In my relentless pursuit of these *Star* legends, I tracked down
the reporter who had caused this uproar. True, he had taken a
girl home from the party and made love to her on her parents'
chesterfield. Confronted by her parents, the girl confessed and
blamed her fall from grace on the beer at the Van Paassen party.
"The truth of the matter," said my informant, "is that I'd been
banging her on that chesterfield for months. But I didn't think it
was the kind of defense that would go over well with Holy Joe
Atkinson."

Sometimes people got fired but just kept on working anyway.
Morley Callaghan and Gordon Sinclair belonged to this group.
Morley wrote the story of a lake boat crashing into a Toronto
breakwater. The harbor master moved red pins around on his
map for Morley, showing how much the boat was off course.
Shortly after the story appeared, Hindmarsh received a curt note
from Atkinson. The harbor master was a friend of his. He would
never have volunteered information that the boat was off course.
That would be determined properly by a commission investigating
the accident. There was to be a retraction and an apology.

Callaghan was indignant. He hurried into Hindmarsh's office
and said, "An apology is ridiculous."

Hindmarsh glared at him. "Don't tell me what is ridiculous,"
he said furiously. "The harbor master says he said no such thing
to you."

Callaghan started out the door. "I'm going right down to his
office. I'll tell him how he moved those pins around—"

"You'll do no such thing!" roared Hindmarsh. "You'll do what
you're told, do you hear? Now you think you're running this
paper!"

Callaghan said, "You're wrong, Mr. Hindmarsh."

Hindmarsh got red in the face. "Again you tell me I'm wrong. In my own office you keep telling me I'm wrong. Get out of this office. You're fired!"

Callaghan had already been fired once before, for not crying out a cheerful "Good morning, Mr. Hindmarsh!" when the latter appeared each day. Morley survived his "firings" because Hindmarsh saw him as a university man he wished to keep, if he could be broken of his prima donna ways.

Gordon Sinclair, a colorful feature writer who wandered the world for the *Star,* said he was fired several times. Sometimes he would be sentenced to such ignominious tasks as making up the women's page. Sinclair was no prima donna. The punishments simply rolled off his back.

The economy waves were frequently blamed on Hindmarsh's habit of overspending on disaster stories. One such massive team effort was the Moose River mine disaster of 1936—in which three men were entombed in a collapsed gold mine in Nova Scotia. It became a story of incredible suspense as teams of miners and drillers worked to free them over an eleven-day period. Greg Clark, Fred Griffin and a *Star* flying squad of reporters and photographers worked day and night for days on end. As a postscript, famed *Star* photographer Fred Davis crawled down into the condemned mine to take flash photos of the narrow tunnel where the men had been trapped.

It was estimated that the *Star* spent $25,000 on this journalistic saga—and the aftermath was in the Hindmarsh tradition. According to Frank Chamberlain, six reporters were fired and six more had their salaries cut back from $60 to $50 a week.

Hindmarsh was responsible for these spending sprees. As managing editor, he might have done more to protect his men from the resulting economy waves.

Pierre Berton wrote a profile of Harry Comfort Hindmarsh for *Maclean's* magazine in 1952. At about the same time he was commissioned—paid $600—by the *Star* to write the official Hindmarsh obituary. This was held by the *Star* until Hindmarsh died, when it appeared under the head, GREATEST NEWSPAPER-MAN IN CANADA, IS TRIBUTE OF ALL WHO KNEW HIM. While Berton wrote with some balance, he did refer to Hindmarsh as much-misunderstood, as a kind of newspaper genius, a fearless editor, a man with a razor-sharp mind, a man of countless kindnesses to his employees.

I have never known Pierre to be wrong in his opinions, but there are other opinions about Hindmarsh. At one time Frank Chamberlain's desk was near that of Hindmarsh in the newsroom. Chamberlain overheard countless calls that Hindmarsh received from Atkinson. All Hindmarsh said was, "Yes, Mr. Atkinson. I'll see to that. Yes, Mr. Atkinson. Right away, Mr. Atkinson. Yes, Mr. Atkinson."

These calls seemed to substantiate the opinion that Hemingway carried away from the *Star*. He once planned to write a novel about Hindmarsh. He had a simple title for it: "The Son-in-law."

26

I know of nothing as instantly pleasurable as the sight of the bulge and boil of a trout rising to a fly, with the immediate consequence of the curiously sensuous tug on the rod tip.

—*Greg Clark*

Someone once observed that a man had to be lucky with wars. There were usually two in his lifetime. If he were lucky he was born too late for the first one and too soon for the second one.

Greg was not lucky this way, but he was a lucky, happy man in between his two wars. He enjoyed good health. His work was going well. And he found a way to escape back to the world of nature, which had been such a large part of his youth.

He discovered fishing.

His first memory of fishing was sitting in a boat with his father at the mouth of Duffin's Creek near Pickering on Lake Ontario and catching perch with worms. Next were images of rowing a boat at Go Home while his father trolled with a long bamboo rod, the silver arc of a muskie leaping in the sunshine, his father up to his waist in water while working a fighting bass up onto the shoreline rocks.

His father also took him on fishing trips to Algonquin Park and to Georgian Bay streams he himself had fished as a boy. In those days, he told Greg, the fish were counted only in dozens and carried home in tubs.

Up until 1922 Greg enjoyed bait fishing and trolling as one of the minor pleasures of being outdoors. But in that year, by accident, he happened on the wonderful world of fly fishing. For the next twenty years, his calendar year would begin with the opening of the trout season on May 1. Fishing of one kind or another would occupy him and his pals throughout the summer and fall until the ice threatened to lock them in at Go Home Bay. The winters were spent in buying books about fishing, testing new equipment, reading catalogs and acquiring new flies from the great sporting-goods stores in New York and London.

His collection of plugs and flies and line and reels kept outgrowing his tackle boxes. "At last!" wrote Greg one Christmas. "I've been given a tackle box that should last me for life! It's as big as a dog kennel!" Jimmie Frise decorated the box with a caricature of Greg.

Within fifteen years Greg had managed to collect nearly two hundred books on fishing. These included Lanman's *Adventures of an Angler in Canada,* Henshall's *Book of the Black Bass,* Louis Rhead's *The Speckled Brook Trout,* Roosevelt's *Game Fish of the North,* Richard Nettle's *Salmon Fisheries of the St. Lawrence,* Thompson's *Reminiscences of a Canadian Pioneer,* J. M. LeMoine's *Les Pêcheries du Canada,* and scores of other rare books. Greg did not try to collect everything on English and American fishing, but was aiming at a complete collection of Piscatoria Canadiana and felt he needed only another half dozen volumes to complete his collection of Canadian classics.

Among the few he still hadn't found were Volume II of Frederic Tolfrey's *Sportsman in Canada* and Mary Orvis Marbury's *Favourite Flies,* although he felt the latter was perhaps rather modern for his collection.

In the mid-Twenties Greg and John Mossop, a Toronto tackle dealer, did the spadework for the founding of the Toronto Anglers' Association, along with George Warburton, Walter Davison and others. Greg stayed out of the organizational work, but he stirred up interest in the group by stories in the *Star* and other publications.

As a result he was awarded the Number One membership card. When it later became the Ontario Federation of Hunters and Anglers he received an Honorary Life Membership in that organization. In this period his personal writing ambitions were laid aside, but he did write the text for *Game Fishes of Canada,* a book published by the Canadian Pacific Railway Company.

From 1923 to 1926 he and a small group of friends had enjoyed fishing the Mad River at Singhampton, not far from Collingwood, Ontario. In 1926 they leased a stretch of the Mad running north from Singhampton through the farm of a man named Neff. For the next ten years Greg opened the trout season there on May 1 and fished dozens of other streams and lakes throughout the year. His father was a member of a fishing club on the Beaver River in the Cuckoo Valley.

Briefly Greg was a member of the Bourbonnais-Kianicka Club, north of Duhamel in Quebec. The club had a number of birch-bark canoes made in the Indian pattern and Greg ordered a four-teen-footer from their supplier for use at Go Home.

Because of his wide reading and restless curiosity Greg soon became deeply involved in the theory and use of trout flies. European trout were surface feeders and the English flies developed to attract them resembled winged insects. These were largely the kind of flies imported for use by Canadian fly fishermen. Greg felt that Canadian trout were also bottom feeders and would be taken equally well, or better, on flies that resembled the larvae or nymph insect stage.

Greg took some flies made of deer hair and trimmed the hackle, wings and tail until it resembled a nymph. One opening day Greg took eighteen trout with the new fly. He found that it worked well early or late in the trout season and in almost any type of water. Greg named it the deer-hair nymph and his friend John Mossop, the tackle dealer, made them up and sold them by the hundreds.

Greg was a competitive fisherman, recording all fish caught, their size or weight, the number caught by others in the party, and the type of fly. During his heyday as a fisherman, while the children were very young, he was rarely at home on weekends. One summer he noted, somewhat uncomfortably, that he had spent only one Sunday at home throughout the fishing season.

And what a fishing season he observed, from dawn on opening day to the last legal minute at the end of the season. Opening day and every weekend through May were spent on the Mad River with his fishing club companions. The Mad didn't boil with fish as it had a generation earlier, but in seven days fishing there one May, Greg took 42 trout, all but 4 on his own deer-hair nymph.

That same summer included three outings to trout ponds owned by friends and a visit to French River in search of muskie and pickerel, where Greg caught one of each; the muskie weighed 25 pounds. There were invitations to three other private fishing clubs, return trips to the Mad River, and special outings to

Burleigh Falls and Fenelon Falls. This particular season ended with Greg and his friend Billy Milne using bass tackle to catch lake trout at Lion's Head on the Bruce peninsula for the last three days in October.

Helen and the children spent most of the summer at her family's cottage in Muskoka, but they joined Greg for his two-week vacation at Go Home. Here he spent more time with the children, but managed to land 30 small-mouth bass, 35 large-mouth bass, 15 pickerel and 25 pike.

Go Home was still rich with fish. Greg and Billy Milne camped there for six days one summer and caught a total of 117 fish. For Greg the sport was not in killing fish, but in the skill of angling. Of that record 117 catch, 110 were released back into the water. Seven were kept and given away. On that particular trip they didn't eat a single fish.

More so than his companions, Greg was always alive to every facet of the outdoors—the appearance of wildflowers and plants, the songs of the varieties of birds. Along the edges of the lakes where bass lurked, he studied how the dense bayberry bush rooted in the mud and water, and noted the delicate perfume when he crushed its leaves between his fingers. Its companion, the button-bush, he knew from its white flower-ball. Attracted by a bright red carpet of winterberries, which he could not identify, he made notes to take home.

He described himself as only a casual bird watcher, but his life list was already a long one. He knew the 55 species of warbler in North America, and also knew that he was likely to see only 24 of them. He had already seen 11 of those.

His eyes and his one good ear were always tuned to nature and he delighted in discovering the unusual. A groundhog, of all things, at the top of an eighteen-foot sapling. A nighthawk nesting within fifty feet of a whippoorwill's nest. One day he was mystified by a merganser duck nesting on the shoreline which did not fly away at his appearance. Later he paddled over to the spot and discovered a gull's nest with white gull's eggs in it and a third egg—a pale blue merganser egg! A trick of the cuckoo, yes. But a merganser? What would happen when it hatched?

The Mad River ran close by the village of Singhampton and there was a bridge over the river only a stone's throw from the old Singhampton hotel, where the members of Greg's fishing club stayed on weekends. Their lease began at the bridge. Greg regarded it as a "magic bridge" from the day he called a hermit thrush from the woods to light upon it. The bridge provided other "magic moments," such as the morning when Jimmie Frise and his wife materialized there from a heavy mist and the evening when a sudden boil and rise of trout broke the stillness of dusk.

Like Go Home Bay, the bridge was another magic gateway to the unending, changing universe. Along the Mad River, he would find the brush filled with Myrtle warblers, spot one Blackburnian and a Nashville. For the first time on the Mad, he would spot a ruby-crowned kinglet, with its loud, unmistakable song, and he would speculate as to whether it were nesting there or merely on migration. There were many bluebirds, of course, and sparrows: song sparrows, vesper sparrows, swamp sparrows, white-throated sparrows. Winter thrushes were to be seen, and a puzzling, sooty-gray bird, unrecognized until he heard its loud clacking cry—a female cowbird. Greg's one good ear provided full enjoyment of birdsongs and calls.

He did not often succeed in communicating this pleasure to other fishing friends, who were more interested in landing a fat trout or opening another beer on a sunny afternoon. To lifelong friend Billy Milne, an athlete and a soldier now turned lawyer, Greg tried to explain: "The rosebreasted grosbeak, Bill, sings like a robin that has studied at Milan."

"Where's the beer?" said Billy.

At Go Home Bay, during the summer holidays or hunting in the fall, Greg identified mourning warblers, prairie warblers and Parula warblers. There were scarlet tanagers, ospreys and even a bald eagle nesting on one of the islands. Like a musician, Greg seemed able to file away a bird's song, then bring it back on demand. During the winter he played birdsong records. One record involved the many varieties of thrush and Greg noted errors he had made in their songs.

I have been making the mistake of crediting the Veery with both the Veery and the Olive-backed song. Now I am clear. The Veery is vehement, emphasis on the first beat of each phrase, and falling in the scale, not a melody.

The Olive-backed is the same reedy tone as the Veery, but rising steadily to a bursting rocket of notes, and more melodious.

The Wood Thrush ends each stanza in a contralto triplet—

lul-lul-lul! The Hermit is incomparable, fluting, trying one key after another, working up the scales.

After listening to one record, Greg noted, "Except for the chat, the cardinal and the mockingbird, I had all the other songs correct." He added, "Of course, I know many other songs not on the records."

Greg found chickadees easy to call. If one was in the woods, he could bring it to his hand or the tip of his fishing rod, to the amazement of fishermen who did not know the bird. Other birds took more time and patience, but Greg could bring in the whippoorwill, the hermit thrush, even the black-throated blue.

Greg took Helen on some fishing trips and she became an expert fly-caster, but no more than anyone else could she completely share his infatuation with the wilderness, especially birdcalls.

One day Greg became entranced with the presence of a white-throated warbler in the woods and began working it toward them. Helen waited patiently. When the bird showed itself, it proved to be a white-throated warbler, but its sequence of notes was one note different from the call Greg was using. Greg's second note was the high one, whereas the bird *began* on a high note.

"Hmmmm," said Helen dryly, "the bird's got it wrong."

Greg was put down, but laughed. "I suppose I'll never hear the end of that."

Greg's enthusiasms could lead him at times to appear insensitive or even cruel. At Singhampton there was an unfortunate deaf-mute known as Dummy Taylor. He communicated in finger language. Sitting in the hotel beverage room there, after a day on the Mad River, Greg bought the man a few beers. When Dummy asked Greg why he was doing it, Greg volunteered the message, also in sign language, that he was doing it because "the birds sing and you can't hear them."

On absorbing this message Dummy jumped up and went for Greg with tears in his eyes. He was restrained and friends explained that Greg had happened to touch a sensitive nerve. Dummy, when he drank, insisted he could hear the songs of the birds. Even so, it was a tactless remark and Greg reproached himself for it. Greg abhorred thoughtlessness and when he found it in himself he groaned in remorse.

In his notebook Greg described fishing as a form of worship.

All the religion I have left is best felt, best expressed, in that act of approaching the waters, that sense of leaning my whole being forward, as I come down the road from the hotel at Singhampton to the magical bridge; that sudden enfolding experience of peace as I climb the last fence back of the mill and set my feet reverently in the grass along the curving path.

I would like to believe that the priests of Isis, Diana, Venus, of Toledo or Canterbury, possessed a rapture of soul as intense and uprising as mine at that moment. Instead of graven images and arks of the convenant, I have the ever unexpected aspects of tree, cloud and stream; for chalices of gold and censers of ruby, I have wild birds, vessels of a more precious incense, more mystical liquor. My music is not ordained; but it is older. God doubtless did not detail the sound of wind in grass; I doubt if He did not leave to the water thrush the invention of its simple song; it was surely by harking to the song of the Hermit thrush that men invented music.

The golden years at Singhampton were to end unhappily. The eight members of the club had been paying an annual fee of $150, or less than $20 each. For this bargain price they had enjoyed hundreds of happy hours, but when the ten-year lease expired in 1936 and they went to renew it they learned that farmer Willis Neff had sold the farm, including the fishing rights, for $6,000. The ugly thing was that the purchaser was a man named Victor Goad, a man who had been their guest at the club and at one time had been invited to become a member. Goad knew the lease was coming up for renewal and he had secretly negotiated the purchase of the farm.

The members cursed Goad's perfidy and their own stupidity. With mortgage money available at 3 percent, they could have bought the farm themselves and carried a mortgage of $6,000 for only $180 a year—little more than the cost of the fishing rights. Farmer Neff could have had his capital and continued to live on the farm for free.

Homeless, the club disbanded and many friendships melted away. With the others, Greg was bitter for a time. Again, it might have happened for the best. He could never have given up the

Mad River and the magic bridge voluntarily—but perhaps the time had come to leave it.

While Greg had taken Helen and the boys there on occasion, the weekend gatherings at the hotel, accompanied by partying and drinking, had been exclusively for men. Now, for the first time, Greg could think about opening the trout season with his wife and family.

And yet it would be hard to forget the magic bridge. The original members of the Singhampton Club had been Frank Cooper, Dunc Herriott, Jimmie Frise, Ron Hart, Skipper Howard and Greg. Others, such as Greg's younger brother Arthur and Bumpy Lewis, had been alternate members or frequent guests. Greg would remember the different trout pools on the river for the rest of his life. Sing's Spring, the Spring Hole, the High Bend and the Low Bend. First-time guests at the club were always initiated at the Guest Pool. If they caught a trout here they were "in." If not, they were failures.

One famous guest was John Alden Knight, who originated the solunar tables followed by fishermen all over the continent. On the day he fished the Mad it was a hot, brassy summer day, not good for fishing. No one caught anything until Knight produced an unknown fly made up of red and yellow bucktail. With it Knight proceeded to catch 46 trout, a phenomenal figure even for the Mad.

Frank Cooper was employed at the sporting goods store of Larway, Temple and Cooper, a fishermen's hangout in Toronto. There, the next day, Greg learned of Knight's fabulous fly and watched Cooper making up copies of it. As dean of the club Greg insisted on being allowed to name the fly.

At first he christened it the Assassin. However, in the next few days he read about the death of Rudolf Valentino, allegedly killed by an unfriendly bartender who slipped Mickey Finns into his drinks. Greg switched the name of the new fly to the Mickey Finn and it became famous with fly fishermen under this name. The name of the original fly used by John Alden Knight was never determined, but Knight acknowledged Greg's part in providing an imaginative name for its successor.

The happy days that began at the magic bridge were now over, but Greg would never forget them. He wrote in his fishing journal: "There are only 70 May's and June's in a man's life and now 45 of mine are gone."

27

It is quite true that I have invented for myself a good many experiences which I never
really had. But they were all experiences
which belonged to me by right of temperament
and character. I should have had them, if I
had but had my rights. I was despoiled of them
by the rough tyranny of Circumstance.

—*Don Marquis, poet, playwright,
novelist, newspaperman*

Throughout his life Greg was asked if his stories were true. How
could so many funny things happen to one man?

Humor has frequently been analyzed and dissected, usually to
death, but it does often contain exaggeration and selection of one
kind or another. One of Stephen Leacock's funniest pieces was
called "My Financial Career." In it he bumbles around a bank,
trying to make a deposit, then flees with his money. Inasmuch as
Leacock was a professor of economics, it is unlikely anyone
asked him if this story were really true. In "The Treasurer's Report," Robert Benchley had fun with the idea of losing a locomo-
tive—but it's unlikely anyone ever asked him if he had actually
mislaid one.

Possibly people questioned Greg, because his humor was gentle, his stories of a kind that could happen to almost anyone, and
he wrote them as the unvarnished truth. He was not dealing in the
wild flights of fancy of a Wodehouse or a Perelman. Many
evolved from his personal experiences and everyday observations,
polished up, jiggled about and shaped to his market of the moment. One humorist he admired was Jerome K. Jerome, whose

Three Men in a Boat (Not to Mention the Dog) he had read just
before World War I.

Rarely did Greg jot down ideas and then deliberately develop
them into a story. To a remarkable degree he could visualize his
stories before he ever sat down to the typewriter. He did often try
them out on his friends in conversation, for first and last he was a
storyteller. He loved an audience. Many thought he told stories
better than he wrote them. When he got to the typewriter he could
rattle off a story from beginning to end without stopping, much to
the exasperation of his colleagues.

He passed this off with his usual self-deprecation. "I see a man
getting up on a Sunday morning. He picks up a piece of the Saturday paper and heads for the bathroom. So that's the length of
my stories. Just the length of a good shit."

Oddly enough, there is one story, his most famous story, which
can be tracked down to an idea in his notebooks. The story came
to be known as "The Jade Green Monster." Greg told this yarn
hundreds of times, to service clubs, at meetings of editors and
publishers, in auditoriums and smoke-filled rooms and over
campfires. It was chosen as one of the great fish stories of all time
by the Ananias Committee of the Soo Hackle Club.

The incident that sparked Greg's imagination happened on October 15, 1930. Jim Frise and Greg, as was their custom, had
driven to Burleigh Falls to close the muskie season. They had
guides and fished from canoes. Greg had been wearing a black
sweater under his tweed jacket and, as the day was warm, he removed the sweater and placed it in the bottom of the canoe.

As Greg was reeling his bait in after a cast, a muskie grabbed
it, leaped over the gunwale and fell into the canoe. The gang
hooks caught in Greg's sweater as the fish thrashed around. When
the fish leaped out of the canoe, it was wearing Greg's sweater.

When the story appeared in Greg's first book of collected stories (*Which We Did*) it wasn't called "The Jade Green Monster."
It was called "A Sportsman Is One"—and here is what he made
of that afternoon with Jimmie Frise.

A SPORTSMAN IS ONE

by Gregory Clark

The true sportsman is one who not only will not show his own father where the best fishing hole is, but will deliberately direct him
to the wrong one.

Sportsmen, it seems to me, are the last remaining receptacles of
the true human spirit. The natural man, the man who survived
through countless aeons of tribulation such as the Ice Age and
sundry plagues of smallpox, not to mention prophets priests and
kings, must have been a sportsman; by which I mean a creature
given to hunting, fishing, carousing, chasing and loafing. The only
survivals of that natural man in this final era of the decline of the
human species, are the sportsmen. Sure, it's the decline. We show
all the vices common to decline, like horses gnawing their stable
timber or cattle eating bones. And what a lot of nasty gnawing is
going on all over the world nowadays, as with every utterance,
philosophic, social, governmental, the nature of man is being
blasphemed.

We are multiplying enormously, which is another symptom of
decline. When nature grows sick of a species, as she did of the
passenger pigeon or the dinosaur or any of the things we find in
the limestone, she multiplies them incredibly, as if in a last vain
hope. Then the plague takes them. A plague does not work up
much virulence on a lone hermit. But it goes big in crowded London. In terror, the survivors huddle together. But the engendered
plague germs are so many, so strong, that even the sportsmen
among the dinosaurs and passenger pigeons are wiped out to the
last one.

Not that I am fond of sportsmen. Every time I see in my morning paper the one column cut of the gent in a derby hat and a

cold cheesy face with the lines "Well Known Sportsman Passes,"
I know at once that the gent was one of those who never attended
a race or other sporting event except on a free pass, and never bet
on a horse until the owner had tipped him off that the race was a
benefit for the jockeys. I hold no brief for sportsmen. I think they
are the craftiest, most self-seeking, most devious, most nefariously
ingenious of men. But I believe them to be the natural man. And
I prefer their company to all other.

This story of the maskinonge that undressed me has little to do
with the above sentiments except to reveal, in some mystical way
even I do not understand, though I tell it, the deeper nature of
sportsmen.

The middle of October is the legal closing in Ontario of the
maskinonge season. I do not deny that certain sportsmen, notably
Indians and native sons, continue to take this king of freshwater
fishes all through the year both by sporting methods as well as by
spears, nets, pitchforks and dynamite. But those of us who, by
reason of the vices aforementioned such as conscience or social
sense or lack of opportunity, are bound by the law, regard the
maskinonge fishing of mid October to be the most royal angling
of the whole year, befitting the close of all fishing; a sort of Wag-
nerian fourth act upon which the curtain falls, the theatre of our
sport is darkened, and we creep home to hang up our rods in a
cool dry closet.

In mid October, the shores of the rocky maskinonge lakes are
glorious with color. The days are short and full of vim. Hale
winds blow. The chill in the air wakes in our subconscious the
age old instinct to fare forth to slay and fill the cave with hams
and skins against the fated winter. Our blood sings.

And along the hard shores, amid the clefts of rocks, in the cold
shadow of sunken logs, that tiger of freshwater fish, that lithe jade
green lurker, compounded of steel springs and frenzy—the maskinonge—awaits us. Twenty, thirty pounds he goes, commonly.
Sixty pounds he goes in the Lake of the Woods; but that is
heaven and not for such as we. Eight, twelve, sixteen pounds he
really goes, for most of us who go plugging for him in the
tapestried aisle of mid October.

All summer long, the maskinonge have lain secret in the weed
beds scattered all over the lakes. But when the frost comes and
the weeds die and rot and fill the water with a stinking, the

muskies creep shoreward, towards the rocks and gravel beaches where the water is less fouled. There, in two, three, four feet of water, they wait until the sludge of vegetable death subsides and the waters clear. And there, along the shore, we, creeping in Indian paddled canoes and chucking our grotesque painted wooden plugs from our short, clever rods, find him.

Ah, he has no depths to sound. Under him, the rocky bottom. Beside him, rocks and shallows. There is but one element that beckons him. As he feels the sting of hooks, as he senses the dread snare of line challenging that liberty which to a fish must be all in all, he leaps. Not one of those pretty up and down, in and out leaps for which the bass is so justly famous. But a savage, mad, oblique, any-old way leap that will carry him sliding and skidding across the surface a distance of twenty feet. And shaking and fighting every foot of the way, he boils, leaps, jerks, furiously exerting every ounce of his steely energy in every possible direction at once.

And to him who holds the lithe rod to which all this fury is fastened, comes a great timidity; a great, weakly-smiling, pale-jawed sense of terror. It must be the contrasts of sport that addict us. The sudden explosion of the grouse amid the frosty calm. The bound of a deer after the long patient stalk. The savage boil of a muskie to break the rhythmic monotony of the cast, cast, cast. Oh, lovely spirit-jolting shock of sport.

Jimmie Frise, that insufferable and inescapable cartoonist to whom I have been linked by Fate in as happily a misspent life as falls to any man, was successfully commissaried by me to our favorite muskie water for the closing day of the season. It is quite a trick to get cartoonists anywhere. Their favorite condition is heels on the table, chez lui. But dawn of closing day rose dull and soft, and Jimmie and I joined forces with an American gentleman who was staying at the hotel, a muskie addict fifteen per cent. overproof, an elderly man by the name of Mr. Scholtz from Pittsburg who carried around seven hundred dollars' worth of rods and tackle; and his guide was Old Noah. Jim's guide was Abe, as usual. Mine was Scotty Hoggarth, a Caledonian from Peebles who was married to an Indian and who was equally fluent in the Scottish and the Ojibwa.

Scotty is perhaps the greatest guide in the world. Both of us think so. As we creep silently along the shore, forty feet out, with nary a sip from the paddle as Scotty handles it, and nary a scrape or a dunt from boot of me, Scotty looks at a spot on the edge of the shore, and so great is his art, I place my lure exactly in the spot he was looking at.

"It's a forrrm of mesmerism," explains Scotty, whenever we marvel at this wonder. "I stare at the spot. It is, obviously, the best spot. I stare and stare. And then you cast, sputt, square into that verra spot. It's een-credible. No wonder we get so many fush."

And this soft, dull October day, with the shores like a faded old Paisley shawl for color, and a fitful little wind ruffling the water amid the rocky islands and channels, Scotty and I had the luck. The three canoes of us proceeded in follow-my-leader order, Mr. Scholtz first, with Old Noah humped darkly over the paddle and Mr. Scholtz with his beautiful tackle and clever forearm, casting three times a minute, smoothly, rhythmically; fifty yards behind him, covering the same water, I with Scotty; fifty yards behind me, Jimmie and Abe, in a deep Ojibwa silence.

Scotty and I are vocal anglers. We chat. We exclaim and we debate. We tell long tales and wonders. Whiles, we exhort the fish. We dare them to come on. Give us a Chance, we defy them. Scare the both of us.

And forty minutes after starting, our exhortations had the desired effect when a ten-pounder met my plug almost before it touched the water. In a rush like a rugby player getting under the ball, the muskie plunged and met the red and white lure. I struck back. The muskie came straight for the canoe, plunging, slashing, insane. And for ten blazing minutes, I was back where all men belong—about ten thousand, twenty thousand years. Back of all piety and deceit, back of all that veneer the first year psychology students speak of. Veneer, what an ugly, lucid word.

And in due time, the fury passes; the muskie, heavy, fain, is drawn alongside by weak wrists and thumping pulses; and Scotty, very still, very tartany of face and broadswordish of expression, makes a clean sweeping draw with the cleek, as he calls my telescopic gaff hook, and hauls the thudding monster inboard.

Of course Scholtz and Jimmie have ceased fire to watch the battle. That is the etiquette of fishing in parade. And they come alongside to admire the jade beastie and, if I mistake not, to christen it.

*   *   *   *   *

Now, in this lovely October morning, I was clad in garments that are of importance to the tale. I wore plus fours and jacket of a bright rusty red Harris tweed. And under the jacket, contrasting with it so sharply that all men would remember it, a yellow sweater with sleeves.

With sleeves.

Within another half hour, as the result of our continued incantations, another and a bigger muskie boiled savagely to my lure, and Jimmie and Scholtz had the pleasure of suspending activities while, with triumphant cries and tumult of victory, Scotty cleeked for me a thirteen-pounder. We all adjourned for lunch on a rocky point, where the guides gralloched and quartered and cooked my ten-pounder for luncheon. I was, by luncheon end, something of a pain to both my good companions, neither of whom all morning had so much as seen a swirl. And Scotty, I have no doubt, was something duodenal to Old Noah and Abe, as they finished up what was left of leviathan.

At any rate, through narrowed eyes, Scholtz and Jimmie must have had a good look at me as I stood forth on the rocks, in my red tweed and bright yellow sweater, informing them:

"I now have my limit of two muskies. But for the afternoon, gentlemen, I shall keep my position between you, and cast for bass. If any muskie is so disrespectful of the law as wilfully to attack my lure, I can do no more than release him, after he is subdued."

And we embarked, and set forth, full fed, in the hazy afternoon, along lovelier Paisley shawl shores than ever, I contemplating the good humor of God who should not only create small cocky men, but on top of that should permit them to catch the muskies. And my two friends extended their intervals to seventy-five yards either side of me.

Within twenty minutes of starting, I rose, hooked, hand-landed and set free a muskie of seven pounds. Less than a half hour later, I rose and dittoed another of about six pounds. By this time, I was conscious of the almost steady regard of my two friends. They would take their eyes off me long enough to make their cast. Then, as they reeled in, they would turn their heads and stare balefully in my direction. Then look away long enough to select the next spot, and make the cast.

And Scotty and I, aware that this was one of the classic hours of our lives, were suiting the occasion with words and music. We thought up all manner of discussions as to the true characteristics of an angler. Of the psychic power the genuine angler has over fish. But it was not to hear our jibes that Scholtz and Jimmie turned their heads like automatons towards us, one ahead and one behind. It was to see us catch muskies.

It was mid afternoon, and I grew warm. I laid down my rod. Whipped off my jacket. Skinned off my yellow sweater. Tossed it behind me onto the lunch basket. Donned my red tweed jacket. Resumed casting.

The angels who accompany anglers so devised it that the twenty seconds I was engaged in this simple act, both Scholtz and Jimmie were casting and had their heads turned from me and did not see me take off my vivid sweater. Nor was I aware that they had not seen me.

I cast. I felt weeds touch my lure. I reeled in, sitting forward to observe my lure and see if it had caught weeds. I reeled the bright bauble near, drew it alongside, peering down at it.

From below, like a javelin flung vertically up by the devils that inhabit the deep, a muskie rushed.

In a splitting leap, he took my lure from under my face and came like a lightning bolt upward. I flung myself sideways, the muskie slithered against my left shoulder and fell behind me on to the lunch basket. The hooks of my lure entangled in the sweater. With a convulsive leap, the eleven-pounder, all steel bows, flung himself into the air behind my cringing head. And at that very instant, I, recovering my voice, whooped.

Scholtz and Jimmie, just finishing their casts, turned. They beheld, clear, unmistakeable, irrefutable, a handsome muskie in the air above my shoulders, shaking on his fierce snout, my yellow sweater.

"My Goad, man," moaned Scotty, as he watched me recover my senses slowly, and start to fight the impeded muskie.

"Save my sweater," I begged.

"Save the fush," begged Scotty. "It will never be believed. Never in ten thousand years. It's a miracle."

A very brief struggle, and the poor muskie, swaddled in my soaking sweater, was hauled alongside and Scotty lifted it by the gills. And held it, sweater and all, aloft.

And then we saw Scholtz and Jimmie.

They had quit fishing. They had laid their rods in the bows. Their dark guides, Old Noah and Abe, were paddling, crouched and incredulous, towards us. But not so incredulous as their bosses. Scholtz was gripping the sides of the canoe, white and wide eyed. Jimmie was sitting forward, showing his teeth in a brave derisive grin. But there was a mild panic in his face.

"Mon," I heard Scotty behind me, "mon, keep your heid. They think the fish took your sweater off ye. Whush, now."

The two canoes approached, cautiously, and eight eyes stared blankly at the fish, the sweater, Scotty and me.

Scholtz came alongside and put one leg into my canoe to hold us. Jim came alongside and did likewise. The silence was broken only by heavy breathing.

"Gosh," I said, "I reeled alongside to see if I had a weed on. He came straight from below. With that plug all bristling with hooks, he came straight for my face. I was like in a trance. I couldn't move. If he had ever hit me in the face with that plug he'd have torn my face off."

I breathed heavily.

They all cleared their throats.

"Look at the slime on my shoulder," I said, turning to exhibit, in fact, the smear of slime he had left all over my jacket lapel.

"Mon," said Scotty, in a tone full of hidden meaning, "you're in luck today."

"It's the nearest thing I ever had happen," I said, shakily.

Scholtz was the first.

"How," he said hollowly, "did he get your sweater off?"

"Eh?" I said, looking around as if that little detail had escaped me up to the moment. "Oh, I guess the hooks must have caught. I just felt a swipe, and the sweater went over my head."

"But," said Scholtz, who now had the sodden sweater in his hand to see that it was not torn, "it couldn't."

"What's that?" I asked, a little startled.

"I say it couldn't," said Scholtz heatedly. "It simply couldn't take this sleeved sweater off, without removing your jacket."

"Alright," I said, agreeably, "it didn't then."

"But," said Scholtz, "my God, I saw it."

I turned to Scotty and eagerly instructed him to dig the spring scales out of the tackle box and weigh the fish before he let it go. He still had it by the ears, having disentangled the sweater.

I heard Old Noah speak briefly to Abe in Ojibwa. I caught Scotty's eye fleetingly.

"Greg," said Jimmie, with a nice little laugh as between friends, "tell us how it did it?"

"Jim," I said, humbly, "all I know is, I saw the fish coming. I sort of hung in space for a second, unable to move. Then I leaned backwards. It struck me on the chest. I felt a swipe. It was all so instantaneous. Just a kind of swipe, and the next thing I see, is that muskie in the water with my sweater on his snout."

Scholtz looked at Jimmie. Jimmie looked at Scholtz.

"I saw it," said Jim, in a thin voice. "I saw the damn thing rip it right over his head."

"I heard him yell," agreed Scholtz. "And just as I looked, I saw the fish yank the sweater off him."

"But," said Jim, "it's impossible."

"Yes," said Scholtz. "Take a look at it. The sweater isn't torn or ripped in any way."

"Personally," I said, "I'm going ashore for a rest. Come on, Scotty; chuck the fish in and run me ashore."

"Eleven pounds," sang out Scotty, lowering the muskie into the water and picking up his paddle.

Scholtz and Jimmie followed.

"Mon," said Scotty, quietly, "how are we daein'?"

"We'll have them nuts in a few minutes," I replied.

*　　　*　　　*　　　*　　　*

We all piled ashore. My first concern was my sweater. Scotty and I wrung it out and spread it to dry. Jimmie and Scholtz were engaged in sotto voce conversation down by the canoes. I saw Scholtz slowly and carefully going through the motions of pulling off an imaginary sweater without taking his coat off. Then he shook his head.

I saw Jim eagerly going through the same motions, only swiftly.

"I've seen magicians," said Jim, "take a man's vest off without removing the coat. They did it quickly. Maybe if you do it quickly, it can be done."

"Don't be an ass," cried Scholtz, loudly. "It can't be done, any way."

"If you didn't see it," said Jim, "I'm ready to say I didn't see it."

"But," groaned Scholtz in agony, "I did see it. That's the hell of it. I saw it yank it right off him. And it isn't torn."

"Boys," I called, "why worry? It's over. I might have had those hooks in my cheek and an eleven-pound wildcat tearing the face off me. Let's forget it."

"Forget it?" said Scholtz, coming up the rocks. "He says, forget it."

"Yes, I say forget it," I said, a little heatedly. "I don't claim anything. I don't ask you to believe it. If it is going to ruin our last holiday, I say forget it."

Jim came up and put his hands on my shoulders.

"Listen, Greg," he said earnestly. "The thing is absurd. There is something funny about this. Tell us. How did it do it?"

"Listen, Jim, suppose I tell you it didn't do it?" I demanded coldly.

"But it did," said Jim.

"I say it didn't, so let the matter drop," I said tensely. "Let the whole thing drop."

"Gentlemen," said Scotty, who was eager to be in on this marvel, "I saw it happen right before my eyes. How it happened, the Lord only knows. But I agree with Mr. Clark. I say, let the whole matter drop."

Scholtz glared angrily at us. We glared angrily back. Jimmie laughed uneasily, and it was now four o'clock of an October afternoon and a chill was coming into the air. A loon yelled weirdly in the distance. Old Noah and Abe stood speechlessly below us, leaning on their paddles, their patient old faces full of bewilderment.

"Come on, Scotty," I said quietly.

And in silence we all got back into our canoes and pushed off and continued up the shore for three quarters of an hour, with never another rise from the darkling water, and the wind grew, and the chill; and that creeping dusk of October moved up on us, and suddenly Scholtz called—

"How about the hotel?"

And soon, three canoes were striding across the open for the hotel, rods furled, anglers cuddled down, guides bending and shunting in the short Ojibwa paddle stroke.

Scotty and I went directly to my room for the usual amenities. Jimmie and Scholtz went straight in by the log fire-place and boldly and without preamble stated their case to the half dozen others, mostly Americans (they know about this October fishing); and soon Scotty and I, with our door open, could hear the gales of laughter and the incredulous shouts, and above it all, the insistent, protesting, declaiming voices of Scholtz and Jimmie.

Up the stairs came a stumble of many feet, and all the Americans swarmed in to behold the victim of the miracle. A quiet, unassuming little man, I was; reserved, aloof in the best British tradition. I had little to say. Nothing to add. It was obvious I did not wish to discuss the matter.

"I'll make an affidavit," shouted Scholtz, "that I saw it."

He was getting more than angry. There was bigotry in his tone.

"Me too," confessed Jim doggedly.

"Come down," said one of the leatheriest of the Americans. "I'm an attorney. I can draw an affidavit. You can get it properly sworn by a Canadian."

Downstairs they all stamped, laughing, damning; and Scotty and I continued the amenities.

And so it came about that I possess two affidavits declaring before God that a maskinonge removed from my person a yellow sweater with sleeves, said sweater being under my coat, and removed without the coat being removed, or the sweater being torn or damaged in any respect.

And on the affidavits being duly sworn and delivered into my keeping, Scotty and I came clean before the assembled brethren in front of the log fire-place.

And the amenities were general.

28 _____

We are all descendants of successful hunters.
                                              —*Greg Clark*

At the height of Greg's fishing enthusiasm, his father, Joseph Clark, remarked dryly, "It looks as if your career, unique at university, gratifying in your return to journalism, were likely to peter out in some damn frogpond in the country." It was June, and Greg had just toted up his first catch since the opening on May 1: 121 trout, most of them taken on the deer-hair fly he had created—a few on the Black Plamer, Soleskin, Royal Coachman or J. W. Dunne flies.

Few men were ever more conscious than Greg of a man's golden years and the speed with which they would slip past. And few, especially during the Depression Thirties, were better able to take advantage of them.

At the *Star Weekly,* Hindmarsh had gotten rid of Cranston and was remaking the paper in his own image, but Greg was still comparatively safe, because of the relationship of the Clarks with Holy Joe Atkinson, and the popularity of the Jim and Greg feature.

Greg now had his weekly Greg and Jim story down to a science. He and Jimmie could take off for a day's duck shooting at Lake Scugog, fishing at the Mad River, or even a day at the races, a weakness of Jimmie's, and turn it into a story. In fact, Greg could have done the story without leaving the office, but what man in his senses would be guilty of such folly?

During the Depression their salaries rose from around $4,000 a year to close to $10,000—not grandiose in view of their contributions to the paper's success, but good money for those years.

While both were soft touches for panhandlers and hard-luck stories, they had different ways of keeping themselves broke. Jimmie was a compulsive gambler and his disposable income disappeared on the tables, at the track or with bookmakers. Greg spent his money before he got it—on fishing and hunting equipment. He couldn't resist a store window or the magic catalogs from L. L. Bean, Abercrombie & Fitch, Hardy's, Farlow's or Forrest's in London. His collection grew to nineteen fly rods, five bait-casting rods, tackle boxes filled with plugs, spinners, reels, gaffs, some three thousand flies, not to mention the jackets, vests, boots, knapsacks, bandoliers, guns, ammunition, knives and dozens of other special items, stored both at home in Toronto and at the Go Home cottage, or his extraordinary collection of books on birds, flowers, fish and wildlife. There were also the beagle pups being raised for him on Vince Baker's farm at Claremont, for deer hunts and for rabbiting and field trials. For a man who lived for the opening of the trout season—and sometimes closed the fishing season at Go Home just before the cottage was locked in ice—he managed a good amount of hunting.

The annual deer hunt, of course, overlapped on the end of fishing, but there was hunting through most of the year. There were times for hares and rabbits, pheasants and ducks and for just ordinary plinking of squirrels, crows and groundhogs.

The groundhogs, or "grunts," as Greg and his friends called them, were the farmer's pest; the country roads leading from the city afforded ample opportunities to shoot them. On some fishing weekends, Greg and his friends frequently shot twenty, thirty, sometimes over forty.

He was awestruck on his first hunting trip to Pelee Island for pheasant. "It was a blizzard of pheasants," he said. "Even the greatest estates in England could not have shown such numbers of birds." Back in 1924, twelve pairs of pheasants had been released on the island by Ohio sportsmen. Greg estimated that there were now at least fifty thousand birds on the eleven-thousand-acre island.

His brother Arthur and his friend Dr. Alan Secord, the veterinarian, were in a separate party and got sixteen birds between them. A good rifleman, Greg was not particularly good with a shotgun, as he felt he had trouble sensing the shot dispersion and lead. However, he bagged four cock pheasants. The party of D. J. Taylor, then deputy minister of game and fisheries, got more than fifty birds in one morning's shoot. "If they had been taking hens," said Greg, "they might have had five hundred."

Greg's wife, Helen, under Greg's insistent tutelage, had become a good flycaster, and now was becoming a good shot with rifle and shotgun. In 1935, when they were guests of the deputy minister, Helen bagged three pheasants and Greg eight. They stayed at a local farmhouse on the mainland, enjoyed heaping meals of country food and were ferried back and forth to Pelee in the government fisheries patrol boat. It was a wonderful highlight of their outings together. Others in the party added to their bag and Helen and Greg returned home with a wicker basket filled with twenty birds.

Greg's enthusiasm was not dampened by near-accidents or even real tragedies. One of his longtime friends and fishing companions, Ron Hart, out alone with his dog, apparently killed himself in the late 1930s by the accidental discharge of his shotgun, which he had leaned against a fence he was climbing.

Greg's oldest boy, Murray, whom the family called "Baba," was now coming along on fishing and hunting parties. Once he nearly shot Greg. On a rabbit-hunting expedition, Murray took three shots with his .22 rifle at a bounding hare. All missed. As the group continued, another shot came from Murray's rifle; this bullet missed Greg by a few feet. Murray stammered out the classic, "I didn't know it was loaded!" Greg took the matter calmly. Murray was already his favorite.

He recorded the incident in his notebook and wrote in the next paragraph, "I am getting him a .410 for Christmas." The .410 shotgun nearly led to Murray's own death.

On a two-day pheasant shoot near Brampton with Greg, Helen and Skipper Howard, they flushed a few birds in the morning but got no shots. The three adults headed for their car for lunch. Murray trailed them, coming across a farm field. On the far side of the field a party of Brampton men appeared and flushed a jackrabbit. As it bounded over the crest of the field, one of the hunters banged away.

Murray, just over the crest, was in the line of fire. He was hit by a hail of shot and went down, yelling, "Dad!" The other hunters reached him first. Three pellets were sunk into the walnut gun butt of the .410; nine others were in Murray—his hand, leg, shoulder, head and face. They drove him to Toronto General, where the shot was located and dug out with the help of X rays, and Murray was given anti-tetanus serum.

Greg noted the events in his notebook, observing that "no hunter should ever fire at game on a crest." He then went on, "As a result of this, Helen stayed home next day and Skipper Howard and I had to go out alone for the second day of the shoot." No soldier, Helen.

Greg fondly described her years of fishing and hunting as playing the role of "good companion." In all the years of sitting on deer runs while the dogs ran, she had never really expected to be confronted with a deer.

When it finally happened, at Go Home, she had the traditional buck fever. Taking trembling aim, she found she could see nothing past the end of the gun. She had to clear a muddied peep sight. The deer did not go down at her first shot, and the gun jammed. She cleared it and got off three more shots as the deer bounded past her and white-flagged away.

A few minutes later they found the doe, down and dying, not far away in the woods. Greg was delighted and proud that, of Helen's four shots, three had found the mark, but for Helen, that was enough deer hunting.

Murray lived to become a crack shot with both shotgun and rifle. On his very first deer hunt at Go Home, he brought down a huge buck with one shot, straight through the heart, at close to a hundred yards distance. He was then seventeen.

Throughout these busy years, Greg was slowly changing. No one with his curiosity and imagination could spend so much time outdoors without observing the changes coming over the land. Greg, like other hunters and fishermen, was among the first to preach conservation. They did not then have precipitation collectors to study the effects of acid rain, nor were they full-time professors correlating the effects of nutrients and chemicals on fish spawning grounds, nor were they scientists making mathematical models of the effect of cottage encroachment on animal life—but Greg and his friends could see what was happening.

As early as 1926, Greg was writing about the disappearance of the native brook trout from Ontario streams. He reported on an experiment in New York State which favored planting of the European brown trout. They could flourish in warmer water and withstand more pollution.

As well as the *Star,* Greg had many other platforms. He was in demand for speeches to service clubs and before all kinds of groups and associations.

At the Kiwanis Club in Midland, Greg was introduced jocularly by the Honorable William Finlayson, Minister of Lands and Forests: "Greg is one of those fanatics who prevent sleep in government offices but who none the less do good by their extreme ideas." In his speech, Greg gave an example of his "extreme ideas."

"The government," said Greg, "is doing what they charge as a crime to anybody else in the province. They are paying dividends out of capital. Those hundred millions of tourist dollars that the government announces so proudly each year are not profit. They are dividends paid out of the capital of the wildlife of this province. And when all the fish are sold to the tourists the price will be reckoned far too cheap. In the end, we will have to pay back all those millions to try to recover the forests, the rivers and the animals and fish we have so cheerfully sold for a song."

At another meeting of anglers and hunters, Greg warned: "We sportsmen are like speculators sitting down to count our losses. Instead of realizing that the government, the lumber and pulp interests, the Hydro and the tourist traffic are bucketing out wildlife assets in a far more desperate way than the brokers have done in the market."

He railed loudly against the provincial government's granting of logging rights in Algonquin Park, set aside as a reminder of the once beautiful forests that clothed the province. "You see industrialism and tall chimneys making their triumphant march toward whatever destiny such things march toward," said Greg. "I see the forests falling, the wild things fleeing and dying, the bright streams turned to muddy sewers."

He saw the sale of all rights on the Nipigon to the Lake Sulphite Company as the final rape of a great river, and paid a final visit there with Helen and the two boys. He wrote: "It looks to me as if the government of Ontario is incapable of understanding in any degree whatever the value and terrible fragility of its wilderness assets. When they are gone, the government will wake up and spend millions vainly trying to restore what they wantonly wasted." Less than a year after the sale of the Nipigon Rights, he noted grimly, but without satisfaction, that the Lake

Sulphite Company had gone into liquidation in the worst smother of scandal, political and financial, that had arisen in years.

Greg lived to see many of his "extreme ideas" become the minimal ideas of all those concerned with our environment. His warnings have come true—with a vengeance. Greg did not visualize the poisoning of entire river systems by the deliberate dumping of toxic chemicals. Nor was he aware of the airborne acid rain which was bringing slow death to hundreds of Ontario lakes. He probably couldn't have visualized a government seemingly limited to issuing bulletins about which fish were poisonous to eat. However, he did become disenchanted at how little was being done and his own failure to make himself heard, in that time between wars.

29

SUNRISE, SUNSET

Joseph Thomas Clark died on Friday, July 23, 1937, in the cottage at Go Home Bay. He was in his seventy-second year but was still working at the *Star;* when he suffered his heart attack he was on his annual vacation. He had been attended by a doctor and put to bed at the cottage. Greg and his brother Joe had been summoned from Toronto. As their father lay dying, the two brothers sat on the veranda, sharing a bottle of scotch, aware that the end was probably near.

It was a beautiful summer evening. Moonlight rippled across the water. Fish splashed in the bay. Whippoorwills called from the woods. Greg's son Murray, now fifteen, was on the veranda, playing a game with Joe's son, Joe Clark III. The boys were of an age and good companions.

The two men talked for some time—in subdued tones, even though their father was asleep or unconscious. Suddenly a chance remark, perhaps even a joke, caused their old rivalry to flare up once again.

"All right," said Joe. "You may have knocked me about when I was small, but I sure gave it back to you later on."

"Is that so?" said Greg. His eyes narrowed and he rose slowly from his chair. He launched himself at Joe, his arms outstretched. Joe rose to meet him and in a moment the two grown men were wrestling about the porch, knocking over the wicker table and chairs. Their two sons looked on, bewildered and terrified.

They fell heavily to the floor, remained locked together for a moment, then one of them broke the tension with a laugh. They released each other, got back on their feet somewhat shamefacedly and began straightening up the furniture.

It was an incredible deathbed scene. Mercifully Joseph Clark did not waken or regain consciousness. The persistence in Greg of this jealousy, rivalry or whatever it was is hard to grasp. But it was a central part of his being, something he never outgrew. Part of it came from the fact that Joe was handsome, whereas Greg suffered agonies about his own appearance. Part of it was that Greg felt both his parents had admired and loved Joe more, much more, as a small child. He was also jealous of Joe's skill as an athlete.

Not long after their father's death, Joe suffered a minor heart attack while playing golf. Greg made a note of the event in his journal. He was not upset, but rather cold-bloodedly observed ". . . this will be a lesson to Clarks who follow golf instead of the True Faith." He went blithely on in the next sentence, "Tree sparrows in the garden."

Their father left a will disposing of his rather small estate, estimated at about twelve thousand dollars. The cottage at Go Home went to Greg. A lump sum went to Mabel, enough for her to build a cottage of her own at Go Home. The rest of the cash available went to Arthur, the youngest. Arthur had tried hard to follow in the footsteps of Greg and Joe, his older brothers, but without success. He had failed as a reporter in Toronto and as an advertising space salesman in Vancouver. His father left him enough cash to make a modest investment in a printing firm.

For Joe there was nothing. Joe lived well and had borrowed substantial sums from his father over the years, depositing I.O.U.'s against his share in the estate. He came out even.

There was one token bequest to him—a token, but highly significant. In the fashion of his time, J.T.C., as they called their father, had always carried a gold watch in his vest pocket. On the chain there was a shark's tooth and a small gold locket. None of the children was curious about what was in the locket, assuming it was a photo of their mother.

Greg was looking after his father's personal effects after the funeral. He laid aside the gold watch, knowing it was to go to Joe. The locket caught his eye and on impulse he opened it. For Greg it was a blow to the heart, a confirmation of all his terrible fears and jealousies. What his father had carried all these years in the locket was a picture of his brother Joe: the final, ultimate proof.

Greg slipped the locket from the chain and hid it with his own personal possessions. No one will ever know what was in his mind. There is no mention of the locket in his journals or diaries.

So far as is known, Joe did not express any curiosity about the missing locket, perhaps assuming it had been lost or mislaid. He was happy to have the gold watch and chain and the shark's tooth. Greg, having committed the crime, now had to live with the secret; he did so for many years. Perhaps he managed to shut it out of his mind.

If he ever entertained the idea of confessing to Joe, that opportunity slipped away with the passage of time. In 1950 his brother suffered a stroke. He lived on for six years, but without the ability to speak or communicate. Gil Purcell devoted a great deal of time to attempting to cure or alleviate this aphasia. Two or three times a week Purcell visited Joe's home and sat with him in the family dining room, rehearsing him in simple word-and-object recognition—but months of this produced no results beyond a very limited vocabulary and some relief of Joe's depression. Purcell did succeed in teaching him how to say "yes" and "no" and one other essential phrase, "rye and water," which had been Joe's favorite drink.

When Joe died on November 28, 1956, this brief note appeared in Greg's journal.

"My brother Joe died last night, quietly in his sleep. He had a thrombosis in April, 1938, and then in 1950 a stroke that deprived him of his speech and forced his retirement from all active life. He has had six years as a Man in the Iron Mask."

This brief note was buried in a long ten-page account of the November deer hunt. Greg felt that this hunt might be his last and he wanted to record all the details of it in full. Obviously the thought of his brother Joe was not something to which he could address himself for long periods.

The locket's secret remained with Greg for nearly thirty years, until he was clearing out his possessions at 119 Crescent Road for the move to the King Edward. Joe's son, Joseph Adair Porter Clark, was now a man in his mid-forties. He had been a naval officer in World War II and since had become a successful public relations executive. This man, the third Joe Clark, had kept in touch with his famous uncle and occasionally stopped by for a drink with Greg on his way home from work.

On a spring day in 1966, Greg called him up and asked him to make a point of stopping in after work. He found Greg upstairs at his desk.

"I've got something for you," said Greg.

He handed over the locket. His nephew looked at it curiously, not knowing what it was.

"Open it up," said Greg.

Young Joe did so and found himself looking at a picture of his father at about the age of four, posing with a cricket bat.

"Your grandfather wore that on his watch chain," said Greg. "I took it off after the funeral. Your father never knew that it was his picture our dad carried around with him."

Young Joe sensed a certain electricity in the air, even though Greg's voice was flat and without emotion. His mind flashed back to that scene on the cottage veranda at Go Home, nearly thirty years ago, when he had been a teenager watching his father and Greg fighting, while their father lay dying inside.

"You better keep it," said Greg.

He said nothing more and young Joe put the locket in his pocket and left. Greg remained seated at his desk. For some time, before going home, Joe walked the streets, trying to understand the meaning of the incident. Neither he nor Greg ever referred to it again.

The death of Greg's father in 1937 had followed the death of his mother, Sarah Louise Greig, by some seven years. Her death in 1930 had not been as mercifully sudden. She had been in deteriorating health for a number of years and for the final two years of her life she had been in a full-care home near Barrie, Ontario. Her condition was in such contrast to the young woman she had been that friends and relatives found visits very painful. Greg was the most dutiful visitor of all, right to the end.

Greg's acquisition of the family cottage followed closely the loss of the Mad River fishing rights. He began spending more time with Helen and the boys, now in their teens and learning to handle rod and gun. Greg watched their skills grow with pride.

"Murray mastered bait-casting in two weeks. Age 11."

"Young Greg carried the new 14-foot canoe across the Go Home Chute portage, unaided and in style. Age 14."

But Greg's freedom was diminishing. Hindmarsh now had control of the *Star Weekly*. It was easier for him to commandeer Greg and others for daily work.

As a promotion stunt Greg imported a zebra for the zoo and ran a contest for naming the animal. He worked for the *Star*

Greg's son Murray poses with his first deer. Smear on his forehead is traditional "blooding."

Greg's brother Arthur with Dr. Alan Secord, well-known Toronto veterinarian and a hunting and fishing companion of Greg's.

Greg and Helen with Elizabeth and Murray at beginning of World War II.

At the outbreak of World War II, Prime Minister King tried to enlist Greg as a government speech writer. In 1941 he introduced Greg to Winston Churchill, in Washington, D.C.

Greg's sons, Murray and Greg, Jr., donned uniforms early in the war.

Greg brought this machine gun back from overseas and Murray tried it out at Go Home Bay.

Greg was accredited as a war correspondent at the end of 1939.

In London, Greg renewed his friendship with Matthew Halton and the latter's daughter, Kathleen.

Greg, his brother Joe, Dick Malone and Fred Griffin overseas in World War II.

(Left) Greg admires statue in Italy. *(Canadian Army Photo)* *(Below, left)* Greg and brother Joe enjoyed a reunion in Vasto, Italy. Joe had become director of public relations for the Canadian Armed Services. *(Below, right)* Toward the end of the war, Greg switched his coverage to the Royal Canadian Air Force.

TORONTO DAILY STAR

90,000 OUT; R.A.F. RULE DUNKIRK
Tommies Tell Greg Glorious Story

TORONTO DAILY STAR
Village Succors, Hides Wounded Canadian--Greg Clark

TORONTO DAILY STAR
3-Hour Bridge To Carry Army, Canadian Feat---Clark

TORONTO DAILY STAR
"Italians, Loaded Like Donkeys, Surrender"---Clark

THE TORONTO DAILY STAR
RESCUERS ONLY FEW FEET OFF
'We Can Hold Out,' Cries Doctor; Herman Magill Dead

WEARY RESCUE PARTY MAKING FINAL SPURT AGAINST RISING WATER

HOME AND SPORT EDITION

'WE CAN HOLD ON 10 OR 12 HOURS' SAYS ROBERTSON

STAR 'PLANE MAKES DAWN-TO-DUSK DASH 900 MILES TO MINE

Greg's name appeared in many headlined stories. *(Courtesy Toronto Star)*

After the war, Jim Frise and Greg tried fly fishing in Quebec.

After many deer hunts with Greg, Helen finally bagged a deer. It ended her hunting.

Go Home Bay still provided good fishing.

Helen became an expert.

Greg enjoys a reunion with Ross Munro and Dick
Malone. Munro, a leading war correspondent, wrote
Gauntlet to Overlord. Malone wrote *Missing from
the Record;* later he became head of the FP newspaper chain.

The head of the Ontario Society of Artists, Cleeve
Horne, tried his hand at capturing Greg in oils in
1952.

CANADIAN PRESS WAR CORRESPONDENTS ASSOCIATION
Later Canadian War Correspondents Association

First Meeting, Windsor Hotel, Montreal Jan. 5, 1945

Front row: Louis Hunter, Foster Barclay, Ernie Burritt
Back row: Harry Day, treasurer, Ross Munro, president,
Doug How, Bill Stewart, Alan Randal, secretary, Gil Purcell

John Griffith McConnell took over the *Montreal Standard* as publisher when he was twenty-six years old. The ailing weekly developed into *Weekend Magazine,* with the largest circulation of any Canadian publication. *(Jock Carroll)*

Members of the youthful team that revived the *Standard* were Alex Janusitis, Glenn Gilbert and Mark Farrell. Gilbert provided editorial leadership. *(Louis Jaques)*

This trio saw *Weekend Magazine* take shape. Left to right: Phil Surrey, photo editor; Craig Ballantyne, executive editor; Hugh Shaw, magazine editor. *(Charlie King)*

The 1949 staff of the *Standard.* Foreground: Glenn Gilbert, managing editor. Left to right: Lewis Louthood, promotion manager; Craig Ballantyne, executive editor; Kate Aitken, women's editor; Phil Surrey, photo editor; Max Newton, assistant photo editor; Andy O'Brien, sports editor; Alex Janusitis, review editor; Hugh Shaw, magazine editor; Stanley Handman, news editor.

Greg checks his height against that of marathon swimmer Marilyn Bell. *(Jock Carroll)*

Greg covered the Arctic tour of the Duke of Edinburgh. *(Jock Carroll)*

Art director Dick Hersey encouraged Canadian artists to work for the *Standard. (Public Archives of Canada, Ronny Jaques photo)*

Standard reporter Mavis Gallant went on to write novels and short stories. *(Public Archives of Canada, Glay Sperling photo)*

Standard reporter Jacqueline Moore with her son by Brian Moore, the novelist, also once a Montreal reporter.

Weekend sports editor Andy O'Brien interviewed Doug Hepburn of Vancouver when the latter became world heavyweight weight-lifting champion. Both men weighed 280 pounds.

Weekend's vast circulation introduced editorial problems, as lampooned by this Hamilton theater group. *(Jock Carroll)*

Harry Barberian, proprietor of a Toronto steak house, lights a "cigar" for Duncan Macpherson, the artist who worked with Greg after the death of Jim Frise. *(Dick Loek)*

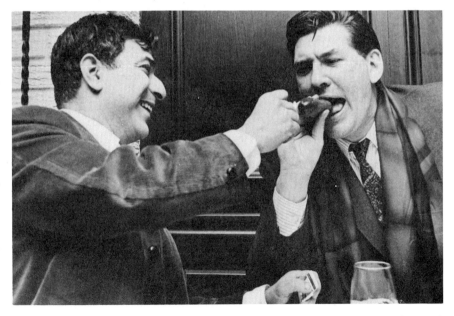

Santa Claus Fund and the *Star* Fresh Air Fund, which provided summer holidays for the underprivileged. He made his pilgrimage to Rome and followed Royal Tours across Canada. Reporter Jimmy Nichol said that Greg called this work ". . . singing the *Star*'s Mammy songs."

But even when he was at home, Greg was not a strong father figure. "With us," said Greg, Jr., "Dad did not play the heavy father, laying down the law or making rules. As a result, I think, we were not a closely knit family. After dinner Murray would go upstairs to his books. I wasn't a great reader at the time—that came later—so I would leave the house and roam around with boys my age. Elizabeth spent a lot of time with Mother."

As a youngster, young Greg was actually a little confused about his father's identity. He saw his name on important news stories. He saw him as the caricature in the Jim-Greg stories. He saw him as a hunter and fisherman. He saw him as an entertainer who loved to tell stories and be the center of attention, and yet as a man who liked to retreat to his attic and sort his outdoor gear.

"I think his strongest relationship was with Mother," said young Greg. "Dad put Mother on a pedestal when they were married and he never let her get down."

Greg had a Victorian attitude toward his domestic life. He did not bring his work problems home, nor did he bring home his drinking and fishing companions. Perhaps he wasn't encouraged to do so. Helen, the minister's daughter, did not drink or approve of Greg's drinking. Her mother, the minister's widow, lived with them from the earliest days of their marriage until she was over ninety years of age. The housekeeper, Hilda Ashcroft, who was with them for twenty-nine years, was also a straitlaced person. Greg did not drink at home, except for the occasional bottle of beer; these he kept hidden behind the furnace or in the attic.

As the firstborn, Murray was the first to learn to fish and shoot. Very early he showed signs of Greg's love of words and Greg's love of the wilderness. During Greg's two-week vacation, the whole family was together at Go Home. The rest of the summer Greg was a summer bachelor. The others went to Helen's family cottage at Lake of Bays, in Muskoka. As Murray grew older, though, he preferred the more primitive surroundings at Go Home, even if he had to stay there alone. This Greg could understand.

Murray also had a lively imagination and shared Greg's love of books. At high school he began writing poetry and plays. Greg came to see him as the heir of the Clark tradition, a newspaperman, perhaps even more. It was perhaps all too human for Greg to let his favoritism show. One would have expected him to be wiser in view of his own traumatic experience, but history repeated itself and young Greg and Elizabeth became aware of it.

However, Greg did exhibit the same overly protective attitude toward Elizabeth that he had about all women. An incident at Go Home became a joke that circulated among the Clarks' relatives.

On a walk through the woods, trailing behind Greg were Elizabeth, Greg, Jr., and one of the Drew-Brook boys. A rifle was discharged accidentally and the bullet whizzed past Greg's ear. Furiously he turned on the two boys. "You stupid little buggers! Are you trying to kill me? Haven't you been told how to carry a gun?" Greg did not get angry very often, but the shot had frightened him. The tirade went on and on and the two boys remained silent.

Finally Elizabeth interrupted, "But Daddy, it was *my* gun that went off." In a flash Greg changed from the angry man to the doting father. "Awwww, Dids darling," he said, "you must try to be more careful."

Greg felt Elizabeth must be sheltered from life just as much as Helen. In her teens Elizabeth laughingly referred to herself as "The Princess" because, in her parents' eyes, she could do no wrong. She complained to friends, "They tell me everything I do is wonderful. I know it isn't, but I just can't get an honest opinion."

Elizabeth returned from a shopping expedition one day with a new outfit. She put it on and came downstairs to model it for Greg, Jr. "Just tell me honestly how you think this looks on me."

Young Greg glanced up and said unhesitatingly, "It looks like hell."

Elizabeth said, "Thanks. That's just what I wanted to know."

When she went back upstairs, Greg, Jr., was scolded by his mother for talking to his sister in such terrible fashion.

More and more Murray became Greg's companion on hunting and fishing trips. Greg wrote in his notebook: "Murray is a solitary and shy young man whose poverty of companions may even now be due to his close association with me in recent years. But how I love that young man."

Very suddenly the days of peace were over. The signs of impending war had been obvious, but Greg had been pushing them to the back of his mind.

On September 1, 1939, Greg drove Murray home from a trip to the cottage. It was Murray's eighteenth birthday. It was also the day Hitler's panzer divisions rolled into Poland. Greg saw it as an ominous coincidence.

30

WORLD WAR II

Three days after Canada entered the war, Greg received a phone call. It was the Prime Minister of Canada. Mackenzie King wanted to know if Greg would take on the delicate task of writing speeches for himself and his cabinet colleagues. Greg was flattered but reluctant to commit himself. He told King he would discuss the matter with *Star* publisher Atkinson and get back to him later.

When Greg went to Atkinson's office to discuss the offer, the publisher placed no obstacles in his way. In fact, he said he thought Greg would end up broadcasting for the government sooner or later during the war. Greg was much sought after as a speaker and had been doing more radio work in recent years.

Still Greg hesitated. He was appalled at the return of war—something he had known at its worst—and he was reluctant to disturb his situation at the *Star*. His collaboration with Jimmie Frise was more fun than work and he was earning more than he ever had before—a ten-thousand-a-year salary, supplemented by radio income. He was still spending money faster than he earned it, and owed $20,000 to his bank. Despite this debt, he had somehow convinced himself that he was now well ahead of the game because he was carrying $40,000 in life insurance.

In celebration of this financial improvement he had moved from Baby Point Road to a large, rambling house at 19 Indian Grove. This he also rented. It had room for his three growing children and his mother-in-law, separate bedrooms for Helen and himself, and even an attic room where he could store his hunting and fishing gear.

Greg finally got around to writing to Mackenzie King. He wrote that he did not think it was in the best interests of all concerned for him to take on the speech-writing job at the present time.

Greg's forty-seventh birthday arrived on September 25, two weeks after Canada officially declared itself at war and twenty-five days after the invasion of Poland. He retreated to his new attic, celebrating his birthday with the annual autumn ritual of unpacking and repacking his haversacks, waxing the heads of matches to make them waterproof, oiling his guns and gear. He estimated he spent ten times the hours in rearranging and cleaning his treasures that he did in the use of them.

His new home backed on a ravine and the yard was filled with birds. Greg became interested in the starling after watching one sitting in the sun at the end of the day and listening to its queer, confidential mutter. It was, Greg felt, much like the Indian's night song, a résumé of the day's happenings. In the starling's conversation Greg recognized the song of many other birds, the chatter of sparrows, the cry of meadowlark and flicker, even a hermit thrush imitated *sotto voce*. There were other familiar sounds he could not quite place. He determined to learn the speech of this small, black, chuckling, whispering parrot.

He added a new wicker game basket to his collection—his fourth. He had been looking at this particular basket for years as it sat in an Eaton's showcase. It was a beauty, made of English willow with a heavy brown canvas cover. Greg didn't really need another basket, and his resolve held as long as the price remained at $18. However, one day it was marked down to $5, a price no man could resist.

Having acquired it, Greg decided it was perfect for carrying decoys, and that therefore he should try making some. In a week he had hacked out two bluebill decoys, the first carpentry he had ever attempted in his life. While working on them his mind kept coming back to war. His own war of twenty years ago seemed remote and strange, like some fairy tale he had heard.

Even the current war seemed remote. There was the occasional parade, watched in curious silence by people on the streets. The nation was pathetically unready for war. The recruiting depots had to be closed temporarily, because there was no way to handle the volunteers. The army was allegedly equipped with a handful of Bren guns and anti-tank rifles. Reportedly, there were only fourteen tanks and ten naval vessels in operating condition.

There was talk at the office of Greg becoming a war correspondent. His response was a flurry of trips with the family: he and Murray and Helen shooting pheasant in October; the deer hunt at Go Home Bay in November; all three children and Helen to the Muskoka cottage for Thanksgiving.

His notes on the plants, the flowers, the water levels at Go Home, the appearance of black squirrels in the area became more frequent. Perhaps the death of his own parents had given him some sense of his own mortality, a feeling that the "frabjous" days were drawing to a close. Murray was entering his last year of high school. Greg, Jr., was just beginning. Things were moving so quickly. Greg made more notes about the starling:

> Today I listened for a long time to a starling only 12 feet distant on the apple tree and I must say I really love the international song this bird sings.
>
> Among the reminiscences of a better season that he indulged in, unmistakable and most artistically rendered, were robin call, goldfinch wing song, sparrow, meadow lark, grackle and several pianissimo and rapid passages, fairly long sustained, that were without question an effort on this bird's part to reproduce the sound of an early summer day with *all* the birds singing; a solo effort at symphony.
>
> Three times now I have noticed sparrows coming and sitting nearby, all fluffed out and attentive, like an audience for the starling's performance.

Meanwhile, back at the *Star* office, Joseph Atkinson was being forced into a reappraisal of his ideas about Russia. Like many liberals during the Thirties, he had seen Hitler and Mussolini as a greater menace than communism, and he had seen hope in the Russian experiment, not knowing the cost. As recently as 1938 Atkinson had been trying to get Matthew Halton and Greg into Russia, but they had been refused visas. Now he was upset by the Russian-German non-aggression pact, which paved the way for the drive into Poland. He was stunned when Russia attacked Finland on November 30, 1939.

Matthew Halton was dispatched to the Finnish front. Greg was accredited as a war correspondent. On December 19 he was sent to England with the second contingent of the First Canadian Division.

It was the period known as the Phony War. Greg toured army camps and airfields in Britain and visited British and French troops in France, crossing battlefields he had known in World War I. He was alarmed at the complacency of the British and French commands and, apart from the Maginot Line, the poverty of modern weapons. When he returned to Canada in the spring of 1940, he conveyed these observations to Atkinson, who probably relayed the information to Mackenzie King. The paper followed government policy in not pressing for conscription until Canada had created a war machine.

Greg was back home but briefly—long enough to note a cardinal in the garden and to check the notes of a song sparrow against those of a tree sparrow. He also managed to acquire, for only $4.50 each, two original John Gould prints—one of the pine grosbeak and one of the starling. Gould lived from 1804 to 1881 and Greg's prints had been published about 1840. Greg framed them and speculated about the hundred-year journey which had brought them to the walls of his den.

For several years now, he had missed the opening of the trout season on May 1. 1940 was to be another such year. Denmark and Norway were overrun in April. Just before the trout season opened, Hindmarsh sent Fred Griffin overseas to attach himself to British Army headquarters. Greg was to go with the 1st Canadian Division into France.

Greg arrived in France on May 10, 1940, the day Germany launched the Blitzkrieg, bypassing the Maginot Line via Holland and Belgium. Greg and some 198,000 British troops, along with 140,000 French and Belgian soldiers, made a miraculous escape from Dunkirk. Despite this debacle, the Allied command now hatched a plan that seems insane in retrospect. A single Canadian division and a single British division were to be sent into Brittany to try to hold a 150-mile line and keep a toehold on the continent.

Greg was moving up from Boulogne with a group of war correspondents to cover this front when the front came back to meet them: they were bombed out of Arras and out of Amiens. At Amiens they had to abandon their kits and flee; the Germans almost had the town surrounded. Greg and the other correspondents were evacuated from Boulogne on a small mine-layer packed to the gunwales with some two thousand British troops.

In the period of inactivity that preceded the Battle of Britain, the *Star* ordered its correspondents home, relying for news on wire service coverage. Greg made a second speech to the Canadian Club in Toronto. "After telling you of the might of the French Army and the readiness of the British Army and of the Maginot Line, I went back to see that might brushed away as though it were dust." He described the retreat, but assured his audience that in the logic of history we would win. It was a difficult thing to believe in the dark days that followed, 1940 through 1942: the blitz on London, the Battle of Britain, Hitler's attack on Russia, Pearl Harbor, the fall of Hong Kong, the disaster of Dieppe.

Meanwhile, in April of 1941, Greg procrastinated on an assignment to return to England. Helen, for the first time in his long newspaper history of sudden departures, had been upset at the prospect of his going.

Sammy Robertson, a reporter with Canadian Press and a friend of Greg's, did leave at this time, on the H.M.S. *Nerissa*. In the normal course of events Greg would have shipped with him. The *Nerissa* was torpedoed en route to England and went down with all hands. In this first year of war, Hitler's submarine pack had sunk over a thousand ships and the Germans were building eight new submarines for every one they lost. Greg felt he had been saved from death by a premonition of Helen's.

In August of 1941, Greg did make another quick trip to Europe, his third since the outbreak of war. He flew the Atlantic with Prime Minister Mackenzie King, three government officials and three other newspapermen.

When King addressed a gathering of Canadian troops in England he was roundly booed, and the high-level political conferences the Prime Minister attended yielded little for publication. Greg found the assignment as hopeless as any he had ever had and was glad to return to Canada.

King was having trouble getting Canada aroused about the war; Canadian troops had not as yet even contacted the enemy. The troops in England were restless and bored with training exercises. These and other pressures played a part in the two debacles that followed in 1942. One was the sending of the Winnipeg Grenadiers and the Royal Rifles of Canada to Hong Kong just in time to be captured by the Japanese. The second misadventure was the disastrous assault on Dieppe, from which less than half the Canadian force returned.

Meanwhile, when Pearl Harbor exploded in December 1941, Greg was sent to California to see what could be learned about possible attacks on North America. From here he was rushed to Washington for Winston Churchill's visit with Roosevelt. He had the honor of being introduced to the Prime Minister of Britain by the Prime Minister of Canada.

Greg's respite from the battlefield was to last until 1943, but meanwhile his brothers and sons were being drawn into the war. His brother Joe had been made director of public relations at National Defense Headquarters in Ottawa. His youngest brother, Arthur, enlisted and sailed for Britain. His son Murray had enlisted in the Queen's Own Rifles and was taking an officer's training course. Greg, Jr., had enlisted in the army reserves, although he would later switch to the Royal Canadian Air Force.

On June 8, 1943, Greg and Murray enjoyed a last day of fishing together. By September Greg was on his way overseas again.

By the summer of 1943, Montgomery's Eighth Army, victorious in Africa, had begun preparations for the invasion of Sicily and Italy. To this point the *Star*'s most active war correspondent had been Matt Halton, who had followed the war to Finland, Greece and Egypt. He'd distinguished himself by making his way through enemy lines to besieged Tobruk and had become a well-known radio personality through his reports for the Canadian Broadcasting Corporation. Now his career at the *Star* ended. There were several versions. One was that Halton was annoyed when Hindmarsh announced that Greg and Fred Griffin would be covering the invasion of Sicily. Another was that Hindmarsh told Halton he would have to drop his radio work and confine his reporting to the *Star*'s pages.

In any case, Halton went to the C.B.C. and Greg and Griffin were posted overseas. Before leaving for the Mediterranean, Greg spent some weeks in England. At Epsom, near London, Greg and a small group of friends spent an evening at a local bar and made history by founding the Epsom Dart and Fart Club.

The club was based on a mastery of flatulence. Rank was established by one's skill in imitating punctuation marks, much as in Victor Borge's classic skit, "Phonetic Punctuation." Borge, of course, used his mouth to make the noises.

In the Epsom Dart and Fart Club a short bip was a period; a

bip that tailed off was a comma; two short, quick bips signified a colon; a long blast was a dash; a prolonged rising and falling blast finished off with a short blip was a question mark. The difficult passages, such as the question mark and the exclamation point (a vertical blast followed by a short bip), were fraught with danger.

The highest rank in this society was established as that of Fart Master, granted only to those who succeeded in farting in the presence of royalty—in the presence of royalty, but not necessarily in the hearing of royalty. Some time later Greg had an opportunity at Buckingham Palace to achieve this exalted rank, but his nerve failed him.

On the somewhat noisy evening when the club was founded, charter memberships were issued to those present. These were inscribed on government-issue toilet paper, perforated with the words "Government Property." For the rest of the war—and even later—the charter members carried these certificates in their wallets, alongside their Short Snorter bills.

The Epsom charter members were Captain Jack Hughes, Captain Fred Payne, Bruce West, then with the Canadian Information Services, Greg and Captain Doug MacFarlane, later editor of the *Maple Leaf, The Globe & Mail* and the Toronto *Telegram*.

MacFarlane was one of many who felt Greg told a story much better than he wrote it. Early in the war, MacFarlane took an officer's training course at Gordon Head, near Victoria, British Columbia. It was a tough course, including drill, maneuvers, lectures and a form of commando training. MacFarlane lost thirty-five pounds in three months.

Greg and *Star* photographer Norm James landed in Victoria on an assignment and MacFarlane joined them for a party in their hotel room. They were drinking "bull cocktails," a mixture of rye and milk, with the milk bottles standing outside on the window ledge to keep cold. MacFarlane was talking to Norm James, but his attention kept wandering because, in another part of the room, Greg was telling a story about a fascinating new army course just launched by the government.

MacFarlane left James and joined Greg's audience, where he listened raptly for ten minutes before it dawned on him. "My God, that's *my* course at Gordon Head he's talking about!" MacFarlane said later, "His facts weren't wrong—it was just that

Greg presented them so romantically, so dramatically that I thought it was another world."

Greg arrived in Sicily in September 1943. Although now over fifty years of age, he adjusted well to life in the field. In the First World War it had been a full-time effort just to stay alive. In this war the morale value of news was gradually being recognized; correspondents were given liaison officers, transport, billets and communication lines to get their stories back home.

At first, in Sicily and Italy, there were problems. The military establishment was sometimes slow to admit the importance of news. And there were inter-service rivalries, as delineated in Colonel R. S. Malone's book, *Missing From the Record*. Malone, a liaison officer attached to General Montgomery's staff, was placed in charge of press relations in Sicily and Italy, and came to know Greg well in that period.

Like many others, Malone was surprised to discover the people whom Greg knew—and who knew Greg—from the Pope, the Duke of Windsor, President Roosevelt and on down the list. Following the liberation of Naples, Malone and Greg had tea with Benedetto Croce, the Italian philosopher, who was considered for the temporary post of President of Italy following Mussolini's fall. Malone sensed a similarity between Croce's philosophy and Greg's feeling that one should lighten the way through life with humor.

Having tea with a philosopher was not the only experience Malone was to share with Greg in Italy. Another was to take place in what had once been one of the largest whorehouses in Naples. Because of the large number of bedrooms it contained, Malone had unwittingly requisitioned it as an officers' mess. He invited Greg there for dinner one evening. Greg took over the dinner, instructing the cook on the preparation of bouillabaisse, telling stories and, halfway through the dinner, marching in a makeshift orchestra he had recruited on the streets of Naples, made up of lame and one-eyed beggars. Malone was only able to bring the evening to a close by placing Greg under mock arrest.

Malone and Greg would meet again in Normandy after the invasion there, under less happy circumstances.

31

Alas, the days of newspaper enterprise in
war are over. What can one do with a censor,
a 48-hour delay, and a 50-word limit on a wire?

—Winston Churchill,
newspaper correspondent
during the Boer War

The *Star Weekly*'s circulation doubled during the war. It was
helped by a wartime ban on the importation of similar U.S. publications, which was intended to conserve currency, but it was also
helped by the war coverage of its Canadian writers.

The *Star*'s overseas staff included Matt Halton, Greg, Fred
Griffin, Bill Kinmond, Claude Pascoe, Paul Morton, Ross
Harkness and others. The invasion of Sicily and Italy created the
greatest concentration of Canadian war correspondents since the
beginning of the war. It was also to bring sharply into focus the
problems of Allied joint operations, inter-service rivalries, press
and communications difficulties.

For these reasons, Lt. Col. Dick Malone was to be placed in
charge of army public relations in Sicily and Italy, gaining experience that would be even more useful in the coming invasion of
France. Malone had the problem of integrating the news coverage
of British, American, Canadian, Polish and New Zealand forces,
each with its own political and national sensitivities.

The campaign in Sicily and Italy was under the direction of
General Sir Bernard Montgomery, the famous "Monty" of Eighth
Army fame, himself a complex and eccentric character who
collected love birds and other pet animals in his personal caravan
as he moved along.

Canada, over the objections of General Andrew McNaughton,

had abandoned the idea of maintaining its army as a complete unit and had committed the 1st Canadian Division to the Eighth Army in Sicily. Within a few days of the Sicily landings, McNaughton announced his intention to visit the Canadian troops—without clearing this with Montgomery. Monty stated that he would place McNaughton, then Canadian Army Commander, under arrest if he set foot on the island without his personal permission.

These territorial imperatives extended to press coverage. Some generals tried to dictate their own coverage; others seemed intent on thwarting any coverage whatsoever. Malone, nearly to the end of the war, was struggling with the upper-class English view that Canada was simply a colony of Britain and that "British and American troops" was sufficient identification of the Canadian presence.

In this battle, Canadian correspondents more than held their own. Ross Munro, of Canadian Press, got beachhead scoops at Dieppe, Sicily, Italy and Normandy. The first story filed from Paris on the liberation of that city was Canadian—and Paris was not even an area where the Canadian Army was operating.

In World War I only a handful of well-known reporters had made it up front. In Sicily and Italy there were many: Ross Munro, Doug Amaron and Bill Stewart of Canadian Press; Ralph Allen for *The Globe & Mail;* Bert Wemp for the Toronto *Telegram;* Fred Griffin and Greg for the *Star;* Matthew Halton, now working for the C.B.C.; Lionel Shapiro, working for NANA—the North American Newspaper Alliance—and *Maclean's* magazine; Sholto Watt for the Montreal *Star* and Wally Reyburn for the Montreal *Standard*—to name only some of the Canadians.

Many of these writers were colorful, eccentric, competitive individuals, some of them with as little knowledge of the military as the military had of them. Both Matt Halton and Lionel Shapiro felt, and said, that they were the greatest war correspondents the world had ever seen. Halton rehearsed his radio broadcasts in press quarters until fellow correspondents cried for mercy. Shapiro, later a successful novelist, tore his stories from the typewriter and cried, "Listen to this beautiful prose!"

Bert Wemp was a somewhat solid citizen who had won the D.F.C. as a pilot in the previous war and had become a mayor of Toronto between wars. When the correspondents discovered The

School of Coral, a church-run guild which produced beautiful cameos and similar items, Fred Griffin had a cameo produced in his wife's likeness. Bert Wemp had one made of his own rather handsome profile.

Wemp was a true-blue Orangeman and reported for the Orange-oriented Toronto *Telegram*. He regarded the muddy roads of Italy as just another example of Catholic squalor. In his Toronto *Telegram* dispatches he concentrated almost exclusively on Toronto soldiers. As they looked forward to the fall of Rome, fellow correspondents had fun composing Wemp's story of that event in advance. They felt it would begin this way: "Rome was liberated today. Among those present from Toronto were . . ."

Sholto Watt was a delicate-looking Cambridge man. He was disdainful of enemy fire and wore a monocle while interviewing privates in the line until embarrassed fellow correspondents persuaded him not to. In the Montreal Press Club twenty years after the war, Sholto managed to puncture Greg's platform personality. Greg had cornered Sholto and subjected him to rather a long story with all the gestures. At the end, Sholto didn't laugh. He simply affixed his monocle and said, "Greg, why do you always address me as though I were an *audience?*" Greg enjoyed the putdown and repeated it.

Another aesthete was Bill Boss, an army information officer later to become a Canadian Press correspondent. Boss had the musical background to conduct a symphony orchestra. Later, in liberated Antwerp, he did just that.

Wally Reyburn later became a Montreal *Standard* editor and wrote a book called *Some of It Was Fun,* a collection of the ribald tales and ironies of war. Reyburn was also a musician. He was one of two Canadian correspondents at Dieppe, and wherever he found a piano he entertained with "The Dieppe Concerto," a dirge of his own composition.

After the capture of Sicily the invasion of Italy loomed. For the invasion, there were press positions available for the wire services and radio, but only two spots open for "the specials"—those correspondents representing individual newspapers or magazines. One spot was open for the U.S. landing at Anzio; the other for the British-Canadian landing on the toe of Italy. The names of the "specials" were written out on slips of paper and dropped into a hat. The name drawn for the Anzio landing was Lionel Shapiro, who capered gleefully about.

The slips of paper were made ready for the second drawing. The name drawn was Greg Clark. After this, the sergeant in charge of the draw casually dumped the remaining slips in the fireplace. Greg claimed later, much later, that he had bribed the sergeant so that all the slips in the second draw bore the name "Greg Clark." The story may not be true, but Greg was capable of a trick of this sort.

One correspondent who became a good friend of Greg's in Italy was Bill Stewart of Canadian Press. For some reason Greg got the idea that Stewart was an orphan and insisted on adopting him as a son. Stewart protested that he had a father and a mother and even brothers and sisters back in his hometown of Rivière du Loup, but Greg, his mind made up, ignored these facts.

Said Stewart, "I met Ernie Pyle in the Pacific Theater later and had a chance to compare him to Greg. They both wrote about people, but were quite different in style. Pyle was a shy, retiring man. Greg was an entertainer. If nothing was happening when he arrived, things began to happen."

There were the usual arguments in messes and bars about the relative values of British and American soldiers. Greg was liable to stir things up by taking whichever side was unpopular at the moment. "He was," said Stewart, "quite capable of defending the Yanks one moment and then afterward telling someone he could take the American Eagle, stuff it up his ass and let its wings thrash around until the great bird died." Greg got away with a lot because of his size and his grandfatherly appearance.

In Italy his conducting officer was a wild, irreverent man from Calgary named Gordon Hutton, a man who feared neither the enemy nor his own brass. Hutton referred to ambitious officers as "men who kept a civil tongue in their colonel."

The driver assigned to Greg and Hutton was a Negro from Port Arthur named Joe Greaves. Greaves was a former Linotype operator with ambitions to be a reporter. He was also a champion scrounger and was usually covered with binoculars, wristwatches, Beretta pistols and other items of trade. In their jeep, these three men looked like three characters in search of an author.

Greaves was a wild driver, even on the Italian mountain roads. Greg, made nervous by these thrilling rides, was constantly shouting, "Watch out! Not so fast!"

This back-seat driving made Greaves nervous. He somehow scrounged an extra steering wheel for the jeep and hid it in the

front seat. One day, on a particularly dangerous road, when Greg
was shouting his usual instructions from the back seat, Greaves
suddenly swung around and presented Greg with the steering
wheel. "Here!" he said. *"You* drive for a while!"

The 1st Canadian Division was committed to advancing up the
spine of Italy, which was the hard way to go. Bridges had been
blown up by the retreating enemy and vehicles had to be winched
down valleys and up hills. Meanwhile reconnaissance forces
found it much easier going up the coastal road and were often far
in advance. Bill Stewart joined the Clark jeep in forays up the
road. When news was hard to come by they would turn inland to
"liberate" some small Italian village.

Greg, with his entourage, his white sideburns and his dignified
mien, would be hailed by the villagers as a general. Wine and
flowers would appear, to cries of *"Il generale! Viva! Viva!"* They
were a miniature version of Hemingway's raggle-taggle band of
Maquis and correspondents who advanced on Paris and claimed
its liberation.

On a somewhat similar foray, Dick Malone would possibly
have had an easier time if he had had Clark, the imitation general, at his side. Malone and his jeep driver entered a garrison
town and found hundreds of Italian soldiers lined up ready to
surrender. Unfortunately, the general in charge, General Achille
d'Havet, felt that as a point of honor he could only turn over his
sword to someone of equal rank.

Lieutenant Colonel Malone did not qualify. Malone, nervous
because he knew the town was scheduled for an imminent Allied
attack, argued with the Italian general. The general was adamant.
Exasperated, Malone finally drew his pistol and took away the
general and his staff at gunpoint—in the general's own staff car.
The capture of a general was another Canadian first.

As a result of one of these village forays, Greg wrote one of his
most moving dispatches. The *Star* headlined it:

BLOODLUST OF GERMANS SATED
IN WANTON SLAUGHTER OF MEN
FROM ITALIAN PEASANT VILLAGE
BY GREGORY CLARK

Somewhere in Italy, Sept 26—(Delayed) Monsters in victory and monsters in flight, the Germans have added to the

imperishable name of Lidice in Czechoslovakia the little name of Rionero in Italy, and I am one of the witnesses. In this tousled town of 10,000 inhabitants the Germans, the night before last, perpetrated one of their foul slaughters of innocent civilians. Twenty-one young men of the town of Rionero, ranging in age from 16 years and most of them in their early twenties, with the exception of a father of a family, aged 40, were lined up and shot in cold blood.

This afternoon I visited the bloodsoaked ditch in which they died and then went up to the cemetery where the pitiful bodies, clad in their rags, were laid ready for burial. Some were riddled with tommy guns, some were shot between the eyes with pistols.

Of this little random selection of townsfolk, those who fell pretending to be dead were sought out by calm cold Germans and four Italian Fascist paratroopers aiding and abetting them, and were shot at pistol point. All but one. Stefano Di Mattia, with his townsmen's blood sluicing him, feigned death so well that he alone of 21 escaped with only a leg wound. Stefano it was who took me to the scene of the slaughter and then led on to the array of dead.

Here is the story to which hundreds of citizens of Rionero bear witness:

On Friday night, Sept. 24, with 8th Army patrols already on the fringe of the town, 60 Germans with a small number of Fascist paratroopers among them were preparing to withdraw north from the town. Ever since the armistice [Italian] the Germans had been lawless and contemptuous of the Italians and looted at will.

About 5 p.m. a party of half a dozen Germans, a sergeant leading, came down the main street and in front of the house of Pasquale Sibilia stopped to shoot a chicken. Little Elena, seven-year-old child of Pasquale, ran in to tell her father and Pasquale came to the door armed with a rifle and shouted to the Germans to get away. The German sergeant laughed and shot Pasquale in the leg. Pasquale fired back and hit the German sergeant in the hand.

In five minutes the town was in an uproar and a party of 16 Germans plus four Italian Fascist paratroopers swarmed on to Pasquale's neighbours and began herding up all the men in the immediate neighborhood.

The whole affair did not take 30 minutes. Let Stefano di Mattia, the only survivor of this gruesome vengeance, speak:

'It was all one confused dream, all in silence, broken only by the yells of the Germans and the outcries of our women, instantly stilled. We were bustled up the street to the edge of town, about 100 yards. There in an open field we were ordered to line up. By the faces and actions of the Germans and those four Fascists we suddenly knew what was going to happen.

'In front of us with tommy guns and pistols were fourteen Germans and those four Fascists. The German sergeant gave a command. The Italian Fascists translated to us with sneers. 'Kneel! Kneel!' Before we could understand the guns opened. We were just in a huddle. I felt the sting of a bullet on my right leg and I fell. Others, I don't know who, fell or struggled over me, drenching me with their blood. I lay still as death. I heard the voices of the Germans as they waded among us shooting at pistol point those still alive. Just across the road at the corner of the village our women folk and a crowd of townsmen and children stared in silence.

'I know,' said Stefano, 'that they intended to burn us right in the ditch on the roadside for they forbade any of the townsfolk to come near us, and I lay there till dark, while a sentry guarded the pile of dead. Then it seems plans were changed when your patrols were reported on the fringes of the town. At midnight the Germans left in a great rush with lorries and armored cars and by morning all were gone.'

On the notice board of the town hall the Germans left written testimony to their crime.

'There have been already killed 15 men who were responsible for having fired against the Germans. This serves as a warning to all rebels of what will happen to them if any further acts against Germans are perpetrated.'

It was, Greg noted, signed with an illegible scrawl by some officer who must have already felt the hot breath of justice on his neck.

Greg called at the house of the little girl where the chicken had been shot. He saw her tiny ragged figure disappear into the inner darkness of the house. He did not press his request to talk to her. He ended his dispatch: 'I merely vowed to remember and remember that ragged little figure against the day these gray-green bastards plead before the bar of humanity.' It was the first time such an epithet had ever appeared in Greg's copy and the first time this word had ever appeared in the pages of the *Toronto Daily Star.*

One day in Italy Greg said to Bill Stewart, "Aren't we lucky to be in the best business in the world?" Another day he said to Dick Malone, "Does it ever occur to you to ask yourself, 'Just what the hell am *I* doing here?' "

32

Now when the pageant of the sun is gone,
And day's last flourish in the west despairs,
Above me darkling steals this other dawn,
This pale, entrancing universe of stars.

—*James Murray Clark*

As the hard fighting in Italy neared its end, Greg and Griffin were transferred back to England in anticipation of the Normandy invasion. During April and May of 1944 Murray was also in England, with a Canadian Base Reinforcement Group.

Whenever he got a 48-hour pass Greg took him to London, where they attended symphony concerts, the theater, Albert Hall. At press billets Greg was constantly pulling snapshots of Murray from his wallet to show off. Murray with his first fish, his first pheasant, his first deer.

June 6, 1944. D-Day. An awesome Allied armada moved into the South of France, to be met by an equally awesome German war machine. The Allied plan called for hundreds of tons of tanks, trucks, and supplies to be landed daily during the initial weeks, but bad weather created days when only a dozen tons came ashore. On D-Day plus 17, June 23, Murray's CBRG camp was moved to Normandy, near Cresserous. Canadian casualties were heavy and officer replacements were needed.

Montgomery, in charge of all land forces, was developing a colossal trap for the counterattacking German forces under his old foe, Rommel. Monty pressed the attack in the Caen-Falaise area with the Canadian troops, while Patton forged farther inland. During this period the Canadians and British suffered the main German onslaught—four Panzer divisions, five S.S. divisions, nine other infantry divisions, including one rushed from Norway, and the 16th German Air Force Division.

Having achieved this concentration of German power, Monty switched his armor to the U.S. sector under cover of night. Patton began a breakout which resulted in the entrapment and massive slaughter of the German forces.

Greg came to Normandy shortly after D-Day and was attached to the press camp at headquarters. He soon discovered Murray at his CBRG camp and began regular visits. For a long time Greg had told himself that the war would be over long before Murray became involved, but this hope was getting dim.

Murray was posted to the Regina Rifles, which had suffered severe losses. Greg was panic-stricken when he discovered that Murray had been posted. He tracked him down and found Murray in charge of a platoon and taking off on his first combat mission.

Up to this point in his life Murray's interests had been classical literature, music and art. He collected books and wrote poetry. In him Greg saw the young man he himself had been thirty years before. He was also, in Greg's opinion, a youth totally unprepared for war, too innocent to survive.

Dick Malone, in charge of Canadian public relations, saw what was happening. "Greg began to visit Murray's unit every day," said Malone. "He wanted to teach him all the tricks of war overnight. On Murray's first night attack, he wanted to go with him to show him how it was done. It was a pathetic situation. We tried to get Greg to stay away from the boy, but the next morning he would race back to his unit. If Murray was in the line Greg would come back and sit up all night with a bottle."

Greg showed a brief flicker of his old humor when a *Star* service message came through requesting a photo of Griffin and Greg together in the field, to run with their *Star* stories. "Greg got up early," said Malone, "got his uniform pressed, his buttons and shoes shined, shaved, got a photographer and woke up Griffin. Griffin was still wrapped in his sleeping bag. Greg shook him roughly and said, 'Get up, get up!' Griffin, still half asleep, his hair tousled, unshaven, wearing the clothes he'd fallen asleep in, stood up beside Greg—and the photo was taken and flown back to the *Star*. Griff didn't know what it was all about until later."

But it was just a flicker of his former self. In a last meeting with Murray he made a desperate suggestion. Should he try to get Murray transferred from his combat unit to the public relations section—out of danger?

In his heart he must have known what Murray's reaction would be: not contempt, perhaps, but a feeling of shame for his father. Putting this down in his journals, years later, Greg said it was the most tragic moment of his life.

Murray's reaction was predictable and understandable. He went to his commanding officer and asked that Greg be kept away from him. Malone talked to Greg, told him the Air Force needed press coverage, assured him he would keep in touch with Murray, and pressured Greg into transferring his operations to the RCAF 39th Reconnaissance Wing, then operating out of Bayeux. Greg's RCAF conducting officer was John Clare, later an editor of *Maclean's* magazine. They had many adventures, including a ribald dinner at the abbey of San Michele, but Greg was still worrying about Murray.

With the liberation of Paris, Greg headed there. In Paris Malone saw him for one brief evening. In search of a drink, they went to the American Bar at the Ritz. They were told there was nothing to drink, the Germans had taken everything . . . except a case of something they wouldn't drink. It turned out to be a case of Seagram's V.O. Malone and Greg bought the whole case. At a nearby table was Marlene Dietrich, who joined them at Greg's invitation. After this magic night Malone went on to the liberation of Brussels.

Meanwhile, the Regina Rifles continued advancing up the French coast—where strong pockets of Germans continued to hold their ground. On the night of September 16, Murray's company was ordered to advance from the village of St. Inglevert to locate and attack an emplacement of large guns which had been used to fire across the Channel at Dover.

Lieutenant Antoine Massé, in charge of the center platoon in the attack, felt there had been some mistake from the beginning. The terrain was not what reconnaissance had described. The coastal road that was supposed to lead them to their objective was nowhere to be found. Their first probing attack on a group of houses on the coast brought back withering machine-gun and mortar fire, which pinned them down and indicated that the Germans were there in totally unexpected strength. "The whole area was thickly mined," said Massé, "and to cap it all, they were able to pivot around at least one of the enormous cross-Channel guns and fire at us point-blank."

The giant shells added to a situation already hopeless and dangerous beyond description. Massé sent a messenger asking permission to retreat. Meanwhile, Murray, under fire, joined Massé for consultation. He had left his platoon under the command of his sergeant. As he joined Massé there was another shell from the Channel gun and both threw themselves down against the side of the sunken road. Murray fell directly on a buried mine, which exploded. The phosphorous grenades which dangled on his chest now ignited and covered him with searing flames.

Massé was himself wounded by the explosion, but staggered to his feet. He attempted to extinguish the flames with water from his canteen, which only added to the flames consuming Murray's body. The two platoons were withdrawn from the position and that night the dead were recovered by a patrol.

When Malone learned the news he sent a message for Greg to meet him in Brussels. Greg left by jeep immediately, knowing in his heart that the worst had come to pass. The news might be of his brother Joe, due on a flight from Canada. It might be of *Star* correspondent Bill Kinmond, who was missing in action. But in his heart he knew.

It took him nearly a whole day to reach Brussels through Chantilly, Cambrai, Mons—the old battlefields of his own war. When he found Malone, Greg was already crying.

He said, "It's Murray, isn't it."

"Yes," said Malone. "It's Murray."

Malone had a map reference indicating where Murray had been buried. He and Greg drove there, but they had trouble finding the battle scene. As they went past a small church graveyard in St. Inglevert, Malone noticed some new boards, nailed in the rough shape of a cross. On inspection they found one that bore the name of Sergeant M. E. Clark of the Regina Rifles.

Murray, of course, was a lieutenant. Oh God, thought Malone. There's been one of those unbelievable coincidences and I have put Greg through this agony for nothing. He left Greg at the grave and hurried to the church, where he found an old French priest inside.

"Is there a Lieutenant Murray Clark in those new graves?" he asked. "Of the Regina Rifles?"

"Yes," said the priest. "I have all the names in the book here."

"But it says Sergeant Clark," said Malone. "I have to be sure—that man out there is his father."

"That's another man," said the priest, showing him the book. "Lieutenant Murray Clark is in the end grave—it hasn't been marked yet."

The priest was a tiny man, Greg's size, Abbé Mermet. He put his arm around Greg, who was crying, and comforted him.

Malone drove to Ypres, where he managed to find two rooms in an old hotel and a bottle of whiskey for Greg. The hotel had the windows blown out—and there were no lights. Malone woke in the middle of the night and went next door to Greg's room, where he found him sitting in a rocking chair, bathed in the moonlight coming through the window. Greg talked until dawn—about Murray, about staying in this same hotel in World War I, about the redheaded barmaid of those days, named Yvette.

Back home in Canada, Greg's wife, Helen, had become increasingly depressed. Greg and Murray were overseas. Greg, Jr., had joined the Royal Canadian Air Force and was training in western Canada. Helen was left alone with her aged mother and thirteen-year-old Elizabeth. Her spirits sank lower and lower. She broke into uncontrollable weeping and began to lie in bed all day in helpless panic and confusion. She was on the verge of a breakdown, if not actually suffering from one, when news of Murray's death arrived. Her collapse was now total.

Greg's sister, Mabel, and her husband, Tommy Drew-Brook, gathered around to help until Greg's return. This was not as immediate as they expected. Days passed. Greg delayed in Brussels, unwilling or unable to make his departure. His brother Joe arrived from Canada and joined him. After another visit to the grave at St. Inglevert, Greg delayed his departure for home again.

"He was," said Malone, "manufacturing reasons for staying. He said he had promised Murray to look up the graves of other Regina Rifles men who had died earlier in the Caen area. He was drinking. He was totally unreasonable. I had signals from the *Star* asking for his return. I told him his place was at home with his wife. But it took us two weeks to get him off to London."

Greg spent a week in London. He accomplished little other than securing some of Murray's kit, a notebook he had given him, a few personal items. Back in Toronto, Tommy Drew-Brook became increasingly concerned about Helen's illness. He phoned Ken Edey, *Star* managing editor, who told him the *Star* would get Greg on a plane right away. Another week passed. Drew-Brook, who worked for Canadian-British Intelligence, phoned friends in Ottawa and asked them on what plane Greg was arriving.

Norman Robertson of External Affairs said, "We have no priority request for Greg at all. I can get him on a plane tomorrow morning, but I must have some sort of confirmation from the *Star*. Tell them to contact me with a message that Greg is being released to the government for war work—something of that kind. In the meantime I'll get Greg on a plane, with your assurance that Atkinson or Hindmarsh will get in touch with me."

Robertson cabled London and Greg was on a plane within hours. Tommy Drew-Brook was unable to contact Ken Edey at the *Star,* so that evening he phoned Hindmarsh in his Oakville home. Hindmarsh's daughter answered and said her father could not come to the phone because he had a bad cold. Drew-Brook patiently explained the circumstances. Holding the phone, Hindmarsh's daughter relayed the information to the next room.

Drew-Brook heard Hindmarsh bellow, "Tell him to get in touch with Edey!"

Drew-Brook said, "Tell your father I have been trying to get in touch with Edey without success. All I need from your father is verbal assurance that he will contact External Affairs."

This message was relayed.

Again Drew-Brook heard the shout: *"Tell him to get in touch with Edey!"*

Drew-Brook said to the daughter, "This is a difficult conversation for you. I'm going to hang up now and get in touch with Mr. Atkinson."

Drew-Brook got Atkinson on the phone and explained the circumstances.

Mr. Atkinson said, "Oh, Mr. Drew-Brook, Harry's been moving heaven and earth to get Greg back!"

Drew-Brook said, "May I have your assurance that someone will contact External Affairs tomorrow morning?"

"Of course, Mr. Drew-Brook," said Atkinson. "Our man in Ottawa will see Norman Robertson tomorrow morning "

In the morning Drew-Brook phoned Robertson in Ottawa.

"No," said Robertson. "Greg is actually in the air on his way home—and I must have some sort of support for my action."

Drew-Brook called Atkinson again, who said, "Mr. Drew-Brook, I thought that had all been attended to—I'll look after it right away."

It was attended to, but an ugly thought arose in Tommy Drew-Brook's mind. It seemed to him that the *Star* had not intended to bring Greg home at all. He was too valuable in Europe as a war correspondent. He and Mabel kept this thought to themselves for the next three years, along with the details of arranging Greg's homeward flight.

33

DEATH SPEAKS:

There was a merchant in Bagdad who sent his servant to market to buy provisions and in a little while the servant came back, white and trembling, and said, Master, just now when I was in the market-place I was jostled by a woman in the crowd and when I turned I saw it was Death that jostled me. She looked at me and made a threatening gesture; now lend me your horse, and I will ride away from this city and avoid my fate. I will go to Samarra and there Death will not find me. The merchant lent him his horse, and the servant mounted it, and he dug his spurs in its flanks and as fast as the horse could gallop he went. Then the merchant went down to the market-place and he saw me standing in the crowd and he came to me and said, Why did you make a threatening gesture to my servant when you saw him this morning? That was not a threatening gesture, I said, it was only a start of surprise. I was astonished to see him in Bagdad, for I had an appointment with him tonight in Samarra.

—*W. Somerset Maugham*

I phoned Greg on September 22, 1972, three days before his eightieth birthday. Without preamble, I said, "Some of your friends are thinking of chipping in and sending you a hundred-dollar call girl for your birthday. Any extras, of course, you'll have to pay for yourself."

"Save your money," laughed Greg. "I've just been told a joke about an old man running a fishing camp, who had a very young housekeeper."

"How does it go?"

"Some young bucks at the camp wanted to take her out but she said she had to be home early every night. 'Why?' they wanted to know. She said, 'The old man and I play a game every night. We stand it up straight and bet on which way it falls.' "

"Not bad," I said. "What are you doing for lunch?"

"Watching the hockey game, of course. Are you coming up?"

"If you haven't too big a crowd . . ."

"No, it will just be the two of us. Hurry up or you'll miss the start."

We were in the middle of the most exciting hockey series in history—the first eight-game match between our NHL stars and the Soviet National Team. Tension would mount unbearably, game by game, until the final minute of the final game in Moscow's Luzhniki Arena. Featuring the brilliant play of Canada's Phil Esposito and Russia's Aleksandr Yakushev, the game would be tied at 5–5. Canada would almost stop breathing. Children would be let out of school to watch the satellite television picture. Thousands would bring radio or TV sets to the office—or simply leave work to watch. An estimated 12 million Canadians and 50 million Russians would be watching. Then, there would be that unbelievable moment, with only 34 seconds to go, when Paul Henderson would bang in the winning goal, as he had in the two preceding games.

Greg had left the door of his King Edward hotel room ajar for me and I walked right in. He was sitting in his corner chair, facing the television, and he looked well.

"You missed it!" he said. "They were skating on to the ice one at a time—and being introduced—and Esposito fell right on his ass!"

"Good God," I said. "It would have to be Esposito."

It was Phil Esposito who had pulled the team, and Canada,

together after defeat in the fourth game in Vancouver. He became the leading point-getter of the series, with six goals and seven assists. It was Esposito who would win possession of the puck with only thirty-four seconds left in the final game and pass to Henderson to make that last, incredible, winning goal possible.

"The crowd had been applauding," said Greg. "But when he fell down, they all stopped."

The announcer said something about "tonight's game in Moscow."

"*Tonight's* game?" I said. "Oh, yes, I'd forgotten. It's been so long since I went to Moscow. You never did get to Moscow, did you, Greg?"

It wasn't very often I got a chance to put Greg down, and I wasn't going to miss the opportunity.

"No," said Greg. "There was one time I was supposed to meet Gord Sinclair there. I was coming in through Scandinavia and Sinclair was to come in from the Far East. But we never did get our visas. I think they wouldn't give them to us because I was just a humorous writer and Gord was one of those troublesome writers. Speaking of troublesome writers, are you employed or unemployed?"

I had to laugh. It hadn't taken the little bugger long to get back at me. "You know damn well that I became Canadian editor of Pocket Books in January."

"I knew that," said Greg. "I just wondered if you were still there."

"I'm still there," I said. "Everything's going fine, apart from the fact I'm about to sue them for some overtime work I did."

"I knew it," said Greg. "I knew it. You're too abrasive."

"But that's not the important news," I said. "I've gotten the paperback rights to Tarasov's hockey book and we'll have it on the stands in a month. He called it *Road to Olympus,* but we're putting a big head on it, *Russian Hockey Secrets.*"

Anatoli Vladimirovitch Tarasov was a Soviet Army colonel, coach of the Moscow Army team and of the Russian Olympic team when I'd been in Moscow in 1964. At that time Tarasov's teams had been sweeping World and Olympic hockey and he began agitating for a match with NHL teams. That was now being realized, although Tarasov had been replaced as coach. Tarasov's theories and training methods had been responsible for much of what Canadians admired in Russian teams: the stamina, superb skating and team discipline.

"Did you meet him in Moscow?" said Greg.

"He was the highlight of my trip. At our first meeting he said he would show me everything I wanted to know about his hockey training, that he would trounce me in a tennis match and then he would take me to the best steam bath in Moscow. He added that he would *not* introduce me to his mistress."

"Did he keep his promises?" said Greg.

"All of them—including not introducing me to his mistress. You would have liked him. He had a great sense of humor. After an hour-long lecture on how he trained goalkeepers, he realized he was getting too serious, so he just stopped and said, 'Of course, every coach goes mad in his own way.'"

"Is his book any good?"

"It should be required reading for every hockey coach in Canada—all those who can read, anyway."

We switched our attention back to the television set. Normally it sat silent, since Greg regarded it as an idiot box. He would watch something like the Kennedy funeral, or perhaps the World Series. He even had an idiot screen for it, which was now folded back over the top of the set. The idiot screen was a present from his daughter, Elizabeth. It was a translucent screen, studded with dozens of convex glass pieces, about the size of marbles. When it hung over the front of the set, with the television on, it changed meaningless programs into meaningless patterns of flashing colored lights—like a jukebox, or a pinball machine gone mad. Greg loved it.

The game which was about to begin was the first Moscow game in the series. The first four games had been played across Canada —and had shattered Canada's pride. The Canadian stars had lost two games, tied one and won only one. Now, by courtesy of a star, as Greg put it, we—and millions of other Canadians—were about to see how our team would do on the larger ice surface of the Moscow rink.

"It'll be a matter of condition," said Greg.

I agreed. I had been stunned by the Russian training and discipline. Their hockey players trained all day, all year. We were now seeing the results.

At the end of the first period it was 1–0 for Canada, and Greg and I relaxed with a scotch and soda. There had only been two penalties, one to each team, which was another good sign, as the Canadians had picked up foolish penalties all through the series.

Greg had a photograph that I hadn't noticed before on the wall of his room. It was a black-and-white enlargement of a northern scene, a wooded point jutting into a rippling, glittering stretch of water. "That's Go Home," said Greg, "shot by my grandson, Andy. It's a view from the hill behind my place, looking across the back of Bain's Island, up the Pittsburgh Channel. I had a bench there—there's no counting the hours I've spent watching the sunsets there."

"With a drink in your hand, I bet."

"Hell, no," said Greg. "I wasn't allowed to drink up there. I had to go to war to have a drink."

In the second period, Canada scored again, but the play seemed to be getting rougher.

"My old friend Billy Milne was the dirtiest player on our team at Varsity," said Greg. "His motto was 'Always keep your elbows up.' When I asked him how he got away with it, he said, 'I always know where the referee is.'"

"What was the first hockey game you ever saw?"

"The St. Pats playing the Montreal Maroons," said Greg. "At the old Mutual Street arena. My dad took me."

"Mine took me there, too," I said. "He and his brother Dick coached the Toronto Arenas—the first team to bring the Stanley Cup to Toronto."

I went to the bathroom adjacent to Greg's bedroom. While I was in there I heard a tremendous roar on the television set. Hurrying back to the sitting room, I learned that Mahovolich had scored a third Canadian goal.

Greg chuckled. "You better have a piss every three minutes. We're going to need the goals."

He was so right. Canada led, 4–1, going into the third period, but then the roof fell in. Russia scored four goals in a row. The game ended. The Canadian team had seemed to run out of steam, much as they had in the first game of the series in Montreal. We sat there depressed, trying to understand how we had gone from a 4–1 lead to a 4–5 defeat so quickly. And we did not know yet about Paul Henderson's miracles that were to take place in the next three games.

We put the idiot screen back over the television set and watched the meaningless patterns. "I told you," said Greg mournfully. "You should have had a piss every three minutes."

Through the window behind Greg's television set we could see St. Lawrence Market, the heart of early Toronto. The view now consisted mainly of parking lots, with what seemed like acres and acres of cars. For some time Greg had been urging me to take a photo of this wasteland, but I kept forgetting my camera. "The sun has to be just right," said Greg. "Then you can get all the cars in, stretching as far as you can see."

He moved slowly to the window and pointed out toward Jarvis Street. "Down there somewhere the McMurrays had their house. That's Grandma Greig's people. She was a McMurray. That's where she saw her baby brother, John, killed by a dog. The dog belonged to old Dr. Allan—the one who gave us Allan Gardens. That used to be the outskirts of town, of course."

He went to the phone and ordered us a belated lunch, pea soup and hamburgers. He was good friends with the girl on room service and he had been keeping her informed of the score throughout the game. Now he began to lecture her about the lunch wagon that would be coming up.

"You know what's going to happen," he said. "The waiter will roll that wagon in here with its black wheels and make black marks all over my rug. Maybe you can send some newspapers up with it. No. Here's what we'll do. I'll get Jock to go to the door and he and the waiter can carry the wagon in."

Putting down the phone, Greg picked up a sheet of paper and handed it to me to read. It was the Maugham vignette which appears at the beginning of this chapter.

"I read that thing forty years ago," said Greg, "and it's haunted me ever since—but I could never find it. Just the other day I picked up this old paperback in a book store—*Appointment in Samarra*—and there was this piece used as a preface. If you keep looking for something, eventually you'll find it. You know I don't read O'Hara, so I tore this preface out and gave the book to the chambermaid."

We talked about Greg's biography.

"I keep thinking of you," said Greg, "with this damn life of mine hanging over your head. You must wish you'd never gotten into it."

"Balls," I said. "With all due respect, of course. How is your work going?"

"I ran into Bill Goodson in the lobby the other day," said Greg, "and I thought to myself, oh-oh, here comes the chop."

Goodson, a former advertising salesman, had become publisher of *Weekend Magazine*.

"But Goodson came up and chatted awhile and didn't mention it. I'm fifteen years past retirement, you know. Still on salary. They've treated me very good. You must mention that in the book."

After lunch I asked him his birthday plans. He was having a birthday dinner in the hotel, with young Greg and his wife, as well as his sister, Mabel, and her husband. I wished him the best and took my leave. On the way out I noticed there was a piece of paper in his typewriter. And the old, familiar sign on the wall above it, in big, bold letters.

GO TO WORK!

34

A SMALL CHARGE FOR FLOWERS

Greg was a long time in nursing Helen back from the shadows and in coming to terms with his own grief. With Helen's nervous breakdown, the chores of running the house devolved on him, something with which he had little experience.

Both he and Helen still found Murray's death unbelievable. The sight of a young man coming down the street was enough to make them feel it was Murray somehow, miraculously, returning. At Go Home Bay the sound of a paddle against the side of a canoe or a laugh floating across the water made them start up from their chairs.

Greg clung to his grief, nursed it even, by going through Murray's books, finding a poem, some scattered notes. His own cable to Helen when Murray died: "He had not a single characteristic of those who survive war. He was too gentle to be a soldier, too noble not to be one."

He remembered every little story and scrap of conversation. The day Murray said he was always last to be chosen for games at school. Murray's remark about war and every soldier having a little boy still inside him. In all these Greg saw signs of greatness and promise. He would have achieved more than Greg or Greg's father. Greg began to see Murray as "a saint, who would one day have been a king among men."

He contacted Murray's regimental comrades, carefully wrote down their warm comments. From Antoine Massé, the lieutenant who'd been wounded by the same mine that killed Murray, he extracted every detail of the day and Murray's death, including Massé's futile efforts to douse the phosphorous grenades with water from his canteen, and the immolation of the torn body.

All these things were kept in a treasure chest in Greg's attic. When Dick Malone and Ross Munro visited his home after the war, he took them upstairs to show them and read to them these agonizing memorabilia. Munro and Malone were aghast at the way he was continuing to torture himself and urged him to forget, but he could forget nothing; he was obsessed. Murray's life, like a movie that would not stop, kept running through his mind.

At work he could see the future only as bleak. The *Star* was approaching the peak of its prosperity, but the legal requirement to reemploy all returning servicemen was placing the paper in an overstaffed position. There was no Newspaper Guild and no pension plan. Atkinson, now an old man of eighty, seemed more preoccupied with his will than with his staff. With Helen ill, Greg could not see himself pursuing a newspaperman's roving life— and yet he knew he would be unhappy if he stood aside while younger men took over the job. He was still making $10,000 a year, but he could not see the *Star* continuing to pay him that salary for some routine task.

Hindmarsh was busy depriving feature writers and war correspondents of their prima donna status. Fred Griffin had been the *Star*'s best reporter for twenty years. He was now fifty-seven years old and had just returned from two years of frontline coverage, emotionally and physically exhausted. He was immediately put to work on spot-news assignments, subject to call at all hours. He died of a heart attack within a year, a very bitter man.

Less than ten years before, Griffin had published a book of his newspaper experiences called *Variety Show*. At that time he was still enchanted with the *Star*. His preface to the book read: "One thing I must say clearly. I owe the *Star* much—of opportunity, outlet, realization. Nowhere else in Canada, certainly on no other newspaper, could I have had the experience, the quickened living, the freshness of interest, the fun." But the *Star* had a penchant for unhappy endings.

Greg had shared Griffin's loyalty and enthusiasm for the *Star*. Because of his father's history with the paper, and a certain naïveté on his part, his was even more of a love affair.

On the famous Moose River mine disaster story, the large *Star* crew had been augmented by the presence of Claude Pascoe, the fixer, the Hindmarsh agent. An Ontario government floatplane had been helping newsmen get stories and personnel in and out of the isolated area. When Ken MacTaggart, a *Globe & Mail* reporter, attempted to use the plane, he was confronted by Pascoe, who said he had a telegram from Mitchell Hepburn, premier of Ontario, forbidding such use.

It was common practice in those days for papers to knock out the competition by almost any means—stealing film, tying up telephone and telegraph wires, even kidnapping people in the news. When MacTaggart returned to his office and related the Pascoe story, the editor said, "Write it. We'll print it." After the story appeared in *The Globe & Mail,* MacTaggart encountered Greg on the street. Greg was furious. "Don't ever speak to me again, MacTaggart," he said. "Writing those vicious lies about the *Star.*"

Greg wanted to move on, in 1945, but was reluctant to appear disloyal or ungrateful to the *Star*. He tendered his resignation, but Hindmarsh offered to continue paying him $150 a week for continuing to do the Jim and Greg stories for the *Star Weekly*. As he was planning to do radio work, this fitted in with Greg's plans and he accepted. It did begin to rankle that, in effect, if the Jim and Greg pieces were worth $150 a week, all his years of chasing news stories around the world had been worth only $50 a week to the daily.

Greg continued this new arrangement of Jim-Greg pieces and radio work into 1946. One of his first radio jobs was for Goodyear Tire. Next came a series of C.B.C. talks on rehabilitation, a subject he had written about during the First World War. Talking came easily to Greg and, at $100 an appearance, his income rose considerably.

During this period Helen was under the care of the family doctor, Dr. Macintyre—and also two psychiatrists from St. Joseph's Hospital. She had become almost completely dispirited, with little interest in life. Greg anxiously fanned every spark and improved things at home by replacing the icebox with an electric refrigerator, new rugs and drapes. Slowly, she responded, with a decreasing incidence of complete depression. At Go Home, Greg enlarged the cottage kitchen and installed a new stove. Young Greg started at the university in the fall and Elizabeth began to attend St. Hilda's. Greg's bank loan rose to $13,000.

On September 17, 1946, the second anniversary of Murray's death, Helen and Greg managed to pass the day without a mention of its meaning, but they both felt as though they were carrying a physical burden between them from dawn to midnight. Greg went through his mementos of Murray.

Knowing that Greg was trying to work free of the *Star* and yet was held back by feelings of loyalty, his sister Mabel and her husband, Tommy Drew-Brook, finally told him their version of getting him back from England after Murray's death, including Hindmarsh's repeated bovine bellow, "Tell him to talk to Edey!"

Greg heard Tommy Drew-Brook out quietly. He did not change color or get excited, yet from that moment he was through with the *Star*. He was thinking. For thirty years he had been able to travel anywhere at an instant's notice because of the *Star*'s influence. Why had they not exerted themselves to get him home after Murray's death?

The next morning Greg talked to Jim Frise, who had his own list of grievances. At the *Star*'s front counter for twenty or thirty years had been a gentle man named Misener. When he suffered a heart attack, the *Star* gave him a year's salary as a good-bye present. When Bill Law, the artist in the room next to Jimmie's, had left, management had put a lock on his door and had a *Star* executive present while he cleaned out his pencils and paints, as though he were a thief.

Jimmie and Greg agreed to take the first opportunity to leave. That afternoon Greg went to see the cashier to find out what I.O.U.'s he had outstanding. After she conferred with H. S. Sainthill, the chief accountant, she informed Greg he owed $1,645. Greg was thunderstruck. He went in to see Sainthill, who explained that Greg's income tax had been unpaid during his last year overseas. When the revenue department garnisheed Greg's wages, the *Star* had paid the taxes and charged it to Greg's account.

Greg went to his bank, borrowed the $1,645 in addition to his existing loan there and paid the *Star*. He then called the income tax department man who handled his file. He was told that the department had written regularly to his home but had gotten no answer. When the garnishee was automatically applied, the *Star* had paid promptly. However, the amount had been $1,630, not $1,645. Greg asked Sainthill about the discrepancy.

"Ah, yes," said Sainthill. "There is an item here for $15 for flowers."

Greg had cabled a request for flowers to be sent to Helen on Murray's death.

"Why wasn't I told about this in the year and a half since the war?" said Greg.

"I was instructed not to do so," said Sainthill.

It was possible, thought Greg, that Hindmarsh or Atkinson had ordered this so as not to add to Greg's problems during Helen's convalescence.

That evening he tried to question Helen without upsetting her. Yes, she had put the income tax queries to one side for his return. No, she had had no phone calls from the *Star*, but she had been very vague and confused in that period. Was there something wrong?

"No," said Greg—but he now felt that the *Star* had known that Helen was sick and confused. Rather than recall him from the war, they had quietly paid the income tax on his behalf and charged it to his account.

Greg contacted John McConnell, publisher of the Montreal *Standard*—a weekly paper which was trying to catch up to the *Star Weekly*—from whom Greg had received an offer many years ago.

He and Frise were immediately invited to Montreal and agreed to go to the *Standard* for the same money they were making at the *Star*, a salary of $125 a week and expenses of $50 a week— for a total of $175 a week. For Jim Frise there was the attractive possibility that the *Standard* could arrange syndication of his Birdseye Center cartoon in the United States.

They chose to break the news to Hindmarsh on Christmas Eve, in memory of the legendary *Star* firings.

Hindmarsh removed the cigar from his mouth. "Aren't you going to give us a chance to bid?"

Frise answered, "Mr. Hindmarsh, you have nothing to bid with."

So ended their thirty years with the *Star*.

This is Greg's version of the dramatic break which saw the *Star Weekly* lose two of its oldest, most famous and most valuable personalities. Greg did not excuse himself of all responsibility for Helen's breakdown. In retrospect he asked himself what he, a fifty-year-old veteran of the First World War, with two sons in the present one, had been doing overseas as a war correspondent while his wife was left at home alone. He had trusted the *Star* to be as concerned with his family's fortunes as he had been with the paper.

He felt betrayed. His love for the paper, like Griffin's, turned to hate. Ten years later, Ralph Allen, by now editor of *Maclean's* magazine, caught a glimpse of this hatred, and was so shocked to find this in the gentle, humorous man he knew that he went home and typed this memo to himself:

This sets down very briefly a remarkable scene that took place in Gil Purcell's office around 6:25 P.M. Thursday, December 20, 1956.

By pre-arrangement, Bruce West, Greg Clark and I had met there to see some colour slides Bruce had made during the hunting season of a few weeks earlier at Alex Forbes' Camp Forty near Sudbury. Gil and I had been there a couple of years earlier, along with Bruce and Greg. They had been back in each of the two ensuing years and Bruce had taken some good pictures.

I got there around 5:45, having had to go to my doctor for a routine check-up a while earlier. The others were in session, having had a drink and waiting for me before having a second.

By then everyone knew about the changes in the *Star* directorate and also about Hindmarsh's having been taken to hospital with what looked like a very grave heart attack.

At around seven Foster Barclay brought in a teletype for Gil's attention saying that HCH had died.

We talked about many things, including this, and then Greg said:

"Harry Comfort Hindmarsh was the most unpleasant man I ever knew."

"Careful," somebody said, "he's looking over your shoulder."

Meanwhile Mary Kibblewhite, one of Gil's secretaries, had come in to have a Christmas glass with us—it being Christmas—and Greg turned his head to where HCH might have been and said quite inaudibly out of the side of his mouth: "F--- Hindmarsh!"

He turned his face away from Mary as he said this but she got it just the same. Greg made a number of angry remarks

—not bitter but angry—about HCH—"gone to meet his maker etc." Much more. Then he told the story of how he and Jimmie Frise quit the *Star*."

Greg's version of his departure from the *Star* has been made clear. No executive at the *Star* has ever commented on it. The delay in Greg's return from overseas may have been partly his own fault, caused by his grief at Murray's death. It may have been partly Hindmarsh's insensitivity or the bureaucratic sluggishness of any large organization. Still, if Greg's wife had been emotionally disturbed and confused for many months one might have expected the paper to be aware of this. Hindmarsh kept himself informed on many less important matters.

Hugh Newton, who handled Greg's wartime dispatches, was one who knew how true this was. When Newton joined the *Star* in 1942, he came from British United Press in Montreal. His furniture was to follow him C.O.D. Shortly before its arrival he realized that he did not have enough cash to pay for it, so he went to see Jim Kingsbury for an advance on his first pay.

"I can get you an advance," said Kingsbury, "but this will go on your dossier and Atkinson will have a report of it in the morning. It will hurt your career here. I advise you to borrow it somewhere else."

At a later date, Newton's wife and young son met him for lunch at the Stoodleigh restaurant on the main floor of the *Star* building. Newton's son was taken violently ill at lunch and rushed to a hospital.

The next morning Newton was summoned to Hindmarsh's office.

"How's your boy?" said Hindmarsh.

"He's all right," said Newton. "But how did you know—"

"I get a report on everything that happens in this building," said Hindmarsh.

While researching this book, I interviewed the widow of Harry Hindmarsh. She was polite, but remembered little about Greg other than that he had visited the Hindmarsh home a few times to instruct the children in fly-fishing. No, she knew nothing about Greg's reasons for leaving the *Star*. Perhaps her husband and her father had sheltered her from the problems at the paper, or perhaps she was being diplomatic. When I asked if her husband had shouldered the blame for orders that came directly from her father, she smiled.

"After my father died," she said, "my husband said the phone on his desk didn't ring the way it used to . . . and he almost missed it a little."

At one time I looked to Ken Edey, the man in the middle, to throw more light on Greg's quarrel with the *Star*. I knew Edey well and he had been a good friend of Greg's. Edey had been managing editor of the *Toronto Star* and later managing editor of the Montreal *Star*. He used to say Greg had thrown "two great blocks" for him and helped him obtain both jobs.

After Edey left or lost these two important newspaper positions I kept suggesting to him that he had an obligation to write a magazine article about his experiences to let the rest of us know what it was like in high places. I even gave him the title—"I Was a Managing Editor—Twice." Edey did not follow my suggestion. Perhaps managing editors get there by *not* writing articles about the newspaper business.

Nor would Ken talk about Greg's departure from the *Star*. "When I left the *Toronto Star*," he said, "I made a lot of enemies because I wouldn't say anything about it. The same when I left the Montreal *Star*. You're one of those who has needled me about it. But my feeling is that if I didn't speak up about it when I was in the business then I shouldn't speak up now."

At the time of this conversation Ken was in charge of public relations for the University of Toronto. He had very interesting tasks, such as trying to squeeze the multi-level prose of Marshall McLuhan into linear print for a university publication known as *Explorations*.

Edey went on, "I could tell you six stories about leaving the Montreal *Star,* all true, but none of which would be the whole truth. Sometimes I wonder, in trying to hang on to my alleged mind, if there isn't a self-protective device in not acknowledging the truth about ourselves. If we admitted all the horrors we know about ourselves, we might lose the power to cope. So why not just leave Greg's version of leaving the *Star* as it is. And the same for me."

A very thoughtful man, Ken Edey. But I would still like to read his magazine story.

When Greg and Jim pulled out of the *Star* the paper's reaction was, if not in character, then somewhat petty or excessively businesslike. Joseph Atkinson announced that the *Star* must never again make the mistake of allowing writers or artists the freedom to become famous personalities in their own right. Harry Hindmarsh made his usual literal interpretation of this. Reporters' by-lines all but vanished from the paper, even on very important stories.

Jimmie Frise might be taking his famous "Birdseye Center" with him, but the *Star* held copyright to the title itself. The paper hired another artist, who set about producing an imitation "Birdseye Center." Jimmie's work in the *Standard* had to appear under a new title, "Juniper Junction."

35

There was a young man who said damn,
It appears to me now that I am
Just a being that moves
In predestinate grooves
Not a bus, not a bus, but a tram.

—Anon.

"How lucky can a man be?"

This was Greg's favorite observation about his newspaper career. He explained, "I was along for two great rides—the rise of the *Star Weekly* between the wars, and then the rise of the *Standard.*"

Greg had been with the *Star Weekly* as it grew from a local paper of 20,000 circulation to a national weekly occasionally topping the 1,000,000 mark. The *Standard* was destined, as *Weekend Magazine,* to top the 2,000,000 mark, the largest circulation ever achieved by any Canadian publication.

Although he didn't know it at the time, Greg was indeed lucky to be along for this second great ride. When it became known that Jim and Greg were available, *Standard* publisher John McConnell called a meeting of his top executives. They were not unanimous on the matter of hiring Jim and Greg. There was some feeling that the *Standard* should remain with its policy of developing its own personalities, rather than buying those long associated with another publication. On a split vote, John McConnell cast the deciding vote to hire them. Greg and Jim came to the *Standard* at the end of 1946, not knowing by what a narrow margin their futures had been decided.

The *Standard* had been founded in 1905 by George Murray and later purchased by Lord Atholstan. It was patterned on the

English illustrated weeklies of the time and sold modestly in Montreal and the Maritimes. In 1946 it was still struggling to reach the 300,000 mark. Some time before that, Lord Atholstan's newspaper properties, which included the Montreal *Star,* had come into the possession of a remarkable Canadian named John Wilson McConnell. Born in Muskoka on July 1, 1877, son of an Irish immigrant, McConnell moved to Toronto at the age of fourteen, where he got a job with Christie Biscuits at $3.00 a week. He became a salesman, moved to Montreal and acquired a great many business interests, including the St. Lawrence Sugar Refineries, the base of an estimated $400 million fortune.

McConnell became a quiet philanthropist. At one point his gifts to McGill University alone totaled over $12,000,000. His three sons died premature, tragic deaths: one as a result of misusing a common pain-killer, one by his own hand and one by drowning alone in his own private lake.

John Griffith McConnell was the son slated to take control of the *Standard* and the Montreal *Star*. He had studied the newspaper business at the *Times* of London, the New York *Times* and the New York *Sun*. In 1938, at the age of twenty-six, he began revamping the *Standard* with the help of a small group of men, most of them still in their twenties. One was A. Davidson Dunton, who later became chairman of the C.B.C. and co-chairman of the Laurendeau-Dunton Commission on Bilingualism and Biculturism.

Others were Glenn Gilbert, Mark Farrell, Lewis Louthood and Phil Surrey. They were soon followed by Craig Ballantyne, Kate Aitken, Max Newton, Andy O'Brien, Alex Janusitis, Hugh Shaw, Stanley Handman, Gerald Clark and others.

The *Standard* encouraged the work of Canadian writers, artists and photographers and set them to work to portray Canada and Canadians on a realistic level. A major advance was the photo-story section, which pioneered the documentary photo-story in Canada. *Newsweek* referred to this section as among the best in the world.

The *Star Weekly* had settled into a different formula. Having escaped the ban on bathing beauties which had existed during Mrs. Atkinson's lifetime, the paper now had a batch of beauties standing by in bathing suits, which they used to illustrate almost any kind of story. A story on tobacco might be illustrated by a model caressing a tobacco plant, with the heading, "Girls like these will soon be harvesting the Simcoe tobacco crop." A model gracing the prow of a yacht meant "Girls like these will soon be opening the sailing season." "Girls like these" became a joke in the trade—and a forerunner of today's TV commercials.

Hindmarsh, who collected stuffed predatory birds, had a mania for animal stories. Stories about leopards, tigers, wolves and elephants littered the pages. Artist Gal O'Leary once joked, "We're suspending publication this week! Our gorilla has escaped!"

At the time when Jim-Greg stories began appearing in the centerfold of the *Standard,* there were many who believed that the *Standard* was a better weekly newspaper, although it trailed badly in circulation.

Meanwhile, Greg and Jimmie were getting to know the *Standard*'s staff. It was not as eccentric as the early staff of the *Star Weekly,* but was composed of interesting characters.

Editorial director Glenn Gilbert was a fun-loving man and not a rigid disciplinarian. If an employee was drinking too much Gilbert would call the offender to his office and deliver his standard lecture. "There is room for only one drunk on this paper," he would explain patiently, "and I was here first."

Executive editor Craig Ballantyne was tall, handsome and an able newspaperman. Like Greg, he was a bird watcher and a fisherman. He liked to climb mountains and play chess. And he liked women. His on-again, off-again love affair with staff writer Mavis Gallant was followed with interest by the office. Mavis finally wrote the end of the affair in a short story and went off to Europe, where she wrote short stories for *The New Yorker* and serious novels.

Other women on staff included women's editor Kate Aitken, cooking editor Helen Gougeon, writers Doyle Klyn and Jacquie Sirois, the latter married to the emerging novelist Brian Moore.

Craig Ballantyne was the best chess player in the office. His favorite chess anecdote was Grand Master Bogolyubov's explanation of why he always won, whether he was playing the white pieces or the black. "When I play white," said Bogolyubov, "I win because I am white. When I am black, I win because I am Bogolyubov."

Magazine editor Hugh Shaw was a Queen's graduate and an ex-navy man. He came to the *Standard* from *New World* magazine in Toronto, another pioneer publication in photo-journalism. Shaw was a great friend of Greg's and worked hard at fitting him into the *Standard*.

Photo editor Phil Surrey was an artist in oils and also played chess. His section featured outstanding photographers from across Canada and he developed his own staff of Louis Jaques, Ronny Jaques, Charlie King, Bert Beaver, Bruce Moss, Michael Rougier and others.

Art director Dick Hersey was one of the first to make extensive use of Canadian artists for illustrations. Previously many illustrations had been second-run work purchased from U.S. sources. Oscar Cahen, Ed McNally, Harold Town, Doug Wright and Aileen Richardson made early appearances in the *Standard*. Duncan Macpherson said Hersey kept many artists afloat until their careers were established.

There were lots of family arguments at the *Standard,* generally dissolved in a martini lunch or suspended because there was a staff party at someone's house. However, sports editor Andy O'Brien and Montreal photographer Al Foreman settled one differently in a Newfoundland hotel room which they were sharing on an assignment. They agreed to stand face-to-face and take one punch at each other.

O'Brien, a university football player and boxer, was a monumental man. Al Foreman was much smaller, but he had also been a boxer—in fact, a lightweight champion. They took their positions and O'Brien courteously granted Foreman the first punch.

There was only one punch.

Foreman's blow took O'Brien and a nearby lamp to the floor and broke O'Brien's jaw. The pair then had to repair to the local hospital, get O'Brien's jaw wired up and carry on with their assignment.

There was a son-in-law at the *Standard,* but he was not cast in the same mold as the son-in-law Greg had left behind. His name was Peter Laing and he had married the only McConnell daughter. Laing was a literate, pleasant lawyer who worked on the McConnell family interests. He seemed to enjoy raffish editorial company, frequently dropping in to the Montreal Press Club for drinks and conversation. One of his favorite rhymes was the one on free will and determinism that appears at the head of this chapter.

Laing had been studying law in London at the outbreak of war and had gone to North Africa with the 9th Lancers as a tank squadron leader. In 1942 his jeep was blown up by a mine. Later the same day, the ambulance he was in was blown up by another mine. Both his lower legs had to be amputated. Laing made his way about with two artificial limbs.

The general manager at the *Standard* was Mark Farrell. As a student Farrell had traveled to Moscow, where he was arrested, or nearly arrested, for throwing snowballs at Stalin's statue. Farrell had voted against hiring Greg in the beginning, but came to admit this was a mistake and became one of Greg's fishing companions.

Lew Louthood was another longtime *Standard* employee, one of many bilingual people on the staff. In 1959 he helped put together *le magazine Perspectives,* a French-language version of *Weekend* edited by Pierre Gascon. Louthood was publisher of *Weekend* when the publication dissolved in 1980.

Publisher of the *Standard* and of *Weekend* through its successful years, and of the Montreal *Star,* was the middle McConnell son, John Griffith McConnell. He was a handsome, intelligent man who had great personal charm and a warm sense of humor. As a publisher, he did not have Atkinson's remoteness. He drank and dined with many on his staff, played golf and chess with them. Unlike Atkinson, McConnell did not fire people for attending staff parties. He attended them himself.

McConnell took as much interest in the editorial content of his papers as he did in the bottom line. When Roy Thomson breezed into his office one day with his usual offer to buy, McConnell said, "We are not in the shoe business, Mr. Thomson."

You could argue with John McConnell without getting yourself fired. When I questioned the large amounts of money he spent on modern art, he simply explained: "The accountants tell us how much we can spend each year. If you put the money in old masters it benefits only the dealers. With modern art, at least some of the money goes to an artist who is still alive."

He was interested in books and authors and especially liked the writings of newspaperman Don Marquis. When I said I was also a Marquis fan, John presented me with his copy of *O Rare Don Marquis,* a book long out of print.

By accident I became one of McConnell's chess companions.

On my visits to Montreal we played at his home and at other times he would phone me from Montreal and keep the line open while we played into the night, frequently until dawn. His phone bills must have been staggering as these games went on for many years.

When he visited Toronto, McConnell stayed at the Park Plaza or the King Edward, where we also played. One of our games in the Royal Suite at the King Edward was interrupted by a shot. A number of McConnell's executives and publishing friends were watching our game when a phone call came in for John from Montreal. He turned white as he took the message and said, "Oh God, no." He gave some instructions and then relayed the news to the rest of us. One of the Montreal *Star*'s editors had shot himself. Ken Edey, then managing editor of the Montreal *Star*, was in the room and John's first question to Ken was, "You weren't pushing him too hard, were you?" Edey shook his head. "No, I don't think it was that."

John liked to sip brandy while he played, which did not improve his chess. This was evident in some of our long-distance games and as a result of them I formulated Carroll's Law, which I believe is an original contribution to chess theory. "One ounce of liquor is equal to the square of two pawns."

Despite treatment, McConnell's ability to handle alcohol deteriorated. For his relatives and friends it was a painful thing to watch over the years. When drinking heavily he did not have an abrupt personality change, but he seemed to drink to submerge himself, almost as a form of self-destruction. He gradually lost effective control of his newspapers and one day was found floating face downward in the private lake on his estate north of Montreal. It was a sad ending for a very likable man.

As the only two Toronto employees of the *Standard*, Greg and I had a natural community of interests. We shared some assignments and made trips together to Montreal, where we would meet writers from other *Standard* bureaus: Walter O'Hearn and Frank Lowe from New York or Washington, Steve Franklin from Vancouver, Bruce Moss from Winnipeg, Robert McKeown from Ottawa and Swifty Robinson from Halifax. David Willock, my predecessor in Toronto, was now an editor at the Montreal head office.

As Greg had made it a lifelong habit to avoid exercise, except where fishing and hunting were concerned, one event we did not share was the annual *Standard* golf tournament, an all-male company bash of classic proportions, which took place at golf clubs north of Montreal, usually Lachute or Rosemere. There were few serious golfers. In fact, advertising manager Bill Taylor is the only one I can remember. Sports editor O'Brien was hopeless. He spent a lifetime trying to break a hundred.

A unique annual award at the golf tournament was the Potfor Trophy. It was a gold-plated chamber pot, presented to the person judged to have made the biggest goof of the year. Not surprisingly, general manager Mark Farrell won it twice. I was the only other two-time winner. After the banquet, this golf tournament went on into the night, with gambling, drinking, putting contests held under car headlights—and arguments.

One year art director Dick Hersey continually harangued publisher McConnell about some magazine problem until McConnell decided he had heard enough and headed for the parking lot. Hersey finished his drink, thought of something else he wanted to say and followed.

McConnell started up his Cadillac and did not notice that Hersey had followed him. When he shot backward out of his parking space he ran over Hersey, breaking his right leg. At this point someone uttered a cry or a shout of warning. Perhaps it was Hersey. Hearing this, McConnell changed gears and shot forward, running over Hersey for the second time. This accident was regarded as a great stroke of luck for Hersey, inasmuch as his job would probably now be assured for life. Like so many things, alas, this didn't work out as foreseen.

As an out-of-towner at these tournaments, I was at the mercy of these inebriated golfers for a ride back to my hotel room. My first year, I selected Mark Farrell as a driver, figuring he had the most to lose by any car accident. Unfortunately, Farrell turned out to be a frustrated race driver who drove his European sports cars as fast as they would go. When I saw what was happening, and nearly happening, I crawled into the back seat and lay down on the floor for the rest of the trip.

The next year I avoided Farrell and accepted a ride with Andy O'Brien. O'Brien was one of the world's great drinkers. This night I believe he had also lost his spectacles, for, after circling a cloverleaf two or three times, he bumped his car across a plowed field and got us on the Auto Route heading south toward Montreal, but unfortunately in the northbound lanes. Our erratic progress to the south terrified many northbound drivers, as well as photographer Louis Jaques, who was the other passenger, and me. We also startled a uniformed officer in charge of a tollgate when we came upon him from the rear. He made us get over on the right side of the highway.

I do not know what divine power guided O'Brien through his many merry adventures and enabled him to survive long enough to be elected to the Canadian Sports Hall of Fame in 1980. On another evening in Montreal he decided to drive me home by what he thought was a shortcut, through a park. It was a bumpy ride, as this was not a park with roads in it. I used to attribute his luck to a St. Christopher medal dangling from his rearview mirror. Maybe it was a St. Jude's medal.

In any case, those were the days and it was a happy crew which Greg and Jim Frise joined in the spring of 1947. Things went well for them. The Jim-Greg stories were used as center spreads. "Juniper Junction," the new version of "Birdseye Center," appeared in full color, which was a longtime ambition of Jim's. Things rolled along smoothly until June of 1948.

On a Saturday afternoon of that month, Greg took his wife and daughter on a fishing trip to Tidy's Pond at High Lake. The fish were not rising to the fly, but Greg made three remarkable discoveries in the woods. He found a pair of showy orchids in the shade of a beech tree; the first oven-bird's nest he had ever seen; and a jack-in-the-pulpit which was of giant, almost tropical size. The stem was half the thickness of Greg's wrist and the stalk a good thirty inches in height.

Before the party left for home Greg revisited his three finds. He examined them again and wondered to himself if he had been shown these three things because there was little time left in his life. It wasn't a morbid thought as much as a whimsical one.

They returned to the city at about 11 P.M. and Greg went to bed. Oddly enough, the thought about the time left in life recurred to him. It bothered him a little, for he placed quite a bit of faith in premonitions and omens.

At 3:45 A.M. Greg was wakened by his housekeeper, Hilda Ashcroft. She informed him that Jimmie Frise, his friend for thirty years, had died of a heart attack.

36

Macpherson is the best political cartoonist in the world today.

—*Beland Honderich*
Toronto Star *publisher*

The artist now chosen to work with Greg was Duncan Macpherson, later to become known as the best political cartoonist in Canada. Some thought he was the best in the world.

In 1948 Macpherson was still trying to get over a rather dismal career in the Royal Canadian Air Force and rehabilitate himself at an art school in Boston, Massachusetts.

Getting paired up with Greg Clark in the *Standard* was the first big break in Macpherson's career. That he was even in the running for the job was thanks to the *Standard*'s art director, Dick Hersey.

Macpherson went from high school to the RCAF with the hope of making aircrew, but unfortunately flunked a navigation exam and got sidetracked to Britain and the routine job of loading bombs. A compulsive sketcher since childhood, Macpherson tried to get attached to the RCAF magazine, *Wings Abroad,* with "Ricky" Richard, the creator of the Air Force cartoon character Joe Erk. This attempt failed. He did win a prize for a drawing in a war bond contest, the prize being a war bond. He was discharged on April 1, 1946. Trying to catch up on art, he enrolled at the Boston Museum's School of Fine Arts, on the Fenway in Boston, Massachusetts.

In a show of wartime sketches in Ottawa, Dick Hersey had been impressed with some done by a Duncan Macpherson, cartoons hastily sketched on Y.M.C.A. notepaper. No one in Canada had ever heard of an artist named Duncan Macpherson and Hersey went to extraordinary trouble to run him down in Boston. He was attending art school there on his wartime service credits. Some weeks he got by on a few cans of beans or spaghetti.

Hersey persuaded Macpherson to submit some sample illustrations for Greg's stories along with other established artists who were trying to land the job. Macpherson's were boldly original; they were the eventual choice of the *Standard* editors and Greg himself.

Greg's stories no longer included Jim Frise, but he invented a series of comic characters—Cousin Madge, Darky Daniels and others—based on friends, relatives and neighbors. "I was a tall, skinny kid at the time," said Macpherson, "largely because of my Boston diet. The first time I met Greg, he took me out to lunch and I wolfed down several helpings of everything in sight. One of his next stories, I noticed, featured a cadaverous minister, who not only resembled me, but had the same appetite."

They became good friends and when Macpherson married Dorothy Blackhall at the St. Clair Avenue Presbyterian church in 1949, Greg attended. As with anyone who had grown up in Toronto during Greg's days at the *Star Weekly,* Macpherson regarded him as an institution and never got over the habit of addressing him as "Mr. Clark."

Macpherson's illustrations for Greg's stories were what first attracted national attention to his work.

"I was only getting fifty dollars for these full-color spreads," said Macpherson, "but I pulled out all the stops, and tore off into a kind of Byzantine frenzy."

It would have been fatal for an artist to try to imitate Jimmie Frise—and Macpherson certainly did not do that. His illustrations were huge, grotesque, funny, sometimes searing, a foretaste of his future political cartoons.

As well as the main illustration, featuring Greg or Cousin Madge, he would sometimes pack in half a dozen little characters carrying the story line. It was more than fifty dollars' worth, but Macpherson loved it. He worked so hard and long at them that he sometimes had to ship them off to Montreal in wooden crates to make his weekly deadlines, because the oil paint was still wet.

Macpherson's relationship with Greg remained friendly and harmonious during their partnership. This is remarkable, because Macpherson's relationships—with friends, employers or anybody —rarely do. At his best, or worst, Macpherson was an impressive character. Almost anything you wanted to say about him would be true, in some circumstances. In other circumstances, the opposite would be equally true.

At one time Macpherson asked me to write an introduction to one of his annual cartoon collections, a piece of about 250 words, for which Macpherson said he would pay me $250, or a dollar a word. I began, "Macpherson is kind, cruel, gentle, rough, charming, terrifying, shy, boisterous, puritanical, hedonistic, generous, canny, chivalrous, crude, gay, somber . . ." My plan was simply to go on until I had 250 adjectives describing Macpherson, but he protested he was not going to pay me a dollar a word just to pick words out of a dictionary. Nevertheless, Macpherson is all those things and more.

For a sensitive man, he could become very violent. He claimed it was because he was sensitive. In his heyday as a sensitive artist and barroom brawler he was rather awesome. He had filled out to the size of a black Russian bear, and exhibited about the same social graces. A lot of incidents, some of which involved the wrecking of restaurants, arose from his abhorrence of white space, which he felt compelled to fill up with cartoons. When this happened to be a tablecloth, the wall of a restaurant, the naked thigh of a lady customer or the bald head of some stranger, it sometimes led to misunderstandings.

Tablecloths caused him trouble in another way. Macpherson suffered from the delusion that he could whip off a restaurant tablecloth without disturbing the wine glasses, dishes, cups and saucers on it. It would have been an impressive bit of magic, except it never worked. Instead, whole dinners flew into the air, landing on nearby tables and customers. This led to altercations. One of Macpherson's victims happened to be a visiting Russian ambassador and his security men. Macpherson seemed to be drawn irresistibly toward those who understood artists least.

For a time, Macpherson was the patron saint of Harry Barberian's Steak House on Elm Street; he and Barberian became good friends. Eventually, however, Barberian barred him from the restaurant, as he realized he would soon have only Macpherson left as a customer. At one point Macpherson had been barred from the Toronto Men's Press Club three times, twice for life. Those figures have since doubled at least.

Most of Macpherson's damage was wrought on strangers, casual acquaintances or people he saw as stuffed shirts. He never attacked his friends. Well, hardly ever.

As a typical friend, I have had him tear my suit in half, run away with my tie while I was still in it—little things like that. Another time, we were thrown out of Dorothy Cameron's gallery for creating a disturbance. We were having a simple discussion about the role of the artist in society. He had me in a wrestling hold and I was trying to choke him to his senses. Outside, we staggered across the sidewalk and bumped into a store window. "I could put you right through that window," panted Macpherson. Instead he took me to his house and cooked me bacon and eggs. Now, a total stranger or even a casual acquaintance would probably have gone through the window. That's one advantage of being a friend of Macpherson's.

Dick Hersey, the *Standard*'s art director, who had discovered Macpherson, once commissioned him to paint the official flowers of each province for a *Standard* series. It was the first time this had been done and the project involved Macpherson in considerable research and a lot of painstaking work.

Hersey came to Toronto and was in a room on the tenth floor of the Lord Simcoe Hotel when Macpherson showed up with the series of paintings. Hersey was entertaining some other Toronto artists and, to Macpherson's growing annoyance, began to make some criticisms of the paintings. He didn't like the background used in one, the colors of another.

Macpherson suddenly grabbed up all the paintings, went to the hotel window and hurled them into the night.

"So you don't like them?" he said. "Then we'll get rid of them."

It was a windy night and the paintings fluttered gaily along King and University. A panic-stricken Hersey aroused the hotel manager and his staff and managed to recover them all from the streets and adjoining rooftops.

That Greg Clark, a gentle soul, should have gotten teamed up with such a wild man was one of life's little comedies. Even their basic artistic drives were at odds. While Greg was trying to sugarcoat the pill of life, Macpherson was trying to peel it like an onion. Later, in his political cartoons, he went for the jugular. They respected each other's work on the *Standard* and got along well, though. What eventually broke up the partnership was a change in the paper's format.

Following the pattern established by *This Week* magazine in the United States, the *Standard* contracted with a score of daily newspapers across Canada to carry an abbreviated version of the *Standard* in their Saturday editions. The member papers raised the price of their Saturday editions to pay for *Weekend* and came to share in *Weekend*'s advertising profits. The new publication was christened *Weekend Magazine* and the first edition appeared on September 8, 1951, some four years after Greg joined the paper.

The new package was an instant financial success and left the *Star Weekly* far behind in circulation. The editors soon found out it was a mixed blessing. Along with a score of member newspapers, they'd also acquired a score of daily newspaper editors and publishers accustomed to deciding what appeared in their local papers.

If a *Weekend* article displeased them, they said so loudly or took draconian measures. John Bassett once tore an article out of more than 200,000 copies of *Weekend* before distributing it with his Toronto *Telegram*. And what pleased the Toronto *Telegram* might not please the Medicine Hat *News*. As a result of this situation, *Weekend* eventually became a bland, noncontroversial entertainment package.

The decreased number of editorial pages nearly ended Greg's career. *Weekend* did not have space for the long, illustrated stories Greg had been doing with Macpherson. These were reduced to one a month and then discontinued entirely.

Macpherson was by now established as a successful free-lance artist in other markets and was on the brink of fantastic success as a political cartoonist, but Greg wondered about his own future. He was approaching sixty and beginning to feel the weight of his years. His radio work had fallen off since joining the *Standard*. His only other outside work had been a collaboration with C. L. Burton, the owner of Simpson's, on Burton's autobiography, *A Sense of Urgency*.

Weekend's editors, notably Craig Ballantyne and Hugh Shaw, worked to keep Greg alive in the new *Weekend*. While using him for Royal Tour coverage and other general articles, they encouraged him to try to produce a shorter, one-page story which could become a regular weekly feature. Greg didn't see how he could properly tell a story in the number of words they suggested.

"Have smaller adventures," said Ballantyne.

At first doubtful, Greg did try and soon found he could produce short humor pieces on a wide range of subjects in less than a thousand words.

These ranged from current events to anecdotes about fishing and hunting or his war and newspaper experiences. As space was not available for artwork, a decision was made to use a photograph of Greg at the top of each story. Louis Jaques was assigned to build up a file of photos, which featured Greg in fishing clothes, hunting clothes, with a favorite pipe, in rain gear, turtle-necks or other costumes. From this file a suitable picture could be taken each week, depending on the subject of his story.

What had looked like disaster blossomed into a great new career. "The Shorties," as the editors called them, assumed a regular position on the inside back page of *Weekend* and became one of its best-read features.

Weekend's coast-to-coast circulation climbed to more than two million copies a week. The assumption then was that a newspaper averaged 2.5 readers per copy, so Greg's weekly audience now numbered in the millions. With his photograph appearing over every story his pixie-like appearance also became known across Canada and he was recognized almost everywhere he went.

However, despite the various changes in the format of Greg's stories, he would long be remembered as part of the original Jim-Greg team. In February of 1955 the student humor magazine at McGill University lampooned *Weekend Magazine*. Their take-off of Greg was not of his current work, but of the old Jim-Greg features, which had not appeared for years.

This was their irreverent spoof:

Greg Crock
Tells About

THE EGGNOG

Just before New Years I phoned up my pal Jim Fried and said, "Jim, come on over, and on your way buy four dozen eggs and five quarts of cream. We're going to make an egg-nog."

Half an hour later Jim staggered in under his load and set it down next to my massive punch bowl. I produced the goods in 40 oz. brown bottles and suggested a wee dram to warm us up. Jim agreed. Well, then we started to mix and added a little of this and a little of that to make it just a perfect eggnog.

"Here Jim," I said, "Taste that." Jim did.

"Here Greg," Jim said, "Taste this." I did.

We had another nip to keep out the cold. Then Jim remembered a game.

"Take this egg," he said, "and throw it to me."

I did, he caught it, took a step back and threw it to me. I caught it, took a step back and threw it again. When we were backed against the walls, I threw the egg and caught him right on the nose—was that funny! Then we took a nip to warm up the cold. Then he broke an egg and haired my rub in it.

"Taste thish," shaid Jim. I did.

"Tashte that," I shaid. Jim did.

Then we nipped a little more to cold out the warm. Jim egged a great face in my throw. I took my eggnog and headed it turnwise all over his cup. His eyes looked delirious running down between his hairy eggnog. Eggy jimmed a throw and shouldered me all hit over. I egged Jim all over. Jim laughed. I laughed. Eggy were we. Nip for the cold.

"Ha-ha my nogegg old nog," shed Egg.

"Nog Nog—ha eggy me, poor noggy hairy eggy Jim," shed me.

Jim punched massive hairy bowlwise over my top. Hairy Jim's eggy nog laughter heaved. I fell Jimwise hairty over eggy corpsrate prost on florey nog.

37

THE ROBIN

A Story by Greg Clark

It was exactly twelve years ago yesterday afternoon that Franklin Delano Roosevelt died. I was home from the war, so I took a night plane to Washington to see them bring him from the South and bear him through their city.

Six snow-white horses, with little black tapping hoofs, drew him, so tiny a package there on the gun carriage, in a procession that took two hours to pass through hundreds and hundreds of thousands of his people; and it was the only time in my life I saw 10,000 men weep.

Then all of us who had permission fled north to Dutchess county, N.Y., to the little village of Hyde Park, high on the cliffs above the Hudson river. For there in the rose garden his grandfather had laid out they were going to bury him.

The rose garden is just one hundred yards north of the Roosevelt farm house, a quarter-acre of good clay loam. It is walled in by a solid hedge, eighteen feet tall, of Norway spruces that the grandfather planted. For roses must be sheltered from the blasts that blow down the Hudson and along its high cliffs.

There are twenty-eight beds of rose bushes in this high, sombre-walled and quiet garden. In their midst stands a sundial. I went over to see what inscription there might be on it. There was none. Not even "I tell only the sunlit hours."

It was ten o'clock in the morning that the train from Washington was to arrive down in the valley, on the Hudson river level.

A farm lane runs from the farmhouse past the rose garden, on past the barns and sheds, across a couple of fields and then down steeply over the cliffs to the river road far below.

It was up this lane, gravel and dirt, that the young men of West Point were to haul the gun carriage.

But long before ten o'clock of this glorious April morning, with the redwings and the meadow larks, the song sparrows and chipping sparrows making a small clamour over the fields and in all the cherry trees and hawthorns in bloom, new hedges were springing up, minute by minute, along the farm lane and down the steep cliff.

Hedges of men: marines, sailors, soldiers.

He was to come home to his boyhood playground the way he never, in his wildest boyhood dreams, foresaw.

Inside the dark-walled rose garden, the rose bushes were stumpy and pruned, and only the first leaflets showed. But in every corner of every field as far as you could see, the lilac bushes drooped heavy with their blossoms. And all along the grass banks of the farm lane, millions, yes, millions of violets made a blue carpet.

Into the rose garden, through the gap in the eighteen-foot spruce hedge, threaded the great of our world—the prime ministers, chief justices, ambassadors, members of his Cabinet, famous men all, powerful with the dread power war confers: for the war was still on.

At ten o'clock, all was still save the birds. Their clamour was like bright bells, far off.

And then we in the rose garden heard surely the strangest sound ever devised by man. The muffled drums.

They beat one, two, three, four, five; and then a ruffle of three quick beats.

The drums are muffled. The drumsticks are muffled. The slow, stately beat is like the beat of your heart.

Far off it sounded like a partridge drumming. Of all those men of might in the rose garden and all those thousands elbow to elbow in the human hedges along and down the farm lane, not one but held his breath. And the slow drums came minute by minute closer and closer as the youths of West Point drew their gun carriage up the steep cliff, their fellows pacing slowly before and behind, to the measure of the drums.

Even the birds stopped singing.

When the gun carriage reached the level fields, the band of West Point, sixty instruments, broke into the Dead March, Mendelssohn's; and no fields in the wide world, young in April, ever heard such music. And foot by foot and yard by yard, they drew him along the farm lane and into the rose garden.

There the clergy waited by the open pit in the rose beds, with all the notability of the free world bunched close around them.

The youths from West Point, in their light blue-grey, with the white cross-belts across their chests, and the hard visors of their caps tilted low over their eyes, bore their commander-in-chief to the grave. They stood by, the guard of honour.

The thin voice of the immemorial service rose up out of the midst.

And a robin flew out of the high spruce hedge and landed on a space of open lawn, back of the farthest notable.

It picked up some dead grass in its beak and scooped a little mud.

". . . First Corinthians," came the thin voice.

The robin flew up into the secrecy of the tall hedge.

In a moment, with a low chirp that was clearer than the voice of the clergyman, it flew out of the hedge again, and down to the ground, where it ran a little way, picked up some more grass and some more mud: and flew back up into the hedge. It was building its nest.

I could not keep my mind on the service, faintly intoning. Nor on the notables, whose grave faces turned this way and that.

The robin was stealing the show.

I glanced cautiously along the faces of the marines standing stiff, elbow to elbow, a living hedge all around the foot of the Norway spruce hedge. Their faces were poker faces. Not a muscle moved.

But every eye was on the robin.

Out of the tall hedge it dropped again in its graceful swoop, listened, peered, head on one side, ran a little way, picked up more grass and mud, and flew back up into the spruces, over the heads of the mighty.

Phrase by phrase the old, old service went its way.

The rifles crashed out over the grave.

The robin flew wildly around the rose garden, uttering cries of alarm.

Slowly, the assemblage broke apart and moved out through the gap in the hedge.

The robin flew down and ran more freely over the vacated turf. It selected another beakful of grass and earth.

I went over and spoke to a sergeant of the marines: they were still standing fast.

"Notice the robin?" I inquired.

"That bird," said the sergeant, "has no sense of history."

We studied each other a minute.

"Or has it?" we both said together.

38

A case in point is the failure of Dr. Claude
Bissell to include a single piece of Greg's in
his collection of *Great Canadian Writing* for
the Centennial Library. You have only to skim
the list of authors in the book to conclude Bissell must have been totally unfamiliar with
Greg's work. It represented all fields of writing from the esoteric four-letter poets to news
dispatches from Dullsville, Sask.

The Old Guard of the Literati in Toronto
should include Greg in the small pantheon it
has been acclaiming and guarding instead of
brushing him aside as if he were some kind of
puckish gnome.

—*Hugh Shaw*
Weekend *editor*

From 1950 to the early 1960s, Greg enjoyed a busy period of
work and play, comparable to the decade of the Mad River
fishing club.

Following the breakup of his collaboration with Duncan Macpherson, Greg soon got into the swing of writing the Shorties for
Weekend—and found energy for a new kind of writing. He began
a series of columns for daily newspapers called "The Packsack."
These were under five hundred words in length and were a return

to the essay form he had favored when young. Subjects included birds, cars, skunks, anthropomorphism, weddings, nostalgia— almost anything—usually handled with lightness and humor. About once a week Greg liked to slip in a serious message, perhaps about conservation, car drivers or pollution. Sometimes it was life right around home. In one Packsack Greg wrote:

Excessive talkers are apparently totally unaware of their fault. This is proven whenever two of them meet, and they go their way afterwards, each remarking what an awful talker the other is.

One of the quiet, mischievous pleasures of life is to bring two blatherskites together, watch the fun, and then await your chance afterwards to hear the verdict of each of them on the other.

Being a notorious blatherskite myself, I had the good fortune early in life to catch onto this little game. It is practised, as a rule, by reserved and inarticulate people with a sense of humour. I married one of them, and after the first flush of connubial bliss had passed, I was puzzled by the sort of people my wife used to invite to our home. *They were awful talkers*. You could hardly get a word in edgeways.

Right in my own house, I nearly strangled to death with unuttered sentiments when these frequent guests were being entertained. My wife seemed to be struggling to conceal an expression of great glee.

My own sister was one of them, she having inherited the same lively larynx which runs with the short, stubby strain in my family. When I knew she was coming for the evening, I used to rearrange the chairs so as to place the one she preferred in a sidelines position, leaving my own favourite chair in a central and more commanding location. I used to line up some books and magazines I thought might intrigue her, so that by handing them to her, at strategic moments during the evening, I could bury her for a few minutes in book or magazine and thus reorganize the conversation more to my advantage. None of my schemes worked. My sister has the trick of getting up and sitting on the arm of a chesterfield, or even pacing up and down the middle of a room when the competition gets tough.

Now, when there is a blatherskite in the company, I let him or her have the show. If I am going to blather, I want the floor to myself.

The Packsack columns added to Greg's national reputation. At various times, between twenty and thirty newspapers across Canada carried the column. It was satisfying to Greg and provided him with much more freedom of comment than the Shorties, but it was not calculated to make him rich. Some papers paid two, three or five dollars per week for the six columns, and Canada Wide Syndicate, owned by *Weekend,* took the normal syndicate share of 50 percent of this. Greg's first check for the Packsack was for $79, covering a two-week period. So, for writing a small daily column, Greg was increasing his income by approximately $40 a week—not a large sum, considering his name and reputation.

In 1955, Greg earned $18,000—$14,000 from newspaper work and $4,000 from radio. It was the highest annual income he would ever achieve.

Honors came his way. Back in 1928 he had been made the first honorary life member of the Toronto Anglers' Association and later an honorary life member of the Ontario Federation of Anglers and Hunters, as well as a director of the Audubon Society of Canada. He was now made an Honorary Life Member of the Toronto Men's Press Club. The University of Western Ontario made him a doctor of laws. The Canadian War Correspondents Association made him an Honorary Life Member. *Weekend* held a banquet in Montreal to celebrate his fifty years in the newspaper business. He received the J. V. MacAree award as Columnist of the Year.

Greg spent much time at Go Home because he could see change overtaking his Shangri-la. Utility poles were creeping up the shore of Georgian Bay, sticking up grotesquely from Greg's beloved rocks. For a time the cottagers at Go Home held out against electricity, then voted it in over Greg's protests. He saw that telephones, radios, television would soon follow—perhaps even a highway. Already boatloads of tourist fishermen were cruising Go Home waters, tossing their garbage overboard.

Greg, Jr., and Elizabeth were creating their own lives, with the usual generation conflicts. After the war, Greg, Jr., had completed his university work and entered law school. After one year there he became convinced that it was not a calling in which he would find lasting satisfaction.

He made an appointment with his father for a downtown lunch at which he intended to break the news that he was switching careers. They met, but unfortunately, as they walked to lunch, Greg caught sight of Osgoode Hall with its ornate iron fence and special gates designed to keep out stray cows when it had been built a hundred years before.

"Ah," said Greg dramatically. "The palace of justice. Who knows where you may go when you finish law school. Perhaps a judge, a chief justice like the original William Osgoode, perhaps a member of the Supreme Court."

Young Greg was appalled to learn how much Greg was expecting of him in the field of law and he did not tell him of his decision to drop out that day. For the first time he realized what his university degree meant to his father. Greg had failed university twice. Murray had put in only one term before joining the *Star* briefly and then joining the army. Young Greg was the first Clark in memory to have gotten through university.

Greg, Jr., did leave law school and worked as a traveling salesman for several years. He found life on the road monotonous. He put in another year at the Ontario College of Education to become a teacher and settled into a successful career as a high school teacher and later as a principal.

Young Greg's fiancée was a young woman of twenty-one named Doreen Rew. Along with some of Greg's relatives, she did not approve of the Victorian atmosphere Greg maintained in his home. One Sunday dinner there particularly stuck in her memory. It was a stilted affair with no liquor served. Greg hovered around Helen and carefully steered the conversation away from anything he felt might upset her. Helen's own sister, Beth Fasken, had quarreled with Greg over his excessive protectiveness, to no avail. Greg had, of course, become even more protective after Helen's breakdown at the time of Murray's death.

Following the dinner, Greg was scheduled to depart on a fishing trip from Gil Purcell's house. Doreen and young Greg drove him there, with his gear, and were invited in briefly.

"I was stunned at the metamorphosis which took place in front of my eyes," said Doreen. "I was shocked! Greg actually turned into a human being."

Young Greg said it was probably because Greg had been relaxed by having a drink at Purcell's. "A bottle of beer, I think," said Doreen. "But it was more than that. Seeing him drinking and joking with his male friends, I realized that his wife was deliberately kept in a totally different world." When she and young Greg left in their car, Doreen said, "Don't ever do *that* to me."

Doreen and Greg, Jr., were married on Friday, June 22, 1951. Greg, of course, could not bring himself to offer his son any advice on the physical aspects of marriage. He did manage one tiny bit of advice at the railroad station as the couple left on their honeymoon. He took young Greg aside and explained that the toilet cubicles in train compartments offered limited privacy. He suggested that young Greg make use of the men's room at the end of the car to spare his bride any embarrassment. Young Greg nodded solemnly.

He and Doreen had three children in the next six years: Andrew Evan Murray Clark, born on August 17, 1952; Dorian Louise Clark, on May 16, 1954, and Andrea Lesley Clark, on October 24, 1956. Greg's first grandchild, Andy, grew up to become a news photographer.

In 1953, when he was sixty-one years old, Greg enjoyed the best deer hunt of his life at the Tyson Lake lodge of his friend Ack Forbes. George Alexander "Ack" Forbes had become a friend of Greg and Jimmie Frise's when they visited Preston in the late Twenties. The Preston Springs Hotel, run by Edwin and Gordon Hogmeier, was famous across the continent for its mineral waters, which bubbled from a fountain in the hotel lobby.

Forbes took them bass fishing at nearby Puslinch Lake and enjoyed their friendship throughout their lives. Ack's father had been a wealthy industrialist and the first mayor of Hespeler, where he once operated the largest woolen mill in Canada. The family fortune came to Ack Forbes. He gradually disentangled himself from business to enjoy the outdoor life he found so much more attractive.

From his father he had inherited a membership in an exclusive 2,800-acre duck hunting club near Chatham, Ontario, founded by Sir Casimir Gzowski in 1860, next to one owned by Henry Ford. In 1930, on a private island in Tyson Lake, southwest of Sudbury, he built a beautiful fishing and hunting lodge to which friends were flown in his private floatplane over the next thirty years. A famous Toronto physician once said, "I accept only two invitations a year. Salmon fishing with Sam McLaughlin and deer hunting with Ack Forbes." This doctor was Dr. John Oille, the father of Dr. William Oille, who became Greg's doctor and friend.

Forbes admired Frise greatly, not only for his humor and kindness, but for his skill as a duck hunter. On an outing with Jim and Greg at Burleigh Falls one year, Forbes saw Frise bring down a flight of five bluebills with one shot.

On the 1953 hunt at Tyson the party included four doctors; a mammalogist; Keith Acheson, regional forester; Bruce West and Gil Purcell. The party took seven deer, with Greg getting a buck and a doe. Bruce West, who had hunted before, but not with success, dropped two bucks. While Greg found it satisfying, his pleasure was now less in the hunt than in the simple joy of being outdoors and studying plants, animals, birds.

On this hunt he was fascinated by a passage of about a hundred and fifty snow buntings, which streamed down a valley some forty feet below his position on a hill. It was about four in the afternoon and in the graying light the birds assumed a silvery appearance. Their flight was slow, silent, undulating. This stream of silver birds remained a magical picture in his mind.

Helen's mother, known affectionately as Dodo, still lived with the Clarks at the age of ninety-two. She had been getting deaf for some time and now suffered periods of slight confusion. Talking to Greg, she muttered impatiently one day, "Aaah, I'd sooner die than get too old."

Greg noticed that the hearing in his good right ear was beginning to diminish in the high registers. He could not hear the flight notes of the siskins or finches any longer, as well as some notes of the warblers.

He had long nourished an ambition to fish Sutton Lake on the shore of Hudson Bay, site of the best trout fishing in the world. Greg, Bruce West, Ralph Allen and Gil Purcell were invited to accompany a government inspection group flying in to this remote area on July 31, 1952, but snow and freezing rain caused their planes to land at the Hudson's Bay Company post of Lansdowne House, far short of Sutton.

Despite this, Greg enjoyed many other fishing expeditions in the Fifties, from Newfoundland to British Columbia, including the festival of Les Petits Poissons at Ste. Anne de la Perade, near Three Rivers, Quebec. At the Adams River in British Columbia, he and Helen landed four-, five- and six-pound Kamloops trout.

In 1954, Greg achieved another lifetime ambition when he was assigned to follow the Duke of Edinburgh on a northern tour which led to Coppermine at the edge of the Arctic Ocean. En route, Greg marveled at the might of the Yukon and Mackenzie rivers, as well as the miles of barren land he had thought he might never see, and he took care to dip his feet into the Arctic waters at Coronation Gulf.

This spate of traveling and fishing was well timed. His *Weekend* work was well in hand. Greg, Jr., and his family had gone to Manitoba for a new teaching job. Elizabeth had left the Ontario College of Art to study at Bath, in England.

Greg undertook some extra radio work and speechmaking to finance a trip to England for himself and Helen. A ten-day speaking tour in Northern Saskatchewan in 1955, during which he made twenty-eight speeches, left him very tired.

For the past ten or fifteen years, he had noticed an occasional indigestion pain. It usually began with an ache in the chest, moved into his shoulders—and disappeared after a short while. This time the pain spread from his shoulders down into his arms and did not respond to treatment. The family physician called in heart specialist Dr. William Oille and Greg was put to bed. After electrocardiograms, Greg was advised to postpone the trip to England and was ordered to spend his summer at Go Home resting completely—no activity, not even fishing. However, the illness passed without further incident.

In the summer of 1958, Helen and Greg had Andy, the number one grandson, and his sister, Dorian, for two weeks at Go Home. They made the uncomfortable discovery that they were past the baby-sitting age. Greg wondered if television and other influences inspired a constant need for entertainment in young children. "What can I do now?" was a constant cry. Greg and Helen felt utterly exhausted, baffled and inadequate to the situation.

Elizabeth, Greg's youngest and feyest child, returned from her study of art in England. Now she switched her interest to set design and secured work with the Birmingham Civic Ballet in Alabama. While there she met a young Japanese photographer from New York City named Hiro Wakabayashi and they fell in love.

Hiro was a talented and creative photographer who had become extremely successful in the highly competitive editorial and fashion fields in New York. His work was appearing in *Life, Fortune, Time, Newsweek, Holiday, Look, Harper's Bazaar* and other magazines. In a few years he would be named Photographer of the Year by the American Society of Magazine Photographers.

Greg and Helen were taken aback when their only daughter, still a baby in their eyes, brought Hiro to Toronto as a potential son-in-law. Helen, a minister's sheltered daughter to begin with, and sheltered by Greg throughout their life together, found the adjustment particularly difficult. In the Clark home Elizabeth had been the rebellious child, a free spirit, an artist, and Helen at first viewed the romance as another form of rebellion. For Greg, too, it was a long leap forward to face up to the idea of a Japanese son-in-law. It seemed only yesterday that his father had been writing editorials warning Canada against the "yellow peril" that threatened from the west.

Elizabeth and Hiro were married in May of 1959 and on May 9 Greg wrote only this in his journal: "Hiro and Elizabeth married in a quiet ceremony. I got in the doghouse."

Greg's second grandson, Gregory Thomas Wakabayashi, was born on April 27, 1960. As Hiro was out of town on an assignment for *Look* magazine, Greg and Helen had flown to New York to be with Elizabeth.

The natural instincts of grandparents took over. Greg observed that this new Greg was a little beauty, Japanese enough to please Hiro, Caucasian enough to please the Clarks. When he was first placed in a crib he managed to propel himself forward enough with his feet and hands to bang his head on the end of the crib. Greg saw this as a sign that an infusion of Japanese blood was good for the Clark strain. Helen stayed on in New York to help with the baby and she and Elizabeth became closer than they had been for some time. Greg noted that if the new arrival should become a writer and find Gregory Wakabayashi an unwieldy by-line, he could translate it to Gregory Young-Forest. Not bad.

On July 6, 1961, another Wakabayashi baby arrived; this one

was named Hiro Clark Wakabayashi. With the three children of Greg, Jr., and Doreen, this now made five grandchildren. At the Christmas gathering where all five were together for the first time, Greg stared around in some surprise. Suddenly he was a grandfather—five times a grandfather.

However, others were passing on. Greg's mother-in-law, the formidable Dodo, died at the age of ninety-seven. Helen's closest friend, Margaret Trowern, died suddenly. She was married to Billy Milne, Greg's friend of schooldays, and the two couples had maintained their friendship for fifty years. A few years later Billy Milne died, too. A fishing friend, Skipper Howard, was killed in a car accident. Greg was now the sole surviving member of the Mad River gang.

"It is getting," wrote Greg, "that I have a wider and more familiar acquaintance among the dead than among the living."

39

He's the kind of guy that if you ordered a carload of sons-of-bitches, and you opened up the boxcar and found only this one guy inside—you would have to admit the order had been filled.

—*Mark Farrell*
Weekend Magazine

I don't know who Mark Farrell had in mind when he told me this story. It always made me think of Harry Hindmarsh and Gil Purcell. Greg came to hate Hindmarsh. Purcell became one of his best friends.

Each of these men seemed intent on creating a legend that he was a hard-hearted son-of-a-bitch about work, but really a swell guy underneath. My observation of sons-of-bitches is that they are usually sons-of-bitches all the way through.

Star Weekly writer Charles Vining had a style for writing about difficult subjects. Used on Purcell, it would come out like this.

Gillis Philip Purcell was born November 25, 1904.
You better spell Philip correctly.
He drinks Sugar Cane Brandy with water.
He is a one-legged son-of-a-bitch.
His artificial leg is known as Barney.
At the University of Manitoba he wrote a three hour trigonometry examination in one and a half hours and then left the room.
Of a possible 100 marks on this examination he got 100.
He has missed only one Grey Cup game since the war.
In Latin and Greek his marks averaged 95 per cent.

His father was a newspaperman.

He is a Catholic.

Stuart Keate says he combines the more fascinating qualities
of Monsignor Fulton J. Sheen and Mack The Knife.

He is a one-legged son-of-a-bitch.

As a young man his favourite sports were baseball and
hockey.

He once won the chess championship of the Toronto Men's
Press Club.

He buys and reads great batches of new books, rushing
through them before Christmas so he can give them away
as presents.

He terrified CP's male employees.

He was terrified of CP's female employees.

He married Charlotte Frances Fleming on April 5, 1934.

They had five children.

He called his wife "archy," lower case.

She died on Sunday, May 12, 1968.

A week later Purcell cried.

Before the Red Cross barred him because of his age Purcell
made 65 blood donations.

He has stumped the world on CP business—Britain, Russia,
India, Australia, the Caribbean. Anywhere there is good
fishing.

He is a one-legged son-of-a-bitch.

During his university years Purcell had a job, of sorts, with the
Winnipeg *Free Press,* where his father was telegraph editor. He
did casual reporting and the occasional newspaper cartoon for the
sum of $5.00 a week. His real interest in the job was a free rail
pass which enabled him to become one of the best-traveled university students in Canada.

Upon graduation, he headed east and obtained a job at $25 a
week doing sports for the Windsor *Star.* While there, he answered
an ad for managing editor of the Oshawa *Times.* His application
was drawn to the attention of J.F.B. Livesay, then general manager of Canadian Press. Livesay offered Purcell a job at $40 a
week—and his choice of CP bureaus in Ottawa, Toronto or Winnipeg.

Purcell chose his hometown of Winnipeg. In three years there

Meticulous craftsmanship marked Duncan Macpherson drawings.

ORDINARY LOGIC

Greg's Cousin Madge sets out to rid her garden of stray dogs and falls foul of a hefty sling-shot

By Gregory Clark

ILLUSTRATED BY DUNCAN MACPHERSON

"IS THERE some stuff," enquired Cousin Madge, hotly, "you can buy to keep dogs off your property?"

"I believe there is," I reflected. "But why don't you just instal a 25-cent catch on your gate?"

"Gate? Heck," snorted Cousin Madge, "they jump the fence. But it isn't only my back yard they're invading. It's my lovely dahlias out in front."

"Those dahlias," I demurred, "are six feet tall. No dog . . ."

"Do you know how much I paid for those dahlias?" snarled Cousin Madge. "Those are prize dahlias."

"But look," I reasoned, "no dog can hurt those great big . . ."

"Hurt them?" cried Madge, furiously. "This morning, I happened to look out the parlor window and what did I see? Four dogs — FOUR dogs — jammed right in the middle of my dahlias, scratching, scooping earth in all directions, rolling amid the stalks, chasing each other round and round in that one little patch of prize dahlias. PRIZE dahlias!"

"It won't happen again," I soothed. "It was just one of those whims dogs are subject to, when they are fresh home from the country."

"I'll whim them!" gritted Cousin Madge.

"Remember, nearly all the dogs on this street," I pursued, "have been away with the families for the summer. They've been romping and ranging far and wide in the open country. It's kind of hard to suddenly settle back into the confines of city life . . ."

"The same with kids," said Cousin Madge, darkly.

"Same thing," I agreed. "Just for a few days, you'll notice both dogs and children a little riotous. But they will soon sink back into the city pattern."

"I wish," mused Cousin Madge, "there was some sort of stuff you could buy at the drug store to keep both children and dogs off your property. Why should a person like me, who chose NOT to marry, and NOT to further encumber the earth with children —why should we not have some rights? Why should I have to bear some of the burden of all the fecund females for blocks around . . .?"

"DON'T FORGET," I reminded, "that you have been away all summer, in that cottage hide-away of yours, where there are no kids within a quarter mile. You've got to get acclimated to the city again, just like the dogs . . ."

Cousin Madge slid her spectacles down her nose and examined me over the top of them shrewdly.

"Do you want to do something for me?" she clipped.

"Certainly," I offered.

"Make me a sling-shot," she wheedled. "A catapult."

"What for?" I protested.

"Dogs," said Cousin Madge.

"Now, just a minute . . . " I exclaimed.

"Don't get excited," soothed Cousin Madge. "It's quite proper. It's perfectly legal. I was reading an article only yesterday about training dogs. Do you know what the best dog trainers do? The real expert dog trainers? They use a catapult. When one of the prize dogs they are training disobeys a command when it is at a little distance, the trainer takes the catapult and lets it have it . . ."

"That's a very different thing," I insisted. "Those are their own dogs they are training."

"The logic," scoffed Cousin Madge, "of you men! All I am proving is that a catapult can't hurt a dog. It only stings it, for a minute . . ."

"Catapults," I stated, "are illegal."

"If so," riposted Cousin Madge, "how do dog trainers use them?"

"On their private property . . ." I cut in.

"This is my Continued on Page Twenty-six

Cousin Madge upped the crotch of the sling-shot in Amazonian style, at full arm's length.

Macpherson saw Greg differently than Jim Frise did.

"We ran over the melon patch, squashed the squash, chased 40 hens, scandalized 15 pigs, burst 50 pumpkins . . ."

SQUASH

By Gregory Clark

ILLUSTRATED BY DUNCAN MACPHERSON

"FARMERS," deliberated my sly businessman neighbor, Gibbs, "are, as a class, the last free men on earth."

We were driving past some beautiful farms at the moment. My ill-natured neighbor, Parker, was in the back seat, and I was up beside Gibbs. We were en route to Gibbs' cousin's, Mert Hopkins. He has a beautiful orchard. And we had hopes of coming home loaded with bushel baskets of Northern Spies.

"Free," pursued Gibbs, "in the old, true meaning of the word. Apart from enjoying all the political freedom that the rest of us enjoy, farmers have a personal freedom that has almost vanished from the cities and towns, and from practically all other trades and professions on earth."

"Free?" scoffed Parker, from the back seat. "They've got to get up at five o'clock in the morning. Do you call that freedom?"

"If you call it freedom," I put in, "to be tied body and soul to 14 cows that have to be milked every evening . . ."

"Not to mention four horses," snorted Parker, "that have to be fed and watered . . ."

"And maybe 40 hens," I noted, glancing out the car window, "that have to be coddled and petted and kept from the cold and the croup."

"Roupe!" corrected Gibbs.

"And six hogs," enumerated Parker, watching out the window at the passing farms, "that are eternally yelling for food. And 15 turkeys, and about twelve geese . . ."

We passed a farm where three men were high up on the barn roof, repairing the large metal sheets with which the barn was covered.

"Farmers are not free," I mentioned, "to telephone the hardware man to come and repair the roof; nor the electrician to come and fix the switches; nor the plumber to repair a tap. According to my understanding of farming, every mortal thing around the farm, from acting as midwife to a cow to installing machinery, all HAS to be done by the farmer himself. Otherwise there is no profit in farming."

"Anything else?" inquired Gibbs, cheerfully.

"I'd say, offhand," summed up Parker, "that a farmer has less actual freedom than almost any other class of men in the country. They are slaves of their beasts. Slaves of a terrible routine, not only every day, but all the year through. Slaves of chance. Frost, storm, drought. Their whole lives are ruled by a program of the seasons; yet everything they do is subject to the whim of the weather — the most fickle thing known to man."

"I figure," began Gibbs, "that you two characters don't know what freedom is. Freedom, to you, apparently means being free to go to the movies at 7 pm. Freedom, if I understand you, has to do with ease and comfort, and an absence of any personal responsibility. Freedom means leisure, does it?"

"Well, uh . . ." Parker and I both submitted.

"A farmer," pursued Gibbs, "has 14 cows. He is tied to them, of course. They have to be milked, as you say, every evening. But the farmer is free to sell the cows and go into some other line. Can you do that in your business? A farmer does his own machine repairs, he fixes his own engines he repairs his roof, his plumbing, his electrical equipment. You say he is not free to call a plumber or an electrician. I say he is free of plumbers and electricians, whereas you and I and all the rest of the city and town dwellers are helpless without these fellow-members of the great slavery of city and town. In fact, it is against the law for you to tinker with your water mains or your gas or electricity supply. You've got to send for the officials."

"We don't HAVE to get up at 5 am," insisted Parker.

"No, but we do HAVE to be in the office at 9 am or lose our jobs," retorted Gibbs. "If a farmer doesn't get up at five, he doesn't lose his job. He is a free man. He is free to get up when he likes. And he likes to get up at five."

"Oh, yeah?" Parker and I chorused.

"In the cities and towns," went on Gibbs, "we are all slaves in a great inter-locking system called business and industry. Nine hundred and ninety-nine of us out of every 1,000 are clinging rather desperately to our jobs. It is not merely the boss who can fire us; we can be let out of our jobs by shifts and changes in the great system of slavery that might occur in cities or towns 1,000 or 5,000 miles away. We are helpless robots in a great, grinding machine called the economic structure. Not one of us owns

Greg and his pals try life on the farm and get into a mess

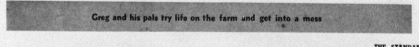

Macpherson's illustrations during the late Forties were wilder than Greg's stories.

Graphologists would find clues to Greg's character in this dinnertime doodle of December 6, 1955.

One of many presents received by Greg on his fiftieth year in journalism was this cartoon by Merle "Ting" Tingley of the London *Free Press*.

Greg's fiftieth anniversary in the newspaper business was celebrated at a black-tie dinner. *Weekend* editorial director Craig Ballantyne is at left; publisher John McConnell is seated at right. *(Richard Arless)*

In 1965 Greg was awarded the Stephen Leacock
Medal for Humour, at an Orillia ceremony atten-
ded by Greg Clark, Jr., and his wife, Doreen. *(Jock
Carroll)*

A cartoon by James Reidford of the *Globe & Mail* was presented to Greg
when he was given a life membership in the Toronto's Men's Press Club.
(Toronto Telegram)

Four choirboys of Canadian journalism in their red flannel fishing night-gowns: Ralph Allen, Greg, Bruce West and Gil Purcell. *(Canadian Press)*

Greg watches a Pierre Berton television tribute with friends Bruce West, Jock Carroll and Gil Purcell. *(Toronto Telegram)*

The Governor-General of Canada, Roland Michener (center), presented the Service Medal of the Order of Canada to Greg and John Gibbons Counsell in a special ceremony.

Greg's lively sister, Mabel, attended his Order of Canada investiture with Greg Clark, Jr. *(right). (Toronto Telegram)*

Greg was made an honorary life member of the Canadian War Correspondents Association. *(Cartoon is by Merle Tingley.)*

Greg's son-in-law, photographer Hiro Wakabayashi, shared Greg's enthusiasm for Go Home Bay and now spends summers there with his family.

Greg takes a ride across Tyson Lake, near Sudbury, Ontario. *(Jock Carroll)*

Greg's granddaughter, Lesley Clark, shared his pleasure when he received an honorary Doctor of Laws degree at the University of Western Ontario in June 1960. *(Bill Barrett)*

Bruce West, Johnny Fauquier and Jim Vipond took Greg to lunch at the King Edward in a wheelchair. West enlisted wartime flyer Fauquier because Greg complained of West's navigating.

Greg and his grandchildren. Back row: Andy, Lesley and Dorian Clark; front: Greg Wakabayashi and Clark Wakabayashi.

Gil Purcell, Bruce West and Greg were frequent guests of sportsman Ack Forbes *(right)* on fishing and hunting trips.

When Greg's legs weakened his friend Ack Forbes provided a deer carrier to get him through the woods north of Sudbury. *(Ack Forbes)*

With the help of Bobby Gimby, the Pied Piper of Expo 67, Greg and sportswriter Ted Reeve opened the new TMPC quarters on March 29, 1969. Greg became the first member of the Canadian News Hall of Fame. *(Strathy Smith)*

With Professor Claude Bissell in the spring of 1975 when the University of Toronto gave Greg the honorary degree of Doctor of Letters. *(Reg Innell)*

Four faces of Greg Clark. *(Louis Jaques)*

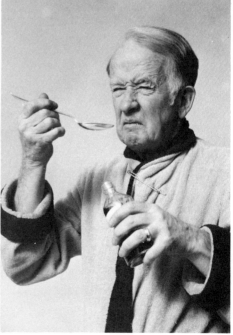

Greg at Go Home Bay. *(Louis Jaques)*

he established himself as an excellent reporter and editor. Livesay brought him to the Toronto head office in 1932 as general news editor; he later became general superintendent.

When war broke out in 1939, Purcell assigned himself to accompany the Canadian 1st Division to England in December of that year to report on their arrival and to set up working arrangements for Canadian war correspondents. Greg Clark was also reporting on the arrival of the 1st Division and, although they had been acquainted before, this was the beginning of a lifelong friendship.

As a result of this trip, Purcell was called upon, a year later, to join the army as public relations officer for the First Canadian Corps. It was an invitation he couldn't refuse, although it put him back to the same $40-a-week salary range he had earned seven years ago and he now had a wife and family.

His army career was brief, cut short by a cruel freak accident. With two movie photographers, Purcell was making an army instructional film of a practice air drop in England. The planes were dropping supply canisters weighing about a hundred pounds, from a height of around a hundred feet. A parachute, attached to each canister, flared open to slow the descent.

On the last drop, Purcell changed the position of his photographic team so the planes would be coming in directly over their heads. As the last canister was dropped, Purcell said, "Now follow this one all the way down!" The advice proved unnecessary. A parachute failed to open and the heavy canister dropped on Purcell. It took his leg off at the knee and knocked him back about thirty feet.

Although the projectile had taken Purcell's leg off, it had not completely severed the cloth of his trouser leg. In shock, Purcell kept standing up and then falling down again. A medical officer, Charlie Letourneau, a former McGill football player, was on the scene shortly. While a tourniquet was being applied, Purcell said matter-of-factly, "If someone would give me a cigarette, I could have a smoke."

Taken on a stretcher to a field hospital, Purcell met CP correspondent Ross Munro, who shared quarters with him. Purcell told Ross to file news of the accident; to bring him the copy of *Time* magazine lying on his bunk; and to find his lost leg, because the boot on it was one of a very expensive Swedish pair he had just purchased.

Purcell retained consciousness until they got him on an operating table to remove the extra bone projecting from his torn leg. Even then, he was still behaving like a newspaperman.

"Where are you from?" he asked the surgeon.

"Kingston."

"Oh," said Purcell, "do you know Rupert Davies? Owns the *Whig-Standard?*"

"Yes," said the surgeon. "I know the son-of-a-bitch."

At this point the anesthetic interrupted what might have been an interesting interview.

Purcell convalesced at Cliveden, Lady Astor's estate-turned-hospital. He was back at his Toronto job with CP in January of 1942, making life miserable again for CP employees. Soon after his return a train crash at Almonte, near Ottawa, left thirty-six people dead. Purcell immediately contacted his Ottawa bureau, where blizzard-like conditions had almost immobilized the city.

He was told the bureau car did not have enough gas to get to Almonte, thirty to forty miles away; that there was no way of getting more gas because of wartime rationing; that the weather had made travel impossible. This exchange of messages was ended by an ultimatum from Purcell that if someone was not on the way to the scene of the train crash in fifteen minutes the entire bureau would be fired.

The bureau members set out, ran out of gas, covered the final miles to the crash on foot and by hitchhiking. By 5:30 in the morning the details of the disaster were chattering across CP wires. The next day, on rereading Purcell's messages, the bureau men began to seethe and were on the point of resigning when another message arrived from Purcell, congratulating them on a job well done. They did not quit. This technique, which Scott Young once described as the one-two punch (a whack in the mouth followed by a pat on the back) was standard procedure with Purcell.

For the balance of the war, Purcell hopped back and forth to Europe many times—working with Greg's brother Joe Clark, Dick Malone and others to resolve the accreditation, transportation, communication and censorship conflicts that developed between the press and the military. This war within a war has a long history.

Although it can be argued that the first war correspondents were early Greeks or Romans, there is a marker in St. Paul's Cathedral in London for William Howard Russell of the London *Times,* which says, "THE FIRST AND GREATEST OF WAR CORRESPONDENTS." Russell began his career covering the Battle of Isted in 1850, in which the Danes repulsed an attempted German takeover. Russell was wounded at that battle, but continued to hunt for more wars to write about. In his day the military were not only unmindful of the importance of getting news home, and unhelpful, but often deliberately obstructive. In the Crimea, Russell not only had to fend for himself for food and lodging, but was actually ordered off the battlefield many times by Lord Raglan, the British commander, who also distinguished himself by ordering the disastrous charge of the Light Brigade.

CP correspondents were outstanding overseas and, just before the end of the war, Purcell and eight other CP staffers founded the Canadian Press War Correspondents Association. Later this became the Canadian War Correspondents Association and membership grew to more than a hundred members. Greg was an honorary life member.

The CWCA is a strange organization. It has a constitution (which has been lost), officers, annual dues and presumably some purpose. Meetings and elections are conducted under conditions that range from dictatorship to anarchy. There is, usually, an agenda, but the most incredible motions are moved, seconded and voted upon in a parody of parliamentary procedure and bombast, punctuated with shouts, dirty songs, insults, drunken reminiscences, irrelevancies, sentimentalities, noble proclamations, obscenities and cachinnation.

New Yorker editor Harold Ross would not allow his writers to use the word indescribable, claiming that nothing was indescribable. Ross never attended a CWCA meeting.

However, there are as many opinions as there are people. Clyde Gilmour, the eminent film critic, attended one meeting and next day he wrote this formal apology to the president:

Dear Mr. President:

I hereby abjectly apologize for my gross discourtesy in

having remarked at last night's meeting of the CWCA that it was "almost as tense, thrilling and exalting as the 1949 quilting bee of the Etobicoke Mothers Guild."

On reflection my opinion is that the meeting was "even *more* tense, thrilling and exalting than the 1949 quilting bee of the Etobicoke Mothers Guild."

Yours truly,
Clyde Gilmour.

Inasmuch as Gillis Philip Purcell roughly divided his time between running the Canadian War Correspondents Association and running Canadian Press, history will judge him on his operation of these two organizations. My personal feeling that he is a reincarnation of Prince Vlad, the Impaler, is of little consequence. I can say that he operated in both milieus with a remarkable economy of words, for a man versed in Latin, Greek, French and English. To the best of my knowledge he used only three expressions: "How about a short, fast one?" "Fantastic, Lady Pamela!" and "Don't panic!"

Authorities in both CWCA and CP have left their assessments of Purcell on the record. He retired on his sixty-fifth birthday, November 25, 1969, after forty-one years with CP. For his blacktie retirement dinner some two hundred publishers, editors, reporters and broadcasters showed up from all across Canada.

Publisher Stuart Keate of the Vancouver *Sun* delivered the eulogy. Keate pointed out that, under Purcell, CP had done more to unite Canada than any other single agency. A personal triumph for Purcell had been the provision of a French-language service in CP. He had played a significant part in the creation of the National Newspaper Awards. Purcell, said Keate, had gained the respect of fellow newspapermen and left behind him things of value to his community and country that would far outlast him.

On December 19, 1969, Purcell was made an Officer of the Order of Canada. In April of 1970 he was elected to the Canadian News Hall of Fame. This happened despite his strenuous objections and despite the fact that he deliberately absented himself from the awards dinner. His son, Bob Purcell, had to accept the award on his behalf.

That's one side of the story. The members of the CWCA also had their opinions of Purcell. Two of them expressed their views in a song about him. These men were Ralph Allen and Charles Lynch. Lynch went on to become a kind of wandering troubadour with the National Press & Allied Workers Jazz Band, Inc., specializing in musical satires of our political leaders. The song, which they composed on the back of an envelope and a discarded cigarette package, is known as "The Purcell Polka" or "The Pisspot Polka." This is how the song ends:

> Purcell, Purcell,
> Is a, is a,
> Purcell, Purcell,
> Is pisspot.

> Pisspot, pisspot,
> Purcell is a pisspot,
> Pisspot, pisspot,
> Purcell is indeed.

> Pisspot, pisspot,
> Purcell is a pisspot,
> Pisspot, pisspot,
> All take heed!

Seldom have words and music come together so beautifully as in this glorious tribute. Ralph Allen's lyrics succeed in capturing the Purcell personality and Lynch's rousing melody makes it ring in memory. The wild, foot-stomping enthusiasm displayed by CWCA members in singing this song at annual meetings is indescribable.

40

AIMLESS LODGE

We were in Greg's room at the King Edward, having a few scotches before lunch.

"This book is short on sex," I said. "People need a bit of scandal in biographies. They want to find out that Eisenhower had a girl friend. That Roosevelt had a girl friend. Hell, even *Mrs.* Roosevelt had a girl friend."

Greg continued to fiddle with his pipe.

"You must be holding back on me," I said. "Look at those bawdy stories you tell some people. That sex lecture you delivered to the troops until the colonel made you stop. That pantomime about the peaceful golden autumn of life, after being dragged helter-skelter through the world by your cock—"

"Just stories," said Greg. "I collected a few funny stories along the way, but they have nothing to do with my personal life. By now you must know I was a one-woman man."

"Take Clyde Gilmour," I said. "He sees all the movies and he knows what sells. Have you heard his story about how he and Joe Levine concocted The Perfect Movie Title?"

"I've heard it three times," said Greg. "And I laughed every time. But I don't want that title on my book. It's perverse."

"A little perversity wouldn't hurt," I said. "Did you ever fall in love with a bear?"

"A bear?" said Greg, incredulous. Then he laughed. "Oh, you're talking about that old *Reader's Digest* joke—the man who got lost, fucked by a bear and found God."

"And quit smoking," I said. "That used to be a joke, but now it's a meaningful relationship. If we handled it delicately we might even win a Governor General's Award."

"Bears are out," said Greg. "I took a shot at a black bear once on a deer hunt. But I missed."

"Then how about us going up to Go Home Bay," I said, "and swimming around underwater until you discover who your father was. We could call it *Submerging*."

"My father was Joseph Thomas Clark, editor of the *Star*," said Greg. "I must have told you that a dozen times, and—" He broke off and glared at me suspiciously. "Have you been drinking?" he asked. "I mean, even before you got here?"

I shook my head. "Drinking isn't my problem," I said. "It's reading. Anyway, here's another idea. It's been suggested there's something vaguely homosexual about you guys who go hunting and fishing all the time. In his column the other day, Richard Needham said his idea of Hell would be to spend eternity sitting around a table at a hunting camp drinking with the boys."

"Spending eternity with Needham might be their idea of Hell, too," said Greg. "Anyway, I didn't even know what homosexuality was until I got overseas and had to defend a couple of poor buggers who got caught playing with each other."

"How about you and Purcell?" I asked. "You're like the Odd Couple. Writing notes to each other. Going fishing and hunting together. Maybe you're latent homosexuals and don't even know it."

"Purcell!" said Greg. "Good God! I'd sooner be linked with a bear! If you want to learn about fishing I'll get Purcell to invite you on our next trip. We're going bass fishing at Aimless Lodge."

"Aimless Lodge?" I said. "I thought Purcell called his place Nameless Lodge."

"He does," said Greg. "But I call it Aimless Lodge."

My invitation—more like the army's daily routine orders—arrived in the mail. Purcell's schedule read:

0617 hours (E.D.T.) Sun rises

0630 " Car No. 2 (Driver—West) departs for Allen residence.

0640 " Car No. 3 (Driver—Carroll) departs for Clark residence.

0700 " Car No. 2 arrives at 16 Rumsey Road. Transfer to Car No. 1.

0730 " Cars 1 & 3 rendezvous at Pickering gravel pit. Relief and refreshment. Moose milk. (Purcell)

0900 " Car No. 1 stops Lakefield for bait. Minnows, worms and hellgrammites.

0900 "   Car No. 3 proceeds and procures fresh-picked corn.

0945 "   Arrival Nameless Lodge. Occupants of Car No. 1 load gear in Boat No. 1.

1010 "   Boat No. 1 proceeds to Barber Pole.

1015 "   Boat No. 2 proceeds to Pescud's Point.

This schedule continued to sunset, at which point, I presumed, Purcell would check the sun to see if it was on time. Nameless Lodge, as I was to discover, was an extension of Purcell's personality. For every item in the cabin there was a shelf, a drawer or a nail. After use, each item had to be put back immediately. Constant reminders were issued by Purcell.

"Would you mind replacing the top on that jar of jam?"

"Would you mind putting that can opener back on the nail?"

"Would you mind putting that chair back where it belongs?"

Eventually, the human spirit rebels. Ralph Allen, a notoriously short-tempered man, once bolted from the cabin with a bottle of whiskey. Outside, he built himself a campfire over which he huddled the rest of the afternoon like some sullen Indian chief.

On this particular day in September, work had fouled up Purcell's transportation schedule. I arrived alone at Nameless Lodge, late in the afternoon. Ralph Allen was not due until the following morning, but Purcell, Greg and Bruce West had finished fishing for the day and were gathered inside. I had brought with me a portable tape recorder to gather evidence of any latent homosexuality. I placed this on the kitchen table, turned it on and then poured myself a drink of rum and water.

After I had settled into a chair, Purcell said, "Would you mind putting the top back on that rum bottle before someone knocks it over?"

I got up and put the top back on the rum bottle.

Greg had been sitting in a boat with Purcell all afternoon, taking his orders about how to steer the boat, where to cast and so forth.

"Some day," said Greg, "I am going to write a story about this place, how you try to take command of everything, bully everyone—"

"It's not bullying," said Purcell. "With people like you and West and Allen, who just drop everything anywhere, I have to spend two-thirds of my time putting stuff back."

From the stove, West said, "Is that tape recorder on?"

"Yes," I said.

"Just cook," said Purcell. "That seems to be more than you can cope with."

West was fussing with the wood stove, trying to start a fire. He intended to roast fresh corn in the husk. Unfortunately, more smoke was backing into the cabin than was going up the chimney.

"There's nothing like watching a great cook at work," said Purcell. "Especially one who can't light a fire."

"It's been my experience," said Greg, "that a man who was any good in the kitchen was no good anywhere else."

West poked angrily at the fire. "Thank you," he said, with some bitterness. "If you, Purcell, or Mr. G. McTrivia Clark there, would like to roast this corn, I am perfectly agreeable. Especially on this stove. The chimney must be full of raccoons."

"No, no," said Purcell. "We're looking forward to this corn. Where did you stumble across the recipe?"

This was a jab at West, who fancied himself as a gourmet cook.

"I found the recipe in Milt Dunnell's sports column," said West. "Where else?"

"One thing about sports columnists," said Purcell, "they're not always sitting around reading their own columns and laughing at their own jokes."

Another jab at West, about his humor column in *The Globe & Mail*.

West was indignant. "I have never laughed at a column of mine in my life," he said. "The trouble is—nobody else laughs either. I'm thinking of putting a new head on it—'No Laughing Matter.'"

By now the smoke had filled the upper reaches of the cabin and was settling lower.

"The cloud ceiling seems to be getting lower in here," observed Purcell. "I hope you can finish that corn before the table disappears."

"I will finish this damned corn," said West, "if we have to eat it lying on the floor."

Purcell and Greg poured themselves another drink and speculated on what calamities Ralph Allen would bring with him tomorrow. In camp, Allen was clumsy and disaster-prone. If he put hand to an outboard motor, it would fall off the boat. If he managed to start the motor, he was likely to sink the boat or get the anchor hopelessly wedged under rocks. Once, before Purcell's horrified eyes, he had knocked the last remaining bottle of liquor off a bridge into a rushing stream.

"Last time he was here," said Purcell, "he got bit by a rattlesnake."

"There are no rattlesnakes here," said Greg.

"I know that," said Purcell. "He'd been on one of those guided tours in Algonquin Park with his son, Glen, so he arrived here with the idea he was now a great expert on trees. He was outside, identifying trees, when I heard a great yell and he came thrashing back, shouting he'd been bitten by a rattlesnake. I just poured myself a drink and told him to sit down while we studied out what to do. 'Has your foot started to get numb yet?' I asked him. 'No,' he said. 'Well, it will,' I said. 'Also you will begin to feel a kind of numbness in the groin. Now,' I said, 'you should tell me just where you want me to take you and, should you pass away before we get there, just whom should I get in touch with?'

"By now," said Purcell, laughing, "he was ready to explode. He said, 'You goddamn unsympathetic son-of-a-bitch!' What calmed him down was when he pulled off his shoes and socks—he couldn't find any mark where the rattlesnake had bitten him. He eventually decided he must have been bitten by a weasel."

"Probably stepped on a twig," said Greg.

After many more drinks, West's corn was roasted and eaten. It was superb, as only freshly picked corn can be. "Fantastic, Lady Pamela," said Purcell. He further expressed his appreciation with an enormous belch. Greg replied with a tremendous fart.

"That's the way I get," said Greg, "if I eat a lot of corn. They're just pure wind. Corn fritters, I call them. That reminds me of Go Home Bay. Up there my sister, Mabel, and her husband, Tommy Drew-Brook—we visit each other for Sunday dinners.

"Last month we were leaving their cottage, just at dusk, me leading with the flashlight to look out for rattlesnakes. As I got out on the rocks I said to Tommy, 'Do you know how the Arabs express appreciation of a fine meal with a big belch?' Tommy said, 'Yes.' I said, 'Okay' and I lifted my leg and I blew the most magnificent goddamn fart you ever heard in your life. Then I walked down the rock to our boat. My sister wouldn't speak to me for a week!"

After more drinks, Bruce West was persuaded to record for posterity his famous story about Churchill in the Casbah. His other most celebrated story was called "The Basket Position," a much more bawdy yarn, and Purcell suggested he also tape this one.

"Well, I don't know," said West. "Takes a bit of a mood for that one."

Greg, always more inhibited with a tape recorder present, felt the same way.

After more bullying by Purcell, West agreed to record "The Basket Position."

Greg went along reluctantly. "Well, all right. I submit. Submisso, that's Latin."

"Submitto is Latin," said Purcell. "Submisso is *not* Latin."

To the accompaniment of more rum and more laughter, West rendered his classic. It was a funny story West had polished up over the years. Inasmuch as this was for posterity, he insisted on hearing it back again from the tape, looking for fluffs or errors.

He laughed uproariously as he listened to himself telling a joke that he must have told a hundred times.

All of us were now completely foxed by the grape, an expression coined by Ralph Allen. Greg took the floor and the microphone. For the next hour he spoke on poetry and farts. He discussed the quality of farts and the effect of various foods on farts, answered technical questions as to whether or not ladies farted, compared Purcell's belches to West's farts, related practical jokes involving the simulation of farts and spoke about the place of farts in history.

After this tour de farts, Purcell said, "It's a good thing Allen isn't here yet. All this shithouse humor would have driven him into the woods."

"I've never been able to understand that about Allen," said Greg. "I laugh at all his sex stories. But he won't even admit outhouse humor has a place in history. Mark Twain wrote an underground sketch called "1601" which was supposed to be a fireside conversation between Queen Elizabeth the First, William Shakespeare, Sir Walter Raleigh. The main topic was a fart."

"I can't believe that," said West.

"You and Allen," said Greg. "God, I'll never forget the first time I saw fart in print. It was in *Portrait of the Artist As a*

Young Man. Joyce wrote that this young man, standing on the steps of whatever university it was, this young man *farted briefly!* God, what a thrill that was!"

"Shocking," said West. "Shocking."

Greg went on. "Phil Smith at *Weekend Magazine* has sent me two clippings—from the *Guardian* and the *New Statesman.* They're about Le Pêtomane—a professional farter who played the Moulin Rouge in the 1890s."

"You're putting us on," said West.

"He could play tunes, blow out candles," said Greg, "and he outdrew Sarah Bernhardt. I'll get a copy of this book and show you. Le Pêtomane."

I had brought along a copy of the *Rubaiyat* on the chance that Greg might be persuaded to read from it. He put on his glasses and began:

"Awake! for Morning in the Bowl of Night
    Has flung the Stone that puts the Stars to Flight:
And Lo! the Hunter of the East has caught
    The Sultan's Turret in a Noose of Light."

Greg cried out with delight. "What a marvelous damn journalist he was, this Fitzgerald! Awake! That cry, Awake! That's absolutely beautiful, you know—not only beautiful English, but beautiful journalism! That punch line right at the top. This guy was a real guy. I wish I'd known him."

Greg read to himself for a while, muttering, "How this man can write. How can he say this with such simple words? What a magical comprehension of the English tongue. Beside me singing in the wilderness."

Greg put the book away for a moment, as though it were too much. "This is taking me a long way back. It's so unstudied, isn't it? It seems to flow naturally from the mind of the poet into our mind. Keats had this, too, this instant communication with the reader."

From memory, Greg recited:

"A thing of beauty is a joy forever;
    Its loveliness increases; it will never
Pass into nothingness; but still will keep—"

Greg broke off. "You know, all my life I've wanted to hear Charles Laughton read that—the first hundred lines of *Endymion*. It would be one of the great things of our time. Now and then you find somebody who can write it—and someone who can say it. Laughton had that gift. Remember his "Gettysburg Address" in, what was it, *Ruggles of Red Gap?* If he could do the *Endymion* as some kind of a tramp character like that—it would shock us. And there are times when we need to be jolted into an appreciation of our treasures."

"How about a short fast one?" said Purcell.

We filled our glasses again. Outside it had begun to rain heavily. There was only the occasional snap and crackle from the fire in the stove and the steady, comforting sound of rain on the cabin roof.

Against this background, Greg read the *Rubaiyat* from the beginning. It was not a reading that Charles Laughton would have given us, rich, resonant and perfect. Greg was now sixty-eight years old, his voice rough and a little gravelly, and occasionally he ran out of breath at the wrong place.

But it was a wonderful reading, a wonderful moment. One verse reminded him of how little time we had. He read it twice, his voice near breaking.

> "Ah, Moon of my Delight who know'st no wane,
>   The Moon of Heav'n is rising once again:
>   How oft hereafter rising shall she look
>   Through this same Garden after me—in vain!"

When he was finished, there was no sound for a while, except the beating of the rain on the roof and the sound of the fire.

"How about a short fast one?" said Purcell.

We all did.

Greg became entranced with the raindrops on the roof. "Isn't that bloody beautiful," he said. "Can you record that?"

I obliged by moving the microphone up into the rafters and recording the sound of the rain on the roof.

"I've heard that so often at Go Home," said Greg. "Now, let's play back my reading of the *Rubaiyat*."

There were groans from around the table. "No, no. We can't sit through that again."

Purcell hypocritically vetoed it on the grounds of Greg's health. "It's for your sake," said Purcell. "You poured your soul into that reading. It's so beautiful that hearing it again would be too much for you."

West produced his best line of the night. "The only part of the tape I would agree to hearing again," he said solemnly, "is that last little bit, the recording of the rain on the roof."

This broke everybody up. We played back the tape recording of rain on the roof while the real thing was taking place over our heads. It seemed very, very funny.

To everybody except Greg, that is. He was annoyed. Hurt, even. After all, he had not only listened to West's dirty stories for the tenth time, but he had listened to them being played back.

He glared at West and said, "Fuck you."

Purcell looked at his schedule and decided it was time to go to bed. He began undressing in a way that was an order. We did the same and got into our respective beds. With a lot of grunting and groaning, Purcell took off his artificial leg and propped it in a corner. Then he hopped around the cabin checking doors and putting out lights.

"While you're up," I said, "would you mind making sure my tape recorder is turned off?"

"Kindly fuck yourself," said Purcell. He switched off the last light and hopped back to bed.

Darkness descended. Purcell belched. West farted. Greg snored. The rain pattered on the roof.

Months later, I made one more attempt to track down latent homosexuality in Greg's fishing companions. This time I went along on the annual Lake Simcoe Ice Fishing Safari, another event organized by Purcell.

I don't know whether it always rains on fishing trips, but it rained again this day—all day. Toward evening I was sitting in a smoke-filled fishing hut in the middle of the lake. There had been no indication that there was a single fish in Lake Simcoe. One ardent fisherman had passed out and was snoring on a bench. All the soggy salami sandwiches were gone. The liquor was all but gone.

The door of the ice hut opened and Bruce West's greasy, unshaven face appeared in the door. He beckoned and I followed him outside. It was still pouring rain, but I was so wet already it didn't matter. We stood in about six inches of icy slush and water that covered the real ice underneath.

West had a glass in his hand and that strange solemn look he puts on his face when he's about to say something funny.

"I was just wondering," he said. He paused to take a drink. He licked his lips. Then he waved his arm around to indicate the rain, the bleak expanse of Lake Simcoe, the ice huts, the whole miserable day.

"I was just wondering," he repeated, "if there isn't something vaguely homosexual in all this."

Then he doubled up with laughter, laughing so hard he almost choked. He really does laugh at his own jokes.

That was the end of it for me. And so far as I'm concerned, that's the end of homosexuality in this book. As soon as I get to the bottom of this page.

41

If Greg had been born before Shakespeare,
Shakespeare would be quoting Greg.

—Ralph Allen
Maclean's *Editor*

The journals in which Greg recorded his thoughts, his observations, the trivia and tragedy of life were first given him by his father, Joseph Clark. In later years, the journals were presents from
his own children, Murray, Greg, Jr., and Elizabeth. Now, they
were filling up more slowly. He didn't get around to using a journal given to him by Elizabeth in 1953 until nearly ten years later.

Now, more and more, he was looking backward. In 1963 he
wrote:

Looking back at old diaries I am impressed with the decline in my handwriting. I wonder how many million words
these old fingers have written in longhand and on typewriter
. . . how many million words that were printed and published.

I have just done some figuring. My *Star Weekly* articles
with Jim ran from 1929 to 1946, and were an average 3000
words. That is 2,652,000 words. From 1919 to 1929, I had
better than 3000 each week, as I usually did two features.
Say, 4000. That is another 2,080,000 words. Between 1919
and 1936 I did very little Daily work, other than Santa Claus
and Fresh Air Fund and other appeals. Let us say one million words.

Then on *Weekend* my Shorties are around 1000 words.
From 1949 to 1962, that is 676,000. My Packsacks averaged
300 words a day, six days a week, from 1948 to 1962.
1,395,000 words. I overlooked my Daily work from 1936 to

1946 that includes huge output at things like Royal Coronation, Papal Coronation, the war and scores, if not hundreds,
of other news stories. The founding of the United Nations,
the execution of Hauptmann, far too many to enumerate. But
I figure 5000 a week for the 11 years comes to 2,850,000.

Now, not counting all the words done for advertising, for
radio, for magazines and odd jobs, the total of words written
and published appears to be 10,653,000. Ten million, six
hundred and fifty-three thousand words! HOLY SMOKE!

On March 19, 1963, Greg wrote, "There is nobody I have to
hurry home to, ever, anymore. Helen, my wife, my love, but
above all my dearest companion and very closest friend, died yesterday morning at 9:00 A.M. of a coronary thrombosis."

Helen's unexpected death followed a few short days of illness
which she and Greg had mistakenly attributed to a recurrence of
gall bladder trouble, for which she had been operated on some
fifteen years before. Dr. Frederick Harrison examined her and
prescribed for the pain. A severe pain began in her shoulders and
spread to her chest. The medication seemed to help, but she was
in distress again early Monday morning. The doctor arrived at
8:30 in the morning and administered a hypodermic to relieve the
pain.

Downstairs, the doctor talked with Greg. "I am afraid it is the
gall bladder. As soon as she is well enough we will have X rays
taken. You say she hasn't been vomiting?"

"No," said Greg.

At that moment, they heard Helen retching upstairs in the
bathroom. They rushed upstairs and got Helen back into bed. She
was dead within the hour. Her last, whispered word was "Greg."

She was buried in Mount Pleasant Cemetery. It was a month
before Greg could again commit his thoughts to paper.

In April, he wrote, "I am in my 71st year, have done everything I intended to do, had a colorful and adventurous life, enjoyed the love and companionship of a beautiful, generous and
understanding woman, sired interesting children, and now I await
the Hammer of God, and hope He hits me square!"

The hammer of fate was not long in coming. In July, Greg himself was struck by a heart attack, his second, and hospitalized for
five weeks. Out again in the fall, he insisted on a recuperative trip

to Go Home on the Thanksgiving weekend. There he awoke at 5 A.M. with severe pain, which his nitroglycerin capsules failed to relieve. A vacationing doctor treated him and he was taken by boat and ambulance back to the hospital for another four-week stay.

The next month his brother Arthur, his junior by seventeen years, died after a long illness. Greg, too, was ready to die and was suffering from great loneliness, even when with his children and grandchildren. The most serious effect of his illness was on his work. He had been forced to drop the "Packsack" daily column during his hospitalization. His second heart attack was another setback which weakened his desire to write. It was easy to put it off one more day.

In the year following this first serious heart attack, he turned in only four stories to *Weekend*'s editors. The news from head office was ominous. As an associate editor, he had been receiving a salary of $15,000 a year. They were going to reduce this to $12,000 and continue him on salary for another year, to see if he could get back into production.

It wasn't disastrous, but Greg felt humiliated. The loss of the "Packsack" column had meant a loss of some $3,000 a year in income. The loss of another $3,000 a year in salary was serious. He wrote a letter to the head office, questioning the cut in view of his years of service. *Weekend*'s editors responded. Yes, he had made a large contribution and they knew he had turned down other radio and advertising work that would have added to his income. They would carry him at full salary and expenses for the coming year.

Greg was now seventy-two, in September of 1964, but he could see no way to retirement. His thirty-five years at the *Star* had earned him no pension at all, and his pensionable time at *Weekend* would have yielded little. He thought less of retirement than he did of death. He seemed, daily, to be waiting. Nothing triggered his old initiative. He had little desire to get up in the morning, dressing was an effort, it was too much trouble to meet anyone or go for a walk. He compared himself to a watch with a broken spring.

As Christmas of 1964 approached, he felt certain he had only a little time to remedy those things that were still undone. Helen and he had planned to visit the military cemetery at Leubringhen in Normandy, where Murray's body had been moved. The first of his heart attacks, back in 1955—a warning really—had prevented them from taking that trip. Now he convinced himself he must go. Against the wishes of his son and daughter, he made reservations to fly to England and to visit Murray's grave on Christmas Day.

It was a strange journey, and his letter to Gil Purcell did not tell the whole story. On December 30, 1964, he wrote:

Dear Gil—

Mission *not* completed!

I got over to Calais Christmas Eve in good time to buy flowers. When I woke Christmas morning, a Channel gale was blowing, it was snowing *slush* not sleet. The hotel people said the radio reported it would get worse. At 11:00 A.M. I took a taxi the 14 Kilometres out to the cemetery. We could not get up the access road on account of the snow, slush and mud, so I clambered with my bouquet up a 12-foot bank, reached the high iron gates. They were locked. Visibility less than 50 yards up the slope. There for about 15 minutes I stood cursing myself for not having made enquiries at War Graves in England. My taxi driver said if he helped me over the fence farther along, I couldn't find my particular stone because all would be plastered with snow.

There was wire securing the stems of my bouquet and the evergreen boughs in it. So with the wire, I fastened the bouquet to the bloody iron gate. I had some bloody strange thoughts standing there in an utterly deserted landscape, like old mad Lear on the blasted heath.

I came back to Calais, dried out my soaked coat, pant legs soaked to the knees, then phoned the gendarmeries at St. Inglevert and even Boulogne. But nobody knew where the cemetery caretakers could be found. The storm continued all night. It was no use calling London. All offices closed Boxing Day. So I came back Saturday and Monday Morrison put me in immediate touch with War Graves and Vet. Affairs who made every offer to take me back and have cemetery open. But the weather had been continuously foul, gales, snow. So, as I told Elizabeth in a letter today, I realize after all that there is more than an iron gate, gales and blizzards between me and my son. I left my flowers on the iron gate.

Aff. — Greg

From this low point, this failure to place his flowers on Murray's grave, Greg gradually rebounded. He was now under the personal care of Dr. William Oille, a renowned heart specialist, who visited him regularly and became a close personal friend.

In view of his heart condition, Greg wondered whether or not he should take the occasional fishing trip.

"Greg," said Oille, "you haven't a thing to worry about. One of these days you are simply going to drop dead." Oille's treatment included a daily ration of scotch, and this had a beneficial effect. Another boost for Greg was a message from Craig Ballantyne, now *Weekend*'s editorial director. *"Weekend* is going to continue you on salary as long as you live."

During his darkest days, Greg had continued to live alone at 119 Crescent Road, with only Mrs. Doris Armstrong, the Clarks' housekeeper since the early Fifties, as company. Surrounded by his photographs, souvenirs and memories, Greg had tended to look to the past too often, too long. He passed too many days in his dressing gown. In 1966 the family house was sold and Greg moved to a small suite in the King Edward Hotel.

For a man with so many souvenirs and treasures, Greg made the change with amazing ease. His rods, guns and fishing flies went to Greg, Jr., some for disposal to old friends. The family pet, a Corgi named Chelsea, was taken by Mrs. Armstrong, who was moving to Fort William. Greg took only his clothes and a few favorite books.

Among these were *Old Mr. Flood* by Joseph Mitchell; *Farewell, Miss Julie Logan* by James Barrie; *The Voice of Bugle Ann* by Mackinlay Kantor and *Wild Life of The Highlands* by Dugald Macintyre. He read these books over and over and once said he would be happy on a desert island with them alone, provided that the Gideons had already left a Bible there.

His library, including the fishing books of which he had been so proud, was given to the University of Western Ontario. Of these angling books, one of his favorites was Plunket Greene's *Where the Bright Waters Meet*. Arthur Ransome's book, *Mainly About Fishing,* he found one of the most perceptive books about the sport. Ransome's other book, a small one called *Rod & Line,* Greg felt should be in every fisherman's pocket. In his own copy, he wrote on the inside cover, "Ransome is one of three or four literary anglers I wish I had known."

Greg moved into Room 683 at the King Edward Hotel on Saturday, July 2, 1966. The room was called a suite. In effect it was a very large bedroom, with a wooden lattice dividing the bedroom section from the sitting room. Both were of good size—and there was a small foyer.

It was on the northeast corner of the hotel and looked down King Street and over to Toronto's old St. Lawrence Market area. Greg also had a good view of St. James Cathedral, where his great-grandfather, Thomas McMurray, had been baptized in 1813 by the Reverend John Strachan. In the cathedral hung the tattered colors of his old regiment, the 4th CMR.

He had difficulty at first in taking his mind away from death. He was not afraid, but seemed to feel he had little time left. In fact, Suite 683 at the King Edward would be a small but happy home for him for nearly ten years.

42

In Brighton it was Alice,
The sweetest of the bunch,
But down on his expense account
She was "petrol, oil and lunch."

—*Anon.*

On a sunny autumn day in 1970, Greg and I were continuing our tour of the Toronto houses he had lived in—eight different ones. Greg mentioned that he had never owned any of them.

"You've lived in Toronto for seventy-eight years," I said, "and never owned a home? This is a city of homeowners and you are a typical Torontonian, if not archetypal."

"I wouldn't lie to you," said Greg. "Well, hardly ever. I was born in a red brick house that my father rented for eighteen dollars a month. Today I live in the King Edward Hotel, where the room rate begins at eighteen dollars a day. I still don't own a home." He said thoughtfully, "You know, I must have paid out a small fortune in rent."

"What about all those houses in between?" I asked. "Indian Road? Woodside Avenue? Baby Point? Indian Grove? Crescent Road?"

"Crescent Road was owned by my daughter Elizabeth," said Greg. "And the others were all rented. I had a horror of owning anything. The moment I made a down payment on a house, I thought some publisher would offer me a big job in Winnipeg or Vancouver or maybe Medicine Hat."

"Listen," I said. "When you were very young—about a hundred years ago—you wrote this in your diary. Quote—Before I become old and exaggerative—unquote."

"I should never have let you read those diaries," said Greg. "All right. The truth is I never had the down payment. I was a working newspaperman. And you know what that's like."

"I know what it's like now," I said. "But what about a hundred years ago?"

"I went to work for the *Toronto Star* in 1912," said Greg. "At a salary of twelve dollars a week. I gave five dollars to my mother for room and board."

"But later," I said, "you became one of the *Star*'s star writers."

"Somehow," said Greg, "I never got out of debt. I remember when Joseph E. Atkinson appointed me promotion manager. I said to him, 'But what about my *Star Weekly* stories? Do I give them up?' Atkinson replied quickly, 'Oh, no, Greg. *In addition* to your *Star Weekly* stories!' "

Greg went on. "I survived the way we all do. On assignment I put the *Star*'s expense money in my left-hand pocket and my own money in my right-hand pocket. Then I made it a point never to reach into my right-hand pocket."

Children were playing on the sidewalk outside 147 Indian Road when we arrived there. The third-floor flat here was the first home occupied by Greg and his wife, Helen, when he returned from World War I. Here his first son, Murray Clark, was born. His second son, Gregory Clark, Jr., was born after Greg moved to his first house. This was 90 Woodside Avenue, a street running east off Runnymede, just below Annette.

After I had taken pictures, Greg said, "It's fifty years ago, but it seems like yesterday. It was a day like this. I was out front, raking leaves, when a man called hello from across the street." He continued, "It was Dr. Horace Macintyre, who practiced from his house at the corner. He came over and said, 'I guess you're the new neighbor. Tell me, Mr. Clark, do you know anything about hockey?' I said, 'Nothing. Absolutely nothing.' So Dr. Macintyre said, 'Good. Then you're just the man I'm looking for. I need a new director for the West Toronto Hockey Team. We've got Harold Ballard and a bunch of other directors who know all about hockey.' "

Greg served as a director on the hockey club for some years and fully lived up to Dr. Macintyre's expectations. Greg's wife became a close friend of the doctor's wife, Kathleen Macintyre.

From Woodside, Greg and I drove to 3 Baby Point Road, where he lived when his daughter, Elizabeth, was born. Next, he moved down the street to 47 Baby Point Road, where his backyard looked out on the backyard of Jimmie Frise, his friend, fishing companion and collaborator on *Star Weekly* stories. Baby Point Road runs down to the Humber River, in the area of the Old Mill.

"I always loved this area," said Greg, "from the time I was a young boy. From my father's house back on Howland Avenue, my chums and I used to walk out here on Sunday afternoons, digging for Indian arrowheads along the Humber and collecting insect and plant specimens."

The house Greg moved to next was not far away. It was a large, rambling house at 19 Indian Grove. As we took photos, the current occupant, a Mr. Bob Grossi, came out and chatted with Greg.

"Does it still slope from north to south?" asked Greg. "We used to drop a marble in the north end and it would run all the way to the other end."

"It hasn't changed," laughed Grossi.

"We used to call it the Halton County Old Folks' Home," said Greg, "because a visitor once said you could walk around in it for three days without meeting anyone. But it was great for the children. A badminton court in the backyard. And a funny little building in the backyard which someone had used as an aviary. Made a great playhouse. We had some of our happiest years here."

Although Greg did not mention it, there had been unhappy times, too, at Indian Grove. It was there that the family had lived during World War II, when Murray was killed. In Greg's attic room, filled with fishing gear, Murray had written a short poem and pasted it on the wall. When Greg moved from Indian Grove he had carefully shaved the poem from the wooden wall, glued it together again and taken it with him.

Leaving the Indian Grove area, we headed for the El Capricio Restaurant at 580 College Street. It had been recommended to Greg by his doctor's daughter, Jennifer Oille, after he had reported on our last disastrous adventure in seeking out good Italian food.

The restaurant was on the second floor; there were only six customers in it. The decor was not too encouraging: a lot of mirrors and gold-flecked wall tiles apparently supposed to represent marble. Imitation philodendrons and fake palm trees tried to hide a huge air conditioning machine against the wall.

"Looks a bit like a Moscow restaurant," I said. "There they

stick white refrigerators right in the middle of the most elaborate dining rooms."

The waiter explained that there was no scotch—they had no liquor license. In lieu of his usual noon medicine, Greg swallowed a small pill. "It's a kind of refined nitroglycerin," said Greg. "I get a pain in my chest these days from any kind of exertion— even climbing those stairs."

After ordering a bottle of wine, Greg asked about my assignment in Montreal for the Toronto *Telegram,* on the kidnapping of James Richard Cross and Pierre Laporte.

"The usual trouble with proofreaders," I said. "There was a mention of the Queen Elizabeth Hotel—Le Reine Elizabeth—and I underlined the masculine article. But some proofreader or editor changed it to La Reine Elizabeth. The fan letters were all about my ignorance."

Greg shook his head sympathetically. "I know. It's bad enough being blamed for your own mistakes. I had one Jim-Greg story ruined for me that way. I was quoting an illiterate character who used very bad grammar. Some proofreader went through the whole story, automatically correcting all the grammar—and ruined the whole damn story. When I tracked him down I said from now on any mistakes in my copy are *my* mistakes—not *your* mistakes. Remember, we writers are the troubadours, tramping the hills and valleys of the world in search of the golden pheasants. When we bring them to you—they're for you to cook—not cook the shit out of them!"

Greg looked appreciatively at the wine when it was poured. "Come fill me with the old familiar juice," he said. "Methinks I might recover by and by."

We both ordered the antipasto. One portion would have done the two of us. The plates were heaped with ham, tomato, black olives, pickled cauliflower, shrimp, cucumber, cheese, salami, mushrooms and tiny green peppers.

The rest of the meal was just as good. Greg sprinkled his cannelloni with grated Parmesan cheese.

"It's pronounced parmigiano," said Greg. "Aged until it's so hard you can't eat it, only grate it and sprinkle it on."

Because of Greg's warmth and humor, our table became a center of attention. Greg discussed the food with the waiter, which in turn brought out the chef, a man named Giacomo Davico, who'd worked his way over via Geneva. His home was in Torino.

One of the diners came over to talk to Greg. He was a Torontonian named Charles Taylor, who'd met Greg in 1940, when Taylor had been a private in the 48th Highlanders. Greg is not easy to forget, even after thirty years.

After he had left us, Greg said, "The 48th was on that rescue mission that went in from Brest shortly after Dunkirk. They got in about a hundred and fifty miles before they were recalled. It was all in vain. They were lucky to get out and so was I."

We paid the bill and left. On the drive back to the King Edward, Greg was thoughtful; the tour of his homes had stirred up memories.

"As you know," he said, "Masefield is one of the writers who still thrills me. It's fifty years ago I happened across his *Reynard the Fox*. Then I got hold of *The Everlasting Mercy,* then *Lollington Downs,* a collection of sonnets and little pieces.

"But he has a one-act play I was reading again the other day, *Tristan and Isolt*. I don't think it's ever been performed, which I can't understand. When the curtain comes down, it immediately rises again and this character addresses the audience with a short verse. It ends:

"Not as men plan nor as women pray do things happen
Unthought of, unseen, from the past comes the ill
      without cure,
By the spirit of man and the judgment of God it is shapen
And its end is our pride in the dust . . . it is just,
      it is sure."

Greg rolled the lines off his tongue and then said, "Jesus, what a beautiful four lines."

I left him at his hotel, but he called me at home, as he often did after a visit. We had been arguing about the exact meaning of the word "ineluctable," and we had not been able to figure out the equivalent or the origin of the chef's first name, Giacomo.

Greg took up the conversation as though we hadn't parted.

"Eluctare," he said, "means to struggle or to fight. So, in this case, ineluctable means inescapable, inevitable. Now, about Giacomo. I went down to the barbershop—they're all Italians there. Giacomo is as plain as the nose on your face. It's Jacob. What a couple of dumbbells. Arrivederci."

43

If laughter shared is the cement of friendship, then there is no question about it: Gregory Clark has more friends than any man in Canada.

Greg is a man of special character and diverse talents, a person with great foibles and particular integrity, marvellous prejudices and deep understanding, a tolerant observer and a philosopher, a humorist and a heckler, a respecter of tradition and a nose-thumber, an extraordinary mixture and a man so Canadian no other land could possibly have produced him.

—*Craig Ballantyne*
Editorial Director
Weekend Magazine

Greg was careless with his correspondence. He did not file away letters he received and rarely, it seems, did he make carbon copies of his own letters to others.

Gil Purcell religiously filed away every letter, note and postcard he received from Greg, in a Canadian Press file folder labeled 24-1-X-Clark. The letters presented here are largely from that file folder, along with some correspondence with his *Weekend* editors, Craig Ballantyne and Hugh Shaw, and a few other fans and friends.

The first is actually Greg's typewritten copy of a telegram he sent to Purcell. While Purcell was on a fishing trip in Canada a beetle found its way into his artificial leg and inflicted a painful bite on his stump. Purcell captured the beetle and sent it to Greg for identification. Greg's telegram caught up with Purcell in San Francisco, where he was taking off for a trip to Australia.

Gillis Purcell   June, 1951
Mark Hopkins Hotel
San Francisco

Beetle that bit you positively identified Royal Ontario Museum as dermestes lardarius stop popular name larder beetle and known as pest of pantry especially fond of hams and bacon stop picture appears page 301 Lutz's Fieldbook of insects stop bon voyage.

Gregory Clark

119 Crescent Road   September 25, 1953
Toronto

The Canadian Press
55 University Ave
Toronto

Dear Mr. Purcell:

You may have heard some stories about sex in the first war, most of which are exaggerated. But here is one I would like you to know about, and it is authentic. In the early stages of my service as Adjutant of the 4th CMR I fell off the Colonel's second horse which was a brown bastard nobody else would ride because he was too tame, and I was persuaded to accept Cpl. McPheerson's little black mare, Pissin' Jinny, 15 hands high, and known as a tartar because she detested riders of more than 130 lbs or so, such as stall fed officers, and I only weighed 106½ lbs, so we became very good friends.

Jinny was a very touchy horse, and the whole regiment used to turn out to watch her being thrown and laid flat in order to be clipped. She was a farter. And I must say that such small gifts as I brought her such as oats, etc., were designed to increase this talent in her.

On the march, it is the Adjutant's duty to ride beside the commanding officer, and periodically to leave the head of the column, ride down it, chiding any company officers whose companies are straggling, report to the 2 I/C at the rear of the column, see that the transport is all present and correct, and ride with the 2 I/C for a little while, and then, at a smart walk, ride back up the column to the commanding officer and report all present and correct, sir.

Well, it was my custom, on this return journey to the head of column, to greet each officer as I passed with a small salute from Jinny. Two farts for a lieutenant, three for a captain, and the whole works of whatever Jinny had on hand for a major. All I had to do was give Jinny a small touch with my off heel (I never wore spurs, and Jinny was extremely touchy) and I could play her like a dulcimer. In eight months, she never failed me.

This little whimsy created no end of good morale in the regiment, the marching troops loved it like a play, and Jinny was the best beloved of all the horses in the regiment.

Yours truly,
G. Clark

119 Crescent Road   December 14, 1956
Toronto

Dear Mr. Purcell

As you know, I, in a quiet way, am a collector of walking sticks, and have many curious acquisitions as the consequence of widows, or more particularly, the maiden elderly daughters of namely old men, knowing of my hobby, sending me paternal relics in the nature of waddies (Austral: Roget.) truncheons, bludgeons, billies and cudgels.

Among a recent bequest was the outer hide, epidermis or encasement of a flask-stick, or drinking staff. It is like the others you and I wot of. But it has no bottle in it, and it wants the silver screw-on knob or top.

It occurs to me that you might share with me the obvious project of visiting some glass-blower, Ryries, or conceivably Hartz & Co. who venture into the field of providing specialized glass receptacles for Science, to obtain the necessary enclosure; and then, without much trouble, having a Mechanic fit a suitable silver, Gold, or jewelled cap.

When finished, we might offer it to our old Friend, George Carpenter, on the discreet understanding that it would accompany him to the Incinerator, full, perhaps, with the true, the Blushful Hippocrene, or perhaps Sugar Cane Rum (which, I forgot to tell you, we drank to Absent Friends up at Alec's on the deer hunt,) and you can tell by now that I have been Secretly drinking up in my attic, with my guns, my rods and my camping gear.

But I think you and I might organize a DO in this case.

Greg.

119 Crescent Road   April 27, 1959
Toronto

Dear Mr. Purcell

The saddest time of life is when you reach the age that you smuggle a spare bottle of beer up the back stairs so your wife wont see you, and then hide it. And cant find it. And then, about half an hour later, you realize you have already drunk it.

Yours truly,
G. Clark

119 Crescent Road   November 3, 1958
Toronto

Craig Ballantyne
Weekend Magazine
Montreal

Dear Craig

When I suggested I write you a good humored memo outlining our conversation of two or three weeks ago about Big Money, you said: "Not TOO good humored!"

Well, in some ways it has to be good humored. Because what started the subject in my mind was a conversation I had with Jock Carroll. I said I could not afford a certain trip we were discussing, and he snorted his disbelief. I asked him what he thought I was making at Weekend. He couldnt hazard a guess. "But," he said, "the Packsacks alone . . ."

I then told him that Family Herald (which has been doing very well!) bought the Packsacks each week and selected three from the six to use as a feature opening each issue. They had been doing this for two years since the reorganization. Jock said he knew them well.

"What do you figure I get for them?" I asked.

"Well, hell," he said, "the by-line alone, there, as a feature. About $100?"

I then informed him that Canada Wide got $5 a week for the lot, of which I got $2.50.

"Good," said Jock, "God!"

Now, if I *had* been getting $100 a week, in two years that would have been $10,000 and I would have been out of debt.

However, it is Weekend I have my eye on. You and others have been most kind in your remarks about my contribution. Weekend has been a great success. My wife points out that, despite illness, holidays, travels and absences, in all this time I have never missed an *issue,* nor ever a Packsack. I admit that production is not enough. That is remarkable production. But quality, excellence, have to be assessed by you Brass. Is my present income a full and fair measure of my share, in production AND quality, for my contribution to Weekend's success?

If the survey readership figures that you get are right, they have been *right* for a long time. Do you not think this calls for special consideration? Or do you get letters like this from everybody?

The main point is, I have debts. In 1951, 53 and 54, I made annual fees ranging from $1,500 to $3,000 from radio and TV, of which I got, due to taxes, only about half. This addition to my income enabled me to pay off some debts, but as you know most offers of radio and TV sidelines are turned down by you.

It is not Jock alone who thinks of me as a columnist and character, in the Big Money. The public does. I was moved three years ago by the Red Feather campaign into the Special Names list. The public thinks I am in the Big Money, along with Sinclair and Pierre Berton, who are rumored to be making $35,000 and $40,000 a year. I live in a fine house (owned by my daughter!) I appear to be a sporty old gent.

An old war horse like me should be coming down the home stretch with my tail up. In your opinion, is my income from Weekend as a columnist and character with the widest regular readership in the history of the business what it should be?

This is a fair memo of our conversation. Let me know how you feel about it.

Aff.
Greg

119 Crescent Road   April 26, 1960
Toronto

Dear Mr. Purcell

Were I not to be cremated, I have just hit upon the epitaph I would choose for my stone:

GREGORY CLARK
1892 1960
NAPOO

It is epigrammatic, historic, biographic, perfect.

Yours truly
G. Clark

(A World War I British army song ended with these lines:

> Bonsoir, old thing,
> Cheerio, ching ching,
> Napoo, toddle-ooo, goodbyeeee!

Napoo is believed to be a corruption of the French phrase, *"il n'y en a plus,"* meaning "there's no more, it's over.")

119 Crescent Road   January 10, 1961
Toronto

Mr Purcell

This is NOT a cockfighting chair. It is a reading chair such as Lord Nelson and other gentlemen of his era favored for reading attentively but in comfort.

The cockfighting chair was built on the same principle, with arm rests, but was not all upholstered up like a living-room chair. It was usually of plain wood, like a stable-chair. One sat spraddle of it, facing over the back.

Respectfully yours
G.C.

119 Crescent Road   April 4, 1964
Toronto

Dear Gil

The name of the flower is Freesia, named after a Swedish botanist E. M. Fries (1794–1878) who found it in Africa. It is just about the *last* of the flowers you can buy that have retained *perfume* despite improvement! They cost around $3.50 or so a dozen stems (Toronto, N.Y. etc.) and an *arranged* bouquet of 1½ doz.

is about right. Yellow, white, &, if you are lucky, mauve. Mixed, 1½ doz of each.

Aff.
Greg

119 Crescent Road   September 28, 1965
Toronto

G P

This is a letter I did NOT send to the Telegram. But I thought you might enjoy it.

Greg

The Editor   September 27, 1965
The Telegram

Sir:

Nobody interfered with us English, Scottish and Irish as we battled with each other through the centuries, until we worked out some kind of accord—minus a lot of Ireland. Nobody interfered with France, Germany, Italy and Spain when, over even longer centuries, they fought it out, for one cause or another. Why, then, do we appear to deny the black people, the brown people and the yellow people the prerogative we white people have so jealously preserved? Our proud histories consist largely of wars, and manoeuvring for wars. In nature, the males of all species are warlike; but man is obviously the most warlike of all, for he fights even outside the rut. To us human males, the prospect is horrifying. Might the solution of our universal problem be not political at all, but surgical? Eh?

Gregory Clark

119 Crescent Road   March 27, 1966
Toronto

G P

Here's one for your collection:

Excerpt from the table talk of G. Clark, Esq with his editorial director, C. Ballantyne Esq.—

"When I was born, Napoleon had been dead only 71 years. What an extraordinary change in the style of men's hats!"

G C

King Edward Hotel   August 14, 1966
Toronto

G P

Enclosed is postcard George McClellan brought me from
Calgary. And then you had to pull the rug from under us by telling
us you had an ORIGINAL in glorious technicolor.

George's best story was about the well drillers in Alberta going
5000 feet and getting a dry hole. But the farmer was a true
Westerner waste not want not; and he took the biffy and moved it
over the hole.

Grampaw went out, and didn't come in for some time. So they
went out and found him dead, on the seat. The coroner came and
the doctor and everybody; but nobody could figure out how
Grampaw had died on the seat.

Then one of his daughters, as they sat around the bier, exclaimed:

"I know what happened! Grampaw always held his breath until
he heard the first one land!"

                                    With God's blessing and mine,
                                    Greg

King Edward Sheraton Hotel
Toronto   October 21, 1966

Jock Carroll
Weekend Magazine
2 Carlton Street
Toronto

Dear Jock:

You caught me off balance on my Greek last night. It is *kalles*,
beautiful, and *puge*, rump.

In anglicizing Greek, they put a 'y' for the 'u'. But *puge* is pronounced pew-gee, the gee being hard G.

Callopygian really means someone with a beautiful rump—not
us admirers.

                                                Aff.
                                                Greg

King Edward Hotel   January 10, 1967
Toronto

Hugh Shaw
Weekend Magazine
Montreal

Dear Hugh

Next attached is a letter from young Peter Worthington, which
I had Purcell Xerox for me because I intend to keep the original.
Also a couple of fan letters. I hate to bug you with fan letters and
forward only the few interesting ones.

Jack McClelland phoned me that Lawrence Earle suggests he
do a biography of me as a book. I cleared with Craig the idea
Earle came up with of doing a piece for Reader's Digest. But this
new one needs some thought. I have for years promised Jock
Carroll that if he was so minded, he could borrow my diaries from
my son Greg in case I popped off. Jock has done some recordings,
including that one about the Papal coronation to the Managing
Editors meeting.

I also suggested to McClelland that he might discuss with you
the preparation of a new collection in hard cover as well as paperback of some of the stories we have missed in previous lots—
Miss Bruce, the one about my father burning my ass with his
cigar as soon as I was born, the one about the chamber pot that
slipped from my grasp into the bathtub in that strange silent
house in Barrie etc etc. I am sure we could get a bagful of forgotten ones.

How about my love story? The Fair Sex. Did it get the axe?

Looking forward to seeing you in Toronto one day soon.

                                                      Aff.
                                                      Greg

The Telegram   January 3, 1967
Toronto

Dear Greg:

This may strike you as a rather curious letter, nevertheless it
may interest you.

My father died a couple of weeks before Christmas from cancer in the bowels. Actually he had been living on a sort of 24-hour life-expectancy since the end of August.

It was a hell of an autumn watching him fight a lonely and hopeless battle that was marked with constant pain. At one stage he remarked to me that he would like to die, but didn't know how. It wasn't that he was afraid of dying, so much as he desired to live: Life and he were good friends.

For my mother especially those days at the hospital watching him slowly starve to death were a special agony. We suspended all treatment in September, but still he hung on.

There was only one pleasure my father had during those months . . . one pleasure which would take his mind off the pain: That was being read to.

There were only two books—or rather authors, who succeeded in distracting him. One was Kipling, and his Jungle Books. The other was yourself.

What little comfort there was in those final months was the result of your books. It may mean little to you, but it meant a great deal to the Worthington family, and for what it is worth you will always have our gratitude for your utterly charming books.

Dad would always laugh, or become thoroughly immersed in your tales. And when my mother had read them all to him, she would start again. She must have read them all three or four times, and they never failed to give pleasure to my father.

Again, for the comfort you gave us all, our great thanks.

Yours,

Peter Worthington

King Edward Hotel   April 3, 1967
Toronto

Craig Ballantyne
Weekend Magazine
Montreal

Dear Craig

Saturday, Robarts threw a luncheon for the press, TV and radio for the presentation of the News Hall of Fame to Grattan O'Leary, Joseph Howe and Ralph Allen. Being the first member of this notable senate, I sat with Grattan and we had fun.

I met Jim Kingsbury, who is one of my best few memories of The Toronto Star, and he asked me if it might be possible for me to contribute a piece about The Star's war service in wars one and two to some publication they have in mind for an anniversary of some kind. I told him that due to the present conflict between our papers I thought it doubtful, but he should write you. If he does, I suggest you demur, because I am too darn tired to undertake anything beyond my skinny contribution to US. I also met Honderich who asked if he could come over and have lunch with me to talk about Ralph Allen. I of course agreed. I think they have in mind some sort of biographical book about Ralph made up of anecdotes and so forth. I think it possible you would agree to this, if it was not tied in with The Star. But you should advise me how to navigate these little matters.

Bronchitis bad as ever, nine bloody weeks of it. What a winter!

Aff.
Greg

Toronto Star Limited
Office of the President

April 10, 1967

Mr. Mark Farrell
Managing Director
Weekend Magazine
231 St. James Street West
Montreal, P. Q.

Dear Mark:
The Daily Star will be 75 years old on November 3 next and to observe the occasion we plan to publish a special 75th Anniversary Edition which we hope will include articles written by former Daily Star reporters.
We are particularly anxious to obtain an article from Greg Clark and I am writing to ask if you could possible see your way clear to grant him permission to write this article for us.
With kind regards, I am

Yours sincerely,
Bee
(Beland Honderich)

Weekend Magazine   April 13, 1967
Montreal

Mr. Beland Honderich
President
Toronto Star Limited
80 King Street West
Toronto, Ont.

Dear Bee:

Thank you for your letter of the 10th re Greg Clark.

I discussed this with Craig Ballantyne and he in turn discussed it with Greg Clark. Greg tells him that he is simply too tired to undertake anything beyond his contributions to Weekend Magazine.

However, subject to Greg OK'ing your choice of the piece, you have our permission to publish anything that Greg has written for either Weekend Magazine or The Standard.

I am looking forward to having a chat with you when I am in Toronto CP-CDNPA week.

Yours sincerely,
Mark Farrell

Weekend Magazine   March 12, 1968
Montreal

Sister Elaine Doiron, S.C.I.C.
Mt. St. Bernard College,
Antigonish, N.S.

Dear Sister Doiron:

Thank you for your letter addressed to Gregory Clark.

Greg tries to answer all his own mail as soon as he receives it but frequently it gets ahead of him as it has since we published his piece, May Your First Love Be Your Last, and I hope you will accept this acknowledgment as a substitute for his personal word of thanks. He was delighted to have your letter and has asked me to tell you so.

Sincerely,
Hugh Shaw
Executive Editor

King Edward Hotel   April 8, 1968
Toronto

Dear Gillis

I have not been a Trudeau man, due to the fact that in recent weeks or months I have kind of dried up on my French brethren for fear of the union of Canada.

But I saw him from time to time on TV and his many pictures in the press, and I had to confess to myself that something there stirred me.

At the Saturday convention I watched the whole damn thing from 2 to the end. I saw Trudeau with ever increasing attention as time went by. Watched him in his seat, and coming and going, and with that carnation that some girl had flung him, in his teeth. I suddenly became aware of a strange sense of recognition. Who the hell was he? Who did he remind me of?

Well, sir, I went all the way back to the museums of Rome and Naples and Pompeii where they have the busts of the Romans. Maybe it was the hair-do.

But it eluded me. There was SOMETHING there . . .

It was when the little son of a gun, with the sly, sideways smile, in his speech of thanks, when he referred to what he owed to the press and the communications media.

Elizabethan! He was the Elizabethan man, Raleigh, who could write a poem, throw a flower, or a quip, circumnavigate the globe. He was Shakespearian, not an actor, but a CHARACTER, speaking his smiling lines in the epilogue of one of the comedies, (let us hope not one of the tragedies.) Say, one of the dramas. But THERE by God he was, pure Elizabethan.

Naturally, in my ignorances of worldly things, I dont know how good he is. I would say he is a man not out of a new mould, but a man out of an antique mould.

Let us say God bless him.

Aff.
Greg

King Edward Hotel   August 26, 1968
Toronto

Craig Ballantyne
Weekend Magazine

Dear Craig
    Our letters crossed. Yours enclosing the memo re deferment
[of retirement] for another year from Keith Buckland.
    Mine bewailing how little fishing I have had this season. I
barely put that letter in the box before I realized the enclosed
snapshot of Bill Oille would be a little incongruous unless I told
you the picture was taken last May 28 when we were up at
Forbes's. The eminent doctor is away fishing for steelheads in the
Dean River in North BC, lucky bugger.
    I sent a note of thanks to Keith for his memo.

                                                                    Aff.
                                                                    Greg

King Edward Hotel   November 14, 1968
Toronto

Craig Ballantyne
Weekend Magazine
Montreal

Dear Craig
    The small Armistice Day story was a smash in these parts. I
took a laurel wreath on Sunday to put under the colors of my regiment which hang in St James Cathedral. When the Dean of
Toronto took the pulpit, he referred in an impassioned sermon to
the Royal Regiment of Canada, whose church parade it was, to
the Weekend Magazine and the story of Gregory Clark, com-
mending it to a crowded cathedral. On the way out, humbly, I encountered St Clair Balfour, chatting with some ladies, and as he
gave me a frosty look, I said "You cant BUY plugs like that!"
On Monday, actual Armistice Day, Gordon Sinclair, gave it another beautiful plug to his enormous audience, and at a dinner at
the Military Institute, crowded, Keiller MacKay was the guest or-
ator, and at the conclusion of a beautiful and flowery address,
Prof. R M W Lower, of Queens, was called upon to reply to the
address; and being not the poetical and flowery type, he asked all

present to be sure they read Weekend Magazine and the warm and kindly piece by Gregory Clark. This is real stuffing. Please don't use any of this in your column without first enquiring from Dean Gilling, Sinclair and Lower exactly what they said, because I got it all second hand, being a little deaf, and my pew mate had to whisper to me what the Dean had just said.

Aff.

Greg

Weekend Magazine   December 19, 1968
Montreal

Mr. G. Clark
Room 683, King Edward Hotel,
37 King St. East,
Toronto 1, Ontario.

Dear Greg,

Enclosed is some Christmas Cheer including the annual Turkey Money.

I must point out that it has been decided that regular Christmas bonuses will be discontinued in the future so that no-one can count on it for next year.

Have a good Christmas and save me some Grant's for my next trip.

All the best,

Craig Ballantyne

165 Maplewood Avenue   September 25, 1972
Toronto 10
Ontario

Dr. Gregory Clark
King Edward Hotel
Toronto
Ontario

My Dear Gregory:

Gordon Sinclair said it all for me and many, many others but let me repeat: Congratulations on your 80th birthday! I was about to say "heartiest" but, you see, I must save the superlatives up for the birthdays ahead . . . I recall your encouraging attitude to the newcomers:

November 24, 1941: 8-col section page Star—Railway Section Hand Captures Three Escaped Nazis. By you know who.

November 25, 1941: Telegram to James Y. Nicol, Nickel Range Hotel, Sudbury—What a peach of a story in last night's paper stop It had everything stop Three cheers Greg Clark

Three cheers to you, sir!

Most sincerely
Jim Nicol

The Premier of Ontario　　　　　　　　September 25, 1972
Parliament Buildings
Queen's Park
Toronto, Ontario

Mr. Greg Clark,
c/o King Edward Sheraton Hotel
37 King Street East
Room 683
Toronto, Ontario

Dear Greg:

May I join in offering congratulations as you mark your 80th birthday today.

Your writings with their unique combination of humour, pathos, warmth, and understanding of human nature, have struck a responsive chord in the hearts of millions of Canadians and many of us look upon you affectionately as an old and dear friend. As one of your faithful readers and admirers, I wish you a Happy Birthday and continued good health.

Sincerely,
William G. Davis

Gordon Sinclair's Office　　　　　　　July 14, 1976
CFRB
Toronto, Ont.

Greg:

Can't tell you when I've enjoyed stories, repartee and luncheon, etc. more. You certainly haven't lost your memory or way with funny and interesting stories!

Also . . . this is just between us . . . there is *no one* who can keep Gordon Sinclair quiet and listening to stories for an hour and a half! As you know he can get bored if not doing at least half of the talking, if not more! You certainly *can* and *did* hold his attention to a greater degree than anyone I have ever met! Gordon told me he sure was glad to see you and have lunch with you.

Take care, I'll keep you posted on items of interest!

If I may say so . . . you are one great, warm, humorous individual!

Talk with you soon.

Affectionately
Pat

44

Art is long, life short, judgment difficult, opportunity transient.

—*Johann Wolfgang von Goethe*

Greg was sometimes asked how he managed to live in the small suite he occupied at the King Edward. He pointed out, "I should be able to manage. I've spent half my life in hotel rooms."

At the King Edward he was a celebrity from the day of his arrival. Friends and readers greeted him on every appearance in the lobby or dining rooms—even on the short elevator ride from the sixth floor. Readers who had never seen him in the flesh recognized him from the Frise drawings, the Macpherson drawings or the Louis Jaques photos.

He took frequent strolls on the downtown streets. One day, in a single block, half a dozen fans halted him to chat briefly. At the end of the block he was stopped by an American tourist who tried to press a dollar bill into Greg's hand. The man said, "I saw you approaching those people, but you didn't seem to be having much luck."

Greg was aghast. The man thought he was a panhandler! Indignantly Greg said, "Those people were approaching *me!* I'm a writer and they wanted to talk to me about my stories."

"Oh, excuse me," said the tourist. "I didn't realize you were a local celebrity."

Even more indignantly, Greg said, "I am not a *local* celebrity! I am a *national* celebrity!"

Greg was usually a soft touch, but was sometimes put off by a panhandler's manner. In this case Greg would cup his hand around his ear and feign deafness.

"What is it?" he would say loudly. "Speak up, my man! What

do you want?" The panhandler would quickly slip away into the crowd.

One of Greg's ports of call was Gil Purcell's Canadian Press office at 55 University Avenue, a drop-in center for newspapermen of all kinds, including Lord Thomson of Fleet. It was a large office with a conference table. Against the north wall was a large red leather sofa. Above this hung a realistic Roloff Beny painting of some wheat stalks against a prairie sky. The office was well equipped with books and liquors, especially rum.

At the King Edward the staff treated Greg as one of the family. One elderly bellman became a good friend. He was a Maltese by the name of Emmanuel DeBattista. Greg called him Manny. He gave Greg extra attention in Room 683 and did shopping errands. Even after Manny retired from the hotel he visited Greg once or twice a week.

There were other permanent guests in the hotel with whom Greg formed friendships. One was John Gibbons Counsell, who had been shot in the spine at Dieppe. He was paralyzed from the waist down. After the war, along with Conn Smythe, Louis M. Wood and others, Counsell founded the Canadian Paraplegic Association and served as first president. Both Counsell and Greg had the Military Cross and in 1967 both were awarded the Service Medal of the Order of Canada. As they were not strong enough to make the trip to Ottawa for the formal presentation, Governor-General Roland Michener made a special trip to Toronto and presented their medals in a private ceremony at the hotel.

Greg's hotel days had a kind of pattern, but not a rigid one. Purcell and West made a point of coming in on Mondays for drinks and yarns and sometimes stayed for lunch. Tuesdays Greg worked or visited friends in the hotel. Wednesdays and Thursdays were his "open" days. There were always people wanting to see him or interview him and he tried to work them in on these two afternoons.

Friday lunches were reserved for Dr. William Oille, friend and physician. Greg's son and his wife, Doreen, came by on Saturday mornings, often staying for lunch. Sundays Greg kept for himself; he stayed in his dressing gown all day and relaxed.

On July 24, 1976, Bruce West and I arrived for lunch. Greg had left the door ajar for us and was listening to Gord Sinclair going on about the news. We poured our drinks without interrupting this ritual. After Sinclair was finished there were greetings and the conversation turned to books. Greg's biography first, of course.

"You poor guy," he said to me. "You must be sick of it by now. Purcell says you'll never finish it."

"Probably not," I said. "But look at all the free lunches I've gotten out of you."

Greg looked at me severely.

"You bugger," he said. He turned to Bruce.

"Remember your book on Toronto? You typed and typed, but it piled up slowly. You began to wonder why the hell you ever started it."

"Yes," said Bruce. "And I remember what you said to me. Columnists were just song-and-dance men. A few quick steps, a twirl of the hat and then skipping offstage—finished for the day. A book was a whole new ball game."

West has a very good memory, which he describes as "total recoil." He came up with another memory of Greg.

"Remember that publishers' luncheon at the Royal York? Wes Hicks was acting as master of ceremonies, wandering around the tables with a microphone in search of authors. When he got to our table he said, 'Ah, here's an author! Mr. Gregory Clark!'"

Greg said, "Then what happened?"

"What happened? You jumped up on your chair so everyone could see you. And you said, 'I am *not* an author. I am simply an old newspaperman. Old newspapermen sometimes achieve a benign air which might lead you to mistake them for authors. It was an honest mistake, Mr. Hicks, and I bear you no ill will.'"

"Did I say that?" said Greg. "Well, the mind works better when you're younger. Now mine slithers around like a kid on roller skates."

Greg's writing had slowed in recent years. *Weekend* continued to pay his salary, but did not push him for material. Now, Greg had fallen victim to "writer's block." He sat in front of his typewriter with the old "Go to Work!" sign above it, but his fingers would not move. In all the years of meeting deadlines, in all the years of effortless production, nothing like this had ever happened to him.

Purcell did his best to help. He pointed out that Greg had always rehearsed his stories and tried them out on his friends before he went to the typewriter. He visited with Greg, talked to him on the phone, tried to get Greg to talk out his stories, but this didn't work.

Clyde Gilmour brought a tape recorder to Greg's room, one that was simple to operate, to see if Greg could work out a story on the machine, but this didn't help either.

The situation was not without irony. For sixty years Greg's failure at the University of Toronto had preyed on his mind. In the spring of 1975, the university announced that it was going to award him the degree of Doctor of Letters (*honoris causa*). Greg was delighted with this honor, but the event itself overwhelmed him. There had been a long, glowing introduction by Professor Claude Bissell. Greg was greeted with a standing ovation from the students. Talk had flowed from Greg all his life, but when he tried to make a speech now he was overcome with emotion. His voice almost totally failed him. He managed only a few almost incoherent words, about his early failure at the university and about the swift passage of time. He was assisted from the platform to another standing ovation. Since then he had been unable to write a word.

"I think I suffered a kind of mini-stroke," said Greg, trying to explain it to me as we sat with our pre-lunch drinks. "Not a paralyzing stroke, but one of those things that hits executives and seems to make them lose their grip. Bill Oille says maybe I'm just written out."

Greg looked at his watch. "Look," he said, "I've made a lunch reservation in the Oak Room for one o'clock. Down the hatch with your drinks."

West and I protested that we needed another drink first and were given a respite by the arrival of Greg's friend Manny DeBattista, who had purchased some bottles of scotch for him. Manny was as careful with Greg's money as Greg was carefree with it; he agreed that we should have another drink before going downstairs.

"Down there," said Manny, "you pay a dollar ninety-five for a drink, another twenty-five cents for the waiter."

This led to West telling Joke Number 96—the one about the kangaroo going into a bar in New York and ordering a scotch.

"Finish your drinks," said Greg impatiently, "and get my wheelchair. It's now ten after one."

West assumed a pained look. "It's like being with Purcell," he said. "Jock, do you remember that dear old friendly Clark we used to know? Now it's Major Clark, giving orders—"

"Get the wheelchair," Greg commanded. Obediently we gulped the balance of our drinks and got out the wheelchair, which John Counsell had loaned Greg. We assisted Greg into it and Bruce piloted the chair out the door and down the hall toward the elevator, to the accompaniment of Greg's front-seat driving. Some months before, Greg had complained that West, a qualified aircraft pilot, was not very good at flying a wheelchair. On his next lunch date West had brought along Johnny Fauquier, the most decorated living Canadian airman of World War II, who guided the wheelchair to the dining room to Greg's satisfaction.

As Bruce wheeled Greg to a table in the Oak Room I made secret arrangements with the *maître d'* to pay for the lunch. It was almost impossible to get a meal check away from Greg without a wrestling match and I didn't relish the idea of wrestling an old man in a wheelchair in the middle of the Oak Room. It might raise a few eyebrows.

Our luncheon order began with more drinks to make up for those which Bruce and I had been forced to gulp upstairs. In the meantime, unaccountably, Greg got onto the subject of his brother Joe and began telling us of the day nearly eighty years ago when Joe had been spanked for making fun of Alexander Muir, the composer of "The Maple Leaf Forever."

It was a story both West and I knew by heart. Another day we might have pointed this out somewhat rudely, but this day we let it go. At the end of the story Greg began to sing "The Maple Leaf Forever" in a quavery voice: "The thistle, shamrock, rose entwined, the maple leaf forever . . ."

"Please notice," said Greg, "how the Scotch thistle is in there first."

He and West argued about the exact words of the song and West won the argument. West now seized the stage and began to bore Greg and me with a column he was planning to write, about the growth of mediocrity in society. West always confused being serious with being ponderous.

Greg took the conversation back. "What we should do is start a campaign to get rid of those so-called artists who put down their random stream of prose and call it a poem. When people run on about Ezra Pound or Eliot I ask them to quote me two consecutive lines from Pound or from *The Wasteland*. They can't, of course. Then I ask them for the first lines of Keats' *Endymion* or even *In Flanders Fields* and they reel them off. To encyst a moment of truth or beauty in the amber of memory, it has to be memorable, to have meter and rhyme."

West tried to get the conversation back to his side of the table by describing the speeches on journalism that he'd been delivering to high school groups.

"There are really only three things I can tell them," he began modestly. "These are: one, technique; two, sensitivity—"

"Awareness," said Greg.

"No, sensitivity," said West. "And the third is this unbearable compulsion to write it so you can share this thought or idea with someone else. I think that's about all I can tell these young people."

"You must make a lot of short speeches," I said.

West didn't even notice this remark. He repeated his three great principles of journalism all over again, very slowly, so we could grasp them. Next he began a debate with himself as to whether, just maybe, his number three principle should go in the number one position, and the number one principle should go into the number three position. Greg interrupted this dreary debate.

"Well, you can write, as we do, for the passing wind, but for something to live it must have form and beauty. Like Hadrian's farewell to his spirit." Greg recited it in Latin.

> "*Animula vagula blandula*
> *Hospes comesque corporis,*
> *Quae nunc abibis in loca*
> *Pallidula rigida nudula*
> *Nec ut soles dabis iocos!*"

Greg's recitation of this piece, which he had long felt should be his own epitaph, was so emotional it left a hush.

Trying to relieve the tension, I said, "Would you literary lions permit me one quotation?"

"All right," said West, "but just one."

I quoted Sir Alan Herbert. "If nobody ever said anything unless they knew what they were talking about, a ghastly hush would descend upon the earth."

They laughed.

"I quite agree," said Greg. "If you have nothing to say, shut up. That's why I've been so quiet and reticent all these years."

This brought another laugh.

"In my case," said West, "the godawful frightening part of it is that every now and then I think I *do* have something to say."

Greg asked for the luncheon check. When the waiter told him I had already paid it, Greg gave me an outraged look. "I invited you two here today to be my guests. Guests can't pay."

He was still muttering about this after we had gotten him back to his room and settled in his chair by the window. As we left he shouted after us, "Next time *I* pay!"

45 _____

Good night, sweet Prince.

—Shakespeare

For a man in his eighty-fifth year, Greg was in reasonably good condition. His mind was still active, but his body was beginning to fail him. Muscular atrophy in his legs caused a few falls in his hotel room. In addition, he was experiencing pains in the lower back. In January of 1977 these became severe and he entered Toronto General Hospital.

Upon his arrival a jovial intern greeted him. "Don't worry, Mr. Clark. We'll have you up and out again in no time."

Later Greg reported this to Purcell on the phone. "He doesn't seem to know that the last thing I want is to get up and out again."

Almost two years earlier, in an interview with Frank Rasky of the *Star,* Greg had said, "I'm all packed and ready to go. I'm an aged agnostic, unafraid of death and undeluded with thoughts of a life hereafter."

Young Greg and Doreen visited him regularly. On one of Doreen's visits she found him curled up on his side in a fetal position. She touched him lightly. He opened his eyes and whispered hello, but that was all.

One day young Greg found his father in deep pain. He said he had been given an enema which had hurt him internally. There had been a showing of blood. For most of his life young Greg had not known his father to complain of aches and pains—he seemed to take them in his stride—but this day he lay quietly and said, "Oh, Greg, it hurts."

The fact was that Greg had intractable cancer of the rectum. This had been an incidental finding; his chief disability was the progressive angina which had caused his three previous coronaries.

The end was not long in coming. There were three doctors in the room when he died on Thursday morning, February 3, 1977. They were still there when young Greg arrived on the scene. The doctors explained that his father had been under sedation and had died quietly.

Greg had left specific instructions. He was to be cremated. There would be no formal funeral service, only a small gathering, limited to relatives, at young Greg's home. When Elizabeth arrived from New York, she and her brother did a lot of soul-searching about carrying out the instructions to the letter. There were relatives who could not be reached easily, friends who might think a more elaborate service was called for. In the end they decided to follow Greg's request, with one change: they invited Gil Purcell, Bruce West and Manny DeBattista to the family gathering.

On Saturday young Greg welcomed the gathering. He explained Greg's last requests, including the one that a bar be provided for the guests.

His father, although he had lost a sense of formal religion, had admired much of the writing in the King James version of the Bible. During one of young Greg's last visits to him in the hospital, he'd asked him to read from the Second Epistle of Paul the Apostle, the verse beginning, "I have fought a good fight, I have finished my course, I have kept the faith." Young Greg read this selection and then Bruce West delivered the eulogy.

"We are gathered here this afternoon to pay our respects to a loving relative and a loyal friend.

"We who were his companions and colleagues can assure his family that his passing is a blow that is as cruel and sharp to us as to those who were more closely bound to him by blood.

"In a way he was a kind of father to all of us. He taught us many things, which had a profound effect upon our lives and will be remembered all of our days.

"As a hunting and fishing companion he gave each one of us who were lucky enough to be with him, a new and richer appreciation of the beauties and mysteries of nature . . . he made us stop and look again at the glories of the forests and the fields and the lakes and the streams and those humble creatures which dwelt within them. For that alone we shall always be grateful. Through his wise and understanding eyes, a whole new world was opened to us.

"Those of us who happened to be clumsy followers of the craft he performed so superbly—the art of the story-teller— owe him a double debt. He gave us all good advice—not in a preachy kind of way, but with the deep warmth and humour which seemed to make such advice all the more valuable to us.

"Not one of us who ever had the privilege of associating with him was not a better newspaperman for this experience.

"We can, of course, take some small comfort from the certain knowledge that Greg Clark was a brave and noble man. He did not fear death—even as a young warrior, when the wine of youth was sweet and so much lay before him. Later, with an extremely full and useful life lying behind him, he was ready to look calmly down toward the end of the road, like the gallant philosopher he was.

"As I say, this is some comfort to us—but will never, of course, do much to alleviate the terrible gap his passing has left in all of our lives.

"Twenty-five years ago—almost to the day, on February 7, 1952—the whole world listened to the announcement by Prime Minister Winston Churchill of the passing of King George the Sixth. I would imagine that, as a staunch royalist, Greg would not mind me quoting from the statement of the great man who was one of his heroes—as he was of mine:

"'During these last months,' said Churchill, 'the King walked with death as if death were a companion—an acquaintance whom he recognised and did not fear. In the end, death came as a friend—and after a goodnight to those who loved him best, he fell asleep . . . as every man or woman who strives to fear God—and nothing else in this world— may hope to do.'"

Throughout his life Greg thought about death from time to time, even joked about the manner of his departure and a suitable epitaph. In an early story he did with Charles Vining, Greg said:

"I want to be dressed in my fishing clothes, waders and jacket. Then I want them to lay me out with a rod in my hand and all my other rods and flies and reels spread out around me. Then I want them to cremate me and all my things and put the ashes in the centre of a great big concrete boulder. The boulder will be dumped in the Hawthorn pool on The Mad River. My fishing friends will come along and see the boulder and say, 'There's Greg out there—let's try a cast there.'"

In later years he became fond of the dying Hadrian's address to his soul, which he had committed to memory in the original Latin and sometimes recited. There are more than a hundred translations and versions of this literary fragment. Greg and Gil Purcell read many of them and debated their correctness or poetic feeling. Here is one version Greg liked.

> Little pleasant wandering soul,
> Guest and companion of my body,
> Where will you go now—
> Pale, stiff, naked—
> Never to play around again
> The way you used to!

46 _____

EPILOGUE

Greg left specific instructions about the disposition of his ashes. They were to be scattered at three different locations: Helen's grave at Mount Pleasant cemetery, the family cottage at Go Home Bay and the grave of his son Murray in France.

Young Greg and his sister Elizabeth placed some of the ashes on Helen's grave not long after Greg's death. That summer, Elizabeth scattered more at some of Greg's favorite places around the cottage at Go Home.

It was not until the following year that young Greg could arrange to make the trip to Murray's grave in France. In the meantime, he placed the rest of his father's ashes in a small metal canister from Greg's fishing equipment—a waterproof container that Greg used to keep matches dry when in the woods.

Young Greg and his wife, Doreen, landed in Calais in August of 1978. They rented a car and drove about ten miles to the village of St. Inglevert, not far from the place where Murray had met death.

During the drive, young Greg thought about Murray and tried to recapture some of the boyhood scenes and experiences they had shared forty years ago. There were not very many, as Murray had been four years older than young Greg, with his own set of companions. Murray had also been more intellectually inclined at the time. There were memories of their homes and of fishing and hunting expeditions with Greg, though.

One of these afternoons had always remained vividly alive in young Greg's memory. The three of them had been out partridge hunting at Go Home. As they emerged from the woods, Greg and young Greg had trailed behind Murray as he walked down a long, flat rock that ran into Clark's Bay, a few hundred yards from the cottage.

Murray had nearly reached the water when two partridges jumped. One swung left toward a nearby island. The other flew right, along the shoreline.

Young Greg and his father had halted at the drumming sound of the birds' flight. They saw Murray snap his gun to his shoulder and swing on the bird to the left. He fired and the bird dropped. Without pause his gun swung to the right and fired again. The second partridge dropped. This double was a fine display of marksmanship and the memory of it had always remained clearly etched in young Greg's mind.

Not far from St. Inglevert, Greg, Jr., and Doreen came upon the sign indicating the Canadian War Graves cemetery. They parked the car and walked up a long, grassy path to the gate of the cemetery. The path was lined with Canadian pine trees and the grounds were beautifully kept.

The headstone on Murray's grave had a maple leaf inscribed on it and these words:

Lieutenant
J. M. Clark
The Regina Rifle Regiment
17th September 1944 Age 23

Below the cross on the headstone was a short poem of Murray's, one chosen by his father:

Ah, Gentle Sky
In Thy Blue Bend I See
Thee Stoop To Kiss That Spot
That's Dear To Me, J.M.C.

Greg, Jr., emptied the canister of ashes on the grave and mixed them in with the loose earth. Afterward he and his wife went to the small building where the grave records were kept. Greg, Jr., signed the register; he also signed it for his father.

He and Doreen closed the cemetery gate and began to walk back along the path lined with pines. Suddenly, only a few feet ahead of them, a partridge broke cover and drummed down the path, finally veering out of sight through the trees. They were both startled. Greg, Jr., was almost frozen to the spot. Instantly there had flashed into his mind that scene at Go Home Bay when

Murray had flushed the two partridges. He was not a superstitious person, but he was emotionally shaken by the appearance of the partridge. He felt that a sign had been given, a circle had been closed, a story was ended.

Appendix

BOOKS BY GREGORY CLARK

1936   *Which We Did*   Reginald Saunders
1937   *So What?*   Reginald Saunders
1959   *Best of Gregory Clark*   Ryerson Press
1961   *Greg's Choice*   Ryerson Press
1963   *Hi, There!*   Ryerson Press
1964   *Gregory Clark War Stories*   Ryerson Press
1969   *May Your First Love Be Your Last*   McClelland and Stewart
1971   *A Bar'l Of Apples*   McGraw-Hill Ryerson
1971   *Outdoors With Gregory Clark*   McClelland and Stewart
1973   *The Bird of Promise*   Infocor Limited
1974   *Grandma Preferred Steak*   Infocor Limited
1975   *Fishing With Greg Clark*   Optimum Publishing Company
1976   *Things That Go Squeak In The Night*   Optimum Publishing Company
1977   *The Best of Greg Clark And Jimmie Frise*   William Collins Sons & Company Limited
1978   *Silver Linings*   William Collins Sons & Company Limited
1979   *Greg Clark & Jimmie Frise Outdoors*   William Collins Sons & Company Limited
1979   *Ten Cents Off Per Dozen*   Optimum Publishing Company
1980   *A Supersonic Day*   McClelland and Stewart
1980   *Greg Clark & Jimmie Frise Go Fishing*   Today Books

Index _____

Gregory Clark entertained Canadians for more than fifty years with his news stories, columns and humorous writings, becoming one of the best-known personalities of his time. He and his cartoonist partner, Jimmie Frise, first became famous in the pages of the old *Star Weekly*. Later in *Weekend Magazine,* Greg's stories were illustrated by outstanding political cartoonist Duncan Macpherson.

Greg's honors and decorations were many. In the First World War he won the Military Cross in action as an infantry lieutenant at the Battle of Vimy Ridge. In World War II, he distinguished himself as a war correspondent in Sicily, Italy and Europe. He was named an officer of the Order of the British Empire and was awarded the Service Medal of the Order of Canada. He received the Stephen Leacock Award for Humor for one of his many books and the J. V. McAree Award for his syndicated columns.

He was elected an honorary life member of the Ontario Federation of Anglers and Hunters; the Royal Canadian Military Institute; the Toronto Men's Press Club and the Canadian War Correspondents Association. The University of Western Ontario made him an honorary Doctor of Laws and the University of Toronto an honorary Doctor of Letters. He was the first person named to the Canadian News Hall of Fame.

Jock Carroll, the author of this book, is a Canadian writer-photographer who shared Greg's years on *Weekend Magazine.* Carroll's assignments have taken him across Canada and much of the United States as well as to the Arctic, the Caribbean, Europe, Russia and the Far East. Some of his adventures provided material for a novel, *The Shy Photographer (Bottoms Up!),* a funny, irreverent satire of the magazine and motion picture worlds.

Carroll became an RCAF pilot during World War II and served as a war correspondent in Korea. A former all-around athlete, he now plays golf, tennis, handball and chess.